Regional Organisations and the Development of Collective Security

This book examines the development of collective security by regional organisations particularly after the Cold War. It analyses the various constitutional developments that have occurred within regional organisations such as ECOWAS, African Union, SADC, OAS, and NATO and looks critically at how these developments have propelled regional organisations to depart from the normative framework of regional arrangements contained in Chapter VIII of the UN Charter. Through a comprehensive examination of practice, the book evaluates the impact of regional organisations' newly asserted powers to authorise enforcement action and determine when situations within member states warrant their intervention. It inquires into the legal justifications for these developments from within both the UN Charter and regional treaties and practice and asks whether consensual intervention, that is the use of force by regional organisations on the basis of their members' consent, contravenes or constitutes an exception to the prohibition of the use or threat of force under Article 2(4) of the Charter. The book also analyses the regime of complementarity between the UN and regional organisations.

VOLUME 6 in the series Studies in International Law

Studies in International Law

Volume 1: Between Light and Shadow: The World Bank, the International Monetary Fund and International Human Rights Law *Mac Darrow*

Volume 2: Toxics and Transnational Law: International and European Regulation of Toxic Substances as Legal Symbolism *Marc Pallemaerts*

Volume 3: The Chapter VII Powers of the United Nations Security Council *Erika de Wet*

Volume 4: Enforcing International Law Norms Against Terrorism *edited by Andrea Bianchi*

Volume 5: The Permanent International Criminal Court *edited by Dominic McGoldrick, Peter Rowe and Eric Donnelly.*

Volume 6: Regional Organisations and the Development of Collective Security *Ademola Abass*

Regional Organisations and the Development of Collective Security

Beyond Chapter VIII of the UN Charter

Ademola Abass

University of the West of England

HART PUBLISHING

OXFORD AND PORTLAND, OREGON

2004

Hart Publishing
Oxford and Portland, Oregon

Published in North America (US and Canada) by
Hart Publishing c/o
International Specialized Book Services
5804 NE Hassalo Street
Portland, Oregon
97213-3644
USA

Distributed in the Netherlands, Belgium and Luxembourg by
Intersentia, Churchillaan 108
B2900 Schoten
Antwerpen
Belgium

Hart Publishing is a specialist legal publisher based in Oxford,
England.
To order further copies of this book or to request a list of other
publications please write to:

Hart Publishing, Salter's Boatyard, Folly Bridge,
Abingdon Road, Oxford OX1 4LB
Telephone: +44 (0)1865 245533 or Fax: +44 (0)1865 794882
e-mail: mail@hartpub.co.uk
WEBSITE: http//www.hartpub.co.uk

British Library Cataloguing in Publication Data
Data Available
ISBN 1–84113–480–5

Typeset by Hope Services (Abingdon) Ltd
Printed and bound in Great Britain on acid-free paper by
TJ International Ltd, Padstow, Cornwall

To my mum and my late dad, Dandy.

Preface

This book was originally submitted as a PhD thesis to the School of Law, University of Nottingham in 2003. I commenced my doctoral studies in the same decade as the international community reposed a great confidence in the Security Council to rescue collective security from the Cold War stranglehold and live up to its name as the arch custodian of international peace and security. This hope was neither misplaced nor ill-informed. At the opening of that decade, the world witnessed a reinvigorated Security Council stamp its authority against quarrelsome Iraq and expelled that country's invading troops from Kuwait. Sanctions and military measures were authorised and imposed on an unprecedented scale.

As it turned out, the hope was short-lived. At the close of that decade, the Security Council, once again, found itself a hostage of its veto when it contemplated authorising enforcement action against Milosevic's Yugoslavia. Around the same time, Liberia, Sierra Leone, Haiti and the Democratic Republic of Congo (DRC), exploded into civil conflicts of varied magnitude. The responses of the Security Council were as confounding as they were flabbergasting. In 1994, the Security Council prevaricated while ethnic conflict decimated nearly one million Rwandans, three years after it declined invitation to intervene in the Liberia conflict. The Security Council informed the world that the nature of the Liberia conflict was not such that it could mediate in, a stance it would repeat at the initial stages of the Sierra Leone crisis. At the turn of the century, the Security Council authorised a mere 5,000 peacekeepers for Congo, a country the size of Western Europe, and where there was no peace to keep. The Security Council was lacklustre when Ivory Coast erupted into a major armed conflict. Notably the attitude of the Security Council had been different in Haiti and the Federal Republic of Yugoslavia in the early 1990s.

In default of Security Council-led actions, certain regional organisations have assumed responsibility for the maintenance of peace and security in their regions. ECOWAS, AU and NATO typify organisations increasingly resisting allowing the iniquitous invocation of the veto power, or the notorious selectivity of the UN collective security to hold the world hostage. Inevitably, this development has deeply impacted (and continues to impact) the UN Charter as well as threatening the cohesion of the Charter collective security system.

Although there is enormous literature on the theme of regional organisations, there is a lack of a monograph that studies the development of collective security by regional organisations, particularly after the Cold War, through the prisms of the UN Charter and Constitutions of regional organisations. For a long time, academic analysis of regional organisations has always excluded normative development within regional organisations. Much less is even said about, or written on, the contributions made by organisations such as ECOWAS, to the development of collective security. This book therefore is intended to be a comprehensive and authoritative study on the subject matter. It responds to existing theories on the Charter principles governing regional organisations and advocates new understanding of such principles in the contemporary order. It approaches its subject not only from the premises of the UN Charter, as most other works do, but also through an appreciation of the evolving constitutions of regional organisations. Whilst the book does not advocate discarding the UN Charter, it urges greater autonomy for regional organisations than Chapter VIII of the UN Charter affords them.

A A
Bristol, March 2004

Contents

Acknowledgements

One of the satisfactions to be derived from publishing one's doctoral research is the opportunity to repay a debt of gratitude owed to all those who stood by one in those moments of redoubtable trials. In my case, my debt is huge and can hardly be paid off on these few pages.

I thank the School of Law and the International Office of the University of Nottingham for granting me scholarship and a lump sum respectively to undertake doctoral research. My profound gratitude goes to my two supervisors, Professor Nigel White, Professor of International Organisations and Head of School of Law, University of Nottingham, and Mr Dino Kritsiotis, Reader in Public International Law in the same university. Without their support and encouragement, it would have been difficult to complete the research. Special thanks are also due to Professor White for allowing me to teach his postgraduate classes in Collective Security Law. The stimulating discussions with the students helped greatly in shaping the thoughts put down in this book. I thank my *viva voce* examiners, Professor Rein Müllerson of King's College, London, and Dr Rob Cryer, University of Nottingham, for a very memorable viva and for their comments and suggestions.

I am grateful also to Professors D J Harris and Sue Arrowsmith of University of Nottingham for their support at various stages of my research. Thanks to Professor Robert McCorquodale for advice on specific aspects of my research. My appreciation to Joanne Wright, the Warden of Lincoln Hall, University of Nottingham for support while I was a tutor in the hall for three years. I must also thank the Cambridge Commonwealth Trust for funding my graduate studies at the University of Cambridge and Professor Vaughan Lowe and Dr Susan Marks for their support. It was under the tutelage of these two that the first ideas of this book were conceived. It was indeed a great privilege to have been taught by both at Cambridge. My appreciation also goes to several colleagues in the Academic Council on the United Nations Systems with whom I discussed my ideas at various ACUNS meetings and workshops at different stages of my research.

I acknowledge the library staff of the University of Nottingham and The Hague Academy of International Law, the Netherlands. I thank Alison Simpkins and Maureen Welch Dolynskyj, both staff of the School of Law, University of Nottingham, for their constant readiness to assist. Although many more deserve to be mentioned, I take the liberty to say a big 'thank you' to all those fine colleagues at Nottingham with whom I shared such a memorable time and space.

I am also grateful to the authorities of the Economic Community of West African States (ECOWAS), particularly the Director of Legal Affairs, Mr Roger Laloupo, and his deputy, Mrs Halima Ahmed, for their support while I interned at ECOWAS Headquarters in 2000. Thanks to Ambassador Sam Ibok of the Africa Union for providing helpful comments about the organisation's activities. I also thank Mr Richard Hart, Melanie Hamill and the rest of the team at Hart Publishing in Oxford.

My sincere appreciations to Uncle Akin Adewuyi and Aunty Nike, Adeleke Sorinmade, Funmi Adaramola, Rolanda Oostland, Margaret Cunningham, Cynthia Walker, Mashood Baderin, Tian Kuanrong and Jackie Jones. Special thanks to Charlotte Baker. My warmest wishes to Inma.

Table of Cases

International Courts and Tribunals

National Courts

Table of Treaties, Conventions and Declarations

Introduction

THE END of the Cold War precipitated the increased involvement of regional organisations in the maintenance of peace and security. This development, launched by ECOWAS intervention in Liberia in 1990,[1] has been hailed by the United Nations as opening a new era in which 'regional arrangements or agencies can render great service if their activities are undertaken in a manner consistent with the Purposes and Principles of the Charter, and if their relationship with the United Nations, and particularly with the Security Council, is governed by Chapter VIII.'[2] The main principles of the Charter to which the activities of regional organisations are expected to conform are contained mainly in Chapter VIII, Article 2(4) and Article 103 of the Charter.

Chapter VIII empowers regional organisations to settle disputes amongst their member states using peaceful means.[3] This they can, and are encouraged to do entirely on their own initiative and without resort to the Security Council. However, this Chapter forbids regional organisations to take enforcement action without the authorisation of the Security Council.[4] In addition, Article 2(4) obligates states to 'refrain in their international relations from the threat or use of force against the territorial integrity or political independence of any State on in any other manner inconsistent with the Purposes of the United Nations',[5] subject to

[1] On ECOWAS intervention in Liberia, see Anthony Chukwuka Ofodile, 'The Legality of ECOWAS Intervention in Liberia' (1994–95) 32 *Columbia Journal of Transnational Law* 381; Georg Nolte, 'Restoring Peace by Regional Action: International Legal Aspects of the Liberian Conflict', 23 *ZaöRV* 53/3 603; Kofi Oteng Kufor, 'The Legality of The Intervention in the Liberian Civil War by the Economic Community of West African States' (1993) 5 *African Journal of International Law* 525; Kofi Oteng Kufor, 'Developments in the Resolution of the Liberian Conflict' (1994–95) 10(1) *The American University Journal of International Law and Policy* 373; Clement Adibe, 'The Liberian Conflict and the ECOWAS-UN Partnership' in Thomas Weiss (ed), *Beyond Subcontracting: Task-Sharing with Regional Security Arrangements and Service-Providing NGOs* (London, Macmillan Press Ltd, 1998) 67; David Wippman, 'Enforcing the peace: ECOWAS and the Liberian Civil War' in Lori F Damrosch (ed), *Enforcing Restraint: Collective Intervention in Internal Conflicts* (New York, Council of Foreign Relations, 1993) 165; Funmi Olonisakin, *Reinventing Peacekeeping in Africa: Conceptual and Legal Issues in ECOMOG Operations* (The Hague, Kluwer Law International, 2000); Margaret Vogt (ed), *The Liberian Crisis and ECOMOG: A Bold Attempt at Regional Peacekeeping* (Lagos, Gbajumo Publishing, 1992).

[2] A/47/277–S/24111, 17 June 1992. *An Agenda for Peace, Preventive Diplomacy, Peacemaking and Peace-keeping*, Report of the Secretary-General pursuant to the statement adopted by the Summit Meeting of the Security Council (at the level of Heads of States and Government), 31 January 1992.

[3] Article 52(2).

[4] Article 53(1).

[5] Articles 1–3.

permissible exceptions under the UN Charter.[6] Article 103 enjoins all members of the UN to accord primacy to their obligations under the UN Charter if such are in conflict with their obligations under other international agreements.[7] Although the obligations contained in Articles 2(4) and 103 are addressed to states *per se*, such individually assumed obligations do not cease when states congregate as collective groups.

However, contrary to the UN's expectation, regional organisations have not generally conducted their activities in a manner consistent with the principles of the Charter. On many occasions, regional organisations have taken enforcement actions without Security Council's authorisation. Furthermore, these organisations have assumed the competence to determine the existence of threat to or breach of the peace, a power explicitly allocated to the Security Council under Article 39. The most significant indication of the radical departure of regional organisations from the regulatory framework of Chapter VIII manifests in their concluding audacious treaties the provisions of some of which not only codify the iconoclastic practices mentioned above, but also constitute direct challenges to the time-honoured principles of the UN Charter.

For several reasons, the current trend in regional collective security portends dire consequences for Chapter VIII in particular and for the cohesion of the UN collective security in general. There has been a sharp increase in the number of regional organisations engaged in collective security task. This is due, not only to the emergence of new regional organisations after the Cold War, but also to the transformation of erstwhile defensive alliances into collective security organisations (see Chapter 3). This means that the number of potential 'violators' of Chapter VIII and other Charter rules governing regional organisations has multiplied.

Apart from the proliferation of regional organisations, certain deficits associated with Chapter VIII present regional collective security with enormous problems. To start with, Chapter VIII envisaged *only* pacific roles for regional organisation, save occasional uses of force as may be authorised by the Security Council.[8] Nothing in that Chapter or elsewhere in the Charter foretold the peace enforcement role regional organisations currently play in their respective regions. Nor did Chapter VIII envisage the kind of relationship that developed between regional organisations and the UN after the Cold War. On its own part, the UN does not have, nor particularly desires, set rules for guiding the development of its relationship with regional organisations. As explained by a UN Secretary-General, it was not the purpose of the *Agenda for Peace* to set forth 'any formal pattern of relationship between regional organizations and the

[6] Articles 51, Chapter VII, and Article 107, now obsolete.
[7] Article 103.
[8] Article 53 (1).

United Nations, or to call for any specific division of labour.'[9] This, according to the UN, was in order for joint operations to adapt to the realities of each case with flexibility and creativity.

In the absence of guidelines for regulating regional organisations' activities and directing their interaction with the UN, regional collective security has been implemented haphazardly. For examples, in the actions taken by organisations such as the Economic Community of West African States (ECOWAS)[10], the North Atlantic Treaty Organisation (NATO),[11] and the Southern African Development Community SADC),[12] there has been a significant drift from the UN Charter, and a gradual but powerful drive towards a decentralised collective security.[13] A decentralised collective security, as proposed in this book, is a process whereby regional organisations assume the legal competence to authorise enforcement actions under their constituent instruments, and beyond the formalistic framework of Chapter VIII. This is different from a decentralised enforcement action, contained in Chapter VIII, whereby the Security Council delegates enforcement powers to regional organisation.[14]

Regional organisations justify their new practices on many grounds. Some argue that the selective nature of the collective security administered by the Security Council under Chapter VII leaves them with no other choices. Many jurists, such as Professors Elihu Lauterpacht[15] and Martii Koskenniemi,[16] have noted the uneven nature in which the UN applies itself to members' conflicts. Some organisations insist that the wanton use of the veto power by the permanent members of the Security Council prevent this organ from discharging the responsibility entrusted to it by

[9] Above note 2, 10 of 13.

[10] *Treaty of Economic Community of West African States* signed in Lagos, Nigeria, on 25 May 1975, (1975) XIV *International Legal Materials* 1200, as amended by the *Revised Treaty* 24th July 1993, (1996) *International Legal Materials* 660. The Member States of ECOWAS are The Republics of Benin, Burkina Faso, Cape Verde, Côte D' Ivoire, The Gambia, Ghana, Guinea, Guinea Bissau, Liberia, Mali, the (Islamic Republic of) Mauritania, Niger, Nigeria, Senegal, Sierra Leone, and Togo. See the Preamble to the Revised Treaty, *ibid.*

[11] The North Atlantic Treaty, 4 April 1949, 1949 34 *United Nations Treaty Series*, 243. NATO comprises 26 member states viz; Belgium, Bulgaria, Canada, Czech, Denmark, Estonia, France, Germany, Greece, Hungary, Iceland, Italy, Latvia, Lithuania, Luxembourg, Netherlands, Norway, Poland, Portugal, Romania, Slovakia, Slovenia, Spain, Turkey, United Kingdom, and United States.

[12] Established August 17 1992. See Treaty establishing SADC, (1993) 32 *International Legal Materials* 116. SDAC members are: Angola, Botswana, Democratic Republic of Congo, Lesotho, Malawi, Mauritius, Mozambique, Namibia, Seychelles, South Africa, Swaziland, Tanzania, Zambia, and Zimbabwe.

[13] See Chapter 5. This concept is alternatively referred to in this book as regionally authorised enforcement action.

[14] See Chapter 3.

[15] Professor Elihu Lauterpacht's *Foreword* to Marc Weller (ed), *Regional Peacekeeping and International Enforcement: The Liberian Crisis*, Cambridge International Documents Series, vol 6, (Cambridge, Cambridge University Press, 1994) at ix.

[16] Martii Koskenniemi, 'The Place of Law in Collective Security' (1996) 17 *Michigan Journal of International Law* 455 at 460.

states under Article 24(1) of the Charter.[17] Although the sporadic invocation of the veto power has abated since the end of the Cold War, the use of the 'hidden veto'—the continuous threat of the veto by permanent members of the Security Council—continues to achieve practically the same effect as its actual invocation. Twice between 1999 and 2003 (specifically Kosovo and Iraq crises), the threats of veto by Russia and France respectively prevented the Security Council from acting under Chapter VII.

The view has also been expressed that the provisions of Chapter VIII have fallen out of step with the challenges facing states in modern society. For instance, ECOWAS argued that the speed with which conflicts explode in Africa (the Rwanda genocide is a perfect example), coupled with the often innocuous nature of African conflicts, does not afford African states the luxury of waiting for the Security Council authorisation.[18]

This book examines the development of collective security by regional organisations, particularly after the Cold War, within and beyond Chapter VIII provisions. Whole libraries have been written on regional collective security. However, the province of this book must be distinguished from such works in two principal respects: the substance of its engagement and its analytical imperatives. Most legal analysis of regional intervention has always been conducted within the framework of peacekeeping operations.[19] This is despite frequent evidences to the contrary.[20] The legality of such action is invariably determined within the rules of the UN Charter only. As one writer noted, 'when regional organizations have engaged in the use of force the legality of such action has been assessed by the rest of the world not in terms of the organization's own constitution but rather in terms of the UN Charter and general international law'.[21] The immediate consequence of such restrictive approach is that where a regional enforce-

[17] In two separate interviews conducted by this writer with the Director of Legal Affairs Department of ECOWAS and the African Union in April 2000 and February 2004 respectively, the interviewed affirmed this view. Transcripts of interviews are available with the author.

[18] *Ibid.*

[19] Christine Gray, *International Law and Use of Force* (Oxford, Oxford University Press, 2000); Hilaire McCoubrey and Justin Morris, *Regional Peacekeeping in the post-Cold War Era* (The Hague, Kluwer Law International, 2000). See for instance the treatment of the Symbolic Arab Security Force in the Lebanese conflict in 1976 by Hassouna, 'The League of Arab States and the United Nations: Relations in the Peaceful Settlement of Disputes' in Berhanykun Andemicael (ed), *Regionalism and the United Nations* (1979); *The OAU and the UN: Relations between the Organization of African Unity and the United* Nations (New York, Africana Pub Co, 1976), published for the United Nations Institute for Training and Research.

[20] A clear example of this is the ECOWAS intervention in Liberia whereby, despite ECOWAS's claim that its action in Liberia did not require consent by conflicting parties (thus excluding peacekeeping), most analysts prefer to regard the action as an exercise in peacekeeping operation. See Chapter 5.

[21] See Gray above note 19 at 209.

ment action has *not* been authorised by the Security Council, such action is promptly dismissed as violating the UN Charter.

Undoubtedly, Chapter VIII remains cradle to all regional actions. However, this does not, and *should not* be taken to mean, that the development of regional collective security terminally depends on that Chapter, regardless of changes in the social and political configuration of the society in which the UN Charter operates. Such a constrictive vision of the Charter not only obscure the contributions made by regional organisations to the development of collective security law, but also underestimates the capacity of the UN Charter to adapt itself to new situations. This book challenges such orthodox positions on regional collective security.

There is another major academic predilection challenged by this book. Despite the unwillingness of the UN to call for specific division of labour between the UN and regional organisation, as noted above, writers continue to calibrate the UN / regional organisation interaction under preconceived epithets.[22] The consequences of this are many. First, as analysis in Chapter 5 shows, no single conceptual epithet sufficiently or accurately explains the nature of the relationship that has developed between the UN and regional organisations. Second, collapsing the entire UN / regional organisation interaction under specific conceptual epithets often results in undesirable conclusions. For instance, writers have described as joint-peacekeeping operations cases in which the UN plainly played a second fiddle to regional organisation.[23] This is different to situations whereby the Security Council 'specifically authorize regional arrangements or organizations to take the *lead* in addressing a crisis within its region'.[24] Sometimes, it is claimed that the Security Council delegates its enforcement powers to regional organisations while, in reality, no such powers have been delegated.[25]

The most disturbing consequence of confining legal analysis of regional enforcement action to the UN Charter is the unmistakable marginalisation of the emerging principles of intervention engendered by current developments in regional collective security. These include a considera-

[22] Eric Berman, 'The Security Council's Increasing Reliance on Burden-Sharing: Collaboration or Abrogation?' (1998) 4 (1) *International Peacekeeping* 1; David O'Brien, 'The Search for Subsidiarity: The UN, African Regional Organisations and Humanitarian Action' (2000) 7(3) *International Peacekeeping* 57; Thomas Weiss (ed), *Beyond UN Subcontracting: Task-Sharing with Regional Security Organisations and Service-Providing NGOs* (London, Macmillan Press Ltd, 1998).

[23] For a similar view, see MacFarlane, 'The CIS and the OSCE in Georgia's Wars' in Thomas Weiss (ed), *Beyond Subcontracting*, above note 22 at 122.

[24] Agenda for Peace, at 10. See Chapter 5.

[25] Danesh Sarooshi, *The United Nations and the Development of Collective Security: The Delegation by the UN Security Council of its Chapter VII Powers* (Oxford, Clarendon Press, 1999) 248–49, fn 4. Cf Clement Adibe, 'The Liberian Conflict and the ECOWAS—UN Partnership' in Weiss, *Beyond Subcontracting*, above note 22, 67 at 83.

tion of whether the fact that regional organisations have developed treaties, which empower them to authorise enforcement action on their own, constitutes a possible re-interpretation of Chapter VIII in practice; and, whether regional organisations' practice whereby they determine for themselves that a threat to or breach of the peace has occurred, has any legal basis in the Charter or general international law.

Furthermore, there is a compelling need to determine the response of third states to the new powers asserted by regional organisations, especially to authorise enforcement actions outside Chapter VIII framework. Specific issues to consider include: whether state practice of regional organisations presently disclose any particular trend; how the Security Council, whose authority is constantly eroded by regionally authorised enforcement action, views this development; which regional organisations are involved in authorising collective security on their own, and what their justifications are; how these practices fit into the normative framework of the UN Charter and general international law; how to reconcile regionally authorised enforcement action with the prohibition of the use of force in Article 2(4) of the Charter.

One prominent feature of this book, which deserves immediate explanation, is its considerable attention on African regional organisations, especially ECOWAS,[26] the African Union[27] and SADC[28] amongst several other discussed regional organisations. The selection of these organisations is guided by certain considerations. Most existing works on regional organisations have dwelt substantially on western regional organisations such as the Organisation of American States (OAS), the North Atlantic Treaty Organisations (NATO), the OSCE, and so on. Although these latter organisations feature substantially in this book, commentary on them is restricted to where their current practices reinforce this book's thematic occupations or provides an instructive contrast to such. In contrast little is ever written on the contribution of African states to the development of regional collective security. Thus, this book attempts to redress the imbalance that currently exists in this area of international law.

Moreover, the practice of ECOWAS, as well as the development of its laws since the end of the Cold War, constitutes by far the greatest challenge to the Charter principles governing regional organisations. As to be seen later, whilst in certain areas ECOWAS continues to enrich our understanding of how the UN and regional organisations should interact in the present legal order, many of its actions have warranted a critical

[26] Above note 10.

[27] See the *Sitre Declaration and the Decision Assembly of Heads of State and Government on the Constitutive Act of the African Union* EAHG/Dec 1 (V), p 1.

[28] See J Cilliers, 'The Evolving Security Architecture in Southern Africa' (1995) 4 *African Security Review* 40; McCoubrey and Morris, above note 19, 140–50.

rethinking of both the Charter rules on regional collective security and the practice of regional organisations in general.

A caveat is appropriate at this juncture. This author does not propose that regionally authorised enforcement action has definitely become a new norm of general international law. Much less that state practices of regional organisations since the end of the Cold War, even if they disclose a departure from Chapter VIII framework, warrant a total disengagement of regional organisation from the UN Charter. The simple remit of this book is to understand the development of collective security by regional organisations and map out how this can enhance the overall scheme of collective security in the Charter in the contemporary world order.

A few words must be said about the basis upon which the author grounds his proposition that, given certain circumstances, regional organisations may take collective security measures without the authorisation of the Security Council (see Chapter 4). The idea is that the Security Council's primary competence over collective security is subject to its ability to discharge its responsibility in accordance with certain conditions laid down in Article 24(1).

In developing this theme, I have benefitted immensely from the works of eminent scholars such as Thomas Franck, Louis Sohn, Michael Reisman, Michael Glennon and Oscar Schachter on analogous themes. At various times, these scholars advanced, or countered, the thesis that the deficit in the operation of collective security by the Security Council has made the prohibition of force in Article 2(4) obsolete. If this book does not specifically rehash their views, it is because these views are too numerous and widely varied to encapsulate in this work. Furthermore, the book profited from the works of David Caron and Sean Murphy whose writings on legitimacy of the Security Council, as those of Thomas Franck, provide the foundation on which some ideas of Chapter 3 are built. Finally, it is from Thomas Weiss's constant placing of the post Cold War collective security on the academic agenda that this book draws inspiration.

The book's structure is woven around an introduction, six chapters, and a conclusion. Chapter one deals with a conceptual analysis of regionalism, regions and regional organisations. There have been radical changes to the notion of regionalism since the San Francisco Conference where all definitions of regional organisations were rejected. For example, the concept of 'new regionalism', which connotes regional organisations that perform multi tasks, developed shortly before the end of the Cold War. Organisations which subscribe to this new concept perform a wide variety of activities ranging from economic integration to collective security. This chapter therefore is an elaboration of the general meaning of regionalism. By analysing various approaches to the concept from international law and international relations perspectives, this chapter illuminates the actual and normatively desirable place of regional organisations in the collective security system. By rejecting the narrow conceptions of regionalism, this chapter advances a conception of regionalism much broader and useful in the present context.

In terms of method, this chapter examines a broad range of theories, spanning from international relations to international law. By so doing, the chapter demonstrates that states make little or no distinction between a region as an abstract concept and regional organisations under the auspices of which they sometimes act. Thus, the conflated treatment of the terms 'regions' 'regionalism' and 'regional organisations', and the adoption of an analytical approach that compares divergent materials, is a deliberate strategy to reveal the interwovenness of these terms and illuminate the problems that writers often encounter when they embark upon scientific classification of concepts.

Chapter 2 focuses on the specific provisions of the UN Charter on regional organisations. This chapter examines the general structure of Chapter VIII and analyses the role of regional organisations with respect to both pacific settlement of disputes and enforcement action. Rather than stating the obvious, emphasis is placed on the interpretation that regional organisations have accorded to Chapter VIII provisions in the context of present collective security order. Such issues as retroactive authorisation, whether economic sanctions can or should constitute enforcement action, the limit of regional enforcement action when authorised by the Security Council, are critically analysed. So also is whether the Security Council can utilize regional organisations beyond their territory or ask them to perform roles not contained in their constitutions. The intention of the analysis in this chapter is to reveal the substantive and structural weaknesses of Chapter VIII, which make it inadequate to the contemporary needs of regional organisations.

In Chapter 3, the decentralised enforcement action is examined. This is the means adopted by the Security Council in order to implement the provisions of Chapter VII through models that do not exactly match the Charter provisions. This chapter demonstrates that, despite its flexibility, the decentralised enforcement model is not a credible replacement of collective security.

One of the core ideas of this book is the focus of Chapter 4. This chapter discusses the concept of collective security. It proposes mainly that contrary to widespread belief, collective security does not belong exclusively to the province of the Security Council. This chapter also challenges the view that states cannot undertake collective security measures in the absence of Security Council authorisation. It proposes that regional organisations can residually act in the default of the Security Council action and in situations where the in-built Charter protective mechanisms fail to protect states.

Chapter 5 analyses the practice of regional organisations since the end of the Cold War. This is aimed at establishing that the use of force by regional organisations, without the authorisation of the Security Council, is not just an accidental occurrence that will soon cease to be. This chapter examines the emerging principles in regional collective security. Such principles include the replacement of the Host State consent with a treaty-based consent enabling regional organisations to use force on the territories of their members. The particular benefits to be derived from decentralised collective security, as well as its limitations, are also discussed.

An observation is necessary here concerning the structure of this chapter. While it may be more desirable to approach the analysis here by focusing on particular instances of regional interventions, this approach presents certain difficulties. Most of the legal principles analysed here features virtually in every case study that could have been adopted, while no single of these cases explains the principles exhaustively. The approach of this chapter is therefore, to consider instances of regional intervention within the analysis of various legal principles concerned herewith as and when they arise.

Chapter 6 embodies another major idea of this book. It discusses the impact of regionally authorised enforcement action on the prohibition of threat or use of force. Generally speaking, regional enforcement actions constitute an exception to the prohibition of force in Article 2(4) of the Charter, insofar as such actions are authorised by the Security Council. However, in the light of state practice to the effect that regional enforcement actions have taken place outside Chapter VIII, these actions can no longer be simply regarded as *just* exceptions to the Charter rule. Rather they challenge the rule in Article 2(4). This chapter therefore argues that consensual military intervention by regional organisations does not violate any peremptory norm under Article 2(4).

The conclusion brings together all the cogent points made in the chapters and develops further the advantages to be derived from decentralised collective security. It emphasises that while Chapter VIII has evidently become inadequate in the context of the modern world, regional organisations must continue to defer to its provisions wherever possible, especially Article 54 which obligates them to report to the Security Council at all times.

This book does not advocate that regional organisations should discard the UN Charter and replace it with their own constitutions. Rather, what it proposes is a more pragmatic relationship between the UN and regional organisations based on the provisions of the UN Charter and constitutions of such organisations in a manner that will bring out the best in the two regimes for the overall health of collective security.

1

The Meaning of Regionalism

INTRODUCTION

THE UNITED NATIONS Charter allocated to regional organisations powers for the maintenance of peace and security in a way that its predecessor, the Covenant of the League of Nations, did not. These powers are contained in Chapter VIII of the UN Charter and are entrusted to what the Charter refers to as 'regional arrangements and agencies'.

The phrase 'regional organisations' is ubiquitously found in academic writing today to refer to those entities differently named in Chapter VIII. Yet, the term 'regional organisation' has a different connotation in international law, in contrast to, say international relations, and is accorded a technical meaning in the UN Charter.

Furthermore, there have been great changes to the normative conception of 'regional organisation' and 'regionalism' in contemporary society, compared to what was intended in 1945 when the UN was formed. It is therefore worthwhile to commence analysis of regional organisations by first appreciating the usage of the terms 'regional organisations' and 'regionalism' by writers across disciplines, and by states in their daily interactions. Such a preliminary exercise is intended to illuminate the actual and normatively desirable place of regional organisations in the collective security system, being the preoccupation of subsequent chapters.

1.1. REGIONAL ORGANISATIONS: AN HISTORICAL OVERVIEW

Historically, states co-exist on the basis of association.[1] Such associations are often defined by the linear distances that exist between states. Hence, it is common to speak of state groupings on universal, regional and sub-regional bases. These associations are often denominated by political,

[1] See James Mayall, 'National Identity and the Revival of Regionalism' in Louise Fawcett and Andrew Hurrell (eds), *Regionalism in World Politics: Regional Organization and International Order* (Oxford, Oxford University Press, 1995) 169 (hereafter Fawcett and Hurrell); Wolfgang Friedmann, *The Changing Structure of International Law* (London, Stevens, 1964) 213, quoting Phillip Jessup, *A Modern Law of Nations* (1948) at 7.

social or economic interrelationships.[2] Yet, the study of international organisations focusing on the dynamics of states' relations did not attract serious academic interest before the emergence of the League of Nations (hereafter the League)[3] and the United Nations Organisations (hereafter the UN).[4] Most academic writings on international relations before this period centred on the substantive questions of international law, conceived as the law governing the relations between states. Principal intellectual concerns at that time were *inter alia*, issues such as the law of treaties, recognition in international law, the law of neutrality, and jurisdiction over territorial waters.[5]

That is not to say that there were no international organisations prior to the emergence of the League and the UN. Certainly, European and American States had, long before the League and the UN, organised themselves into some kinds of regional associations such as the Congress of Vienna[6] and the Rhine Commission,[7] both formed in 1815. The International Telegraph Union[8] and the Universal Postal Union[9] are examples of universal organisations that existed since 1865 and 1875 respectively. Nevertheless, studies of international organisations before the UN concentrated predominantly on economic issues.[10]

The outbreak of the First World War necessitated the organisation of the international community of states under a more effective, universal umbrella. The League was the first universal organisation of its kind in terms of political salience. Its Covenant recognised and preserved the pre-existing regional basis for states' co-existence.[11] Thus, regional arrange-

[2] See Fawcett and Hurrell, above note 1, 1.

[3] For an excellent review of the early development of regionalism, see AH Robertson, *The Law of International Institutions in Europe* (Manchester, Manchester University Press, 1961); RJ Harrison, *Europe in Question: Theories of Regional Integration* (London, George Allen & Unwin Ltd, 1971). For the statistical chronology of the increasing relevance of international institutions to world politics see Michael Wallace and David Singer, 'Intergovernmental Organisations in the Global System, 1815–1964: A Quantitative Description', (1970) XXIV *International Organisation* 272.

[4] For similar views, see Robertson, above note 3, Fawcett and Hurrell, above note 1, *et seq.*

[5] Robertson, above note 3, 1.

[6] See Genevieve Peterson, 'Political Inequality at the Congress of Vienna', (1945) 60(4) *Political Science Quarterly* 544; Harold Jacobson, *Network of Interdependence: International Organization and the Global Political System* (New York, Alfred A Knopf, 2nd edn, 1984).

[7] See David O'Brien, 'The Search for Subsidiarity: The UN, African Regional Organizations and Humanitarian Action', (2000) 7(3) *International Peacekeeping* 57, arguing particularly on page 59 that 'arguably the first attempt to allocate political authority in a tiered regime comprising sovereign states and an intergovernmental body dates to the creation of the Central Commission for the Navigation of the Rhine in 1815'. See also Robertson, above note 3 at 4 *et seq.*

[8] Robertson, above note 3 at 4.

[9] *Ibid.*

[10] Fawcett and Hurrell noted that 'there has been a great deal of attention devoted to the economic issues associated with schemes for free trade and economic integration', above note 1, 2.

[11] Article 21.

ments such as the Inter-American System[12] flourished alongside the League. However, although mentioned in its Article 21, the League Covenant did not allocate any significant role to regional organisations, and neither the League itself nor these organisations received any major academic attention.[13]

The formation of the UN in 1945[14] was a turning point in the status (and the study) of regional organisations in international law. Not only did the UN Charter, like the League Covenant, preserve the place of regional organisations, it went further to allocate crucial roles to such organisations in the emerging international legal order. These roles have to be performed within specific legal parameters. Hence, Chapter VIII of the Charter contains provisions regulating regional organisations.[15]

Several factors have been adduced for the rise in the political importance of regionalism after the formation of the UN. The 'developments within Europe (the EC decision to press ahead with the completion of the Single Market, the negotiation of the Maastricht Treaty, and enlargement of the Union towards Scandinavia and Central Europe)'[16] have been given credit for the rise in regionalism. The regionalist wave in the 1960s has also been attributed to the growth in the number, scope, and diversity of regionalist schemes,[17] causing an unprecedented intermingling of microeconomic organisations and macroregional political organisations.[18] It has also been argued that the dividing line between economic and

[12] Inter-American System is the appellation by which the trio of the Charter of the Organisation of American States (OAS), adopted at Bogota in 1948, the Rio Treaty of 1947 and the Treaty on Pacific Settlement (Pact of Bogota) 1948 is commonly referred. The Texts of the OAS can be found in Treaty Series No 1 1-A (OEA/Ser-A/2(SEFP) Add.), as amended by the Protocol of Amendment to the Organisation of American States 'Protocol of Buenos Aires', signed on February 27, 1967 at the Third Inter-American Conference; Protocol of Amendment 'Cartagena Protocol' signed at Indias de Cartagena, approved on 5 December 1985 by the Fourteenth Special Session of the General Assembly; Protocol of Amendment to the OAS Charter 'Protocol of Washington', approved by the Sixteenth Special Session of the General Assembly 14 December 1992; and the Protocol of Amendment of the OAS Charter 'Protocol of Managua' adopted at the Nineteenth Special Session of the General Assembly 10 June 1993. OES/Ser. X/11 (English) Treaty Series No 61. See also (1986) 25 *International Legal Materials* at 529; General Assembly Document OEA/Ser. P. AG/doc. 16 (XIV-E/85) rev. 2, 26 February 1986.

[13] Robertson argued that '[t]he League of Nations found a small place in the textbooks . . . [but] that was practically the end of it, except for the specialist who pursued his studies so far as to learn about the Central Commission for Navigation on the Rhine', above note 3, 2.

[14] See Ruth B Russell, *A History of the United Nations Charter: The Role of the United States 1940–1945* (Washington DC, The Brookings Institution, 1958), for a comprehensive account of both the Dumbarton Oaks Meeting and the San Francisco Conference leading to the formation of the United Nations Organisation.

[15] Articles 52 and 53 of the UN Charter.

[16] Fawcett and Hurrell, above note 1, 1, *et seq.*

[17] Paul Taylor, *International Organization in the Modern World: The Regional and Global Process* (London, Pinter, 1993) 24–28.

[18] See Joseph Nye, *Peace in Parts: Integration and Conflicts in Regional Organizations* (Boston, Little, Brown & Co, 1971).

political regionalism became harder to draw. Hence, 'security cannot be considered separately from the regional economy'.[19] Some writers have even suggested the failure of universalism as being directly responsible for the growth in regionalism.[20]

Whatever is responsible for the rise in regionalism after the UN, there is no doubt that the traditional conception of regional organisations as unidimensional entities gave way to new regionalism,[21] which is multidimensional in character. Thus, classical regional organisations such as the Organisation of American States (OAS 1948) and the Organisations of African Unity (OAU 1963) were joined by the Caribbean Community and Common Market (CARICOM, 1973), the South African Development Coordination Conference (SADCC, 1980), the Economic Community of West African States (ECOWAS, 1975), and the Gulf Co-operation Council (GCC, 1981) shortly before the end of the Cold War. The pedigree of these latter organisations consists in their rejection of the integrationist pretensions of the older organisations and subscription to limited numbers and goals, while at the same time embracing a diversity of purpose.[22]

In 1945, several states met in San Francisco to discuss the Dumbarton Oaks Proposals[23] in order to establish a constituent instrument for the UN. Some of these states attempted to define regional organisations under the UN Charter and lay down criteria for determining such.[24] These efforts failed. The majority of participating states felt that laying down criteria at that stage might thwart the future development of regional organisations.[25] In addition there were disagreements about the relationship between pre-existing regional organisations, such as the Inter-American

[19] Yochi Funabaschi, 'The Asianization of Asia', (1993) 72(5) *Foreign Affairs* 81, also cited by Fawcett and Hurrell, above note 1, 4.

[20] See Robertson, above note 3, (arguing that a 'universal system of international cooperation will not function without mutual forbearance and respect and a willingness of all parties to abide by the basic rules of the game. It was these qualities which were found to be lacking during the troubled years immediately after the war. The excessive use of the veto by the Soviet Union, culminating in its boycott of the Security Council, and the refusal by a number of the satellite States to participate in the work of the Specialised Agencies or, in some cases, their actual withdrawal from membership struck a severe blow at the concept of universalism.') 4–5.

[21] 'New regionalism' is a term used by several writers to describe the set of regional arrangements that emerged shortly before the end of the Cold War. See Michael Keating, *The New Regionalism in Western Europe: Territorial Restructuring and Political Change* (Cheltenham, Edward Elgar Publishing Limited, 1998); Norman Palmer, *The New Regionalism in Asia and the Pacific* (Lexington, Mass., Lexington Books, 1991); Björn Hettne, 'Neo-Mercantilism: The Pursuit of Regionness', (1993) 28(3) *Cooperation and Conflict.*

[22] Louise Fawcett, 'Regionalism in Historical Perspective' in Fawcett and Hurrell, above note 3 at 16.

[23] Russell, above note 14 particularly Chapters VIII–XXI on the Dumbarton Oaks proceedings. See the text of invitation in US State Department, *Foreign Relations of the United States: The Conferences at Malta and Yalta,* 1945, Publication 6199 (1955).

[24] Below.

[25] The British for instance argued that it was unreasonable to discriminate against possible later treaties of the same character. See Ruth Russell, above note 14, 691.

System and the UN.[26] Unlike the League Covenant which had explicitly mentioned the Monroe Doctrine (upon which the Inter-American peace system was based)[27] the UN Charter did not incorporate any of the pre-existing organisations by name. This was despite the fact that it was recognised at Dumbarton Oaks that the existence of regional bodies for dealing with peace and security matters should not be precluded.[28] In the end, the states participating at the San Francisco Conference unanimously rejected all proposed definitions of regionalism, including the Egyptian proposal, perhaps the most challenging of them all.[29]

Since the inception of the Charter, writers across various disciplines[30] have continuously engaged in the task of defining and conceptualising regionalism. For international lawyers, the need to define regionalism grew stronger with the relationship developing between the UN and regional organisations after the Cold War. During the Cold War, legal writers hardly conducted doctrinal inquiry into regionalism. Most Cold War literature on the subject matter[31] focused on the interpretation of the Charter provisions concerning regional organisations.[32] The extremely small body of doctrinal works[33] in existence at this time made little or no

[26] As we shall see in the next chapter, debates about the place of the pre-existing regional organisations such as the Inter-American System, in the political equation of the UN came second only to the question of the veto among the issues that very nearly thwarted the creation of the United Nations.

[27] Robertson, above note 3, 5.

[28] For the attempts by American States to have the Inter-American System encrypted in the Charter, see US Department of State, *Postwar Foreign Policy Preparation*, Publication 3580 (February 1950); Russell, above note 14, 552 *et seq.*

[29] See Chapter 2.

[30] Robert Clawson, (ed), *East-West Rivalry in the Third World: Security Issues and Regional Perspectives* (Wilmington, Del., Scholarly Resources, 1986); W Rostow, 'The Coming Age of Regionalism', (1990) 74(5) *Encounter*; Robert Sato, J Wanadi, and S-J Han (eds), *Asian Security Issues: Regional and Global* (Berkeley, Institute of East Asian Studies, University of California, 1988); Iver Neumann, (ed), *Regional Great Powers in International Politics* (London, Macmillan, 1992); Charles Pentland, *International Theory and European Integration* (London, Faber & Faber, 1973); Ernst Haas, 'The Challenge of Regionalism', (1958) 12(4) *International Organization.*

[31] Leonard Meeker, 'Defensive Quarantine and the Law', (1963) 57 *American Journal of International Law* 515; Carl Christol, 'Maritime Quarantine: The Naval Interdiction of Offensive Weapons and Associated Matériel to Cuba, 1962' *Ibid*, 525; Abraham Chayes, 'Law and the Quarantine of Cuba,' (1962/63) 41 *Foreign Affairs* 550; A Eide, 'Peace-keeping and Enforcement by Regional Organizations,' (1966) 3 *Journal of Peace Research* 125; WT Mallison, 'Limited Naval Blockade or Quarantine Interdiction: National and Collective Defense Claims Valid Under International Law', (1962) 31 *George Washington University Law Review* 339–43.

[32] For instance, the major preoccupation of legal writers in the 1960s Cuban Missile Crisis and the Dominican Republic conflict was to interpret enforcement action under Chapter VIII for the purpose of determining whether the OAS ought to have obtained the authorisation of the Security Council before imposing naval interdiction on the High Seas and whether the economic sanctions imposed by the OAS on Dominic Republic and Cuba in respect of alleged subversive activities of the former and the ideological practices of the latter violated Article 53(1) of the UN Charter.

[33] Hans Kelsen, 'Is the North Atlantic Treaty a Regional Arrangement?' (1950) *American Journal of International Law* 162 and Eric Beckett, *The North Atlantic Treaty, the Brussels Treaty*

real attempt to match theoretical propositions with empirical developments such as state practice.[34] Conversely, legal writings after the Cold War have concentrated far too much on the practice of regional organisations, in the context of collective security, almost to the exclusion of doctrinal analysis.[35]

With the unprecedented empowerment of regional organisations by the UN Charter comes the need to understand, in the clearest terms possible, what these organisations are and who they represent. Are they regional organisations predating the Charter or new ones to be formed? Could these organisations be the signatories to the mutual pacts and defence treaties[36] agreed after the First World War?

In the following sections, an examination of how regionalism has been conceived by states and writers is undertaken.[37] For instance, it will be shown here that the fear expressed by early functionalists like David Mitrany[38] that regionalism is at odds with universal organisations, is unfounded and has been made obsolete by the development of a partnership between the UN and regional organisations. Certain issues, which will be taken up elsewhere in this book, will also be introduced. An example of these is the contention that the use of force by regional organisations without the authorisation of the Security Council invariably violates Article 2(4) and Article 53(1) of the UN Charter.[39] Finally, this chapter highlights how political debates have come to shape the legal creation of regional organisations within the Charter framework, and how legal

and the Charter of the United Nations (London, Stevens & Sons, 1950) are the best known attempts by lawyers at doctrinal analysis of regionalism during the Cold War.

[34] Michael Akehurst, 'Enforcement Actions by Regional Organisations with Special Reference to the Organization of American States', (1967) 42 *British Yearbook of International Law* 175, is perhaps the most significant attempt by an international lawyer to undertake a doctrinal and empirical analysis of regionalism during the Cold War.

[35] Karsten Nowrot and Emily Schabacker, 'The Use of Force to Restore Democracy: International Legal Implications of the ECOWAS Intervention in Sierra Leone' (1998) 14(2) *American University Journal of International Law Review* 32; A Conteh, 'Sierra Leone and the Norms of Non-Intervention: Evolution and Practice' (1995) 7 *African Journal of International and Comparative Law* 166; Georg Nolte, 'Restoring Peace by Regional Action: International Legal Aspects of the Liberian Conflict', 23 *ZaöR V* 53/3 603; Kofi Oteng Kufor, 'The Legality of the Intervention in the Liberian Civil War By the Economic Community of West African States', (1993) (5) *African Journal of International and Comparative Law* 525; Funmi Olonisakin, *Reinventing Peacekeeping in Africa: Conceptual and Legal Issues in ECOMOG Operations* (The Hague, Kluwer Law International, 2000).

[36] Treaty of Alliance and Mutual Assistance of 10 December 1944 between France and Soviet Union, (1944) *American Journal of International Law*, 83; Treaty of Alliance of 12 Dec 1943 between Soviet Union and Czechoslovakia (Friendens-Warte 45 (1945), 73); Treaty of Alliance of May 26, 1942, (1942) 36 *American Journal of International Law* 216.

[37] In his article, 'Of System, Boundaries, and Territoriality', (1986) 43(1) *World Politics*, Fredrich Kratochwil pointed out the importance of undertaking groundwork aimed at clarifying thoughts thus: 'An examination of shifts in the functions of boundaries is particularly helpful for a better understanding of the origin and evolution of the present territorial system'.

[38] David Mitrany, *A Working Peace System* (Oxford, Oxford University Press, 1944).

[39] Below, Chapter 6.

issues have influenced the states' perception of regionalism in the Charter. It demonstrates how certain considerations help in understanding—and hence in defining—regionalism. This will be the focus of Chapter 2.

1.2. REGIONS, REGIONAL ORGANISATIONS AND REGIONALISM: CONCEPTUAL ISSUES

The terms 'regions', 'regional organisations' and 'regionalism' are ambiguous[40] and elusive.[41] What constitutes a regional organisation may very well be a function of whether a particular organisation is geared towards economic, political or military goals.[42] As Hurrell has noted, '[t]here are no "natural" regions and definitions of "region" and indicators of "regionness" vary according to the particular problem or question under investigation'.[43]

The problems of defining regionalism received a great deal of academic attention in the late 1960s and 1970s but the results yielded few clear conclusions.[44] In this period,

> [r]egionalism was often analysed in terms of the degree of social cohesiveness (ethnicity, race, language, religion, culture history, consciousness of a common heritage;) economic cohesiveness (regime type, ideology), and organizational cohesiveness (existence of formal regional institutions).[45]

As Oran Young once observed, there is emerging a pattern of linkages between various regions of the world which focus leaders' attention upon extra-regional interests and activities.[46]

Writers' attempts to define regionalism show that there is little gain to be derived from seeking scientific definitions of concepts.[47] Bruce Russett, for instance, attempted to calibrate regionalism in definitive terms in his pioneering work in 1976.[48] Described by Paul Taylor as having used a

[40] Andrew Hurrell, 'Regionalism in Theoretical Perspective' in Fawcett and Hurrell, above note 1, 38.

[41] Michael Keating, above note 21 at 9.

[42] See generally, Jack Plano and Robert Riggs, *Forging World Order* (New York, 1967); JS Nye, *International Regionalism* (New York, 1962). But see specifically, JS Nye, 'Regional Institutions' in Cyril E Black and Richard A Falk (eds), *The Future of International Legal Order: The Structure of the International Environment* (Princeton, Princeton University Press, 1972) Vol 4 at 429, (noting that 'there are no absolutely naturally-determined regions').

[43] Above note 40.

[44] *Ibid*. See also Fawcett and Hurrell, above note 1, 10.

[45] *Ibid*. See also U Wannop, *The Regional Imperative: Regional Planning and Governance in Britain, Europe and the United States* (London, Jessica Kingsley, 1995).

[46] Oran Young, 'Political Discontinuities in International System' (1968) 20(3) *World Politics* 369 at 392. Also cited by Taylor, above note 17, 11.

[47] Hurrell, above note 40, 38.

[48] Bruce Russett, *International Regions and the International Systems: A Study in Political Ecology* (Chicago, Rand McNally and Co, 1976); Bruce Russett *et al*, *World Handbook of Political and Social Indicators* (New Haven, Yale University Press, 1964); Bruce Russett, *Power and Community in World Politics* (San Francisco, WH Freeman, 1974).

'highly sophisticated quantitative methodology',[49] Russett's work soon became 'one of the reasons for the decline of interest in the subject'.

Regionalism is often conceptualised by reference to extrapolative conditions.[50] Regional organisations are thus sometimes perceived as any arrangements not 'globally inclusive in their membership'.[51] Using this element alone, organisations such as the Commonwealth are perceived as regional, notwithstanding that its membership is scattered all over the globe with no real links except incidents of shared historical experience amongst members. According to this reasoning, regionalism occurs where the requisite number of congregating states falls short of universalism.[52]

There is also a manifest problem with the way in which states conceive regionalism and regional organisations in their international relations. During the Cold War, the Soviet Union consistently denied that NATO was a regional organisation.[53] This was in order to prevent NATO members (especially the United States) from intervening in European conflicts. Yet, during the conflict leading to the disintegration of the Socialist Federal Republics of Yugoslavia (SFRY), NATO had responded to Security Council Resolution 816.[54] The Security Council had called upon states 'acting nationally or through regional organizations or agencies, to take all necessary measures in the airspace of Bosnia and Herzegovina, in the event of violations, proportionate to the specific circumstances and the nature of the flight'.[55] NATO states did not respond *nationally*, a choice that would undoubtedly have prevented them from making a *collective* appearance under the auspices of NATO. NATO's appearance was based on the second part of that provision: 'acting through regional organisations'. Neither the UN nor any states participating in the operation or otherwise, protested against NATO's intervention under the auspices of Chapter VIII.

[49] Paul Taylor, above note 17, 9.

[50] See generally George Downs (ed), *Collective Security beyond the Cold War* (Ann Arbor, Mich., University of Michigan Press, 1994).

[51] Nye, 'Regional Institution', above note 42 at 430.

[52] See George Downs, above note 50.

[53] See Russell, above note 14, Chapter 27.

[54] In fact, NATO had expressed its readiness to support the UN in an operation as early as 17 December 1992. In a letter sent by the Secretary-General of NATO on behalf of member states to the UN, in response to an earlier letter sent from the former to the latter, NATO states said that 'We confirm today the preparedness of our Alliance to support, on a case-by-case basis and in accordance with our own procedures, peacekeeping operations under the authority of the Security Council, which has the primary responsibility for international peace and security. We are ready to respond positively to initiatives that the UN Secretary-General might take to seek Alliance assistance in the implementation of UN Council Security Resolutions'. See Final Communiqué, Ministerial Meeting of the North Atlantic Council, NATO Headquarters, Brussels, 17 December 1992. Also cited in the *Atlantic News* 2484, Annex 19 December 1992.

[55] UN Doc. S/RES/816. On this point see, Rosalyn Higgins, 'Peace and Security: Achievements and Failures', (1995) 6 *European Journal of International Law* 445 at 452–53.

Furthermore, in its case against ten NATO member states, instituted before the International Court of Justice (hereafter: ICJ), the Federal Republic of Yugoslavia (FRY), argued that NATO was a regional organisation.[56] The motive behind the FRY's classification of NATO is Article 53(1) of the UN Charter. If NATO thus were a regional organisation, then its use of force against the FRY without the authorisation of the Security Council would have violated Article 53(1) of the UN Charter.

These examples demonstrate the intermingling of political and legal elements when states consider whether or not an organisation is a regional one. NATO chose not to regard itself as a regional organisation for political reasons: it did not wish to subject its enforcement actions to the authority and control of the Security Council.[57] Article 54 of the Charter obligates regional organisations to report whatever measures they take or contemplate under regional arrangement to the Security Council. It is thus tempting to agree with the assertion that 'it is how political actors perceive and interpret the idea of a region and notions of "regionness" that is critical'.[58]

1.3. CRITERIA FOR CONCEPTUALISING A REGION

Writers have proposed several theories in order to define what regions and regional organisations mean.[59] These theories differ widely, both in their depth and significance. In the following sections, an analysis of some of these theories is undertaken with the intention of revealing the inherent weaknesses of such theories. A functional definition of regionalism is adopted and this will be used throughout the book.

1.3.1. Geographical Proximity

It has been advocated that there should be geographical proximity between states forming a regional organisation.[60] The rationale for this

[56] See Legality of Use of Force (*Yugoslavia v Belgium*), International Court of Justice (ICJ) *Press Communiqué* No 99/17 (29 April 1999).

[57] See Nigel White, 'The Legality of Bombing in the Name of Humanity', (2000) 5(1) *Journal of Conflict and Security Law* 27.

[58] Hurrell, above note 40, 38.

[59] For an excellent analysis of regional integration theories, see particularly Reginald Harrison above note 3; Grove Haines, *European Integration* (Baltimore, The Johns Hopkins Press, 1957).

[60] See Nye, above note 42, Russett, above note 48, and Ellen-Frey Wouters, below note 64; DW Bowett, *Self-Defence in International Law* (Manchester, Manchester University Press, 1958) 219; Waldemar Hummer and Michael Schweitzer in Bruno Simma (eds), *The Charter of the United Nations: A Commentary* (Oxford, Oxford University Press, 3rd edn, 2002) 807 at 820 *et seq*.

view consists, *inter alia,* in that territorial proximity justifies claims to regionality.[61] This criterion, in the context of international law, first attained prominence at San Francisco. The Egyptian delegate to the San Francisco Conference had proposed an amendment to the Dumbarton Oaks proposal relating to regional arrangements. In it he stated that:

> There shall be considered as regional arrangements organizations of a permanent nature grouping in a given geographical area several countries which, by reason of their proximity, community of interest or cultural, linguistic, historical or spiritual affinities, make themselves jointly responsible for the peaceful settlement of any disputes which may arise between them and for the maintenance of peace and security of their region, as well as safeguarding of their interests and the development of their economic and cultural relations.[62]

The United States objected to this definition on the ground that while it addressed 'obvious legitimate and eligible factors',[63] it fell short of covering all possible cases that could come under the concepts of regional arrangements or agencies. The United States gave no examples of such possible cases. It is however interesting to note that in its response to the Egyptian definition, the United States had apparently made no distinction between regionalism as a concept, and regional organisations, as a legal phrase engendering a different connotation altogether. It would appear that, by basing its notion of a regional organisation on the consistency of regional actions with the purposes of the United Nations, the United States subscribed to a liberal interpretation of regionalism in contrast to the restrictive definition offered by Egypt.

Several writers have expounded theories of region similar to the one proposed by Egypt at San Francisco.[64] Joseph Nye defined an international region as 'a limited number of states linked together by a geographic relationship and by a degree of mutual interdependence'.[65] He then went on to define regionalism as 'the formation of interstate groupings on the basis of regions'.[66] Nye proceeded to conceptualise a

[61] See J Beaufays, *Théorie du régionalisme* (Brussels, S Story-Scientia, 1985).

[62] *United Nations Conference on International Organization* (hereafter UNCIO), *Documents* vol XII, 850.

[63] *Ibid*, at 858. *UNCIO, Summary Report of the Fifth Meeting of Committee III/4,* 8 June 1945, *Doc* 889, III/4/12, 1.

[64] See especially Inis L Claude, *Swords into Plowshares: The Problems and Progress of International Organization* (New York, Random House, 4th edn, 1971); Joseph Nye, above note 42; Ernst B Haas, *The Uniting of Europe: Political, Social, and Economic Forces, 1950–1957* (Stanford, California: Stanford University Press, 1968); *ibid, Beyond the Nation-State: Functionalism and International Organization* (Stanford, Stanford University Press, 1964); Ellen-Fry Wouters 'The Prospects for Regionalism in World Affairs' in Cyril E Black and Richard A Falk (eds), the *Future of International Legal Order,* Vol 1 (Princeton, Princeton University Press, 1969), 465–594; Hans Kelsen, *Collective Security under International Law,* International Studies, Naval War College 1954 (1956), particularly at 49, (1957) 259–60, also cited by Hummer/Schweitzer, above note 60 at 821.

[65] Nye (ed), *International Regionalism* (Boston, Little, Brown & Co, 1968) xii.

[66] *Ibid*, vii.

regional organisation as one whose membership is restricted in principle and in practice on the basis of geographical contiguity (i.e., there are no non-regional members); and this contiguity involves a *proximity* and compactness.[67] He defined as 'quasi-regional organizations' those whose membership is in part on the basis of geographical consanguinity or a geographical area of concern; but which in *practice* included non-regional members. All other restrictive membership organisations—including universal ones—he treated as non-regional.[68]

Apparently Nye placed a great emphasis on geographical proximity. However, in distinguishing between regional and quasi-regional organisations, he referred to the importance to be accorded 'principle' and 'practice'. Whereas in principle states can claim to belong to a regional organisation by virtue of their physical proximity, where such states, in practice, include non-regional members—that is non-proximate members—they are deemed to be quasi-regional organisations. NATO would be deemed to be a quasi-regional organisation under this theory by virtue of the membership of the United States and Canada. Whether these parameters are realistic or useful in classifying organisations is debatable. However, to assert that a regional organisation becomes a 'quasi' one because it contains one or more 'non-regional' members is to give geography an undue prominence in defining a region. This is even more so when a regional organisation can also lose its regional quality, according to Nye, if it consists of non-regional members or operates in a non-regional geographical area of concern.

In contradistinction from other advocates of geographical proximity, Nye urged that there is the need to measure this proximity in terms of physical distance. This assumption that regionalism implicates a spatial dimension appears anachronistic, and is demonstrably contradicted by the technorealities and interdependency of the contemporary world. Once again, NATO is a good example of a case where physical distance amongst member states does not seem to affect the effectiveness of the organisation. Few would doubt that the evolution of weapons of mass destruction (WMD), long-range ballistic missiles and rapid communication facilities have shrunk linear distances between countries. The true determinant test of a region, it is submitted, cannot inhere solely or substantially in the *physical* nearness of states, even if we accept this criterion for its symbolic

[67] In support of this theory, Nye referred to the 'precise pedigree of contiguity', demanded and concluded that this was entirely a matter of choice. He then gave the example that '6000 miles between the most distant capitals (half the maximum distance between capitals of UN members) and no country more than 1500 miles from the other makes NATO "regional" would require a threshold of 3000 miles', Nye, 'Regional Institution', above note 42, fn 19.

[68] *Ibid* (Emphasis added).

importance.[69] It is not surprising therefore that Nye himself noted, and rightly too, that '[p]hysical contiguity can be misleading, not only because technology, history, and culture can make "effective distance" differ from linear distance, as some writers put it, but also because images of what constitutes a region are affected by different political interests'.[70]

Consideration of national interests, be they political, social, economic or even military, influence states in their conception of regionalism more than considerations of distance. 'Our purpose in promoting a world of regional partnership,' said President Johnson of the United States, 'is not without self-interest. For as they grow in strength inside a strong United Nations, we can look forward to a decline in the burden that America has had to bear in this generation'.[71] The concept of a region being so promoted by statesmen is one that seems to actually operate without the constraints of boundary. Hence President Charles de Gaulle of France was perfectly in harmony with this belief when he enthused that 'it is in keeping with the conditions of our times to create entities more vast than each of the European States'.[72]

1.3.2. The Multidimensional Conception

Some writers have proposed the operational scope of regional organisations as the main criterion for defining a region. Bruce Russett's approach, while conceptually similar to the trend prevalent among several scholars, shows distinctive qualities in its practical implications. 'The notion of a region either within a single country or a region of the world embracing a number of nations', he writes, 'has provided a venerable tool in the workshed of political and social research.'[73] While this tool 'like most ancient implements originally designed for specific purposes by their inventors' has quickly assumed different responsibilities, it has been refined in time by different workers for particular tasks. Curiously enough, 'while they usually kept the basic name "region" for what they were working with, the implements became so specialised that, like the innumerable breeds of *Canis familiarus*, one would hardly know that they all belong to the same species'.[74]

[69] Hurrell, for instance, argued that 'geographical proximity and contiguity in themselves tell us very little about either the definitions of regions or the dynamics of regionalism, but they do helpfully distinguish regionalism from other forms of "less than global" organization', above note 40 at 38.

[70] Nye, above note 42, citing Karl Deutsch and Walter Isard, 'A Note on a Generalized Concept of Effective Distance', (1961) *Behavioural Science* 308–10.

[71] Lyndon Johnson, *Department of States Bulletin* (September 26, 1966) 4453.

[72] Press Conference, September 9, 1965. Quoted by Nye, 'Regional Institutions' above note 42.

[73] Russett, 'International Regions' above note 48, 1.

[74] *Ibid.*

Russett's metaphor, however, does not illuminate the definitional *problématique* of a region. Europe and Africa are two distinct regions that are relatively politically and socially homogeneous within themselves. Nevertheless, as Russett himself has noted, it is difficult to draw the boundaries as to maximise the similarity within each group and minimise that between them.[75] Roderic Davinson dramatically underlined the problem of defining a region in a 1964 article symbolically entitled 'Where is the Middle East?'.[76] Russett asked if it extended from Morocco to Pakistan, or whether a line should be drawn somewhere between. 'What do we do,' he queried, 'about Israel which, though right in the middle of any geographic delimitation of the region, still does not fit by any cultural criterion?'[77]

According to Taylor, rather than subscribing to geographical proximity for its own sake, 'a selection has to be made'.[78] However, this cannot overlook the 'recurrent theme'[79] which is a 'concern with that particular scale of geographical area which is best fitted to the performance of tasks judged crucial for the welfare of individuals, or for the advantage of government. That area may extend beyond the boundaries of existing states, or be a part of their territory, or even be coterminous with their frontiers.'[80]

More important is the reason for seeking a definition of a region, which, in the words of Taylor, is a 'concern with finding that area in which function might be most efficiently performed and because of this it is a utilitarian concept'.[81] Taylor suggested that the geographical delimitation of a region has some connection with the dimensionality (in contradistinction from the nature) of the tasks that a particular organisation wishes to perform. Therefore, if the particular task to perform *extends* beyond the geographical confines of member states, there is logic in extending the region beyond that which geography ordinarily defines it to be.

Having correctly noted that 'no generally accepted definition of regionalism exists', Ellen-Frey Wouters defined a regional organisation 'as a permanent, both inner- and outer-directed multifunctional association, located in a particular geographical area, serving a number of states which are mutually interdependent and share certain interests, needs, characteristics, and loyalties'.[82] She then identified two types of association commonly called regional organisations, but which, in her opinion, do not fit into the foregoing definition.[83]

[75] *Ibid.*
[76] Quoted by Russett.
[77] Russett, above note 48.
[78] Above note 17.
[79] *Ibid.*
[80] *Ibid.*
[81] *Ibid.*
[82] Ellen Frey-Wouters, above note 64 at 466.
[83] *Ibid*, 461.

> The collective security arrangements such as the Northern Atlantic Treaty Organization and the South East Asia Treaty Organization are primarily single-purpose associations oriented towards externally motivated power factors. While on paper committed to the development of their regions, they have in practice made little or no contribution to the political or economic integration of their regions.[84]

It is worth mentioning one or two points about Wouter's reference to NATO. First, her classification of NATO as a 'collective security' arrangement is incorrect.[85] NATO is not a collective security, but a collective self-defence arrangement since its constituent treaty does not task it to restrain its members from using force against one another.[86] Whereas collective security organisations restrain their members from using force (ingressive) collective self-defence organisations are concerned with acting against external aggressors (eggressive).[87] As a collective self-defence organisation, NATO's main objective is to use force to repel any attacks directed against any of its members from outside sources.[88] It is this distinction between ingressive and eggressive uses of force that differentiates collective security arrangements, such as the Organisation of the American States and the Economic Community of West African States (ECOWAS),[89] from defensive alliances ones, such as NATO.

Second, an organisation does not fail the test of 'regionalness' simply because it performs a single function.[90] Although it is true that at inception NATO embraced a monolithic vision—responding to outside attacks with force—that does not mean that all regional organisations must be multi-purpose oriented.[91] If the 'single-task' of NATO serves any judgmental value, it is to distinguish NATO from the new regional organisations such as ECOWAS, CARICOM and SADC which emerged during the mid-1970s. Moreover, the extent to which one may continue to regard NATO as a monolithic organisation is now questionable in the light of its

[84] Ellen Frey-Wouters, above note 64 at 461.

[85] For a definition of collective security, see Chapter 3.

[86] For similar view, see Erika De Wet, 'The Relationship between the Security Council and Regional Organizations during Enforcement Action under Chapter VII of the United Nations Charter', (2002) 71 *Nordic Journal of International Law* 1 at 8; Hans Kelsen, above note 33.

[87] But see Yoram Dinstein, *War, Aggression and Self-Defence* (Cambridge, Cambridge University Press, 3rd edn, 2001) 246. The adoption of the terms 'ingressive' and 'egressive' (Cf Dinstein's 'introverted' and 'extroverted',) is explained by the literal meanings of the two terms. An 'ingression' suggests the *right* or *act* of going in, whereas 'egression' is the converse.

[88] See De Wet, above note 86 at 8.

[89] ECOWAS was founded on 28 May 1975. Text of the Treaty of in (1975) XIV *International Legal Materials* 1200, as amended by the Revised Treaty 24th July 1993, text in (1996) 25 *International Legal Materials* 660.

[90] But see Dekker and Myjer, 'Air Strikes on Bosnian Positions: Is NATO also Legally the Proper Instrument of the UN?' (1996) 9 *Leiden Journal of International Law* 413.

[91] Taylor, above note 17 at 7.

declaration in Rome in 1991.[92] By this instrument, NATO reorientated itself in recognition of the fact that the causes and consequences of instability extend to the economic, social and political arena. Accordingly, it empowered itself to perform certain tasks such as peacekeeping operations.[93]

1.3.3. The Neofunctionalist Approach

For the Neofunctionalists, of which Ernst Haas[94] is the leading voice, the deterministic factor in conceptualising a region is deducible only by reference to the dynamics of integration.[95] This theory emphasises the totality of the situational variables that direct the course of regionalism.[96] The principal argument of neofunctionalism is found in its view of the expansive logic of integration.[97] In its simplest form, neofunctionalism posits that the joint activity, which brought sovereign states together, must be larger than the sum of the original independent activities.[98] To the Neofunctionalist therefore, there is a greater need to understand the factors that tend to increase a propensity to tackle problems at regional levels.[99]

In approaching the subject in this manner, Ernst Haas, according to Taylor, self-consciously signalled the 'obsolescence of regional integration theory'[100] in 1976, though a great number of dissenting voices thought that in doing so he was a bit premature. Karl Deutsch, after conceiving regional integration as the 'attainment within a territory, of a "sense of community" and of institutions and practices strong enough and widespread enough for "a long" time, dependable expectations of "peaceful change"

[92] *Declaration on Peace Co-operation* issued by the Heads of State and Government participating in the meeting of the North Atlantic Council (NAAC), 8 November 1991.

[93] Wallander, 'Institutional Assets and Adaptability: NATO After the Cold War' (2000) 54 *International Organization* 712.

[94] Ernst Haas, *The Uniting of Europe* above note 64.

[95] See also Leon Linderg, *The Political Dynamics of European Economic Integration* (Stanford, Stanford University Press, 1963).

[96] Haas expressed his task in *The Uniting of Europe* as mainly to dissect the actual 'integration process' with a view to deriving propositions about its nature. Hence, he focussed more on the situational variables of regionalism rather than the achievements and failures of specific regional organisations.

[97] *Ibid*, 283–317.

[98] *Ibid*; see also, Harrison, above note 3, 76.

[99] For a systemic analysis of functionalism, see Amitai Etzioni, *Political Unification: A Comparative Study of Leaders and Forces* (New York, Rinehart & Winston, 1965); AJR Groom, 'Functionalism in World Society' in AJR Groom and Paul Taylor (eds), *Functionalism: Theory and Practice in International Relations* (London, University of London Press, 1975); John Burton, 'Functionalism and Resolution of Conflict' *ibid*.

[100] Ernst B Haas, *The Obsolescence of Regional Integration Theory* (Berkley, The University of California Press, 1976).

among its populations', conceptualised the combined territory of the United States and Canada as an integrated 'pluralistic security-community'.[101]

Despite its contribution to the regionalism debate, one major weakness of neofunctionalism is its inability to predict the development of regional integration in Western Europe.[102] The situational variables which Haas, Etzioni[103] and Lindberg[104] had adopted in pursuing their theory of region did not act out in Europe as they had predicted. Apparently, by adopting the European Coal and Steel Community (ECSC)[105] as his analytical framework, Haas had hoped to prove that integration within that community would be achieved through the vehicle of pressure groups, businessmen and political parties.[106] Contrary to this assumption, evidence in Europe disclosed that it was the treaty establishing the ECSC, 'its institutions and the goals laid down in the text, plus a number of important external factors, [that] have provided a focus for, and have thus helped to sustain, a rather vague political will to unify'.[107]

1.3.4. The Teleological Approach

Teleology connotes the method by which the meaning of a treaty provision or an idea is derived from the purpose for which that treaty is established or the idea exists. In proposing at San Francisco that the purpose and principles for which the United Nations is established should be the dominant criterion to guide the conceptualisation of regional organisations as opposed to mere geography, the United States set the stage for the teleological school of regionalism.

Bruce Russett was at the forefront of the group of scholars who focused their idea of region upon the development and application of various indicators. This approach seeks to measure the existence of a region by gauging the *consequences* of the practice of it. Russett placed much emphasis on 'socio and cultural homogeneity; that is regions composed of states which are similar with respect to several kinds of internal attributes'.[108] He

[101] Karl W Deutsch, et al, *Political Community and the North Atlantic Area* (Princeton, Princeton University Press, 1975) 6, cited by Ellen-Frey Wouters, above note 64 at 468, 5–6.

[102] Taylor, above note 17 at 9.

[103] Above note 99.

[104] Above note 95.

[105] For analysis, see Gardner Patterson, *Discrimination in International Trade: The Policy Issues 1945–1965* (Princeton, Princeton University Press, 1966) 75–90; Andrew Wyatt-Walter, 'Regionalism, Globalization, and World Economic Order' in Fawcett and Hurrel, above note 1, 74 (arguing on page 80 that 'the European Payments Union (EPU) and the European Coal and Steel Community (ECSC), both established at the beginning of the 1950s, represented the first major steps on the road towards regional integration').

[106] Haas, above note 94, xii.

[107] Harrison, above note 3, 89.

[108] Above note 48 at 3.

identified two elements of such homogeneity: *similarity* of nations in grouping, rather than *identity*, is usually sufficient; and secondly, the concept is multidimensional rather than unidimensional (the similarity should apply over more than a single set of cultural characteristics). The elements which such congregating states share only need to be such that all such states have some closeness to in contradistinction from the ones they share identically. According to Russett, '[c]lose has to be sufficient criterion because, in the real world of social complexity, no two units are ever *identical* in anything of importance.'[109]

It is possible to challenge the notion of multidimensionality proposed by Russett, within the framework of the teleological theory. Russett's idea is premised on the assumption that the multidimensional nature of the socio-cultural variables binding congregating states evidences a stronger desire (and desirability) of a region than a single factor. It is submitted that a single, strong identical culture could actually forge a greater unity amongst several states than do a cluster of cultural indicators to which all those states, even if they are only two, *feel* close. Our objection to Russett's theory is that, while it is agreed that cultural compatibility of some sort—rather than mere spatial affinity—should be accorded greater significance in determining regions, stressing the multidimensional nature of such cultural variables is fraught with serious consequences.

The reality of global politics and regional integration apparently does not support Russett's thesis on the 'multidimensionality' of socio-cultural variables as a criterion of regionalism. All communist states of the world, at the height of the communist ideology, could have congregated as a region more conveniently, regardless of their geographical locations, bound by a single ideological commitment, than the divided States of Africa which actually share a few close cultural values and political aspirations. The thesis being proposed here is that the internal cultural variables that must serve as indicators of a region need not be multidimensional in nature. It is enough to have one strong binding ideology or culture, which may be political, social, or economic. It is unrealistic to assume that the congregating of the States of Western Europe was achieved on the basis of *several* cultural practices rather than an abiding culture of democracy. In fact, the question may be asked, out of the several contending cultural practices, which ones should confederating states give greater weight to, and by what means may such a decision be reached? The presence of a single overwhelming factor, such as ideological fraternity, eliminates the need to engage in a futile exercise of trying to seek common denominators among a multitude of cultural values.

The very divergent circumstances in several countries that move towards federation may present a stumbling block towards the realisation

[109] *Ibid*, at 15.

of a collectivity of shared values. 'Because of the complexity of the integrative process', Wouters noted,

> few coherent models have been worked out. Most of the existing images of regional community formation are fragmentary, consisting of isolated concepts, hypotheses, or generalization. They are almost exclusively based upon the Western European integrative process and do not provide us with theory applicable to other regions as well.[110]

One agrees entirely with this observation. It might be much easier to discern common values in the Western European markets where some measure of political and economic stability exists. Yet, to seek to apply this approach wholly to the regions of the African continent would be a mistaken adaptation of the comparative process.

1.3.5. The Structuralist Perspective

According to Taylor, prediction and prescription, which may be differentiated according to the weight given to each, may denominate a region.[111] Structuralism[112] focuses on distinguishing between the regional integration needs of the North and the South and prescribing different modalities and levels of development for them based on the outcome of such investigation.[113] Structuralism derives from the view that globalism inevitably involved exploitative relations between North and South and that therefore, the various regions in the South should be encouraged to develop stronger relations economically and politically among themselves.[114] Underlining this criterion is the dependency theory.

Other scholars who, as Taylor observed, are not so self-consciously structuralist often deal with this criterion in their work. According to Rajni Kothari, 'there is need for much greater regional co-operation among the various small and weak countries of the world, pooling their political and military resources, entering the world power structure on the basis, and ultimately upsetting the system through which a handful of states are able to dominate the world'.[115]

However, some have argued that a structuralist classification of the universe into North-South poles is no longer tenable as a viable analytical

[110] Above note 64, 470.

[111] *Ibid*, at 11

[112] For an excellent survey of structuralist literatures, see Clive Archer, *International Organization* (London, Routledge, 2nd edn, 1992) 118–24.

[113] See James Mayall, *Nationalism and International Society* (Cambridge, Cambridge University Press, 1990).

[114] See Andre Gunder Frank, 'The Development of Underdevelopment' (1966) *Monthly Review* (September) 369–92.

[115] Rajni Kothari, *Footstep Into the Future: Diagnosis of the Present World and a Design for an Alternative* (New York, The Free Press, 1974) 135.

category.[116] Robert Gilpin pointed out that the Third World (South) 'no longer exists as a meaningful entity'.[117] Mayall also thought that the Third World had lost much of its erstwhile homogeneity and that the show of strength by Third World countries in organisations such as the Organisation of Petroleum Exporting Countries (OPEC) and the Non-Aligned Movement (NAM) had waned.[118] This despondent picture[119] of integration in the Third World prompted other theories, like sub-regionalist grouping, put forward by Rajni Kothari.[120]

1.3.6. The 'Diversity' Approach

Several other criteria have also emerged from the criticisms levelled against those proposed by other scholars. Since these criteria do not readily fit into the already identified conceptual frameworks, they are grouped here under the label 'diversity-approaches' insofar as they emphasise the lack of a unifying theory. Rather than subjecting the idea of a region to predetermined conceptual frameworks, with the aim of deciphering specific attributes or setting out trite requirements, the views classified under the diversity approach emphasise the various indices of regions that are often marginalised in the frenetic world of theorisation.

Louis Wirth rejected altogether attempts to generalise the concept of regionalism, especially from the point of predetermined criteria. According to him,

> [r]egionalism is not one thing, but many things. The failure to discriminate the many distinct factors that underline the emergence and persistence of regions is a serious fault of present day research. Areas of homogeneity have been mistakenly represented as an area of integration.[121]

On the contrary, Rupert Vance deferred to the relationship that exists between man and his natural environment in conceptualising a region. He quoted a geographer's reference to '*an ensemble de rapport* between man and natural milieu in conceptualising regionalism'.[122] Howard, like Moore, conceived of a region as a 'mechanism for providing an economy

116 See for instance, Robert Gilpin, *The Political Economy of International Relations* (Princeton, Princeton University Press, 1987).

117 *Ibid*, 304.

118 Mayall, above note 113, 141.

119 But see Marc Williams, 'Re-articulating the Third World Coalition: The Role of the Environmental Agenda' (1993) 14(1) *Third World Quarterly* 7.

120 Rajni Kothari, above note 115.

121 Rupert Vance, 'The Regional Concept as a Tool for Social Research' in Merrill Jensen (ed), *Regionalism in America* (Madison Wis, University of Wisconsin Press, 1951) 392 at 123.

122 *Ibid*, at 123.

for the decentralization of political power'.[123] Overall, the beauty of the diversity approach lies in the fluidity it brings into the debate about regionalism and regional organisations.

1.4. REGIONALISM AND THE DISCIPLINE OF INTERNATIONAL LAW

There is a dearth of doctrinal works by legal writers on the subject of regionalism. Most legal literature on the subject is based on the provisions of the UN Charter governing regional organisations. It may be that the futile attempt to define regional organisations in San Francisco was responsible for this apathy towards doctrinal analysis amongst legal writers. It may also be argued that the fact that in the world of *Realpolitik* theory and practice hardly converge is another reason for the few doctrinal works on the subject outside the normative guidelines of the UN Charter.

Whatever factors may be responsible for the scarcity of legal materials in this area, there are certain benefits to be derived from, and certain mistakes to be avoided, when legal writers undertake doctrinal exposition of regionalism. As will be developed more fully in the next chapter, it is not entirely useful to always allow one's conception of a region to be guided mainly by what organisations declare themselves to be. As noticed in the NATO example, political, rather than legal factors influence states in such matters.

Furthermore, the increasing involvement of the UN with regional organisations warrants a careful explication of regionalism and regional organisations by legal specialists. When the need arises, the UN often subordinates its own law to the overbearing demand of politics. When the UN allowed NATO to operate in Bosnia/Herzegovina, pursuant to a resolution specifically addressed to regional organisations, the UN did not, by so doing, make a value judgement about the status of NATO under the Charter. It apparently succumbed to the political exigencies of the moment. If the UN means to treat an organisation as regional within the spirit of Chapter VIII,[124] it will unambiguously say so as it did when it

[123] Odum W Howard, *Southern Region of the United States* (Chapel Hill, NC, University of North Carolina Press, 1936); Harry Estill Moore, *American Regionalism: A Cultural-Historical Approach to National Integration* (New York, Henry Holt, 1938) 27.

[124] See *UNCIO Documents* III, 488, 620; *UNCIO Documents* XII, 835–36. See also Bruno Simma (ed), *The Charter of the United Nations: A Commentary* (Oxford, Oxford University Press, 1994) 689. Some states indeed attempted to give to the UN the competence to qualify a 'typical' union of states as a regional agency (Cuba) (see *UNCIO Documents* III, 488, 620); the General Assembly, the charge to examine conformity with the provisions regulating regional arrangements (New Zealand) (see *UNCIO Documents* XII, 793, Russell, above note 14, 703). Some suggested even the Security Council, *UNCIO Documents* IV, 884. However, all these proposals were rejected on the ground that reserving the approval of regional arrangements and agencies for the Security Council might delay the functioning of such arrangements. See Russell, above note 14 at 703, Bruno Simma's *Commentary* above note 124, 689.

accorded the Arab League an observer status in 1950,[125] although it was less explicit when it accorded the OAS the same privilege in 1948.[126]

Finally, relying exclusively on the objectives declared by the constituent treaties of organisations may present certain difficulties. The problem may arise whether an organisation can alter its original *casus foederis* merely by consensus or other informal processes,[127] and if it could do, whether such has the capacity to alter the nature of the organisation as declared in its treaty.[128]

A doctrinal analysis of regional organisations, as Hans Kelsen once undertook,[129] helps to avoid the pitfalls identified above. Then, it is possible to make value judgements and measure practices against set rules and standards and not *vice versa*. Conversely, a legal analysis of regionalism entirely based on the provisions of the UN Charter may not achieve such objective results.

1.5. THE PLACE OF REGIONALISM IN COLLECTIVE SECURITY

Traditionally, regionalism was considered antithetical to the idea of collective security, which was linked, by several writers, to the concept of international government.[130] This was the core objection of functionalism to regionalism.[131] According to the leading exponent of functionalism, David Mitrany, '[t]here is little promise of peace in the mere change from the rivalry of powers and alliances to the rivalry of whole continents . . . Continental unions would have a more real chance than individual states to practise the autarky that makes for division'.[132] Hence, to the Functionalists and Universalists as well, regionalism is inimical to universalism, and except in the sense of regional devolution of functional administration, it has no place in the functional universe.[133]

[125] GA Res 477 (V), 1 Nov 1950.

[126] General Assembly Resolution 253(III). *Repertoires of Practice of the United Nations Organ*, II, 443.

[127] Dekker and Myjer take the position that such an alteration can only be effected through an amendment of the constituent treaty of NATO. See above note 90 at 414–15. But see De Wet, (above note 86) contending that such views as expressed by Dekker and Myjer presents 'an unnecessary static image of the possibilities offered by the constitution of an international organization, which is a living instrument that must be capable of adapting to changes occurring in practise', 8. See also Blokker and Muller, 'NATO as the UN Security Council's Instrument: Questions Marks from the Perspective of International Law' (1996) 9 *Leiden Journal of International Law* 419.

[128] But see Michael Akehurst, above note 34 (arguing that 'the only way in which one can be certain that an arrangement is covered by Chapter VIII of the Charter is to see whether the parties to the arrangement have claimed that it is a regional arrangement, and whether this claim has been accepted in practice by the United Nations') 178.

[129] Above note 33.

[130] See Louise Fawcett, above note 22, 11–12.

[131] See Harrison, above note 3, 27.

[132] David Mitrany, above note 38, 45.

[133] *Ibid.*

As will be seen in the next chapter, the picture of collective security that emerged after the Second World War did not justify the functionalist thesis. As Stanley Hoffmann has noted, '[o]ne reality of post-war world politics [was] the division of a huge and heterogeneous international system into subsystems in which patterns of co-operation and ways of controlling conflicts are either more intense or less elusive of controlling global system'.[134] Thus, the regional organisations that emerged after the Cold War are not a mere reorganisation of universal rivals into contentious regional conclaves.

Certainly, legal writing has not adequately reflected the reality of the post-war developments of regional organisations and the dynamics of their activities under the UN Charter. Regionalism is still mostly treated by writers as meaning the *regionalisation* of collective security: an analytical method which inevitably pitches regionalism against universalism in the context of the UN Charter as though they are at war with each other.[135]

Some writers favour the use of regional organisations in achieving peacekeeping purposes in conformity with the provisions of the UN Charter[136] but decry the incidents of regional organisations operating outside the prescriptions of the Charter.[137] Such writers tend to dismiss regional organisations as lacking both in military and required financial capacities to undertake collective security actions like enforcement actions.[138] For these writers, activities of regional organisations must conform to peacekeeping rules lest such activities are illegal. Other writers argue in favour of total replacement of UN collective security.[139] In a

[134] Stanley Hoffmann, 'International Organization and the International System' in *Janus and Minerva: Essays in the Theory and Practice of International Politics* (Boulder, Col, Westview Press, 1987) 293.

[135] On the theme of regionalism/regionalisation of collective security, J Wolf 'Regional Arrangements and the UN Charter' 6 *Encyclopaedia of International Law* 289–95; R Yalem, 'Regionalism and World Order' (1962) 38 *International Affairs* 460–71; J Moore 'The Role of Regional Arrangements in the Maintenance of World Order', in Cyril Black and Richard Falk (eds), *The Future of International Legal Order* VL III (Princeton, Princeton University Press, 1972) 122; Muthiah Alagappa, 'Regional Arrangements, the UN, and International Security: A Framework for Analysis' in Thomas Weiss (ed), *Beyond Subcontracting Task-Sharing with Regional Security Arrangements and Service-Providing NGOs* (London, MacMillan Press Ltd, 1998) 3.

[136] See John Burton, *Peace and Theory* cited by Joaquín Tascan, 'Searching for OAS/UN Task-Sharing Opportunities in Central America and Haiti' in Thomas Weiss (ed), above note 135.

[137] See Christine Gray, *International Law and the Use of Force* (Oxford, Oxford University Press, 2000) 216.

[138] *Ibid*, See also Weiss and McFarlane, 'Regional Organizations and Regional Security' (1992) 2(1) *Security Studies* 5; Eric G Berman, 'The Security Council's Increasing Reliance on Burden-Sharing: Collaboration or Abrogation?' (1998) 4(1) *International Peacekeeping* 1, especially at 8.

[139] Maurice Bertrand and Daniel Warner (eds), *A New Charter for a Worldwide Organisation?* (The Hague, Kluwer Law International, 1997); Maurice Bertrand, *The United Nations: Past, Present* and *Future*, (The Hague, Kluwer Law International, 1997). But see Louis Sohn, *Broadening the Role of the United Nations in Preventing, Mitigating or Ending International or Internal Conflicts that threaten International Peace and Security*, (Washington DC, International Rule of Law Center, The George Washington University Law School, 1997).

sense, one may say that for most of the post-Cold War period, many legal analysts continue to stick to the doctrinal objections to regionalism in total disregard of continuous growth in the popularity of regional actions amongst states.[140]

The question as to the future of regionalism in the context of collective security can be answered without conceiving regionalism as antagonistic to universalism. If there is one area in which the future portends some measure of certainty for regional organisations it is most certainly in the field of collective security. The post-Cold War period shows a more favourable environment for regionalism than previously possible.[141] Indeed:

> there are few people today who would argue seriously that the potential of the UN is jeopardized by the growth of regionalism, or that regionalism is merely a halfway house between the nation-state and a world not ready to become one.[142]

Even erstwhile regional and subregional organisations whose objectives have been purely economic at inception are now reinventing themselves to incorporate collective security into their agendas. This is in recognition of the fact that without political stability, there is no question of economic prosperity. Regional organisations are now mostly regarded as a natural outgrowth of international co-operation, compatible with the UN and indeed, as Francis Wilcox observed, an 'indispensable element in its successful growth and functioning'.[143]

The transformation of ECOWAS from a purely subregional economic grouping to one endowed with legal and institutional capacities to undertake collective security measures is a manifestation that regional grouping is much more likely to be encouraged within collective security frameworks.[144] The same can be said for the adoption of the defence protocol[145] by the Southern African Development Community (SADC)[146] in 1994 to expand the objectives of the organisation to embrace collective security.

[140] See Chapter 5 for a review of practice by regional organisations after the Cold War.

[141] See Peter Robson, 'The New Regionalism and the Developing Countries' (1993) 31(3) *Journal of Common Market Studies* 335, also cited by Louise Fawcett, above note 22, 16.

[142] Louise Fawcett, above note 22, 19.

[143] Francis Wilcox, 'Regionalism and the United Nations' (1965) 19 (3) *International Organization* 789.

[144] For an analysis of ECOWAS' new collective security mechanism, see Ademola Abass, 'The New Collective Security Mechanism of ECOWAS: Innovations and Problems' (2000) 5(2) *Journal of Conflict and Security Law* 211, text of treaty annexed.

[145] *Protocol on Politics and Security* (1993) 32 *International Legal Materials* 116.

[146] Established August 17 1992. See Treaty establishing SADC, (1993) 32 *International Legal Materials* 116. For a comprehensive review of the Southern Africa security structure, see J Cilliers, 'The Evolving Security Architecture in Southern Africa' (1995) 4 *African Security Review* 40. See Hilaire McCoubrey and Justin Morris, *Regional Peacekeeping in the Cold War Era* (The Hague, Kluwer Law International, 2000) (hereafter Morris and McCoubrey) 140–50.

The recent emergence of the African Union[147] is another indication that regionalism will probably play a greater role in the future system of collective security. Even within Europe, the adoption of the Nice Treaty (which amended the Treaty of the European Union)[148] appears to continue this enhancement of regional collective security systems. Although this treaty addresses a wide range of issues, it also gives prominence to Europe's security structure, especially the establishment of the Rapid Reaction Force for Europe. These new regional organisations, endowed with multidimensional objectives, echo the 1987 call by Soviet President Gorbachev for a 'comprehensive system of international peace and security'[149] and by ex-American President Bill Clinton for 'open regionalism'.[150]

1.6. CONCLUSION

This chapter aimed at considering the meaning of regionalism as a concept and how it has been imported into the world of regional organisations. The purpose of this was to appreciate the evolving nature of regionalism as a concept used by jurists, and how it has been adapted in practice by states to define regions and regional organisations. As will be seen in subsequent chapters, this conceptual analysis is instrumental to the examination of the normative provisions governing regional organisations under the UN Charter.

The criteria by means of which scholars have tried to define 'region' are multitudinous. There may not be a set of criteria that may be accepted as totally appropriate or rejected as completely useless. It is tempting to opine that whatever criteria one chooses they merely reflect individual preferences. For instance Ellen-Frey Wouters excluded collective security arrangements from her own definition of regional organisation on the ground that neither NATO nor SEATO has been able to fulfil its treaty obligation in the development of their area.[151] According to her, they are

[147] For analysis of this Constitutive Act of the African Union, see Ademola Abass and Mashood Baderin, 'Towards an Effective Collective Security System and Human Rights Protection in Africa: An Assessment of the Constitutive Act of the New African Union', (2002/1) XLIX *Netherlands International Law Review* 1; Corinne AA Packer and Donald Rukare, 'The New African Union and its Constitutive Act' (2002) 96(2) *American Journal of International Law* 365; Gino J Naldi and Konstantinos D Magliveras, 'The African Union—A New Dawn for Africa?' (2002) 51(2) *International and Comparative Law Quarterly* 415.

[148] See text in the *Conference of the Representatives of the Member States*, SN 533/00, Brussels, 12 December 2000.

[149] Cited in Brian Urquart, *Decolonization and World Peace* (Austin, Texas, University of Texas Press, 1989) 226; also in Louise Fawcett, above note 22, 18.

[150] Quoted in Louise Fawcett, above note 22 at 20. For a discussion of this concept, see Rosemary Foot, 'Pacific Asia: The Development of Regional Dialogue' in Fawcett and Hurrell (eds), above note 1, 228.

[151] See above. See also Dinstein, above note 87, Chapter 10.

transitory arrangements that *cannot be expected* to play an important role in the future. While this prediction obviously came to pass regarding the fortunes of SEATO, it has not, as far as NATO's commitment is concerned.[152] Such is the problematic nature of the attempts to characterise regional organisations.

There is definitely a need to have guidelines for determining what regions and regional organisations are. This will not only help to understand the relevant provisions of the UN Charter, but also will be pivotal to a clear appreciation of the nature of the relationship that has developed between the UN and these organisations after the Cold War. Whilst the UN and regional organisations must co-operate to maximise their resources towards peace and security, it is desirable to delineate the legal provinces of the two within the Charter.

In a world in which the UN is becoming increasingly dependent on the previously untapped capacities of regional organisations in order to meet its growing agenda, it is necessary to determine which organisations the UN could make use of and rely on. In setting such guidelines, however, care must be taken not to subscribe to restrictive definitions of regionalism. Certainly, therefore, there cannot be a single definitive rule for determining which organisations are regional. Hence, the 'diversity approaches' as summarised by the statement above is to be preferred.

Accordingly, a regional organisation can be defined as *a notion encompassing entities, which may, but not necessarily, belong to a geographically determinable area, having common and disparate attributes and values, but which seek the accomplishment of common goals*. The distinctive force of this proposed definition is its emphasis on abstract values, over mere physical geographical proximity, and the possibility that states claiming to belong to a region may have divergent values. This definition reflects the reality especially in Africa where members of a single regional organisation experience extremely diverse political cultures, varying from monarchy,

[152] Bruno Simma, 'NATO, the UN and the Use of Force: Legal Aspects' (1999) 10(1) *European Journal of International Law* 1; Thomas Franck, 'Sidelined in Kosovo? The United Nations Demise Has Been Exaggerated' (1999) 78 *Foreign Affairs* 116–18; Edward Lutwakk, 'Give War a Chance', *ibid*, 36–44; Peter Rodman, 'The Fallout from Kosovo', *ibid*, 45–51; William Hagen, 'The Lethal Nationalism', *ibid*, 52–54; Edward Luck, 'A Road to Nowhere', *ibid*, 118–19; Walter Rocker, 'America First?' *ibid*, 119–20; Michael Glennon, 'The New Interventionism, the Search for a Just International Law' *ibid*, 2–7; Michael Glennon, 'Glennon Replies' *ibid*, 120–22; Chris Hedges, 'Kosovo's Next Masters?' *ibid*, 24–42; Vojtech Mastny, 'Did Nato Win the Cold War?' *ibid*, 176–89; Robert Hunter, 'Maximising Nato' *ibid*, 190–203; Antonio Cassese, '*Ex Injuria ius Oritur*: Are We Moving Towards Legitimation of Forcible Humanitarian Countermeasures in the World Community?' (1999) 10(1) *European Journal of International Law* 23; Dino Kristiotis, 'The Kosovo Crisis and NATO's Application of Armed Force against the Federal Republic of Yugoslavia', (2000) 49 *International and Comparative Law Quarterly* 330; Nigel White, 'The Legality of Bombing in the Name of Humanity' (2000) 5(1) *Journal of Conflict and Security Law* 27; Christopher Greenwood, 'International Law and the NATO Intervention in Kosovo' (2000) 49 *International and Comparative Law Quarterly* 926.

democracy to militocracy and and divergent cultural values. It is on the basis of political and economic aspirations amongst states moving towards closer co-operation that an effective system of regional collective security has emerged after the Cold War.

2

Regional Organisations and Chapter VIII of the UN Charter

INTRODUCTION

CHAPTER VIII OF the UN Charter governs regional organisations.[1] This chapter consists of Articles 52–54.[2] In general, Chapter VIII embodies the framework for a decentralised enforcement system. It empowers regional organisations to pacifically settle disputes amongst their members.[3] It also devolves enforcement powers, allocated to the Security Council under Chapter VII,[4] on regional organisations through delegated authority.[5] However, regional organisations may not take enforcement action without the authorisation of the Security Council.[6] In addition, they must keep the Security Council informed of whatever actions they take or contemplate at all times.[7]

This chapter examines the provisions of Chapter VIII of the UN Charter in the light of contemporary world order.[8] It scrutinises how regional organisations have interpreted and applied Chapter VIII provisions.

As will be seen shortly, regional organisations generally seem to show little regard for the practical importance of the normative distinction

[1] See Bruno Simma, *The Charter of the United Nations: A Commentary* (Oxford, Oxford University Press, 2nd edn, 2002), 807 *et seq*; Leland Goodrich, Edvard Hambro, Anne Patricia Simons, *Charter of the United Nations: Commentary and Documents* (New York, Columbia University Press, 3rd edn, 1969); Jean-Pierre Cot et Alain Pellet (sous la direction de) *La Charte des Nations Unies: Commentaire: article par article* (Paris, Economica, 2e édition revue et augmentée, 1991).

[2] See UNCIO XII, at 708; A Salomon *L'ONU et la Paix: Le Conseil de Sécurité et le règlement pacifique des différends* (Paris, Editions Internationals, 1948), 83–84.

[3] Article 52.

[4] See discussion in Chapter 3 below.

[5] On the theme of delegated authority by the Security Council, See Danesh Sarooshi, *The United Nations and the Development of Collective Security: The Delegation by the UN Security Council of its Chapter VII Powers* (Oxford, Clarendon Press, 1999).

[6] Article 53(1).

[7] Artcle 54.

[8] See Fred L Morrison in J Delbrück (ed), *Allocation of law Enforcement Authority in the International System: Proceedings of an International Symposium of the Kiel Institute of International Law, March 23 to 25, 1994* (Berlin, Duncker & Humblot, 1995) (hereafter Delbrück's *Allocation*) at 39.

between Article 52 and 53 measures under Chapter VIII.[9] For instance, during the Liberia snd Sierra Leone conflicts, ECOWAS, whilst pursuing pacific settlement, levelled military actions against rebel factions without Security Council authorisation, although some jurists have claimed that the Council retroactively approved both operations by conduct.[10] Similarly, in the Cote d'Ivoire conflict (2002),[11] ECOWAS threatened the rebel faction of the Patriotic Movement of Cote d'Ivoire (MPCI), to 'engage in the (sic) immediate dialogue with the ECOWAS Mediation Mission with a view to laying down their arms'[12] or face the 'prospect of regional intervention to maintain peace.'[13]

Some writers have tried to distinguish between the type of crises regional organisations can intervene in and those they cannot under Article 52, and the scope of regional organisations' authority when acting under Article 53. The argument is sometimes made that regional organisations can only take action in respect of internal (in contrast to external) disputes between member states.[14] It is often said that the Security Council cannot utilise regional organisations outside their regions and beyond tasks established for such organisations by their constitutive instruments.[15]

Therefore, in order to determine the overall adequacy or otherwise of Chapter VIII in general, it is pertinent to critically evaluate the respective place of pacific measures and enforcement actions in the emerging regional collective security order.

2.1. THE NORMATIVE FRAMEWORK OF CHAPTER VIII

2.1.1. Pacific Settlement of Disputes

The provisions of Chapter VIII of the UN Charter constitute some of the most important compromises agreed to by the states that met at San

[9] Richard Lillich, in Delbrück's *Allocation*, noted on the level of ECOMOG's activity with regard to seeking authorisation from the Security Council, that 'my impression of the situation with respects to ECOMOG's operation, gained from talking to the person who at least last July was administering it, was that there was not really much thought given to the question of whether it needed UN authorization explicitly before intervening.', at 70.

[10] See Goerg Nolte, 'Restoring Peace by Regional Action: International Legal Aspects of the Liberian Conflict', 23 *ZaöR V* 53/3 603. See analysis of this in Chapter 5.

[11] See a detailed analysis of this conflict in Chapter 5.

[12] 'Ghana: ECOWAS forms mediation mission on Cote d'Ivoire', *Accra Daily Mail* (01/10/2002), http://www.africaonline.com/site/Articles/1,3,49911.jsp.

[13] Ofeibea Quist-Arcton, Ecowas, 'Peace Effort Underway in Ivory Coast', allAfrica.com http://allafrica.com/stories/200210010001.html.

[14] See Hummer/Schweitzer in Simma's *Commentary*, above note 1 at 807.

[15] De Wet 'The Relationship between the Security Council and Regional Organizations during Enforcement Action under Chapter VII of the United Nations Charter' (2002) 71 *Nordic Journal of International Law* 1.

Francisco to debate the establishment of the UN.[16] The need to include some compromisory provisions in the UN Charter arose out of the concerns of several states participating in the Conference,[17] especially the Latin-American states, about the relationship of regional organisations and other security arrangements, particularly those already in existence at the time,[18] with the UN.[19] These states were resolutely against the Security Council being given authority over regional arrangements.[20] They were anxious to protect their organisations from what they perceived as an overloading of powers in the hands of a small but omnipotent Security Council.[21] As far as these states were concerned the Act of Chapultepec, which they signed shortly before the conference got underway, contained a 'juridical instrument' to regulate enforcement measures at regional level, which predated the Security Council's authority over regional arrangements.[22] Other states wanted their organisations to occupy a more ambivalent position in the scheme of things to come.[23] These latter states wanted to exempt their organisations from being regulated by Article 52(1) and Article 53(1) provisions,[24] and at the same time wanted them to benefit fully from the provisions of both articles.

[16] See Ruth B Russell, *A History of the United Nations Charter: The Role of the United States 1940–1945* (Washington DC, The Brookings Institution, 1958) 688 *et seq*; Arthur H Vandenberg (ed), *The Private Papers of Senator Vandenberg* (1952) 192 *et seq*; James S Sutterlin, *The United Nations and the Maintenance of International Peace and Security: A Challenge to be Met* (Connecticut, Praeger, 1995) (hereafter Sutterlin) 93; However, on the initial misgivings of the United States on giving too many concessions to regional organisations, see Edward R Stettinus, Jr, *Report to the President of the Results of the San Francisco Conference* (*Department of State*, June 26, 1945) 109; See also *UNCIO Documents*, vol 12, 684.

[17] Ruth Russell, above note 16, 688 *et seq*.

[18] Treaty of Alliance and Mutual Assistance of 10 December 1944 between France and Soviet Union, (1944) *American Journal of International Law* 83; Treaty of Alliance of December 12, 1943 between Soviet Union and Czechoslovakia (Friendens-Warte 45 (1945), 73); Treaty of Alliance of May 26, 1942, (1942) 36 *American Journal of International Law* 216.

[19] Russell, above note 16, 701, quoting from Arthur H Vandenberg (ed), (1952) *The Private Papers of Senator Vandernberg* 192.

[20] Writing about this episode, a commentator noted that the regional security provisions of the Charter (primarily the current Chapter VIII) might well have been dropped from the Charter, but for the insistence of the Latin American states that their existing regional system, then called the Pan American Union, be preserved. See generally Morrison, above note 8.

[21] One such fear was based on the February 1945 Yalta Formula, which became Article 27(3) dealing with the veto power. It was felt by certain states, like the United States, that permanent Member States of the Security Council, not originating from a particular region, might invoke the veto to prevent regional action. See Bruno Simma's *Commentary*, above note 1, 687. See L Goodrich, 'Regionalism and the United Nations', (1949) *Columbia Journal of International Affairs* 10.

[22] See Ezequiel Padilla (Mexican Minister for Foreign Affairs), 'The American System and the World Organization' (1945) 24 *Foreign Affairs* (October), 104. Cf Ruth Russell, above note 16, 688 fn 1.

[23] *UNCIO Documents*, vol 12, 684.

[24] For instance, the Latin American States, which had wanted initially to reserve the settlement of regional disputes for regional arrangements/agencies, insisted that the Inter-American System be exempted from the subordination of regional agencies to the UN. See Bruno Simma's *Commentary*, above note 1, 687.

The other basis of contention related to the specific question of renewal of aggression by former enemy states.[25] This issue was resolved, at Dumbarton Oaks, by providing in Chapter XII, a provision that nothing in the Charter would preclude actions against enemy states[26] a formula which assuaged Soviet anxiety about the Security Council is control over former enemy states.[27] This became the first compromisory provision of the Charter in the context of the UN/regional organisation relationship. However, this provision was criticised at San Francisco.[28] Its relationship with those provisions concerning regional arrangements was not clear to many states.[29] To several European states, this provision with the new paragraph 12 guaranteeing 'individual or collective self-defence' was not an adequate safeguard against aggression from Germany.[30] They wanted greater assurance, in the form of a specific exemption from Security Council authorisation, inserted in the UN Charter.[31]

The second concession to regional arrangements is embodied by the 'first recourse' clause contained in Article 33(1) of the Charter. Though this article does not fall under regional arrangements, it specifically addresses the subject of Chapter VIII—regional organisations. This article provides that

> The parties to any dispute, the continuance of which is likely to endanger the maintenance of international peace and security, shall first of all, seek a solution by negotiation, enquiry, mediation, conciliation, arbitration, judicial settlement, resort to regional agencies or arrangements, or other peaceful means of their own choice.

In paragraph 2, this article imposes an obligation on the Security Council to, 'when it deems necessary, call upon the parties to settle their disputes by such means'. The tenets of this article are further enhanced by Article 52(1) which states that

> Nothing in the present Charter precludes the existence of regional arrangements or agencies for dealing with such matters relating to the maintenance of international peace and security as are appropriate for regional action, provided that such arrangements or agencies and their activities are consistent with the Purposes and Principles of the United Nations.[32]

[25] Now Article 107 UN Charter.

[26] Article 107 UN Charter.

[27] See Russell, above note 16 at 688 *et seq*.

[28] Doc 576 III/4/9, May 25 1945, *UNCIO Documents*, vol 12, at 680.

[29] Russell, above note 16, 688–9.

[30] *Ibid*, 689.

[31] See *UNCIO Documents*, vol 12 at 728. See also Russell, above note 16 at 689.

[32] The wording of this article, especially the part that refers to 'consistent with the Purposes and Principles of the United Nations' is a textual confirmation of the position generally agreed amongst states at San Francisco as discussed in Chapter 1. For the interpretation of this phrase in practice, see below.

Article 52(3), like Article 33(2), obligates the Security Council to encourage pacific settlement by regional arrangements either through disputant states referring matters to their organisations themselves or by the Security Council initiating such a move.[33] Historically therefore, Article 52 was inserted in the Charter to enable regional organisations to undertake pacific settlement of disputes among their members and to resist armed attacks and aggression by defending their members under Article 51. Although nothing in Chapter VIII explicitly entitles regional organisations to benefit from the provisions of Article 51, it was clearly understood at San Francisco that self-defence was primarily inserted in the Charter for the protection of regional organisations.[34] Furthermore, the provisions of Article 51 are cast in the mould of an 'inherent right' of all states so that regardless of wherever the right appears in the Charter, it is available to and accessible by, all states at large. The right, which is inherent, was natural and inalienable, and as such could be exercised by regional organisations.[35]

Although Article 52 (3) addresses regional organisations and obligates the Security Council to encourage them towards pacific settlement, there have been instances of tension and disagreement between the two. These concern the question as to which of the two has primacy over the pacific settlement of disputes,[36] and whether activities of some regional organisations are consistent with the purposes and principles of the UN.[37]

[33] The Security Council indeed initiated the process of regional settlement of disputes amongst member states of a regional organisation in the Lebanon conflict of 1958. The Security Council deferred its consideration of the matter brought before it by President Chamoun of Lebanon over his concerns about the interference by Egypt and Syria over Lebanon's internal affairs until the Arab League had dealt with the issue first. See Hussein Hassouna, 'The Arab League of States and the United Nations: Relations in the Peaceful Settlement of Disputes' in Berhanykun Andemicael (ed), *Regionalism and the United Nations* (Dobbs Ferry, NY, Oceana Publications, 1979) at 310; Brian Urquhart, *Hammarskjöld* (London, Bodley Head, 1973) 261–92; Alan Henrikson, 'The Growth of Regional Organizations and the Role of the United Nations' in Louise Fawcett and Andrew Hurrell (eds), *Regionalism in World Politics: Regional Organization and International Order* (Oxford, Oxford University Press, 1995) 122 at 139 *et seq*; Akindele, *The Organization and Promotion of World Peace: A Study of Universal-Regional Relationships* (Toronto, University of Toronto Press, 1976) at 89–92.

[34] Doc. 576III/4/9, May 25 1945, UNCIO Documents vol 12, 680. According to the Colombian Foreign Minister Lleras-Camargo, serving then as the chairman of Committee III/4 responsible for the para VIII provisions, 'Latin American Countries understood . . . that the origin of the term "collective self-defence" is identified with the necessity of *preserving* regional systems like the Inter-American one. The Charter, in general terms, is a constitution, and it legitimatizes the right of collective self-defence to be carried out in accord with the regional pacts so long as they are not opposed to the purpose and principles of the organization . . . If a group of countries with regional ties declare their solidarity for their mutual defence . . . they will undertake such defence jointly if and when one of them is attacked.' See *UNCIO* documents, vol XII 680–81.

[35] Alan Henrikson, above note 33, 122 at 128. See also FO Wilcox, 'Regionalism and the United Nations' (1965) 19 *International Organization* 790–92.

[36] See the Declaration of the Caracas Inter-American Conference of 1954, *Documents in American Foreign Relations 1954* (1955) 412.

[37] Simma's *Commentary*; Cot and Pellet; Goodrich, Hambro and Simons above note 1.

In 1954, an internal disorder in Guatemala[38] led its leader Jacobo Arbenz to appeal simultaneously to the UN and the OAS. Although the USSR characterised the conflict as arising from an 'aggression' rather than a mere 'local dispute',[39] with the aim of primarily seizing the Security Council of the matter under Article 24 of the Charter, the issue was resolved in favour of conceding primacy to the OAS while affirming that this did not fetter the Security Council's ability to intervene in the matter at any time.[40]

Similar disputes arose between the UN and OAU over the frontier disputes between Morocco and Algeria in 1963,[41] and Somalia and Ethiopia (1964).[42] Whereas the leadership of Morocco initially appealed for an intervention by the OAU,[43] Algeria had appealed to the UN.[44] Pressure by African countries to the effect that the OAU should be resorted to in the first instance, coupled with the reluctance of Western powers to involve themselves in the conflict eventually led to Morocco bringing the matter finally to the OAU.[45]

[38] For an account of this crisis, see Stephen Kinzer and Stephen Schlesinger, *Bitter Fruit: The Untold Story of the American Coup in Guatemala* (New York, Doubleday, 1982); Piero Gleijeses, *Shattered Hope: The Guatemalan Revolution and the United States, 1944–1954* (Princeton, Princeton University Press, 1991); Richard Immeman, *The CIA in Guatemala: The Foreign Policy of Intervention* (Austin, Texas, University of Texas Press, 1982).

[39] SCOR/9th Yr./675 Mtg./June 20, 1954, and supp for April, May and June, pp 11–13. See also Goodrich and Hambro, above note 1, 358. See also Akindele, above note 33 at 80–81.

[40] For a historical perspective of the crisis, see NJ Colletta and L Cullen, *Violent Conflict and the Transformation of Social Capital: Lessons from Cambodia, Rwanda, Guatemala, and Somalia* (Washington, DC, World Bank, 2000); Greg Grandin, *The Blood of Guatemala: A History of Race and Nation* (Durham NC, Duke University Press, 2000).

[41] For a detailed study see Hanspeter F Strauch, 'L'OAU et les conflits frontaliers' (1967) 22 *Revue française d'etudes politiques africaines* 59; Zdenek Cervenka, *The Organisation of African Unity and its Charter* (New York, Frederick A Praeger, 1968) 96 *et seq*; Gino Naldi, 'Peace-Keeping Attempts by the Organisation of African Unity', (1985) 34 *International and Comparative Law Quarterly* 593; Alan Henrikson, above note 33 at 136–39; Ellen Frey-Wouters, 'The Prospect for Regionalism in World Affairs' in Richard Falk and Cyril Black (eds), *The Future of the International Legal Order* vol 1 (Princeton, Princeton University Press, 1969) 463 at 529 *et seq*.

[42] Gino Naldi, 'The Organisation of African Unity and Saharan Arab Democratic Republic' (1982) 26 *Journal of African Law* 152; Berhanykun, Andemicael, *The OAU and the UN: Relations between the Organization of African Unity and the United Nations* (New York, Published for the United Nations Institute for Training and Research by Africana Pub Co, 1976); RMD'Sa, *The Relationship between the UN and OAU in the Fields of International Peace and Security and of Economic and Social Development* (unpublished PhD thesis), Faculty of Law, University of Birmingham (1982), vol 1.

[43] For documentation, see Louis Sohn (ed), *Basic Documents of African Regional Organizations* (Dobbs Ferry, NY, Published for the Inter-American Institute of International Legal Studies by Oceana Publications, 1971–72); Gino Naldi (ed), *Documents of the Organization of African Unity* (London, Mansell, 1992); for analysis of OAU roles in African conflict, see Gino Naldi, *The Organization of African Unity: An Analysis of its Role* (London, Mansell, 2nd edn, 1999).

[44] UNGAOR, 34th Session, 1979, Supp No 23 (Doc. A/34/23/Rev. 1) 106. See Naldi, 'Peacekeeping Attempts by the Organisation of African Unity', above note 41 at 596; Naldi, *The Organization* of, above note 43.

[45] See Berhanykun Andemicael, 'The Organization of African Unity and the United Nations: Relations in the Peace and Security Field' in Berhanykun Andemicael (ed), above note 33, 238.

During the Congo crisis (1963–64),[46] the OAU insisted that the conflict be left to African states to resolve, and rejected intervention by outside states, such as the United States, Belgium and United Kingdom, in Stanleyville in November 1964.[47] Consequently, the Security Council passed a resolution that placed the resolution of the dispute in Congo 'in the lap of the OAU'.[48] With regard to the Somalia/Ethiopia dispute, the OAU claimed primacy over the Security Council following the request by Somalia that the UN intervene in its dispute over lands it believed were wrongfully held from it by Ethiopia. Somalia concurred and notified the Security Council that it was no longer minded to raise the issue in the Security Council 'while the matter is in the hands of the OAU'.[49]

Jurisdictional disputes between the UN and regional organisations have become rare in the contemporary world order for a number of reasons. First is the absence of the Cold War climate of fear and mutual distrust between East and West which fuelled disagreement between the UN and regional organisations. The flipside of this is that the two regional organisations that were usually engaged in this primacy-dispute with the UN—OAS and OAU—became less relevant: the OAS arguably because of the backlash from American States for the US's support for Britain in the Falklands War against Argentina, a fellow American State. The withering of the OAU, on the other hand, was due to a cocktail of factors, not the least being the rise of more proactive sub-regional organisations such as ECOWAS and SADC in Africa. With ECOWAS taking charge of sixteen West African countries and SADC responsible for about a dozen, the OAU fell into redundancy; its natural death in 2001 was inevitable.

Second, more regional organisations have now developed sophisticated regulatory and institutional mechanisms that enable them to tackle members' disputes with more vigour than before. A good example is the development by ECOWAS of a comprehensive dispute settlement mechanism as an important feature of its Protocol on collective security.[50] Under this

[46] For documentation see, Rosalyn Higgins, *United Nations Peacekeeping, 1946–1967: Documents and Commentary* vol 3, Africa (Oxford, Oxford University Press, 1980). William Durch (ed), *The Evolution of UN Peacekeeping: Case Studies and Comparative Analysis* (New York, NY, St Martin's Press, 1993); FT Liu, 'Peacekeeping and Humanitarian Assistance' in Leon Gordenker and Thomas Weiss (eds), *Soldiers, Peacekeepers and Disasters*, (Basingstoke, Macmillan, 1991); Nigel White, *Keeping the Peace* (Manchester, Manchester University Press, 2nd edn., 1997) 207–23, 254–61.

[47] William Durch, above note 46; See particularly Georges Abi-Saab, *The United Nations Operation in the Congo, 1960–1964* (Oxford, Oxford University Press, 1978). White, above note 46, Chapter 7.

[48] Akindele, above note 33 at 98–102. See also, Alan Henrikson, above note 33 at 138.

[49] UN Doc. SCOR S/5542, Feb, 1964, 65–66. See also Alan Henrikson, above note 33 at 137.

[50] For analysis, see Ademola Abass, 'The New Collective Security Mechanism of ECOWAS: Innovations and Problems', (2000) 5(2) *Journal of Conflict and Security Law* 211, text of treaty annexed.

mechanism, ECOWAS established a Council of Elders, dividing its region into four administrative zones, with each zonal office responsible for collating and feeding information on potential troubles to ECOWAS headquarters in Abuja, Nigeria.

The third factor is the explosion of disputes immediately after the demise of the Cold War and the overstretching of UN resources. Naturally, the more conflicts there are the larger the human and material resources required by the UN to discharge its responsibility. Thus, any signal by regional organisations indicating their willingness to deal with crises on their own, especially using peaceful means, is eagerly welcomed by the UN, especially the Security Council members which, in the past, would be the first to challenge such offers. Hence, in the crises in Guinea-Bissau, Cape Verde and at the early stages of the Liberia and Côte d'Ivoire conflicts, ECOWAS acted primarily in seeking an amicable resolution of the disputes. It was not until the situation became more desperate in Cote d'Ivoire that the Security Council adopted Resolution 1464 seizing it of the dispute and prescribing the specific roles to be played by ECOWAS and France therein.[51] The same approach was adopted in the intervention by SADC in the conflict in the Democratic Republic of Congo and the involvement of the CSCE in the crises in Georgia and Akhabiza.[52]

2.2. REGIONAL ARRANGEMENTS OR AGENCIES: CHARACTERISATION AND PRACTICE

Jurisdictional conflicts between the UN and regional organisations, of the nature discussed above, often result from how regional organisations perceive their relationship with the UN. As noted in the last chapter, states deliberately rejected endorsing any specific definition of 'regional organisation' at San Francisco. Thus, the formula resorted to by the Charter drafters in Article 52(1) was simply to refer to regional organisations generically as 'regional arrangements or agencies' leaving the contents of that phrase to be ascertained in practice.[53] However, despite the normative ambivalence of Article 52(1), certain organisations have formally

[51] For analysis of the Security Council intervention in Cote d'Ivoire, see Ademola Abass, 'The Security Council and the Challenges of Collective Security in the Twenty-First Century: What Role for African Regional Organisations?' in Douglas Lewis (ed), *Global Governance and the Quest for Justice*, Volume 1 (Oxford, Hart Publishing, forthcoming).

[52] See discussion in Chapter 5.

[53] Cot and Pellet above note 1 at 801, 810. Bruno Simma's *Commentary*, above note 1 at 691.

declared themselves to be regional agencies. The OAS[54], OAU,[55] CIS[56] OCSE[57] and ECOWAS,[58] are some examples.

The OAS is generally regarded as the first and the most sophisticated regional organisation in existence.[59] Article 1 of its Charter explicitly refers to it as a regional *agency*, one of the specific terms adopted by the UN Charter. Like the UN Charter, the OAS Charter did not explain the term 'regional agency'.[60]

Considering OAS' self-description, Charles Fenwick argued that, 'the delegates at Bogotá were too generous in describing their organization as an "agency" of the United Nations, for in fact it is an agency only in the limited field described in Articles 34 and 35 and Articles 51–54 of the United Nations Charter'.[61] Far from a manifestation of a genuine intention to act as a surbodinate to the United Nations, as the term agency ordinarily implies, the 'delegates were anxious not to have it appear that they were setting up a rival body whose decisions in security matters might conflict with those of the Security Council of the United Nations'.[62] Fenwick further noted that, 'the Organization of American States operates with complete freedom in all other respects than those involving security matters; and while provision is made for collaboration with the United Nations, it is a collaboration that does not involve any degree of subordination or agency'.[63]

Unlike the OAS, the OAU Charter[64] did not explicitly describe the organisation as a regional organisation.[65] Nevertheless, its *travaux préparatoires* indicated that the organisation was intended to be a regional organisation.[66]

[54] The Charter of the Organization of American States, 30 April 1948, *United Nations Treaty Series*, vol 119, 3 (48); (1994) 33 *International Legal Materials* 981.

[55] Founded in 1963. See 479 *United Nations Treaty Series* 70.

[56] (1992) 31 *International Legal Materials* 138; Treaty of Collective Security ('Tashkent Agreement') 15 May 1992, printed in Gazeta, 23 May 1992. See also Vasisli Kononenko, *Heads of Governments Grapple over CIS Charter in Attempt to Salvage Commonwealth*, Russ Press DIG, 13 November 1992.

[57] See below.

[58] Revised Treaty of the Economic Community of West African States, 24 July 1993, (1996) 25 *International Legal Materials* 660.

[59] See Fred Morrison, above note 8 at 42. See also Michael Akehurst, 'Enforcement Actions by Regional Organisations with Special Reference to the Organization of American States' (1967) 42 *British Yearbook of International Law* 175 at 153. For an excellent review of the development of the Inter-American System, see Charles Fenwick, 'The Inter-American Regional System: Fifty Years of Progress' (1956) 50 *American Journal of International Law* 18; Jochen Frowein and Rüdiger Wolfrum, 'Security Council Control over regional Action' (1997) 1 *Max Planck Yearbook of United Nations Law* 129.

[60] See Fenwick, above note 59.

[61] *Ibid*, 27.

[62] *Ibid*, 27.

[63] *Ibid*, 27–28.

[64] 3 *International Legal Materials* 1116. See NJ Padelford, 'The OAU' (1964) 18 *International Organization* 521.

[65] See GA Res 2011 (XX), 11 October 1965.

[66] Alan Henrikson, above note 33 at 130.

The ECOWAS Treaty (as revised)[67] however describes the organisation as a regional organisation to operate mainly in the West African region. Likewise in 1992[68] the Conference on Security and Co-operation in Europe (CSCE)[69] declared itself to be a regional organisation within the meaning of Chapter VIII of the UN Charter.[70]

Like states, writers have also attempted to calibrate regional organisations under the Charter. Akehurst thought that:

> the difference between an *agency* and an *arrangement* would appear to be that an agency possesses an institutional superstructure (e.g. the OAS), whereas an arrangement does not (e.g. the Anglo-Soviet Mutual Assistance Pact). In other words, an agency is simply a more highly developed form of an arrangement.[71]

This view has been endorsed by another scholar,[72] who defined 'regional agencies' as 'formal or informal regional organizations (with physical and organizational infrastructure, staff, budget, etc.) with responsibility for implementing regional arrangements'.[73] In contrast, some commentators perceive 'arrangement' and 'agency' as synonymous while some yet think of them as antonymous terms.[74]

[67] Treaty of the Economic Community of West African States (ECOWAS) 28 May (1975) XIV *International Legal Materials* 1200, (as amended by the Revised Treaty) 24th July 1993. See text in (1996) 25 *International Legal Materials* 660.

[68] See James S Sutterlin, above note 16 at 99 *et seq*.

[69] Established at Helsinki in 1975. See *Conference on Security and Cooperation in Europe: Final Act, The Department of State Bulletin*, 73/188 (1 Sept 1975), 323–50.

[70] (1992) 31 *International Legal Materials* 1385. See also 'Paris Charter for a New Europe' adopted at the CSCE Summit Meeting in November 1990, distributed at the UN as General Assembly Document A/45/859, 12 December 1990.

[71] Michael Akehurst, above note 59 at 177. Emphasis added.

[72] Muthiah Alagappa, 'Regional Arrangements, the UN, and International Security: A Framework for Analysis' in Thomas Weiss (ed), *Beyond Subcontracting: Task-Sharing with Regional Security Arrangements and Service-Providing NGOs* (Basingstoke, MacMillan, 1998), 3 at 6.

[73] It seems difficult to perceive the difference between 'arrangement' and 'agency' in terms of their infrastructural capacities. Perhaps, such a distinction made sense in an age when the OAS was the *only* regional organisation with institutional facilities and organs to dispense its activities. Presently, even subregional organisations have developed such facilities and organs such that could lead them to be regarded as agencies, and not arrangements. For instance, ECOWAS not only maintains an impressive headquarters in Abuja, Nigeria, but also has several mini-secretariats in other member states, with four distinct zonal bureaux. If 'arrangement' as a term, connotes 'a (mere) treaty under public international law', (von Alfred Verdross and Bruno Simma, *Universelles Völkerrecht: Theorie und Praxis* 3, völlig neu bearbeitete Aufl. (hereafter Verdros and Simma, *Universelles Völkerrecht*) (Berlin, Duncker & Humblot, 1984, para. 683, cited by Hummer/Schweitzer, above, at 694) and 'agency' means that 'its functions are exercised by its own organs' (Verdross and Simma, *Universelles Völkerrecht*, at para. 941) then it means that all regional organisations, with *organs* competent to act on their behalf are regional *agencies* within the meaning of Chapter VIII. Applying this test to an organisation such as NATO, with its elaborate structures, *prima facie* means that NATO is a *regional* agency under Chapter VIII. Of course, it is common knowledge that NATO does not regard itself as such.

[74] Pernice, R *Die Sicherung des Weltfriendens durch regionale Organisationen und die Vereinten Nationen. Eine Untersuchung zur Kompetenzverteilung Kapitel VIII der UN-Charter* (1972), cited by Hummer/Schweitzer in Bruno Simma's *Commentary*, above note at 694.

It is submitted that the distinction between 'arrangement' and 'agency' is without a difference and has no practical value under Chapter VIII.[75] The fact that the OAS described itself as a regional agency does not confer on it any additional rights or privileges under Chapter VIII. Conversely, non self-declaration does not prejudice the position of other organisations vis-à-vis the Charter. Provided self-characterisation does not impinge on the provisions of the Charter, it matters not by what term a regional organisation refers to itself.

It could not have been that the authors of the UN Charter intended different consequences to result from adopting the two terms. The fact that the terms are couched in disjunctive terms 'arrangements *or* agencies', perhaps evidences that they could be used interchangeably. Afterall, as one commentator has noted, 'formalistic and declaratory self-qualification along the lines of the UN Charter's Chapter VIII does not . . . establish an actual working relationship with the world body'.[76] The crucial factor is not the nature of the organisation but the type of action that is undertaken and the attitude of the Security Council towards it.[77]

The irrelevance of whether an organisation declares itself as a regional 'arrangement' or 'agency' within Chapter VIII is to be distinguished from whether an organisation perceives itself as a regional organisation under Chapter VIII at all. Due to the 'strong impression conveyed especially by Chapter VIII that "regional arrangements or agencies" are to be subordinate to the UN at least in the matter of 'enforcement action', it matters a great deal whether these organizations consider themselves to be Chapter VIII entities'.[78] If an organisation claims not to be regional, a major legal consequence of this is that it may not be governed by Chapter VIII.

Problems of this nature have arisen mainly in connection with the activities of NATO.[79] NATO regards itself as a collective self-defence organisation, formed under Article 51 of the UN Charter.[80] This self-description has led to a general perception among writers that NATO is not a regional organisation under Chapter VIII of the UN Charter and one which is outward-oriented, that is deals only with attacks coming from external sources.[81]

[75] But see Michael Akehurst, above note 59 at 178 (noting that 'the only way in which one can be *certain* that an arrangement is covered by Chapter VIII of the Charter is to see whether the parties to the arrangement have claimed that it is a regional arrangement, and whether this claim has been accepted in practice by the United Nations').

[76] Henrikson, above note 33 at 131.

[77] Christine Gray, *International Law and the Use of Force* (Oxford, Oxford University Press, 2000) 206.

[78] Alan Henrikson, above note 33 at 130.

[79] See W Lang, *Der internationale Regionalismus. Intergrationale Regionalismus. Integration and Disintegration von Staatenbeziehungen in weltweiter Verflechtung* (Wien, Springer, 1982), 35 *et seq*.

[80] *Ibid*.

[81] See Chapter 1.

During the Security Council debate on the nature of NATO,[82] it was argued that NATO was not a regional agency within the meaning of Article 52 because 'in the absence of elements such as common culture, language, history, geographical proximity, a local dispute as required by Article 52(1)—which then could be settled by measures of regional nature-could never arise.'[83] Further, the view has been severally expressed that obligations of military alliances like NATO were inconsistent with the prohibition of the use of force in Article 2(4).[84] In fact, the Soviet Union representative cited Kelsen to the effect that the learned jurist would have regarded obligations arising from Article 5 of NATO Treaty as incompatible with the Charter.[85]

The obvious implication of the characterisation of NATO as an outward-oriented organisation is that NATO cannot undertake pacific settlement of disputes amongst its members under Article 52 since such disputes arise within member states, and are hence an internal matter. Thus, when a crisis broke out in 1956 between Turkish and Greek Cypriots and NATO's Secretary General, Lord Ismay, suggested that the alliance formed a committee to mediate in the conflict,[86] President Makarios of Cyprus rejected the suggestion, preferring the UN forum instead.[87] United States Secretary of State, Dulles, was later to observe that 'NATO has not been organized as a regional association, nor has it any policy or jurisdiction to deal with disputes as between the members'.[88]

It is submitted that the view that NATO's treaty is incompatible with the Charter is erroneous, and, with respect, insufficient to ground a conclusion that NATO is not a regional organisation under Chapter VIII. Nothing in the provisions of Chapter VIII precludes NATO from being a regional organisation. As noted in Chapter 1, the Charter does not state any criteria for determining which organisations qualify to be regional under Chapter VIII. In addition, under Article 1 of the North Atlantic Treaty, NATO members 'undertake to settle any international dispute in which they may be involved by peaceful means in such a manner that international peace and security and justice are not endangered, and to

[82] UN Doc A/PV1356, para 8; UN Doc A/C1/SC 597, paras 39–40, A/C.1/SC, 599; see Bruno Simma's *Commentary*, above note 1 at 819 *et seq*.

[83] UN Doc A/C1/SC 597, paras 39–40, A/C1/SC 599, para 21; A/C1/SC 603, paras 53–54; A/C1/SC 674, para 51; A/C1/SC 675, para 13, 29; A/C1/SC 676, paras 56–58. See also Bruno Simma's *Commentary*, above note 1, 819 *et seq*.

[84] *Ibid*.

[85] UN Doc A/C/SC 602 para 35.

[86] Roberts Jordan, with Michael Bloome, *Political Leadership in NATO: A Study in Multinational Diplomacy* (Boulder, Colo, Westview Press, 1979) 37.

[87] See White, above note 46 at 44, 162, and 261–2.

[88] See The *Department of State Bulletin*, 34/884 (4 June 1956) 925–26; 'Non-Military Co-operation in NATO: Text of the Report of the Committee of Three' NATO Letter, 5, special suppl to no 1 (1 January 1957) 8.

refrain in their international relations from the threat or use of force in any manner inconsistent with the purposes of the United Nations'.

The fact that NATO declared itself to be an organisation formed under Article 51 only primarily makes it a collective self-defence organisation, and not a collective security organisation. That categorisation does not however preclude NATO from being a regional organisation under Chapter VIII since its identity as a collective self-defense organisation only relates to the type of tasks it may perform and not the scope of its operations. Article 51, as we have already noted, was originally included in the Charter to protect regional organisations.[89] Since regional organisations are not prevented from acting under Article 51,[90] an organisation formed under that article may very well be a regional arrangement under Chapter VIII.[91] In addition, the treaties of several *bona fide* regional organisations such as the OAS and ECOWAS allow them to perform collective self-defence as one of their numerous functions.[92] Can it then be said that the presence of an outward-orientated function—repulsion of armed attacks or aggressions—in the OAS and ECOWAS treaties, means that these are not regional organisations?

The contention that in the absence of common language and culture amongst NATO members, a local dispute,[93] such that regional organisations can deal with, cannot arise, is, with respect, nebulous. There is nothing in the provision or the negotiating history of Article 52 that remotely suggests that a local dispute or a dispute such that regional organisations can deal with, can only arise within organisations composed by *homogeneous* states. Few regional organisations contain more heterogeneous members than ECOWAS, SADC and the African Union. ECOWAS members, for instance, speak languages ranging from English and French to Portuguese, amidst hundreds of local and palpably varied languages.

As the analysis in Chapter 1 reveals, a single abiding factor—such as democracy—is often the real link between members of regional organisations. This is particularly true of the European Union. Moreover, the definition of regional organisations proposed in the last chapter places

[89] Above.

[90] See Hummer and Schweitzer in Bruno Simma's *Commentary*, above note 1 at 695. See also Albrecht Randelzohofer, 'Article 51' *ibid*, 661.

[91] In fact in 1956 NATO formed a Committee of Three (foreign Ministers of Canada, Italy, and Norway), in response to the Suez Canal Crisis. This Committee, amongst others, was committed to submitting disputes amongst Member States to the good offices procedure within the Alliance before resorting to any other agency. See the *Department of State Bulletin*, 34/884 (4 June 1956): 925–26. See also 'Non-Military Co-operation in NATO: Text of the Report of the Committee of Three' *NATO Letter*, 5, Special Supp, to no 1 (1 January 1957), 8, quoted in Francis Wilcox, 'Regionalism and the United Nations' (1965) 19(3) *International Organization* 431–32.

[92] See Article 2 of ECOWAS Protocol on Mutual Assistance and Defence (PMAD, 1981), and Article 3(h) of the OAS Charter, 1948.

[93] Hummer and Schweitzer in Bruno Simma's *Commentary*, above note 1, 824–25.

greater emphasis on the common goals sought by members of a regional organisation while recognising that such states may share disparate cultures and values, and occupy indeterminate space.

It is often said that Article 52(2), unlike Articles 34, 35 and 36 of the Charter, does not invest regional organisations with the competence to handle 'situations' and hence, Chapter VIII is not applicable to situations.[94] Advocates of this view seek to distinguish between 'disputes' which regional organisations can resolve under Article 52(2) and 'situations' which, according to them, go beyond regional solutions. Hence, the conclusion that 'disputes' as appears under Article 52(2) can only mean 'local dispute', defined as disputes not involving third parties.

There is no reason why regional organisations cannot amicably settle disputes involving one or more of their member states and a *third* party, that is a non-member state. The distinction between 'situations' and disputes', in this context, is spurious and their differentiation in legal literature lacks any conviction. Nothing suggests in the *travaux preparatoires* of Chapter VIII that the Founding States intended this kind of distinction between 'situations' and 'disputes' by using the alternative terms in the same provision. The whole text of the Charter is littered with inconsistent uses of words and phrases. It is disingenuous to allow what appears to be no more than a mere incidence of drafting inelegance to dictate the interpretation of the Charter provisions. If the Charter authors really meant to demarcate between disputes that regional organisations can and cannot deal with, they would have used a more precise term, such as 'enforcement action' in Article 53(1), and stipulated the conditions under which regional organisations may intervene in such.

The objection that Article 5 of NATO Treaty—containing its *casus foederis*—is inconsistent with the UN Charter, forms part of a wider debate about the consistency of regional activities with the UN Charter as required by Article 52(1).[95] This issue came to light mainly when the General Assembly considered whether it should grant observer status to some regional organisations and whether the UN should in fact have any formal relationship with them at all. To be sure, the UN Charter did not supply a matrix for co-operation between the UN and regional organisations. Nor did the *Agenda for Peace*,[96] which expressed hopes about the roles to be played by regional organisations in the post-Cold War era.

When the General Assembly decided to grant observer status to the OAS in 1948,[97] some UN Member States protested on the ground that

[94] F Fernandez-Shaw, *La Organización de los Estados Americanos . . . una Nueva Visión de América* (2nd edn, 1963) cited in Simma's *Commentary*, above note 1 at 824.

[95] Article 1 of the UN Charter enumerates the purposes and principles of the UN to include (1) the maintenance of 'international peace and security', *inter alia*.

[96] Boutros Boutros-Ghali, *Agenda for Peace*, (1992) 31 *International Legal Materials* 953. Boutros-Ghali, *An Agenda for Peace* (New York, United Nations, 1992).

[97] GA Res, 253.

there was no provision in the UN Charter allowing such a relationship. States' attitude were a little different when the Assembly moved to recognise the League of Arab States (Arab League) two years later.[98]

Unlike the OAS, the constituent instrument of the Arab League did not expressly declare it to be a regional organisation.[99] However, the League's status as such has been established by several of its own resolutions[100] and declarations.[101] Furthermore, the General Assembly had made an earlier reference to 'regional organizations in the Middle East such as the Arab League' in 1947.[102] Nonetheless, Israel argued that the objectives of the Arab League were inconsistent with the Purposes and Principles of the UN Charter since, according to Israel, the Arab League consisted only of people of a particular race and that its objectives were of an aggressive nature.[103] Others said that the constitution of a regional organisation must specifically refer to the Charter of the UN and that such organisation must hold public meetings and have an identifiable area of jurisdiction.[104] The Covenant of the Arab League did not meet any of these 'criteria'. Nevertheless, the General Assembly granted it observer status.

However, when in 1965 and 1975 the General Assembly granted observer status to the OAU[105] and the Organisation of Islamic Conference respectively, there was no protest by UN member states.[106] This might be because when the Security Council spoke of OAU in 1964, it stated that the OAU 'should be able, in the context of Article 52 . . . to help find a peaceful solution to *all* the problems and disputes affecting peace and security

[98] For a review of the qualification of the OAU, OAS, and the Arab League, see Goodrich, Hambro, and Simons, above note 1; Erkki Kourula, 'Peace-keeping and Regional Arrangements' in Antonio Cassese (ed), *United Nations Peace-keeping: Legal Essays* (Alphen aan den Rijn, Sijthoff & Noordhoff, 1978) 102–6; Gray, above note 77, at 204–6; Akindele, above note 33 at 11. (1976) 22 *Keesing's Contemporary Archives* 28122; Quincy Wright, 'The Middle East Problem', (1970) 64 *American Journal of International Law* 270.

[99] This might be because the organisation was formed shortly before the San Francisco conference took place (April–June 1945), which gave birth to the term regional arrangement or agencies in Chapter VIII. See Alan Henrikson, above note 33 at 130.

[100] League Pact, (1945) 39 *American Journal of International Law* 266. See Y Lukacs (ed), *Documents on the Israeli-Palestinian Conflict* (1984) quoted in IO Pogany, 'The Arab League and Regional Peacekeeping' (1987) *Netherlands International Law Review* 54 at 55. On the historical background to the League, see A Gomaa, *The Foundation of the League of Arab States* (1977) cited in Pogany, *ibid*, at 55. On the assumption of regional roles by the League, see B Boutros-Ghali, 'The Arab League (1945–1970)' (1969) 25 *Revue Egyptienne de Droit International* 67.

[101] League Council Resolution 3456 (9 June 1976); League Council Resolution 3457 (10 June 1976), texts of both resolutions are available in French in *Le Monde* (9 and 11 June 1976 respectively), quoted by Pogany, above note 100 at 61 and 62.

[102] GA Res 120.

[103] See *Repertory of the United Nations Practice*, vol 2, 446; Cot and Pellet above note 1 at 795, cited by Gray, above note 77 at 204.

[104] UN Doc A/C 6/SC 215, paras 21, 44; A/C.6/SC 217, para 28. See Bruno Simma's *Commentary*, above note 1, 818.

[105] 479 *United Nations Treaty Series*, 70.

[106] 914 *United Nations Treaty Series*, 111.

in the continent of Africa'.[107] Such explicit, unprecedented proclamation of the status of a regional organisation undoubtedly presents a *fait accompli* to the world.

The UN practice since the end of the Cold War indicates a trend towards perfunctorily implying the status of regional organisations in the resolutions of its organs. For instance, Security Council Resolution 866[108] expressly stated that the Liberian crisis (1989-1997) was the first time the UN had undertaken a peacekeeping mission in conjunction with another organisation. Similarly, the UN would seem to imply that NATO and the Western European Union (WEU) are regional organisations, when in 1994 its Secretary-General included them in his meeting with regional organisations on account of the crisis in the former Yugoslavia.[109]

In a nutshell, the serious tension that once characterised the relationship between the UN and regional organisations has given way to a greater co-operation after the Cold War. This in turn has considerably encouraged regional organisations to devise more comprehensive and useful legal, and in some instances, institutional, frameworks for pacific settlement of disputes among their members.

However, if the end of the Cold War has meant that jurisdictional conflicts between the UN and regional organisations under Article 52 have abated, the post-Cold War period has raised new tensions between the UN and regional organisations in the context of Chapter VIII. This is in respect of the notion of enforcement action provided for in Article 53(1). It is to a consideration of this issue that the chapter now turns.

2.3. ENFORCEMENT ACTION BY REGIONAL ORGANISATIONS

Article 53(1) of the UN Charter is the legal authority for the delegation of enforcement action by the Security Council to regional arrangements.[110] It states that the

> Security Council shall, where appropriate, utilize such regional arrangements or agencies for enforcement action under its authority. But no enforcement action shall be taken under regional arrangements or by regional agencies without the authorization of the Security Council, with the exception of measures taken against any enemy State.

This provision can be regarded as creating a margin of devolution of enforcement powers, already endowed on the Security Council under Chapter VII, in favour of regional organisations. Except for self-defence

[107] SC Res 199 (1964).
[108] UN Doc S/RES/866 (1993) adopted on 22 September.
[109] 1994 *United Nations Yearbook* 88.
[110] On the theme of delegation of the Security Council Powers in general see Sarooshi, above note 5.

(Article 51) and action against former enemy states (Article 107),[111] regional organisations have no other legal competence under the UN Charter to undertake enforcement outside Article 53(1).

2.3.1. Enforcement Action under Chapter VIII: Analysis of Factors Responsible for the Weakening of the Charter Framework for Regional Arrangements

Enforcement action has been defined as 'any action which would itself be a violation of international law, if taken without either some special justification or without the contemporaneous consent or acquiescence of the target state'.[112] It has also been thought of as 'all coercive actions other than valid defensive action'.[113]

What the founders of the UN intended by the phrase could be deciphered from the initial drafts of Chapter VIII at Dumbarton Oaks.[114] In the early drafts, the phrase 'enforcement action'[115] had appeared alongside 'coercive action' which appeared in the amendment proposed by the Soviet Union.[116] Significantly, there was no disagreement amongst participating states between the use of 'enforcement' and 'coercive' in these drafts. Thus, it is submitted that the word *enforcement* or *coercion* implies the notion of force to exert preponderant pressure on its recipient.

The first attempt to interpret the phrase 'enforcement action' under Chapter VIII emerged during the Cold War period when tension between the East and the West culminated in such incidents as the Cuban Missile Crisis and the Dominican Republic debacle.[117] The issue arose in connection with whether the measures imposed by the OAS on the Dominican

[111] However, the provisions of Art 107 are now thought to be obsolete in the light of the fact that former enemy states (such as Germany, Japan and Italy) are now UN members.

[112] Morrison in Delbrück's *Allocation*, above note 8 at 43.

[113] Inis Claude Jr, 'The OAS, the UN, and the United States' (1964) *International Conciliation* 547 at 548–53; John Norton Moore, 'The Role of Regional Arrangements in the Maintenance of World Order' in (Cyril E Black and Richard Falk (eds), *The Future of the International Legal Order* vol 3 (New Jersey, Princeton University Press, 1971) 122 at 153; John W Halderman, 'Regional Enforcement Measures and the United Nations' (1963) 52 (1) *Georgetown Law Journal* 89 at 96. See also Georg Ress, 'Article 53' in Bruno Simma's *Commentary* above note 1, 722 at 732.

[114] UNCIO Documents vol 3, 601, Doc 2 G/14(w)(1), May 8, 1945.

[115] UNCIO Documents vol 3, 598, Doc 2 G/14 (v) May 6, 1945.

[116] *Ibid.*

[117] Leonard Meeker, 'Defensive Quarantine and the Law' (1963) 57 *American Journal of International Law* 515; Carl Christol, 'Maritime Quarantine: The Naval Interdiction of Offensive Weapons and Associated Matériel to Cuba, 1962' *Ibid* 525; Abraham Chayes, 'Law and the Quarantine of Cuba,' (1962/63) 41 *Foreign Affairs* 550; A Eide, 'Peace-keeping and Enforcement by Regional Organizations' (1966) 3 *Journal of Peace Research* 125; WT Mallison, 'Limited Naval Blockade or Quarantine Interdiction: National and Collective Defense Claims Valid Under International Law' (1962) 31 *George Washington University Law Review* 339–43.

Republic (1960) and Cuba (1962) ought to have been authorised by the Security Council under Article 53(1).

In the Cuban Missile Crisis, the Security Council was confronted with the question whether the OAS interdiction of Soviet ships on the high seas, believed to be carrying missiles to Cuba, amounted to enforcement action under Chapter VIII.[118] The Soviet Union favoured this interpretation, which would have meant that the action violated Article 53(1).[119] Curiously, the Security Council had met,[120] fully aware of the content of the October 23 quarantine resolution, before its adoption by the OAS[121] and a formal proclamation by the US President;[122] yet it took no action against it.[123] Similarly, when the Soviet Union proposed a resolution condemning the action as contravening Article 53 of the UN Charter, the Security Council, by general consent, decided not to take action on it, preferring instead to pursue a political resolution of the issue.

It should be recalled that the Soviet Union had maintained a similar position when the OAS imposed economic sanctions on the Dominican Republic on August 1960.[124] This was in response to a series of alleged subversive activities conducted by the Dominican Republic against Venezuela. The Soviet Union had moved that the Security Council approved the action, which in its opinion constituted enforcement action within the meaning of Article 53.[125] The Security Council avoided giving a direct answer.[126] Instead, it passed the resolution, tabled by the United States and supported by Ecuador and Argentina, that the Security Council should merely 'take note' of the action.[127]

A consideration of the manner in which regional organisations have interpreted 'enforcement action' is important for several reasons. Although states at first resented the General Assembly's initial attempt to classify OAS and Arab League under Chapter VIII, they subsequently 'accepted' that regional organisations could undertake pacific measures[128] even if their constituent treaties do not expressly provide for such action,

[118] (1972) 47 *State Department Bulletin* 715.

[119] For an account, see particularly Meeker, above note 117, 521 *et seq*.

[120] (1972) 47 *State Department Bulletin* 715; see also Meeker, above note 117 at 522.

[121] (1962) 47 *State Department Bulletin* 598–600, 720.

[122] Proclamation 3504 (effective October 24 1962), 27 Fed Reg 10401; (1962) 47 *State Department Bulletin* 717; (1963) 57 *American Journal of International Law* 512, quoted by Meeker, above note 117.

[123] *Ibid*, 522.

[124] See Tad Szulc, *Dominican Diary* (1965); John Bartlow Martin, *Overtaken by Events* (1966), all cited by Akehurst, above note 59 at 204.

[125] SCOR 15th year, Supplement for July, August and September 1960 (S/4477, 5 September 1960, and S/4481/Rev I, 8 September 1960).

[126] For a record of the Security Council meeting on this issue, see SCOR 15th, 894th to 895th meetings, 8–9 September 1960. For a comprehensive review, see Akehurst, above note 59.

[127] SCOR 15th year, 895th meeting, 9 September 1960, 5.

[128] For a similar opinion, see Gray, above note 77 at 210; Akehurst, above note 59.

or contain functions that do not exactly coincide with some principles of the UN Charter.[129]

However, in pursuance of dispute resolution after the Cold War, regional organisations have exerted preponderant pressure on Chapter VIII, raising many question marks about the legality of some of their activities. The problem this time is not with whether their constitutions allow for pacific settlement or whether their *casus foederis* are consistent with the purposes of the UN. Rather, the issue is whether regional organisations can authorise forceful measures, (whether economic or military in nature), under the auspices of Chapter VIII, in the same way they can pacific measures.

This problem arose mainly with the practice of ECOWAS. ECOWAS intervened in Liberia when it deployed its Monitoring Group (ECOMOG) in 1990.[130] For this, it required no authorisation from the Security Council.[131] Whether one argues that peacekeeping operations are an outgrowth of the Charter 'discovered like penicillin'[132] or that the phrase 'pacific settlement' as appears in Article 52(2) implicitly refers to them, the bottom line remains that peacekeeping operations do not require Security Council's authorisation before they can be undertaken.

However, ECOWAS imposed massive economic sanctions on the rebel forces in Liberia, in order to compel them to comply with its actions and decisions of the international community. It adopted this approach as part of its strategy to fight the rebel forces in Sierra Leone. Given the coercive use to which ECOWAS intended to put these measures, the question can be asked whether it required Security Council authorisation before it could validly impose such measures.

It is generally believed by international lawyers that economic sanctions do not constitute enforcement action and thus do not require authorisation by the Security Council for validity. Apparently the OAS had formed the view in the 1960s and the Security Council had refrained from taking a formal position on it.

[129] Provided that an organisation can be said to be regional within Chapter VIII, it makes no difference that its constituent instrument does not expressly contain provisions allowing it to undertake pacific settlement of disputes amongst its members. A regional organisation could rely on Chapter VIII provision as its main legal authority for pacific settlement of disputes.

[130] ECOMOG was established at the First Session of the Community Standing Committee between 6 and 7 August in Banjul, The Gambia. See Decision A/DEC 1/8/90 (art II).

[131] See White, *Keeping the Peace*, above note 46. ECOWAS had claimed that ECOMOG was going to Liberia 'to stop the senseless killing of innocent civilian nationals and foreigners and to help the Liberian people to restore their democratic institutions. The ECOWAS intervention is in no way designed to save one part or to punish another'. See S/21485.

[132] Brian Urquhart, 'The United Nations, Collective Security, and International Peacekeeping' in Henrikson (ed), *Negotiating World Order: The Artisanship and Architecture of Global Diplomacy* (Wilmington, Del, Scholarly Resources Inc, 1986) 62.

Interestingly, when ECOWAS considered imposing economic sanctions on the Sierra Leone rebels in 1997, it approached the Security Council for approval.[133] This raises the question whether regional organisations require Security Council authorisation before imposing economic sanctions.

2.4. DO/SHOULD ECONOMIC SANCTIONS CONSTITUTE ENFORCEMENT ACTION UNDER CHAPTER VIII?

The use of economic sanctions has significantly increased since the end of the Cold War. Whereas the Security Council imposed sanctions twice during the Cold War—against Rhodesia (1966) and South Africa (1977)—it did so on no less than twelve occasions between 1990 and 1999.[134] With regard to regional organisations, the statistic is even higher. During 1990s alone, regional organisations imposed sanctions on their members at least three dozen times.[135] These exclude the OAS action against Cuba (1962),[136] the Dominican Republic (1963), and the OAU on Southern Rhodesia following the Unilateral Declaration of Independence (UDI).

It is often argued that non-military measures under Chapter VIII do not constitute enforcement action. This view is based on the distinction made between military and non-military measures by Chapter VII of the Charter, and the differing consequences of the two.

Advocates of this view refer to the overall structure of the security arrangements of the Charter, which, according to them, favour the concentration of military actions solely in the hands of the Council.[137] The manner in which the other provisions of the Charter use the term 'enforcement action', they argue, indicate that non-military measures are not enforcement action. According to this view, Article 2(5) puts an obligation

[133] S/PV3822, 8 Oct 1997.

[134] Against Iraq (1990), the former Yugoslavia (1991, 1992 and 1998), Libya (1992), Somalia (1992), parts of Cambodia (1992), Haiti (1993), parts of Angola (1993, 1997 and 1998), Rwanda (1994), Sudan (1996), Sierra Leone (1997), and Afghanistan (1999). This list has been adapted from David Cortright and George A Lopez, *The Sanctions Decade. Assessing UN Strategies in the 1990s* (Colorado, Lynne Rienner Publishers, Inc, 2000), 1–2. See also David Cortright and George A Lopez, *Sanctions and the Search for Security* (Colorado, Lynne Rienner Publishers Inc, 2002).

[135] Cortright and Lopez, *Sanctions Decade*, above note 134, 2. For OAS action against Haiti, see David Malone, *Decision-Making in the Security Council: The Case of Haiti* (Oxford, Clarendon Press, 1998); Cornevin Robert, *Haiti* (Paris, Presses Universitaires de France, 2nd Revised edn, 1993). For ECOWAS in Sierra Leone, see Ademola Abass, 'The Implementation of ECOWAS' New Protocol and Security Council Resolution 1270 in Sierra Leone: New Developments in Regional Intervention' (2002) 10(1) *University of Miami International and Comparative Law Review* 177. See Chapter 1 note 35.

[136] Above.

[137] Christian Walter, 'Security Council Control over Regional Action', (1997) *Max Planck Yearbook of United Nations Law* 1 at 142.

on all Member States of the UN to 'refrain from giving assistance to any State against which the United Nations is taking *preventive* or *enforcement* action.'[138] The reference to 'preventive or enforcement action' is thus linked with the provisions under Chapter VII Articles 40–42. Article 40 provides that: 'In order to prevent an aggravation . . . the Security Council may . . . call upon the parties to comply with provisional measures . . . but such shall be without prejudice to the rights, claims or positions of the concerned parties.'

Several authors are of the view that all actions taken under Chapter VII were intended to be enforcement actions.[139] Therefore, under Chapter VII, non-military measures constitute enforcement action. The converse—which is the thesis of this school—is that non-military measures under Chapter VIII do not constitute enforcement action since only the Security Council could regulate enforcement action.

Another group of scholars[140] contends that economic sanctions and embargoes are enforcement action, but as they are *such* that individual states may rightfully and legally take, they do not require the authorisation of the Security Council.[141] This group posits that since states may naturally impose economic sanctions and sever diplomatic relations individually without infringing any norms of international law, economic sanctions do not violate Article 53(1).[142] Thus, 'economic sanctions and peacekeeping activities may be undertaken by regional organizations without Security Council legitimation *if internal law opens* such an option.'[143] This was the same argument the United States relied on during the Cuba Missile Crisis in 1962 in justifying its action on the High Seas.[144]

Regardless of which of the contending views may be correct, there is no reason why economic sanctions cannot be regarded as constituting

[138] (Emphasis added.)

[139] Michael Akehurst, above note 59 at 186; Hans Kelsen, *The Law of the United Nations* (London, Stevens & Sons, 1964) 724; Rama, in *Anuario Uruguayo de Derecho International* (1962), 386; Paolillo, *ibid*, 48–49.

[140] See Hans Kelsen, above note 139 at 724, where he said, in support of this proposition that 'This purpose [of non-military sanctions] is defined in Article 41 as follows: "to give effect to its [Security Council's] decisions"; that means to enforce the decision upon a recalcitrant State. Hence these measures, too, may be considered to be "enforcement measures"'. See SCOR, 15th year, 894th meeting, 9 September 1960, para 57. See also, R Wolfrum, 'Der Beitrag regionaler Abmachungen zur Friedenssicherung: Moglichkeiten und Grenzen', (1993) 1 *ZaöRV* 53 576, at 582. Also cited by Christian Walter, above note 137, at 130 and 137.

[141] Those in favour of this view are: Jimenez de Arechaga, 'La coordination des systèmes de l'ONU et de l'OEA',(1964) RdC 111, 419 at 481; R Gerold, *Die Sicherung des Friedens durch die OAS*, (1971), 131, also cited by Christian Walter, above note 137 at 137.

[142] Eide, above note 117 at 732.

[143] Rüdiger Wolfrum in Delbruck's *Allocation*, above note 8, 91.

[144] For a full explanation of this view, see the United States speech in the Security Council, SCOR 17th year, 993rd meeting, 15th March 1962, especially para 113. See also Chinese speech, SCOR 995th meeting, 20th March 1962, para 24.

enforcement action under regional arrangement if it fulfils the main purpose of enforcement: coercing the will of target states.[145]

The argument is often made that economic force was expressly excluded from being forbidden by Article 2(4) and thus could not be classified as enforcement action under Chapter VIII.[146] This view is problematic. Whilst it is true that the Brazilian attempt to include economic measures in the category of forces[147] prohibited by Article 2(4) was rejected at San Francisco,[148] this was not because states felt that economic sanctions could not in fact amount to coercion. The Belgian delegate, during the discussion of the Brazilian proposed amendment, thought that Brazil was underestimating the reach of the amorphous phrase 'in any other manner' contained in Article 2(4).[149] The *Report of Rapporteur of Committee I to Commission I* contained an indication that 'the unilateral use of force of similar coercive measures is not authorized or admitted'.[150] The rejection of the Brazilian amendment therefore 'may have reflected either opposition to the principle it contained or simply the belief of some of the delegates that the Charter already embodied its principles'.[151] Other writers have noted the ambiguity of the *travaux préparatoires* on this issue.[152]

It is submitted that the place of economic force under Article 2(4) does not affect the construction of economic sanctions as *enforcement action* under Chapter VIII. The legal nature of economic force and economic sanctions under Article 2(4) and Article 53(1) significantly differ. Whereas in the former the issue is whether the use of economic force (which indeed could be in form of sanctions) could amount to force under Article 2(4), this is not so under Article 53(1). What Article 2(4) prohibits is the use of

[145] See our definition of enforcement action, above.

[146] There is extensive literature on the subject of Article 2(4). For the purpose of economic coercion and Article 2(4), see Derek W Bowett, 'Economic Coercion and Reprisal by States', (1972) 13 (1) *Virginia Journal of International Law* 1; OY Elegab, *The Legality of Non-Forcible Counter-Measures in International Law* (Oxford, Clarendon Press, 1988); A Hindmarsh, 'Self-Help in Time of Peace' (1932) 26 *American Journal of International Law* 515; L Damrosch, 'Retaliation or Arbitration—or Both? The 1978 United States—France Aviation Dispute' (1980) 74 *American Journal of International Law* 785; Derek W Bowett, 'Economic Coercion: Past and Present' (1976) 16 *Virginia Journal of International Law* 245; Jordan J Paust and Albert P Blaustein, 'The Arab Oil Weapon—A Threat to International Peace' (1974) 68 *American Journal of International Law* 410; Tom Farer, 'The Political and Economic Coercion in Contemporary International Law' (1985) 79 *American Journal of International Law* 407.

[147] *UNCIO Document* 215, I/1/10, 6 527, 559 (1945).

[148] UN Doc 784, 1/1/27, *UNCIO Documents* 331, 334–35 (1945).

[149] *Ibid.* See also Lee C Buchheit, 'The Use of Nonviolent Coercion: A Study in Legality under Article 2(4) of the Charter of the United Nations', in Richard Lillich (ed), *Economic Coercion and the New International Economic Order* (Virginia, The Michie Company Law Publishers, 1976) 41.

[150] *UNCIO Documents* 885, Vol XI I/1/34, 387, 400 (1945).

[151] See Lee Buchheit, above note 149 at 52–53.

[152] Julius Stone, *Aggression and World Order* (London, Stevens & Sons, 1958), 97–98; Rosalyn Higgins, 'The Legal Limits to the Use of Force by Sovereign States: United Nations Practice' (1961) 37 *British Yearbook of International Law* 269, 277, fn 2, cited by Buchheit, above note 149 at 53, fn 43.

force by states in their international relations. What states rejected in 1945 is the specific inclusion of economic measures within Article 2(4). Under Article 53(1), economic sanctions are construed, not as an instrument of aggression to *invade* a state as with Article 2(4), but as a *penal* measure in response to what the regulating state perceives as a previous illegal act by the Target State. The difference between the two is the difference between *aggression* and *enforcement* action. In legal literature, this distinction is rarely made.[153]

Even if it was the intention in 1945 that economic sanctions were not covered by Chapter VIII, as many American international lawyers argued during the Dominican and Cuban crises,[154] there is no reason why such belief cannot be altered by subsequent state practice.[155]

The OAS imposed economic sanctions on the Dominican Republic on August 20 1960 on the grounds that it had conducted subversive activities against President Betancourt's government in Venezuela.[156] Four days later, the Soviet Union had requested the Security Council to approve the sanctions.[157] In the Security Council, the United States argued that enforcement action as used under Article 53 only referred to *military* action and not the severance of diplomatic and economic relations.[158] With respect to Cuba, the OAS had imposed sanctions to counter the pursuit by that state of the communist ideology, which, in the view of the OAS states, was inconsistent with the principles enunciated by the Inter-American System. In addition, the OAS imposed an arms embargo—thus preventing the export of arms by Member States to Cuba—as a price for encouraging and supporting subversive activities against the Venezuelan State.[159] By 1964, the OAS had intensified its sanctions against Cuba, imposing a complete severance of diplomatic and economic relationships with Cuba[160] and by 1967 ordered a partial boycott of all ships, regardless of their nationality, which might be trading with Cuba.[161] As already noted above, the Security Council had been unable to take an unequivocal position on the Soviet's request for authorisation of the sanctions against the Dominican Republic. The Cuban request that the Security Council should

153 Cf Constantine Antonopoulos, *The Unilateral Use of Force by States in International Law* (Athens, Ant N Sakkloulas Publishers, 1997), at 106.

154 See the discussion above.

155 Article 33 (3) (b) Vienna Convention on the Law of Treaties (1969) states that in interpreting the provisions of a treaty, there shall be taken into account, *inter alia*, any 'subsequent practice in the application of the treaty applicable in the relations between parties'.

156 SCOR 15th year, Supp, (July, August and September 1960) (S/4477, 5 September 1960, S/4481/Rev I, September 1960).

157 *Ibid.*

158 *Ibid*, S/4477, 5 September 1960; S/4481/Rev I, 8 September 1960.

159 SCOR 17th year, Supp, (January, February, March 1962), S/5705, 3 February 1962).

160 Modesto Seara Vazquez, 'La neuvième réunion de consultation des Ministres des Affaires Étrangères et l'affaire du Cuba' (1964) 10 *Annuaire français de droit international* 638.

161 *The Times*, 26 September 1967, cited by Akehurst, above note 59 at 190.

seek an ICJ opinion as regards the sanctions against her was also rejected for purely political reasons.[162]

Academic opinions as to whether the OAS actions constituted enforcement actions under Chapter VIII were divided along predictable lines. The views of State Department lawyers and, indeed most American international lawyers reflected the official position of the United States: that Article 53(1) of the UN Charter did not govern the OAS sanctions. Other scholars demurred to this view. Ruda and Paolillo, for instance, argue that if non-military sanctions were not to be regarded as enforcement actions under Chapter VIII, it would have serious implications for the Security Council.[163] According to them, it would mean that, if confronted with a threat to, or breach of, the peace from circumstances within the territory of a Member State, the Security Council could impose only military actions, and nothing more, since only enforcement measures constitute an exception to Article 2(7).[164]

However, other writers contradict this position.[165] Jiménez de Arechaga argued along the same line as several American international lawyers, although with different reasoning. In his opinion, Article 53(1) admits only two exceptions: self-defence and actions against former enemy states. These, in his view, contemplated military action, and, hence, the principle forbidding enforcement action without the Security Council authorisation must be conceptualised in a similar manner, that is, such enforcement action can only imply military action. Some regard Arechaga's position as 'non conclusive, since actions to forestall a renewal of aggressive policy by a former enemy state, for instance, need not *necessarily* be military'.[166]

In the Security Council debate concerning Sierra Leone in 1997,[167] ECOWAS assumed, as did several Council members, that it required Security Council authorisation under Chapter VIII in order to impose sanctions on rebel factions. ECOWAS informed the Security Council that

> it was left with no option but to adopt a set of measures in the form of sanctions and embargo as a mean of pressuring the regime in Freetown to appreciate the futility of its situation and re-engage ECOWAS in a constructive dialogue which

[162] For a discussion of this affair and the political nature of the debate, see Akehurst, above note 59, 188–97, Christol, above note 117, Meeker, above note 117.

[163] Ruda in *Anuario Uruguayo de Derecho Internacional* (1962), 44–49; Paolillo, *ibid*, 234–36 cited in Akehurst, above note 59, 186.

[164] For a similar view, see Thomas Franck, *Fairness in International Law and International Institutions* (Oxford, Clarendon Press, 1995) 219, 221–22, noting that 'enforcement action may take the form of "measures not involving the use of armed force", and that the "Greenwich foot" by which the actions taken by the Security Council in the name of "collective security" are judged is Article 2(7) of the Charter'.

[165] E Jiménez de Arichaga, 'La Coordination des systèmes de l'ONU et de L'OEA pour de règlement pacifique des differends et la sécurité collective' (1964) 111 *Recueil des cours* 423, 479–80.

[166] Akehurst, above note 59 at 188. Emphasis added.

[167] S/PV.3822 3822nd mtg, 8 October 1997.

> would ensure the early reinstatement of the legitimate Government of President Kabbah.[168]

The organisation then requested 'an enabling authorization of the Council to ECOMOG to carry out its tasks as mandated by the ECOWAS summit'.[169]

Two issues must be noted in ECOWAS's request. First, ECOWAS perceived economic measures as means of 'pressuring' the rebel factions to comply with its decisions. This fulfils the purpose of enforcement action under Chapter VIII. Second, it believed that for it to be legal, such an action required authorisation by the Council.

Several members of the Council formed the same opinion as ECOWAS. The UK and US 'fully'[170] and 'strongly'[171] supported the sanctions respectively, with the US indicating that the draft resolution falls under Chapter VIII.[172] Russia saw the sanctions as 'powerful means of pressure on the junta' and as falling under Chapter VIII when it said 'enforcement action should not be undertaken by regional organizations without the authorisation of the Security Council'.[173] China's[174] and Poland's[175] only had concern about the humanitarian consequences of the sanctions on civilians. Korea endorsed ECOWAS' bringing a 'maximum pressure to bear upon the junta with sanctions.'[176] Egypt[177] and Guinea-Bissau[178] endorse the sanctions wholly with the latter stating them to manifest the resolve of African nations regarding military coups'. Only France regarded the sanctions as part of 'measures intended to promote a peaceful resolution of the crisis'[179] a view also shared by the UN Secretary-General.[180] The reference by Mr Dejammet, the French representative to 'peaceful resolution' is a nuanced response to the use ECOWAS had clearly intended to put the sanctions, as understood by several Council members. Nonetheless despite the fact that France viewed the authorization sought by ECOWAS as 'exceptional', the draft resolution was unanimously adopted.[181]

It is submitted that where a group of states imposes collective non-military sanctions on another state for the purpose of coercing or pressuring it, in order to compel it to desist from, or conform to certain

168 *Ibid*, at 4.
169 *Ibid*.
170 *Ibid*, at 7.
171 *Ibid*, at 16.
172 *Ibid*, at 16.
173 *Ibid*, at 9.
174 *Ibid*, at 14.
175 *Ibid*, at 8.
176 *Ibid*, at 8.
177 *Ibid*, at 12.
178 *Ibid*, at 15.
179 *Ibid*, at 6.
180 S/1997/776.
181 UN Doc S/RES/1132 (1997) 8 October 1997.

behaviours, such an action constitutes an enforcement action. Given the reluctance of many states to use force, economic measures have become an effective instrument through which states can enforce their wishes against others and bring recalcitrant states to comply with their international obligations. The recent announcement by Libya that it would allow UN weapons inspectors unrestricted access into its nuclear facilities indicate the effect immense economic pressures can achieve as a punitive, hence, enforcement action, when well-targeted and effectively implemented.

2.5. THE REQUIREMENT OF 'AUTHORISATION' UNDER CHAPTER VIII AND ITS EFFECT ON THE CHARTER SCHEME OF COLLECTIVE SECURITY

Another very important issue to consider under Chapter VIII framework is the effect the requirement of Security Council authorisation in Article 53(1) was originally intended to have on regional organisations and what it actually achieved.

There is no doubt that the Charter drafters intended to subordinate regional organisations to the overall control of the Security Council by imposing an obligation on them to obtain the latter's authorisation in order to undertake enforcement action.[182] This control becomes important given the empowerment of regional organisations under Article 51 to use force in self-defence without the authorisation of the Security Council. In fact, the only restraint on regional organisations under that Article is if the Security Council takes measures necessary to maintain international peace and security. Apparently, it may be difficult for the Security Council to take measures necessary to truncate an act of self-defence, particularly where the concerned organisation consists of one or more permanent members of the Security Council with an interest in the situation.[183] Therefore, it would have amounted to giving regional organisations too much power if Article 53(1) does not expressly restrict their right to use another type of force, which does not have to be in self-defence.

The original framework and policy consideration underlining Chapter VIII consist in affording regional organisations a margin of operation to take actions in exception to the prohibition of the use of force under Article

[182] Winston Churchill, for instance, said that 'there should be several regional councils, august but subordinate'; speech made at The Hague, May 7, 1948, cited in Inis Claude, *Swords into Plowshares* (New York, Random House, 1984) 113, also cited in Sutterlin, above note 16, 93.

[183] For instance, despite Resolution 687 terminating the Gulf War, the allied states (UK, US, and France) still attack Iraq on a regular basis on the ground that that is in their exercise of self-defence under Article 51. See Peter Daniel DiPaola, 'A Noble Sacrifice? *Jus Ad Bellum* and the International Community's Gamble in Chechnya', (1997) 4 *Indiana Journal of Global Legal Studies* 435.

2(4) with the legitimacy of the Security Council authorisation. Thus, it is possible for the Security Council to refuse to authorise a regional organisation intending to intervene in a conflict occurring within its territory.[184]

In reality, the requirement of authorisation under Chapter VIII has turned out to be a classical case of irony in the UN Charter. Rather than ensuring the subordination of regional organisations to the Security Council, the requirement has inspired regional organisations' circumvention of Security Council's control and their departure from the Chapter VIII framework.

The factor responsible for this development is to be seen in the non-specification of the time and the modality in which regional organisations must obtain authorisation from the Security Council in order to take enforcement action. If we construe the phrase 'without the authorization of the Security Council' as it appears in Article 53(1), it is possible to conclude that the Charter drafters intended that authorisation must precede regional enforcement action. Yet, nothing ordains such a restrictive interpretation. There is nothing in Chapter VIII, elsewhere in the Charter, or in the *travaux préparatoires* of the UN, that suggests that it was the intention of the Charter drafters that authorisation must precede regional enforcement action. Those who argue in support of such an interpretation[185] rest their argument on what they perceive as the organic relationship between Article 53(1) and the power of the Security Council to make a determination as to the state of peace under Article 39. They suggest that 'like all collective security measures, the granting of authorization under Article 53(1) cl.2 depends legally on the existence of a threat to peace, a breach of the peace, or an act of aggression. The SC is empowered to decide on both these prerequisites and on the granting of authorization.'[186]

It is unlikely that the supposed relationship between Article 53(1) and Article 39 justifies the conclusion that authorisation under Chapter VIII must be *prior*. To start with, nowhere in Chapter VIII is it stated that the Security Council must make a determination, such that it must make in order to trigger enforcement action under Chapter VII, before authorising regional organisations under Chapter VIII. Even if it is accepted that the determination of the threat to or breach of peace and acts of aggression must be made before a Chapter VIII action, it is not impossible that a regional organisation can exercise such power on its own. Nothing is

[184] For instance J Wolf, 'Regional Arrangements and the UN Charter' (1983) 6 *Encyclopaedia of Public International Law* 289–95 at 293, observes that the discretion of the Security Council enables it to refuse authorisation both on legal ground as well as on the ground of suitability. See also Georg Ress in Simma's *Commentary*, above note 1 at 733.

[185] WTR Fox & Warner R Schilling, *European Security and the Atlantic System* (New York, Columbia University Press, 1973).

[186] Georg Ress in Simma's *Commentary*, above note 1 at 733. See also J Wolf, 'Regional arrangements and the UN Charter,' (1983) 6 *Encyclopaedia of International Law* 329–93.

contained in Chapter VIII which forbids regional organisations from doing so.[187] Finally, it is not clear how a determination such as ordained by Article 39 dictates *when* regional organisations must obtain authorisation. It is possible for a determination to be made, but without it being followed by a request to intervene, and a regional organisation may request to intervene in a regional conflict *before* the Security Council has even met to consider the case.[188] Thus, the argument proposing that authorisation must be prior, because the granting of it is linked with the exercise of the Security Council's right under Article 39, is a *non sequitur*.

The original basis for empowering regional organisations to undertake enforcement action is to enable them to operate expeditiously, *albeit* with the Security Council's control. Therefore, 'it may be necessary for them [regional organisations] to take action *before* it is possible to obtain an authoritative determination of whether the action is justified. Only after the fact do you then get the blessing of the Security Council or at least the non-curse of the Security Council'.[189] To then argue that authorisation must be prior would appear to compromise the very essence of regional arrangement under Chapter VIII.

2.5.1. Retroactive Authorisation and its Impact on Chapter VIII

The practice of regional organisations, especially after the Cold War, clearly demonstrates that questions as to *when* regional organisations must obtain authorisation from the Security Council in order to undertake enforcement action is now moot. Many regional organisations have formed the view that authorisation under Article 53(1) does not have to be prior to action. Thus, they now act first and later seek to legitimatise the action by indicating that the Security Council retroactively endorsed it. This retroactive endorsement is commonly referred to as the notion of *ex post facto* authorisation. An *ex post facto* approval takes place where the Security Council implicitly endorses an enforcement action taken by a regional organisation without its initial authorisation.[190]

It may be that after finding that a threat to peace, actual breach of the peace or an act of aggression has occurred, the Security Council is unable to proceed to authorise a particular regional organisation to act. As already noted, this could be due to several reasons. It may be that the Security

[187] See fuller discussion of this point below.
[188] See discussion on the Liberia and Sierra Leone crises in Chapter 5.
[189] Morrison in Delbrück's *Allocation*, above note 8 at 101.
[190] See Bruno Simma, 'Regional Enforcement of Community Objectives' in Vera Gowlland-Debbas (ed), *United Nations Sanctions and International Law* (The Hague, Kluwer Law International, 2001) 117 particularly at 118 *et seq*, contending that 'there is the possibility for the Security Council to render an implicit authorisation'.

Council is not interested in that particular conflict or is of the opinion that the conflict is not such that it should engage in at that particular time. This may cause the Security Council to simply 'turn away'[191] from the conflict. Also, the Security Council may meet a real difficulty, in the form of opposition from one or more of its permanent members for instance, preventing it from adopting necessary resolutions to authorise enforcement action. This may make it 'run away' [192] from the conflict altogether.

Whatever may be the case, it is possible for the Security Council to return to the case at a later stage and bestow a belated, but valid, legitimacy on the action by tacitly adopting it. An initial incapacity to authorise a regional enforcement action does not invariably fetter the Security Council's ability to do so at whatever stage in the progression of the conflict it may deem fit. This possibility of subsequent approval of an otherwise illegal action avoids the situation in which the Security Council's control over regional organisation's activities, embodied by Article 54, is permanently circumvented by lack of authorisation *ab initio*.[193] Therefore, the view expressed in some quarters that subsequent authorisation will encourage illegality and present the Security Council with a *fait accompli*[194] does not seem to recognise the flexibility of the requirement of authorisation contained in Article 53(1) and the unlimited obligation imposed on regional organisations in Article 54 to keep the Security Council informed of their activities at all times.

The requirement of Article 53(1) concerning the *time* regional organisations must obtain authorisation is subject to flexible interpretation, and has been so dealt with by regional organisations in practice.[195] However, it is extremely difficult to distinguish when the Security Council is just perfunctorily recognising the efforts of a regional organisation towards resolving a conflict from occasions when it is fulfilling a constitutional obligation to accord authorisation to these organisations. The argument is often made that when the Security Council adopts resolutions welcoming the activities of a regional organisation, which activities include unauthorised enforcement actions, such amount to an *ex post facto* authorisation.[196] This line of argument was pursued by some writers to rationalise the Security Council's dealing with the Liberian crisis in 1993 when it emerged that ECOWAS was pursuing enforcement action contrary to its official position.[197]

[191] Sir Arthur Watt's Comment in Delbrück's *Allocation*, above note 8 at 91.

[192] Rainer Lagoni in Delbrück's *Allocation*, above note 8 at 99.

[193] Meeker argued that 'unless the SC states otherwise, authorization at any stage of action implicitly authorizes the earlier stages of the regional action', quoted by Ress, above note 117 at 734.

[194] See Simma, above note 190. But see Morrison, above note 8 at 101.

[195] See Chapter 5.

[196] Simma, above note 190 at 118 *et seq*; Meeker, above note 117 at 522 *et seq*; White, above note 46 at 231.

[197] See Georg Nolte, above note 10.

While it is legally possible that the Security Council bestows retroactive legitimacy on an initial unauthorised regional action, this does not open a Pandora's box. It does not mean that in every situation a Security Council resolution is 'welcoming the return to Sierra Leone of its democratically elected president'[198] or expressing 'full support and appreciation for the mediation efforts of the ECOWAS Committee'[199] the Security Council is retroactively approving enforcement action taken in the breach of Article 53(1). Nor can such a conclusion be reached only on the basis of the Security Council's acquiescence. Such 'welcoming' statements, as are often made by the President of the Security Council,[200] may indeed be no more than expressions of general satisfaction.

It may also be that the Security Council as a political organ concerned with the maintenance or restoration of peace would quite often have to 'build upon facts or situations based on, or involving illegalities'.[201] Thus, one must be cautious not to automatically assume that an *ex post facto* authorisation exists in every conceivable circumstance since it is not in every situation that states may actually negate such inferences from the resolutions of the Security Council, as Russia did not did concerning the action of NATO in Kosovo. In the Security Council debate leading to the adoption of Resolution 1244 on 10 June 1999, Russia expressly stated that the adoption of that resolution which established the KFOR forces consisting substantially of NATO forces should be taken to mean the adoption of the unauthorised enforcement action NATO took against the FRY forces.[202]

Although retroactive authorisation has been very visible in the development of the relationship between the UN and regional organisations,[203] it has nonetheless impacted the Chapter VIII framework and weakened, rather than strengthened, the Security Council's control of regional enforcement actions. Today, the provision of Article 54 obligating regional organisations to report their activities to the Security Council is mostly honoured in the breach. In reality, only a few organisations, mainly the OAS[204] and ECOWAS[205] ever bother to inform the Security Council of

198 Resolution 1156 UN Doc S/RES/1156 (1998).

199 Resolution 1132 UN Doc S/RES/1132 (1997).

200 *Statement by the President of the Security Council*, UN SCOR, 53rd Sess at 1, UN Doc S/PRST 1998/5 (1998) regarding ECOWAS' activities in Sierra Leone; UN Doc. S/22133 (January, 1991), regarding the activities of ECOWAS in Liberia. See also Georg Nolte, above note 10 at 631–34.

201 Bruno Simma, 'NATO, the UN and the Use of Force: Legal Aspects' (1999) 10 *European Journal of International Law* 1 at 11.

202 Resolution 1244 UN Doc S/RES/1244 (1999). See also ND White, 'The Legality of Bombing in the Name of Humanity' (2000) 5(1) *Journal of Conflict and Security Law* 27 at 32.

203 See for instance how ECOWAS was able to rely on this in its intervention in Liberia and Sierra Leone.

204 (1962) 47 *Department of State Bulletin*, 723.

205 See Chapter 5.

their activities, and when they do, it is always out of time, leaving the UN in the dark most of the time as to what they are doing.[206] Military necessity and secrecy surrounding military operations do not encourage them to strictly comply with the reporting obligation embodied by Article 54.

2.5.2. The Competence of Regional Organisations to Determine the Existence of a Threat to Peace under Chapter VIII and its Effect on Decentralised Enforcement Action

One major development that further undermines the integrity of Chapter VIII is the absence of any Charter provision forbidding regional organisations from making a determination as to the existence of a threat to or the breach of the peace or acts of aggression under Chapter VIII. As briefly noted above, some writers have suggested that Article 53(1) is linked to Article 39 in the sense that enforcement action under Chapter VIII can only be taken after a determination by the Security Council under Article 39.[207] Some[208] have even argued that only the Security Council may undertake enforcement action and as such it alone may make a determination as to threat or breach of peace and acts of aggression under Chapter VIII as well.[209] In our opinion, this position is erroneous. It may be true that only the Security Council may undertake enforcement action, at least as far as the Charter provisions are concerned, but that does not mean that only it may make a determination as to the state of peace. The power to take enforcement action is distinct and separable from the competence to make a finding about the state of peace. The restriction on regional organisations contained in Chapter VIII concerns the *type* of actions they may undertake, not the kind of factual evaluation they may make. After all, the Security Council itself may make a determination under Article 39 but refuse to take action. Likewise, regional organisations may make a determination under Chapter VIII and then apply for the Security Council's authorisation. It is entirely up to the Security Council to decide to grant or refuse authorisation on the basis of its own assessment of the situation. What the Security Council may not do, and in fact, has not done so far, is to impugn

[206] See statement by Pérez de Cuéllar reported in *West Africa* 3581 (1–7 July 1991), 1076.

[207] See above.

[208] See Yoram Dinstein, *War, Aggression and Self-Defence* (Cambridge, Cambridge University Press, 2nd edn, 2001) 251; M Akehurst, *Modern Introduction to International Law* P Malanczuk (ed), (London, Routledge, 1997) 426; Lillich in Delbrück's *Allocation*, above note 8 at 67.

[209] But compare the position under the League Covenant which obliged states to apply sanctions against a member state which had resorted to war in violation of its obligations under the Covenant. However, the Covenant left it to every member state 'to decide whether another member state had resorted to war in violation of its obligation under the Covenant'. See Akehurst's (Malanczuk), above note 208 at 23–26, 426.

the competence of regional organisations to make a finding as to the existence of threats to peace, breach of the peace or acts of aggression.

There is no shortage of instances in which regional organisations have made determination as to the state of peace in the evolution of regional collective security. At the outbreak of conflict in Liberia, ECOWAS determined that what was unravelling in that country constituted a threat to regional peace and security.[210] Similarly, it determined that 'the worsening crisis in Sierra Leone has led to the increase in the number of the Sierra Leonean refugees in neighbouring Member States; thus threatening peace and security in the sub-region'.[211] The United States, purportedly acting on behalf of the OAS, made a similar finding during the Cuban Missile crisis. On 22 October 1962, President Kennedy notified the public that: 'the urgent transformation of Cuba into an important strategic base—by the presence of these large, long-range, and clearly offensive weapons of sudden mass destruction—constitutes an explicit threat to the peace and security of all the Americas'.[212] NATO also found the that activities of the Yugoslav army, such as the repression of ethnic Albanians, constituted a threat to the peace and security of the area.[213] Both ECOWAS and OAS have now developed treaty regimes empowering them to make such determination without any recourse to the Security Council.[214] The implications of this development for collective security will be discussed in Chapter 5.

Support for the practice of regional organisations determining the state of peace can also be drawn from the practice of the General Assembly on the same matter. The General Assembly is not explicitly endowed by the Charter with the legal competence to undertake such tasks as the Security Council may under Article 39, but has developed the power through practice. In 1960 the General Assembly determined that the situation regarding South West Africa 'constitutes a serious threat to international peace and security'.[215] Similarly, it adopted a resolution in 1974 expressing grave concern about 'the continuation of the Cyprus crisis, which constitutes a threat to international peace and security'.[216] It strengthened this practice in 1962 when it declared that the policies of Portugal concerning the territories under its administration constituted a 'serious threat to inter-

[210] Decision A/DEC/8/7/92, *First Joint Session of the ECOWAS Standing Mediation Committee and Committee of Five.*

[211] Decision A/DEC/8/97, *Twentieth Session of the Authority of Heads of State and Government on Sanctions Against the Illegal regime in Sierra Leone.*

[212] 47 *Department of State Bulletin* at 715. Also cited by Carl Christol, above note 117 at 526.

[213] See *The NATO Handbook* (1998) at 148.

[214] See ECOWAS Protocol on Collective Security, in Ademola Abass, above note 50, especially Article 10(2) (a). See Article 116 of the OAS Charter as amended by the *Cartagena Protocol*, December 5, 1985.

[215] UN Doc GA Res 1568, 15 UN GAOR Supp (No 16) 33 (1960).

[216] UN Doc GA Res 3312, 29 UN GAOR Supp (No 31) 3 (1974).

national peace and security'.[217] Also, when the Security Council seemed to prevaricate on the issue of apartheid in South Africa, the General Assembly determined that the 'situation in South Africa constitutes a threat to international peace and security'.[218] This was a radical departure from the General Assembly's previous cautious approach to the issue as typified by its view of the situation as one that 'seriously endangers international peace and security'.[219]

As with the requirement of Security Council authorisation, the development of the power to make a determination as to the state of peace by regional organisations has limited the control the Security Council can exert on regional organisations. For instance, because ECOWAS did not have to wait for the Security Council to exercise its power under Article 39 in respect of its intervention in Liberia and Sierra Leone, it was able to act under its own (ECOWAS) authority, direction and control for most of the period of the Liberian conflict especially. It was able to deploy its troops, impose economic sanctions on rebel factions, and imbue its troops with whatever mandates it deemed fit at any stage of the conflict as well as retain field control of their actions.

2.6. COMPLEMENTARITY BETWEEN THE UN AND REGIONAL ORGANISATIONS UNDER CHAPTER VIII

The vision embodied by the framework of Chapter VIII was forcefully explained by the UN Secretary-General Boutros-Boutros Ghali in his *Agenda for Peace* in 1992.[220] This vision was one of complementarity.[221] Chapter VIII was meant to correct the anomaly of the international legal order that prevailed under the regime of the League of Nations whereby regional organisations were acknowledged but not accorded any particular role in the field of peace and security.[222] The fact that the Inter-American System prevailed in the Western Hemisphere and sustained American isolationism during the first World War, coupled with the non-ratification of the League Covenant by the United States, meant that an effective international legal order for peace and security must elicit the input of regional organisations.[223]

[217] UN Doc GA Res 1807, 17 UN GAOR Supp (No 17) 39 (1962).

[218] UN Doc GA Res 2054, 20 UN GAOR Supp (No 14) 52 (1965).

[219] UN Doc GA Res 1663, 16 UN GAOR Supp (No 17) 10 (1961). For a comprehensive discussion of the practice of the General Assembly as regards the determination of threat to, or breach of the peace, see White, *Keeping the Peace,* above note 46, 161–78.

[220] (1992) 31 *International Legal Materials* 953.

[221] See Tommy Koh, 'Summary and Conclusion' The Singapore Symposium: *The Changing Role of the United Nations in Conflict Resolution and Peace-keeping,* 13–15 March 1991 (New York, United Nations, 1991) at 82.

[222] Article 21. See discussion in the last Chapters 1 and 4.

[223] See Russell, above note 16 and various contributors in Delbrück's *Allocation* above note 8 on the rationale for including regional arrangement in the Charter.

The end of the Cold War unleashed many crises that had been bottled up by the decades of contest between the US and USSR. The dissolution of the USSR meant less antagonism to the work of the Security Council. It also signified less East/West interest in former satellite states such as Somalia, the Democratic Republic of Congo, Ethiopia, and Rwanda, to mention but a few.

For the UN, however, the explosion of civil wars in several member states means that it requires a great deal of human and material resources, far more than ever made available by its members, in order to meet its growing responsibilities. Thus, it was inevitable that the UN would reach out to regional organisations to assist in dealing with conflicts, especially those occurring within their regions. When war broke out in Liberia in 1989 the UN called on African countries to take the lead in the crisis.[224] Complimentarity between the UN and regional organisations in the field of collective security can thus be seen as a logical, necessary and pragmatic way in which the gap between the resources available to the UN and the increasing numbers of conflicts can be bridged, without sacrificing the pivotal importance of the Security Council as the overall custodian of international peace and security.

However, as stated above, neither the UN Charter nor the *Agenda for Peace* lay down ground rules for guiding UN/regional organisation relations. The Report of the *Panel on the United Nations Peace Operations* submitted to the UN by the Committee chaired by Lakhdar Brahimi (hereafter the Report)[225] was also silent on the practical aspects of UN/regional organisation relationship. The Panel was tasked with reviewing the working of the UN peacekeeping operations.

The Report stressed the importance of the UN including 'major regional powers'[226] in its peacekeeping operations in order to achieve optimal success. It also strongly highlighted the lack of commitment by UN-led operations in Africa, attributing this partly to developed states' lack of strategic interests at stake in most African conflicts.[227] Yet, despite these acknowledgements by the Panel of the indispensability of regional powers in the collective security equilibrium of the post-Cold War, the Report says nothing about *how* the UN should relate to regional organisations and *vice versa*.

Regarding complimentarity, the implication of the non-specification in the Charter of the modalities for co-ordinating the relationship between the UN and regional organisations is two-fold. The first concerns the legal limit of regional action in cases where the Security Council authorises

[224] See Chapter 5.
[225] A/55/305—S/2000/809. See also http://www.un.org/peace/reports/peace_operations/docs.
[226] *Ibid*, 2 of 11.
[227] *Ibid*, 4 of 13.

them to operate. The second relates to the scope of operations in situations where regional organisations are not authorised by the Security Council, but are permitted by their constituent treaties to undertake enforcement actions.

2.7. THE LEGAL LIMITS OF REGIONAL ORGANISATIONS WHEN AUTHORISED BY THE SECURITY COUNCIL TO UNDERTAKE ENFORCEMENT ACTION

Can regional organisations undertake enforcement actions beyond their territories when authorised by the Security Council? This question is often asked in another way: can the Security Council authorise regional organisations to act outside their own regions? An ancillary matter to this question is whether regional organisations can perform tasks not prescribed by their treaty. This latter issue touches on the *vires* of regional actions. Although this issue has not received major academic attention, it is one of potential controversy given the growing interaction between the UN and regional organisations, and thus merits attention.

It is often said that regional organisations cannot act outside their regions, except in self-defence, even when they have been authorised by the Security Council.[228] There are many bases for this position. One view is that regional organisations cannot act beyond what their constituent instrument permits, and that the Security Council cannot task them beyond their constitutions. It is thus claimed that 'the Security Council cannot overrule the internal law of a regional organization'.[229] According to Kay Hailbronner, 'insofar as Article 53 refers to Chapter VII, it makes regional organizations' actions dependent upon an authorization of the Security Council'.[230] Where, for instance, the Security Council is prevented from acting by a veto, regional organisations cannot, as Arthur Watts contends, seek to act *outside* of their *casus fœderis* in support of Security Council's decisions.[231] For Watts, it cannot be "appropriate" if the regional arrangement does not itself have the power to do what the Security Council would like it to do.[232]

Apart from constitutional restraints, another major limiting factor has been suggested for the position that regional organisations can neither act beyond their region or *ultra vires* their treaties. Siegfried Magriera argued that in the absence of effective judicial control of the Security Council, its

[228] See Delbrück in Delbrück's *Allocation*, above note 8 at 64, Watts, *ibid*, at 75, Wolfrum, *ibid*, at 90–91.

[229] Wolfrum in Delbrück's *Allocation*, above note 8 at 91.

[230] *Ibid*, 71 at 75.

[231] Sir Arthur Watts, *ibid*, 75.

[232] *Ibid*, at 76.

powers under Chapter VII must be construed in a narrow way.[233] Rationalising this position, Watts noted that 'it is not so much a conflict of obligations that is involved here, but an attempt to confer a power which does not otherwise exist'.[234]

It is doubtful whether this reasoning is cogent enough to warrant a restriction on the type of function the Security Council may ask regional organisations to perform or the scope thereto. Article 39 gives the Security Council enormous powers. It is true that this power is not unlimited, and as has been observed, the Security Council may not rely on this power to intervene in a conflict to enforce contractual debts.[235] Nevertheless, the issue of using regional organisations for enforcement action is so fundamental to collective security that the Security Council's discretion in this regard cannot be restricted on the basis of lack of judicial control of its decisions.[236] To posit the contrary is to subject the Security Council's decision-making process under Article 39 to judicial scrutiny. This, it is submitted, contravenes the history of Article 39. As Paul Szasz rightly noted,[237] the question of judicial control of the Security Council was specifically turned down at San Francisco.

Moreover, refusal by regional organisations to act as directed by the Security Council on the basis of incompatibility with their treaties will breach Article 103 of the Charter according prevalence to the obligations of states under the UN Charter when such are in conflict with their obligations under other international instruments.

There is nothing in Article 53(1) that predetermines which geographical entity it might be 'appropriate' for the Security Council to utilise regional arrangements for enforcement action. Logically, it is generally assumed that Security Council will only use regional organisations in their own regions. This concurs with the expectation that regional organisations will be more effective in dealing with regional disputes involving states which mostly are members of such organisations. Nonetheless, the reality of regional intervention does not bear out this assumption. Often, conflicting parties are more willing to accept solutions from outside if they perceive that certain members of the organisation covertly support one party to the conflict.[238]

However, where regional organisations are not authorised by the Security Council, their actions must be confined to their territories even if

233 See Siegfried Magriera, *ibid*, at 81, agreeing with Arthur Watts.

234 Arthur Watts, *ibid*, at 76.

235 Schreuer in Delbrück's *Allocation*, above note 8 at 152.

236 Case *Concerning Questions of the Interpretation and Application of the Montreal Convention Arising from the Aerial Incident at Lockerbie* (Provisional Measures), ICJ Reports 1992, 114, 126. See also separate opinion of Judges Oda and Lachs at 129 and 139 respectively.

237 Delbrück's *Allocation*, above note 8 at 85.

238 A recent example is the initial refusal by Côte d'Ivoire to accept an intervention offer from ECOWAS.

their constituent instruments empower them otherwise. In this regard, the enforcement action undertaken by NATO member states against the Federal Republic of Yugoslavia (FRY) in 1999 violated the UN Charter.[239] This is because NATO did not obtain the authorisation of the Security Council before acting. Although NATO attempted to justify its action on humanitarian grounds, both at political fora[240] and before the International Court of Justice,[241] whether such justifications are right or wrong is beyond the scope of this chapter, and this book. It suffices for our purpose to conclude that NATO's action violated the Charter.

As yet, the Security Council has not utilised regional organisations outside their regions.[242] In those cases where it could be said that the Security Council *utilised* regional organisations at all, it has only *used* them for functions permitted by their own internal laws. Hence, when the Security Council *permitted*[243] ECOWAS to intervene in Liberia, it was for peace-keeping purposes. Certainly, ECOWAS obtained consent from Liberia and some, if not all of the rebel groups. Whether ECOWAS conformed to the formal requirements concerning the validity of such consent is another issue altogether. When the action transformed into an enforcement one, ECOWAS apparently operated under the provisions of its Protocol on Mutual Assistance and Defence (PMAD) which allow it to put military operations in place.

The Security Council has not fully explored the potential of the complimentarity regime that is enshrined in Chapter VIII. An example of a situation where the Security Council could have done this was to have authorised African organisations with experience in collective security, especially ECOWAS and SADC, to intervene in the genocidal conflict that occurred in Rwanda in 1994. Given the principle of non-intervention, most states are not likely to want to intervene in conflicts they have not been requested to mediate. The reluctance of regional organisations in this regard is understandable. The Security Council must take the initiative to extend its Chapter VII powers to situations that Chapter VIII does not ordinarily allow regional organisations to deal with. In that way the complementarity regime between the UN and regional organisations can be further enhanced, even when regional organisations undertake enforcement actions on their own authority as fully discussed in Chapter 5.

239 See Bruno Simma, above note 201.

240 See the debate in the *House of Commons*, HC Deb, 24 March 1999, col 484.

241 *Case Concerning Legality of the Use of Force* (*Yugoslavia v United Kingdom*), 2 June 1999.

242 A probable exception to this is the involvement of NATO in Kosovo and Bosnia from 1994. However, it is perhaps better to assume that NATO's appearance was in accordance with the part of the enabling resolution of the Security Council permitting states acting under their governments.

243 In reality, ECOWAS decided to go into Liberia without obtaining the authorisation of the Security Council. However, the Security Council subsequently welcomed its intervention, an event that has been interpreted as endorsing the intervention. See for instance, White, *Keeping the Peace*, above note 46 at 231. See also Simma, above note 1 at 118.

2.8. CONCLUSION

Chapter VIII was designed with the intention of facilitating the work of the Security Council in the area of maintaining international peace and security. Its provisions established a formal relationship between regional organisations and the Security Council. However, the picture that has emerged in the dealings between the UN and regional organisations after the Cold War shows that regional organisations have subjected Chapter VIII to overwhelming pressure, forcing most of its provisions to yield to unintended usages.

The net effect of the relative primacy enjoyed by regional organisations over the Security Council in matters concerning pacific settlement of disputes, the development of *ex post facto* authorisation, the non compliance with Article 54, and the frequent imposition of economic sanctions, have all significantly impacted on Chapter VIII. Authorisation by the Security Council is rarely sought by regional organisations. Chapter VIII lays down the rules of engagement, but does not set up the guidelines for their implementation, thereby leaving the gap to be filled on a case by case basis.

As we have seen above, regional organisations do not feel inhibited by the provisions of Chapter VIII anymore. When they like, they threaten force without authorisation of the Security Council, as ECOWAS did in October 2002 against rebel forces in Côte d'Ivoire. When they wish, they apply full force without authorisation by the Security Council as ECOWAS did in Liberia, Sierra Leone, and as NATO did in Kosovo. The framework of collective security embodied by Chapter VIII has therefore become obsolete in the situation that has developed after the Cold War.

3

A Decentralised Enforcement Action: An Evaluation of Surrogate Collective Security under Chapter VII

INTRODUCTION

AS SEEN IN the last chapter, the implementation of Chapter VIII provisions by regional organisations reveals many deficiencies in the scheme of collective security envisaged in 1945.

The problem with Chapter VIII is more telling when viewed against the centralised collective security under Chapter VII. Although Chapter VIII provisions entitle the Security Council to utilise regional organisations for the maintenance of peace and security, the process of making that decision is in fact a matter for Chapter VII regulation. It is necessary for the Security Council to *decide* to use a particular regional organisation, either in a conflict ensuing within its region or outside of it, and in what manner it intends to.[1] If such decisions concern enforcement action, it is necessary for all the permanent members of the Security Council to agree to it or for none to reject it.

As the crises in Liberia (1989–1997), Sierra Leone (1997–2001), Kosovo (1999)[2], Rwanda (1994), and Iraq (2003) illustrate, it is not always possible for the Security Council to achieve unanimity of all, or, absent that, pacificity, of its permanent members with regard to Chapter VII actions. The consequence is, as witnessed in the Kosovo and the Iraq cases, a group of states resorting to military action without the authorisation of the Security Council.[3] Such unilateral uses of force undoubtedly thrive on the inability of the Security Council to act, or its lack of interest in particular cases.[4] In the Rwandan genocide, the initial lack of interest of the Security

[1] Art 25 of the UN Charter.

[2] See Douglas Waller, 'Holbrooke's Next Mission' *Time* (1998) 26 October, at 59.

[3] See Nico Krisch, 'Unilateral Enforcement of the Collective Will: Kosovo, Iraq, and the Security Council', (1999) 3 *Max Planck Yearbook of United Nations Law* 59.

[4] In the General Assembly debate in October 1999, the Netherlands warned the Council that its repeated inaction would push the Organisation (the UN) towards the margin as a custodian of peace, and it called on the General Assembly to demand 'that the veto power be

Council to be involved in the civil strife resulted in the total breakdown of collective security, especially where no other organisation was keen to intervene in the conflict.

The objective of this chapter is to demonstrate how the failure of Chapter VII has impacted the overall scheme of collective security in the Charter, particularly that of Chapter VIII. Also, the chapter examines the surrogate collective security model (decentralised enforcement action) adopted by the Security Council at the height of the Cold War in order to prevent the total collapse of Chapter VII. Although the veto power was mostly blamed for the Security Council's inaction during the Cold War,[5] it will be argued here that post-Cold War collective security, which has witnessed little use of the veto, has proved just as much a daunting task for the Security Council.

3.1. CHAPTER VII OF THE UN CHARTER: CENTRALISED COLLECTIVE SECURITY

Chapter VII of the UN Charter contains thirteen articles.[6] These articles detail the progression of the Security Council from the time it determines that a situation threatens or breaches international peace and security, (Article 39), to when it actually authorises states to undertake military actions (Article 42). Once the Security Council exercises its power under Article 39, it may impose provisional measures, such as cease-fires, ordering disputants to maintain the *status quo*.[7] The Council could then follow this by imposing non-military measures such as economic embargoes and so on.[8] Should this prove ineffective or should the Security Council determine, with the benefit of foresight that non-military measures when imposed would be inadequate, it could take a leap from imposing provisional measures to authorising full military action.[9]

Structurally, Chapter VII of the UN Charter could be said to embody a centralised system of collective security. Article 43 of the UN Charter guarantees the centralised nature of Chapter VII collective security. It provides that:

> All members of the United Nations, in order to contribute to the maintenance of international peace and security, undertake to make available to the Security

exercised with maximum restraint'. UN Press Release GA/9607(1999), also cited in White, below note 66 at 37. See also Bruno Simma, 'Regional Enforcement of Community Objectives' in Vera Golland-Debass (ed), *United Nations Sanctions and International Law* (The Hague, Kluwer Law International, 2001) 117 at 120.

5 See discussion below.

6 Arts 39–51.

7 Art 40.

8 Art 41.

9 Art 42.

Council, on its call and in accordance with a special agreement or agreements, armed forces, assistance, and facilities, including rights of passage, necessary for the purpose of maintaining peace and security.

Therefore, regardless of where a situation arises for action, all members of the UN have an obligation to supply the Security Council with the human and material resources that might be required by it to discharge its obligation.

There is an on-going debate amongst international lawyers as to the nature of the obligation that Article 43 imposes on UN members. Some have argued that the article obligates UN member states to set aside forces for the particular need of the Security Council.[10] Others suggested that the intention of the Charter authors was that states would have ready within their national contingent specific numbers of forces for the use of the Security Council. According to this view, Article 43 does not mean that each UN Member State would dispatch contributed forces before hand, and put them permanently in the charge of the UN before a need has arisen.[11] This latter reasoning is to be preferred. Had it been that Article 43 intended a separate force for the Security Council, Article 44, which *obligates* the UN to consult contributing states before deploying such forces, would be redundant. For in that circumstance, those forces would already legally *belong* to the UN and their deployment and condition of service cannot thereafter be subject to prior negotiations with the contributing states as Article 44 mandates.

Furthermore, the *travaux préparatoires* of Chapter VII[12] disclose that Article 43 did not envisage a standing force for the use of the Security Council. Although the idea of such force was mooted by the Informal

[10] Inis Claude, *Swords Into Ploughshares* (London, University of London Press, 1965), 60. But see Jochen Frowein in Bruno Simma (ed), *The Charter of the United Nations: A Commentary* 1st edn (Oxford, Oxford University Press, 1994) 633 (hereafter Simma's *Commentary*). *Certain Expenses Case*, ICJ Reports (1962) 151 particularly at 167 where the Court rejected the argument that the Security Council could not take action in a situation that threatens international peace and security without the agreements under Article 43 being concluded.

[11] For a similar view see, Yoram Dinstein, *War, Aggression and Self-Defence* (Cambridge, Cambridge University Press, 3rd edn, 2001), arguing, *inter alia*, that the Charter 'does not seem to envisage the establishment of a permanent international force, with troops recruited directly by the UN Organization itself' at 263 *et seq*; LC Green, *The Contemporary Law of Armed Conflicts* (Manchester, Manchester University Press, 2nd edn, 2000) 272; See also John Quigley, 'The United States and the United Nations in the Persian Gulf War: New Order or Disorder?' (1992) 25 *Cornell International Law Journal* 1; Leland Goodrich, Edvard Hambro, Anne Patricia Simons, *Charter of the United Nations: Commentary and Documents* (New York, Columbia University Press, 3rd edn, 1969) at 631; Simma's *Commentary*, above note 10 at 636.

[12] See for instance, the view of Mr Al-Anbari, the Iraqi representative to the Security Council during the discussion of Resolution 678, *Provisional Verbatim Record*, UN SCOR, 45th Sess, 2963rd mtg, at 21, UN Doc S/S/PV. 2963 (1990). But see for instance the objection of the Americans during discussion about Art 43 to the idea of creating a stand-by force in the statement of Senator Arthur Vandenberg in Arthur Vandenberg (ed), *The Private Papers of Senator Vandenberg* (Boston, 1952) 96.

Political Agenda Group in 1944[13] when the Group met to consider the three alternative force arrangements proposed for the use of the UN,[14] the proposal fell through in the final phase of the deliberation. It was agreed, *inter alia*, that the idea of a standing force presented 'general difficulties of maintaining and operating such forces . . . and of more particular constitutional hazards in the United States.'[15] Upon a referral from the Agenda Group to the Joint Chiefs of Staff, the latter endorsed the 'system of national contingents'[16] in which the forces would be used 'only as occasion demanded by virtue of specific agreement.'[17]

The argument is sometimes made that the non-materialisation of Article 43 forces means that Chapter VII collective security has collapsed.[18] Central to that contention is the rationale that in the absence of the forces contemplated by Article 43, the Security Council cannot mandate or decide that states undertake enforcement action.[19] Put differently, without the so-called standing force, the Security Council cannot be said to act under Chapter VII and cannot bind states under Article 25.[20] Proponents of this view assert that whenever the Security Council authorises enforcement action, it does so not under Article 42, but under Article 51 of the Charter.[21] This is because without troops anticipated under Article 43, states are at liberty to accept or decline an invitation from the Security Council to intervene in a crisis. All these assertions are reinforced by the fact that Article 47, which provides for the establishment of a Military Staff Committee to advise and assist the Security Council on all questions relating to the Security Council's military requirement for the maintenance of

13 See generally on this issue, Ruth Russell, *A History of the United Nations Charter: The Role of the United States 1940–1945* (Washington DC, The Brookings Institution, 1958) at 220 *et seq*. See also the dissenting opinion of Judge Bustamante in the *Certain Expenses* case (1962, ICJ Reports at 167) stating that in the absence of Art 43 agreements, the 'Security Council must fill the gap by means of direct measures'.

14 *Ibid*, at 235.

15 See Russell, above note at 258.

16 *Ibid*.

17 *Ibid*, 259.

18 John Quigley, above note 11; But see Nigel White and Özlem Ülgen, 'The Security Council and the Decentralised Military Option: Constitutionality and Function', (1997) XLIV *Netherlands International Law Review* 378 at 380 *et seq* (hereafter White and Ulgen).

19 See discussion below.

20 Jean-Pierre Cot et Alain Pellet (sous la direction de), *La Charte des Nations Unies: Commentaire: article par article* (Paris, Economica, 2e édition revue et augmentée, 1991) 633 (hereafter Cot and Pellet); White and Ulgen, above note 18 at 385.

21 See Julius Stone, *Legal Controls of International Conflicts* (1954), 234–37; Stone, *Aggression and World Order* (1958) 189–92; P Malanczuk, *Akehurst's Modern Introduction to International Law*, (London, Routledge, 1997, Rev edn) 397; EV Rostow, 'Until What? Enforcement Action or Collective Self-Defense?' (1991) 85 *American Journal of International Law* 452, 459–60; R Lavalle, 'The Law of United Nations and the Use of Force under the Relevant Security Council Resolutions of 1990 and 1991 to Resolve the Persian Gulf Crisis' (1992) 23 *Netherlands Yearbook of International Law* 3 at 62.

international peace and security, is yet to materialise.[22] Save the initiative of France in 1992 to make available to the UN 1,000 troops from her national contingents,[23] Article 47 has remained inactive most of the life of the Charter.

It is true that Chapter VII collective security was originally set up to be enhanced by the Special Forces under Article 43 and the superintendent of the MSC under Article 47. However, to conclude that the Charter scheme of collective security collapse entirely for lack of such forces or that the Security Council cannot legally authorise states to act under Chapter VII is to stretch the relationship between Article 42 and 43 beyond all reasonable frontiers. Not only does such a view negate the intention of the Charter authors, it also fails to take into account the regenerative capability of the UN Charter as a living instrument.[24]

When inserting Article 43 into the Charter, it was envisaged that collective security might be subject to *ad hoc* implementation. Two provisions support this view. First, Article 106 of the Transitional Security Arrangements of the Charter states that:

> Pending the coming into force of such special agreements referred to in Article 43 as in the opinion of the Security Council enable it to begin the exercise of its responsibility under Article 42, the parties to the Four-Nation Declaration, signed at Moscow, 30th October, 1943, and France, shall, in accordance with the provisions of paragraph 5 of that Declaration, consult with one another and *as occasion requires* with other Members of the United Nations with a view to joint action on behalf of the Organisation as may be necessary for the purpose of maintaining international peace and security.

Second, Paragraph 5 of the referred Moscow Declaration provides that:

> For the purposes of maintaining international peace and security pending the re-establishment of law and order and the inauguration of a system of general security they will consult with each other and, *as occasion requires*, with other members of the United Nations with a view to joint action on behalf of the community of nations.

Article 106 could be interpreted as empowering the Security Council to embark on *ad hoc* execution of Chapter VII pending the institution of a permanent one, arguably by the military agreements of Article 43. Paragraph

[22] Ralph Goldman, *Is it Time to Revive the UN Military Staff Committee*, Occasional Papers Series No 19, Udo Heyn (ed), (California, California State University, 1990); Benjamin Rivlin, *The Rediscovery of the UN Military Staff Committee*, Occasional Paper IV (New York, Ralphe Bunche Institute, 1991).

[23] SC 3046th mtg, UN SCOR 47th Sess (31 January 1992).

[24] See Louis Sohn, 'The Authority of the United Nations to Establish and Maintain a Permanent United Nations Force' (1958) 52 *American Journal of International Law* 229 at 230, contending that since 'the Security Council may establish a UN Force under Article 42 independent of Article 43' since the latter does not limit the Council's using 'any force' it 'might be able to obtain by other methods'.

5 of the Moscow Declaration contains a similar provision because it subjects the tentative arrangements to the emergence of a 'general security'. In any case, Article 43 agreements are subject to the veto power, hence could still be prevented from coming into being, and if they eventually crystallise, from operating successfully.[25]

While the non-materialisation of the special agreement under Article 43 may not necessarily mean that the collective security system envisaged under Chapter VII has collapsed, it does have certain unneglectable consequences. Without the legal ability to *decide* under Article 42, the Security Council may only recommend enforcement action to member states, which leaves many members the discretion as to their participation. In addition, the Security Council may not be able to control the actions of member states unless those activities are taken upon the decision by the Security Council that member states undertake enforcement action. Thus, where member states accept a recommendation by the Security Council to undertake enforcement action, command and control of such actions may be a matter for those states to direct.

However, it is theoretically possible for the Security Council to *decide* that regional organisations should undertake enforcement action. This is because under Chapter VIII, the Security Council does not need to have forces specially allocated to it by UN member states in order to act under regional arrangement. Thus, the argument that without Article 43 troops the Security Council can only recommend and not decide on enforcement action does not apply to enforcement action under Chapter VIII. In addition, the distinction between *recommendation* and *decision,* recognised by Article 39 with regard to the functioning of the Security Council, does not exist under Chapter VIII. Regional organisations are bound to carry out decisions or recommendations of the Security Council, lest their members violate Article 25 of the Charter.

The difficulty experienced by the Security Council during the Cold War, such as the obtrusive use of veto power by the Soviet Union, prevented it from deciding on enforcement actions in circumstances desirous of such measures. An example of this was the invasion of South Korea by North Korea in 1950. This episode led the Security Council to resort to performing the tasks allocated to it under Chapter VII in a decentralised version. Under this model, the Security Council implements Chapter VII measures without necessarily conforming to its formal procedures.

Though decentralised enforcement action was a child of necessity, its contribution to the development of Chapter VII collective security is significant and as such, deserves an evaluation. In the sections below, we consider the legal basis for decentralised enforcement action, its contribu-

[25] JL Brierly, 'The Covenant and the Charter' (1946) *British Yearbook of International Law* 83 at 84.

tion to the development of collective security and factors that seriously militate against its success as a surrogate Chapter VII model.

3.2. DECENTRALISED MILITARY ACTION: A 'SURROGATE' COLLECTIVE SECURITY SYSTEM

In Security Council practice, three different models of implementing collective security can be identified. First, the institution of peacekeeping, which, although not invented by the Security Council, soon became its most popular method of acting. Second, the Security Council cultivated the habit of delegating to state(s) the power to undertake collective actions on behalf of the international community.[26] Third, the practice whereby the Security Council invites regional arrangements to assist it in implementing decisions taken under Chapter VII.

It is not the intention here to delve into these different models through an examination of the totality of Security Council practice either during of after the Cold War, or tackle these categories separately. The approach here is to conceptually examine the institution of decentralised enforcement action and bring out the problems associated with it. Peacekeeping operations, whether undertaken by the Security Council or the General Assembly or any other international actor, do not involve the use of force to enforce collective decisions, hence, do not fall within decentralised enforcement action. Therefore they are exempted from the discussion below.

3.3. THE REGULATORY FRAMEWORK OF DECENTRALISED ENFORCEMENT ACTION

3.3.1. The Legal Bases

There are at least five legal bases, proposed by this writer, to ground decentralised enforcement action. Firstly, according to the UN Charter, states operating as regional arrangements or agencies are permitted to undertake certain kinds of action.[27] These are actions not involving the use of armed force, but mainly of pacific nature.[28] Indeed these organisations are obligated to first attempt to deal with such matters before there can be a referral to the UN.[29] As will be seen in the next chapter, since pacific

[26] See Danesh Sarooshi, *The United Nations and the Development of Collective Security: The Delegation by the UN Security Council of its Chapter VII Powers* (Oxford, Clarendon Press, 1999).
[27] Art 53(1).
[28] Art 52(2).
[29] See Chapter 2.

settlement of disputes forms part of the collective security system, there is no doubt that Chapter VIII provides a legislative framework for a decentralised enforcement system.

Secondly, the Security Council is empowered, according to Article 53, to utilise regional arrangements to undertake enforcement action.[30] This provision is different from that which enables regional arrangements to undertake limited enforcement action, such as the imposition of economic sanctions, within the framework of pacific settlement of disputes. It may be possible, as already argued, for a regional arrangement to impose non-forcible measures in order to compel parties to its treaty to respect its collective decisions. Article 53, on the other hand, is independent of whether concerned regional organisations are already dealing with a conflict or not. It is an overarching power allocated to the Security Council to enable it to use a group of states outside the purview of Chapter VII.

The third Charter basis for decentralised enforcement action can be found in the transitional provisions contained in Article 106. This provision envisaged the *joint* implementation of collective security objectives by both the Security Council and other member states until Article 43 agreements are realised.

The two remaining bases for decentralised enforcement action are not expressly mentioned in the Charter, but directly derive from it. The first is the possibility of the Security Council being able to act through a '*penumbra* of powers' outside the Charter's formal context. This is the doctrine of *implied power* as generally recognised in international law.[31] This entitles international organisations to adopt means, not explicitly provided for in their constituent treaties, but which are nonetheless considered fundamental in terms of the realisation of their primary objectives.[32] The second basis is what Professor Koskenniemi referred to as the 'last resort' doctrine[33] which could be relied on by states, acting through the General Assembly, to undertake enforcement actions where the Security Council is immobilised by the veto.

The Security Council delegates enforcement action without disclosing the legal basis upon which it is acting.[34] Where the Security Council authorises a group of states to undertake enforcement action, except as

[30] See Chapter 2.

[31] *Reparations for Injuries* case, ICJ Reports (1949), 181. See also Fred L Morrison in J Delbrück (ed), *Allocation of Law Enforcement Authority in the International System: Proceedings of an International Symposium of the Kiel Institute of International Law, March 23 to 25, 1994* (Berlin, Duncker & Humblot, 1995) 39 at 46 (hereafter Delbrück's *Allocation*).

[32] See Niels Blokker, 'Is the Authorization Authorized? Powers and Practice of the UN Security Council to Authorize the Use of Force by "Coalitions of the Able and Willing"' (2000) 11(3) *European Journal of International Law* 541.

[33] See Martii Koskenniemi, 'The Place of Law in Collective Security' (1996) 17 *Michigan Journal of International Law* 455 at 486.

[34] See Niels Blokker, above note 32.

permitted by Article 53(1), it would appear to be acting *ultra vires*.[35] None of the above-identified instances would appear to justify a delegation of collective security powers by the Security Council to states except under Chapter VIII. The Security Council is a delegatee of other members of the UN under Article 24(1) and to delegate the authority to use force to a group of states who are not a regional arrangement violates the maxim *delegatus non poset delegaree*—a delegate cannot further delegate.[36] One agrees with Koskenniemi's observation that by delegating its collective security powers the Security Council abdicates its responsibility.[37] On the contrary, the utilisation of regional organisations by the Security Council does not violate the principle of *delegatus non poset delegaree* insofar as the power of the Security Council to do so is expressly granted to it by the Charter.

The crucial question is whether we can regard the Security Council delegating enforcement powers beyond the purview of Chapter VIII as falling within the rubrics of the *penumbra*[38] *of powers* as necessarily incidental to the execution of Chapter VII provisions. Put differently, does the doctrine of implied powers cover situations in which the Security Council acts outside the formal Charter provisions? The importance of this line of inquiry to our analysis is that if it can be established that the delegation of power outside the normative framework of Chapter VIII is covered by the doctrine of implied powers, such shall be deemed to be a legitimate exercise of collective security functions by the Security Council. Conversely, if the delegation of collective security powers outside Chapter VIII is not such that is absolutely necessary in order for the Security Council to implement Chapter VII, then it acts *ultra vires* and illegitimately whenever it so delegates its powers. In that case, the delegation of power by the Security Council to states outside the normative perimeters of Chapter VIII shall be an illegitimate decentralisation of enforcement action.

The power to delegate enforcement action to a group of states not acting as a regional arrangement is not explicitly allocated to the Security Council by the Charter. However, in order for it to be able to discharge its responsibilities under the Charter, especially under Chapter VII, the Security Council has always assumed that it has the implicit power to do that which is not explicitly mentioned in the Charter. An example of this is the

[35] But see Sarooshi, above note 26, See also Mary Ellen O'Connell, 'The UN, NATO, and International Law after Kosovo' (2000) 22 *Human Rights Quarterly* 57 at 68.

[36] See John Willis (1943) *Canadian Bar Review* 257.

[37] Koskinniemi, above note 33 at 486.

[38] Thomas Franck speaks in similar terms when he observes that the UN 'is a creature of a treaty, and as such it exercises authority legitimately only insofar as it deploys powers which the treaty parties have assigned to it.' He then goes on to say that the powers enumerated in the UN Charter 'may be modestly augmented by a "penumbra" of other powers which are incidental to the effective implementation of the enumerated ones'. See Thomas Franck, *Fairness in International Law and International Institutions* (Oxford, Oxford University Press, 1995) at 219.

adoption of resolutions. No single provision of the UN Charter entitles the Security Council to adopt resolutions.[39] The argument can then be made that in order to enable it to discharge its function, especially if it becomes difficult for it to act through the formal procedures laid down in the Charter, the Security Council should be able to resort to other means.

One of the conditions for resorting to implied powers is necessity. It must be absolutely necessary for the Security Council to *imply* such powers. This is particularly so where there exist explicit powers with regard to such functions. The ICJ affirmed this principle in the *Reparation for Injuries Suffered in the Service of the United Nations*.[40] In a well-noted passage the Court stated that:

> Under international law, the Organization [United Nations] must be deemed to have those powers which though not expressly provided in the Charter are conferred upon it by necessary implication as being essential to the performance of its duties.[41]

In the light of Article 43 concerning the troops by means of which the Security Council should implement collective security, can it then be said that an implied power enabling it to use another method not provided for in the Charter fulfils the condition of necessity? The ICJ has yet to take a stance on this issue. However, the opinions of some of its judges give an indication as to how one should approach the question. In the *Certain Expenses*[42] case, Judge Moreno Quintana noted that the

> Implied powers which may derive from the Charter so that the Organization may achieve all its purposes are not to be invoked when explicit powers provide expressly for eventualities under consideration.[43]

Judge Hackworth endorsed this view in his dissenting opinion in the *Effect of Awards Compensation Made by the UN Administrative Tribunal*.[44] According to the judge, powers not expressed cannot freely be implied; implied powers flow from a grant of expressed powers, and are limited to those that are 'necessary' to the exercise of powers expressly granted.[45] However, Judge Bustamante, to some extent, demurred to this view. In his dissenting opinion in the *Certain Expenses* case, he observed that the United Nations Emergency Force (UNEF) and the *Opération des Nations Unies au Congo* (ONUC) missions were appropriate despite the fact that Article 43 agreements were yet to materialise. However, this judge would not seem to be advocating a general principle that the existence of explicit

39 See Blokker, above note at 547.
40 ICJ Reports (1949) at 182.
41 *Ibid*.
42 ICJ Reports (1962), 151.
43 *Ibid*, at 245, also cited by Blokker, above note 32 at 548 fn 19.
44 ICJ Reports (1954) at 80.
45 *Ibid*, at 198.

provisions does not prevent implied powers as was assumed by the UN in conducting UNEF and ONUC missions. Indeed, Judge Bustamante appeared to have based his conclusion on the nature of Article 43. He contended that the negotiation of an agreement under that article was not such 'a basic one' that could prevent other types of actions in its absence.[46]

Academic opinions on this issue diverge.[47] It has been argued that 'the exercise of powers would have to be such as would not substantially encroach on, detract from, or nullify other powers'.[48] A similar view has been expressed by Terry Gill on the basis of 'the basic canons of treaty interpretation, such as those contained in Article 31 of the Vienna Convention on the Law of Treaties and from general principles of interpretation such as *lex specialis derogat legi generali*'.[49] Dan Ciobanu, however, seems to agree more with the view expressed by Judge Gros in the *South West Africa case* that necessity cannot justify in itself the existence of a power, and to invoke only necessity is to step outside the law.[50] This seems to affirm the earlier opinion of Judge Koretsky in the *Certain Expenses* case that the end does not justify the means.[51]

In the *Conditions of Admission of a State to Membership in the United Nations*, Professor Scelle, representing the French government, observed that

> Une décision arbitraire, c'est la negation du droit, c'est la caprice. L'utilisation d'une compétence discrétionaire, c'est l'application d'un pouvoir juridique. Les deux choses sont essentiellement incompatibles. Faire dégénérer une compétence discrétionaire en une pouvoir arbitraire revient à commettre ce qu'on appelle dans tous les langues juridique un abus de droit, ou, comme nous disons en droit public français, un détournement de pouvoir.[52]

The contention that international organisations may not resort to implied powers arbitrarily was recognised by the Permanent Court of International Justice (PCIJ) in the Jurisdiction of the *European Commission of the Danube between Galatz and Braïla*. Here, the PCIJ resorted to a consideration of the

[46] *Ibid*, at 298.

[47] See AIL Campbell, 'The Limits of the Powers of International Organizations' (1983) 32 *International and Comparative Law Quarterly* 523 at 528, also quoted by Blokker, above note 32 at 548–49.

[48] See Campbell, above note 47 at 528.

[49] T Gill, 'Legal and Some Political Limitations on the Power of the UN Security Council to Exercise Its Enforcement Powers under Chapter VII of the Charter' (1995) 26 *Netherlands Yearbook of International Law* 33 at 71.

[50] *Legal Consequences for States of the Continued Presence of South Africa in Namibia (South West Africa) Notwithstanding Security Council Resolution 276 (1970)* ICJ Reports (1971) 339. See Dan Ciobanu, *Preliminary Objections Related to the Jurisdiction of the United Nations Political Organs* (The Hague, Martinus Nijhoff, 1975) at 68.

[51] At 198.

[52] ICJ Pleadings, Oral Arguments, Documents (1948) at 76. See also Dan Ciobanu, above note 50 at 72–73. See also the *Legality of Nuclear Weapons* (1996) ICJ Reports 66 where the Court made reference to the principle of speciality.

principle of *speciality*—an equivalent of necessity doctrine—to hold that, as the European Commission was not a State, but an international institution with a special purpose, it could have *only* the functions bestowed upon it by the Statute with a view to the fulfilment of that purpose.[53] This view found some support in the writing of Professor Dupuy who explained the principle of speciality thus:

> Ils (les Etats) ne reconnaissent aux organes sociétaires que des pouvoirs déterminés dans certaines hypothèses. C'est ce qu'on appelle la règle de la spécialité, norme qui commande la capacité juridique des personnes morales en droit interne et international.[54]

As would have been noted from the above analysis, it is not totally certain whether international organisations automatically have implied powers. The fact that international organisations may, in special cases, resort to implied powers does not answer whether the Security Council acts out of necessity when it delegates its powers. It may well be that ascertaining the existence of such powers is a matter of common sense and historical experience rather than of legal construction.[55]

If we accept the position that for it to effectively implement Chapter VII provisions the Security Council must exercise certain powers by necessary implication, does that mean that in every situation its does so the Security Council invariably acts legitimately? The answer to this question resonates in the space between the provisions of Chapter VII and their implementation by the Security Council through delegation to states.

However, the view that '[t]he Charter would be open to a serious allegation of inconsistency if the Council were able to delegate its Chapter VII powers to Member States organized as a regional arrangement, but not to Member States acting individually or jointly (that is not organized as a regional arrangement),'[56] it is submitted, neither answers the question nor convinces. Regional organisations, as we have already argued, operate within a particular domain of influence be this of political, social or economic nature. According them primacy in regional matters is based on the ground that the Charter allows them to initiate pacific settlement on their own. This is not so with the so-called delegation of the Security Council's powers to a group of states acting individually, except where they act under Article 51. However, Article 51 does not govern enforcement action. The power *delegated* to the coalition of able and willing states is neither confineable to a particular region nor subject to rigorous supervision. Enforcement powers delegated to states acting as such can be very devas-

[53] PCIJ, Ser B, No 14 at 64.

[54] Dupuy, 'Le droit des relations entre les organisations internationales' (1960) 100 *Recueil des Cours* at 533.

[55] For a similar view, see Dan Ciobanu, above note 50 at 68.

[56] Sarooshi, above note 26 at 148.

tating. Absence of proper normative regulation of such power opens up its use to great danger.

For instance both Resolution 83[57] and 678[58] relating to the Korean (1950) and Gulf (1990–91) crises authorised states not only to repel the North Korean and Iraqi aggressions respectively, but to 'restore international peace and security' to the concerned areas. There is no final word regarding the exact meaning of this phrase. Such a wide-ranging power must have a sound legal basis. It is not enough to found this basis on the 'functional necessity to make the Council's enforcement authority effective'.[59] Quite the contrary, such an illegally delegated power can only beget an illegitimate action.[60]

Where the wording of a treaty is clear, a literal interpretation should be accorded its provisions. Commenting on rules of interpretation, Beatson and Matthews noted that, 'the rule of construction prescribes that nothing is to be added to a statute unless there are adequate grounds to justify inference that the legislature intended something which it omitted to express'.[61] This was a restatement of the *Maxwell Interpretation of Statutes*[62] as affirmed by cases like *Ex p Sharps*,[63] *Peebles v Oswaldtwistle Urban District Council*,[64] *Liverpool Corporation v Hope*[65] amongst others. The approach taken by domestic courts and writers to interpretation of statutes is analogous to that indicated of states in the Vienna Convention on the Law of Treaties (VCLT). Article 31 (1) of the VCLT provides that '[a] treaty shall be interpreted in good faith in accordance with the ordinary meaning to be given to the terms of the treaty in their context and in the light of its object and purpose'. The wording of the Charter is crystal clear on who could be a delegatee of collective security powers.

True, the Security Council does not need to operate with the legal exactitude of Charter provisions.[66] However, this does not mean that the Security Council may delegate powers, the exercise of which it cannot supervise.[67] There is certainly a qualitative difference between the nature

[57] 27 June 1950. See Trygve Lie, *In The Cause of Peace* (New York, Macmillan, 1954) 334. See also ND White, *Keeping the Peace* (Manchester, Manchester University Press, 2nd edn, 1997) at 121 *et seq*; EV Rostow, 'Until What? Enforcement Action or Collective Self-Defence' (1991) *American Journal of International Law* 506.

[58] UN Doc S/RES/678 (1990). See (1990) *United Nations Yearbook* 189.

[59] F Kirgis, 'The Security Council's first Fifty Years' (1995) 89 *American Journal of International Law* 506 at 521.

[60] See John Quigley, above note 11.

[61] J Beatson and MH Matthews, *Administrative Law: Cases and Materials* (Oxford, Clarendon Press, 1983) 130.

[62] 7th edn, 12.

[63] (1864), 5 R & S 322.

[64] (1897) 1 QB 384.

[65] [1938] 1 KB 751.

[66] See Nigel White 'The Legality of Bombing in the Name of Humanity' (2000) 5(1) *Journal of Conflict and Security Law* 27.

[67] Sarooshi, above note 26.

of collective security powers delegated to states acting under the aegis of regional organisations and those acting individually. The former is recognised by the Charter,[68] the latter is a brooding omnipotence in the sky. Collective security powers delegated to regional arrangements under Article 53(1) are subject to the control of the Security Council under Article 54. Collective security powers delegated to states acting as such are hardly ever, if at all, controlled. In the Korean crisis, the UN purportedly delegated its collective security power to states, but the US appointed the commander and generally commanded and controlled the action. A suggestion by Secretary-General Trygve Lie for limited co-ordination by the UN was rejected by the US. In Lie's words:

> The United States promptly turned thumbs down. Later it even proved difficult that the report of the United Nations Commander in Korea should be officially transmitted to the Security Council before being released to the Press by American attachés in Tokyo.[69]

During the 1990 Gulf Crisis,[70] the UN was so frustrated by its lack of control of the collective action that Secretary-General Javier Perez de Cuellar, lamented thus:

> What we hear from the three members of the Security Council which are involved—Britain, France and the United States—which every two or three days report to the Council, after the action has taken place. The Council which has authorised this, is only informed after the military actions have taken place.[71]

A centralised collective security system is a system in which only one supreme organ is empowered with the authority to administer the instrument of collective force.[72] The only exception to this rule is if the competent authority delegates that power in accordance with the constituent instrument of the organisation, or general international law, as and when the situation requires.

It may be that the Security Council can resort to the implied power theory in order to delegate collective security powers to entities not expressly stated in the Charter. Such a delegation may qualify as an exercise of decentralised enforcement action. However, that does not mean that the delegated power must not be regulated. If necessity compels the Security Council to step outside the Charter to imply some powers, legality must compel it to step back into the Charter and take control of its exercise. Failure to do this, it is submitted, makes the action liable to abuse and potentially an illegitimate one.

[68] Article 53(1).
[69] Lie, above note 57 at 334.
[70] Quigley, above note 11.
[71] Leonard Doyle, 'UN Has No Role in Running War' *Independent* (London), 11 February 1991, 2 (interview with Perez de Cuellar). Cited in Quigley, above note 11 at 28.
[72] See Chapter 4.

3.3.2. Enforcement Action through the General Assembly: Analysis of its Collective Security Powers under the Charter

Apart from the Security Council implementing collective security functions in a decentralised model, the General Assembly has also operated collective security in the past. The outbreak of conflict in the Far East, when North Korea attacked South Korea in 1950, led to the Security Council adopting three resolutions.[73] Acting under these resolutions, member states of the UN were able to take measures against North Korea. This was made possible by the absence of the Soviet Union from the Security Council in protest at the presence of Taiwan in the Security Council.[74] Upon its return, the Soviet Union effectively prevented the adoption of further resolutions against North Korea.[75] This situation was eventually remedied by removing the Korean crisis from the Security Council and placing it on the General Assembly's agenda.[76]

The lessons learnt by the UN about the obstruction posed by the veto in the Korean crisis was put to use when the involvement of United Kingdom and France prevented the Security Council from effectively dealing with the Suez Canal crisis.[77] The General Assembly, which had already adopted the *Uniting for Peace Resolution*[78] during the Korean crisis, applied it to the Suez crisis.[79] This enabled it to authorise the first UN peacekeeping operation.[80] Since its inception, the General Assembly has utilised the *Uniting for Peace Resolution* a few times. It convened under the resolution in order to deal with the Hungarian incident in 1956,[81] the Jordan crisis in 1958,[82] and the Congo crisis in 1960.[83]

However, not since the Congo crisis (1960–1963) has the General Assembly authorised any action under the *Uniting for Peace Resolution*. The criticisms that were levelled against the *Uniting for Peace Resolution* by some states and writers have somewhat prevented a return to the

[73] Resolutions 82, 83 and 84 of 25 and 27 June, and 7 July, 1950. See SC 477 mtg, UN SCOR (1950). For analysis, see White, *Keeping the Peace*, above note 57 at 121 *et seq*.

[74] White, above note 57, 121.

[75] *Ibid*, see 5 UN GAOR (1950).

[76] For analysis of this episode, see White, *Keeping the Peace*, above note 57, 172 *et seq*.

[77] See William Durch (ed), *The Evolution of UN Peacekeeping: Case Studies and Comparative Analysis* (New York, NY, St Martin's Press, 1993).

[78] GA Res 377, 5 UN GAOR Resolution 10 (1950).

[79] Durch, above note 57.

[80] SC Res 119, 11 UN SCOR Resolution 9m (1956). For a discussion, see White, *Keeping the Peace*, above note 57, 225–27.

[81] GA Res 1004, 2 UN GAO RESS Supp (No. 1) 2 (1956). See White, *Keeping the Peace*, above note 57, 176–78 on the analysis of the decline in the effectiveness and relevance of the *Uniting for Peace* Resolution.

[82] GA Res 1237, 3 UN GAO RESS Supp (No 1) 1 (1958).

[83] GA Res 1474, UN GAO RESS Supp (No 1) 1 (1960); SC Res 157, 15 UN SCOR Resolution 8 (1960). For analysis see White, *Keeping the Peace*, above note 57, 254–61.

resolution by the General Assembly. That does not mean that the General Assembly may not return to the resolution in the future if needs be, or that it has no power to do so.

The following section discusses the legal authority of the General Assembly to undertake collective security tasks, the problems of which shall then be discussed alongside the problems attendant to the implementation of the Chapter VII collective security scheme as a whole. As the involvement of the General Assembly in collective security functioning is in furtherance of a decentralised implementation of Chapter VII, analysing its gains and losses sheds light on the problems attendant on this mode of enforcement action.

Article 10 of the UN Charter empowers the General Assembly to discuss any question or any matter within the scope of the present Charter or relating to the powers and functions of any organs. It also allows it to make recommendations to member states or even to the Security Council with regard to such issues. Kelsen viewed this as a general competence.[84] Elsewhere, this power was regarded as 'the counterpart of the primary function assigned to the Security Council'.[85] The only limitation on this provision is contained in Article 12(1). It prohibits the General Assembly from making recommendations with regard to disputes in respect of which the Security Council may be exercising its functions.

Suppose the Security Council is not exercising its functions on a particular matter and the General Assembly makes a recommendation that states should undertake enforcement action. Such a recommendation falls within the scope of its authority. In that case, it is not an action taken by the Security Council (which has the primary, but not exclusive authority to act), it is a decentralised one. Though this action falls outside Chapter VII, it is submitted that it is a legitimate collective security function conferred on the General Assembly by the Charter. Thus, whereas the centralised collective security system of the Charter is contained within Chapter VII only, the basis for the decentralised enforcement system is much wider.

The argument that the General Assembly cannot make recommendations for enforcement action has no legal basis in the Charter.[86] Article 10

[84] Kelsen, *The Law of the United Nations: A Critical Analysis of its Fundamental Problems* (London, Stevens, 1964) at 198.

[85] See R Otto Kimminich, 'Article 14' in Bruno Simma's *Commentary*, above note 10, 282, quoting Pasvolsky in *Hearing before the Senate Committee on Foreign Relations, 79th Cong 1st session* (July 1945) 599.

[86] GA 301 Plen Mtg, 5 UN GAOR 332 (1950). The Soviet's representative argued that the proposed *Uniting for Peace Resolution* was unconstitutional. This was because it empowered the General Assembly to make recommendations including the use of armed force, to member states in cases whereby the Security Council, because of lack of unanimity of the permanent members fails to exercise its primary responsibility for the maintenance of international peace and security.

talks about *any question* or any *matter*, and recommendation in respect of either to Member States or the Security Council. It will be absurd if this provision is interpreted to mean that the General Assembly can only make pacific recommendation. This is because the Security Council presumably has no problem taking this sort of decision on its own. Arguably, recommendations for peaceful resolution of any contentious question or matter will hardly attract the veto of the Security Council though legally possible. Conversely, it is contended here that the recommendation envisaged by Article 10 relates to matters that may be susceptible to the veto if the Security Council considers them on its own, such as enforcement action. This reasoning is further enhanced when it is considered that the General Assembly could easily bypass the Security Council and make the recommendation to member states if, for instance, it suspects that the veto might obstruct a particular recommendation. Article 10 may thus serve as a basis upon which states may undertake enforcement action through the General Assembly in circumstances that the Security Council is unable or unwilling to act.[87]

Article 11 further clarifies the intention of the draftsman in Article 10 by providing specifically for the circumstances in which the General Assembly may propose a recommendation to member states or the Security Council. Although it might be contended that Article 11(2) stipulates that the General Assembly has an obligation to refer such matters before or after its discussion on any question or matter that might require action, it is very unlikely that 'action' here refers exclusively to enforcement action. Action as used in Article 11(2) could refer to any action that the Security Council might intend to take as the organ primarily responsible for peace and security. Hence Article 11(4) clearly indicates that the Article 11 provisions do not trump the wider power already conferred on the General Assembly by Article 10. Therefore even if it is assumed that 'action' here means enforcement action, Article 11(4) guarantees the competence of the General Assembly as far as the task of making recommendations is concerned.

Article 12(1) prevents the General Assembly from making any recommendation concerning any matters in respect of which the Security Council may be 'exercising functions'. Two issues emerge from this provision which buttress the argument made in the justification of the competence of the General Assembly in undertaking collective security measures. First, it is only in this provision that the word *any* is used to prefix *recommendation*. This indicates that the General Assembly could legally make *any* kind of recommendation under Articles 10 and 11. The emphasis here seems that Article 12(1) wishes to avert a situation whereby

[87] See more about the residual responsibility of states in Chapter 4. See the opinion of the ICJ in *Certain Expenses* case on the competence of the General Assembly over peace and security.

the General Assembly may want to recommend an action inconsistent with measures considered by the Security Council. If the *only* recommendation the General Assembly could competently make under Articles 10 and 11 are just pacific in nature, it is submitted that there would not have been such an emphasis. This is because the Security Council could prevent a pacific resolution of disputes by the veto. Conversely, since the General Assembly could procedurally deal with a matter and make an enforcement recommendation, the restriction of Article 12(1) thus makes sense. If the General Assembly recommends enforcement action to states, this might present a *fait accompli* case to the Security Council.

A final justification that the General Assembly could recommend enforcement action under Article 10 is to be found in Article 14. This article provides that the General Assembly may recommend measures for the peaceful adjustment of any situation, except if that situation is subject to the Article 12 process. The most important point to note here is that Article 14 categorically mentions 'peaceful adjustment'. This means that peaceful adjustment is either not included at all in the several other types of recommendations possible under Article 10, or only partly so. If Article 10 really limits the General Assembly's power to non-enforcement recommendation, the sensible question to ask is where is the need for Article 14?

The second revelation that emerges from Article 12(1) is that the General Assembly's obligation not to interfere only subsists insofar as the Security Council can be regarded as 'exercising' the function assigned to it under the Charter.[88] So, where it is evident that the Security Council is not acting at all or, for all intent and purposes cannot be deemed to be exercising its functions, the General Assembly is free to make a recommendation.

Characteristically, decentralised enforcement action is erratic and neither conforms to, nor is it guided by, a set of regulatory principles such that are designed for a typical Chapter VII action. Hence there are always stark differences between situations in which it is applied, although there are sometimes remarkable similarities. Nevertheless it is one model that is catered for by some provisions of the Charter as examined and certain principles of general international law.[89] One of the serious problems of organising collective security on an *ad hoc* basis is that its operation is unpredictable. So is its ability to cope with differing circumstances.

Having considered the process of decentralised enforcement action, the next task is to examine the problems associated with its use. In these sections we shall scrutinise whether decentralised enforcement action has yielded the expected results. Such results must be measured in terms of (a) the effectiveness of the action; (b) the ability of the Security Council, being

[88] See Chapter 4 for a discussion of this point.

[89] An example is the implied power theory, See DW Bowett, *The Law of International Institutions* (London, Sweet & Maxwell, 1982); 337 *et seq*; White, *Keeping the Peace*, above note 57, 63–73.

the grantor of the power, to supervise the action in the field; (c) the legitimacy of the Security Council's collective action.

3.4. THE PROBLEMS OF DECENTRALISED ENFORCEMENT ACTION

3.4.1. Command and Control

One real problem confronting decentralised enforcement action is command and control. This problem stems from two sources. Firstly, whenever the Security Council delegate enforcement powers to states not acting under a regional arrangement, such states are not under any specific Charter obligation to report their actions to the Security Council. In such a situation, control by the Security Council can only be exacted in accordance with the terms contained in the instrument of delegation. Thus, where the specific Security Council resolution authorising states to undertake enforcement action fails to spell out the modality for making such states account for their use of powers delegated to them by the Security Council, problems of control arise. Much therefore depends on the ability of the Security Council to supervise and control how the delegated powers are utilised.

However, for several reasons, the Security Council has not been able to discharge this pivotal function. Often, the same states which are the beneficiaries of the delegated powers and who often retain the command and control of the action are also the permanent members of the Security Council that must supervise the operation. The situation is different where the Security Council delegates enforcement powers to states acting under the umbrella of regional organisations. In this case, Article 54 of the Charter requires these arrangements to report actions they may or contemplate to undertake to the Security Council.

The political and factual circumstances in which the various instances of decentralised enforcement actions took place in Korea,[90] the Congo,[91] Iraq-Kuwait,[92] Yugoslavia,[93] and so on are too well known to merit further

[90] See, for instance, Kelsen, above note 84; Dinstein, above note 11 at 41, 44, 137–38, 245; White and Ulgen, above note 18.

[91] See George Abi-Saab, *The United Nations Operation in the Congo, 1960–1964* (Oxford, Oxford University Press, 1978); Durch, above note 77; R Higgins, *United Nations Peacekeeping, 1946–1967: Documents and Commentary* vol 3, Africa (Oxford, Oxford University Press, 1980).

[92] See Nico Krisch, 'Unilateral Enforcement of the Collective Will: Kosovo, Iraq, and the Security Council' (1990) 3 *Max Plank Yearbook of United Nations* 59; J Lobel and M Ratner, 'Bypassing the Security Council: Ambiguous Authorizations to Use Force, Cease-Fires and the Iraqi Inspection Regime' (1999) 93 *American Journal of International Law* 124; C Gray, 'After the Cease-Fire: Iraq, the Security Council and the Use of Force' (1994) 65 *British Yearbook of International Law* 135.

[93] See Dick A Leurdijk, 'Before and After Dayton: the UN and NATO in the Former Yugoslavia' in Thomas G Weiss (ed), *Beyond Subcontracting: Task-Sharing with Regional*

elaboration here. On most occasions, the various legal issues raised in this section such as the problems of command and control and the collective nature of the actions are swamped by discourse as to the legality of decentralised enforcement action under the Charter.

Writers have expressed different views of the Korean crisis. It has been argued that the action was in self-defence rather than a Chapter VII action. Dinstein characterised both the Korean War (1950) and the Gulf Crisis (1990–91) as 'American-led expeditionary forces fought in the exercise of collective self-defence (induced by the Council) as distinct from collective security'.[94] This view was based on the assumption that the Security Council could not *require* States to carry out the measures stipulated in Article 42 of the Charter.[95] Some writers oppose this view on the grounds that an act of self-defence under Article 51 is much narrower than that which Resolution 83 recommended for states.[96] Sarooshi further contended that 'the lawfulness of a military enforcement action being taken under the auspices of the Council does not depend on there being an obligation on States to carry out such action'.[97] The latter was in response to the argument that Korea was an action in self-defence because since Resolution 83 only recommended; it was not a binding obligation on states.

Similarly, questions have been raised about the nature of the UN mission in the Congo in 1960–63[98] where the General Assembly activated its powers to regulate collective security. The Security Council adopted several resolutions at the initial stage of the crisis. Later, the USSR vetoed a resolution proposed by Secretary-General Dag Hammarskjöld.[99] The Security Council became deadlocked. Based on the *Uniting for Peace Resolution*, the United States sponsored a resolution to procedurally transfer the matter to the General Assembly.[100] This was adopted.[101] The General Assembly adopted Resolution 1474 on the basis of the *Uniting for Peace Resolution*. Resolution 1474 requested, *inter alia*, that the Secretary-General should take 'vigorous action' for the restoration of law and order. Whether this phrase envisaged enforcement action was of central impor-

Arrangements and Service-Providing NGOs, (Basingstoke, Macmillan, 1998) 49; Weiss, *The United Nations and NATO in Former Yugoslavia, 1991–1996: Limits to Diplomacy and Force* (The Hague, Netherlands Atlantic Commission/Netherlands Institute of International Relations, 'Clingendael', 1996); C Gray, 'Bosnia and Herzegovina: Civil War or Inter-State Conflict? Characterization and Consequences' (1996) 67 *British Yearbook of International Law* 155.

[94] Yoram Dinstein, above note 11 at 245.

[95] *Ibid*, 295.

[96] Sarooshi, above note 26 at 171.

[97] *Ibid*.

[98] For historical and political context of this mission, see Durch, above note 77; EM Miller, 'Legal Aspects of the United Nations Action in the Congo' (1961) 55 *American Journal of International Law* 1.

[99] UN Doc S/4523 (1960).

[100] SC Res 157 (17 September 1960) (USSR voted against).

[101] GA Res 1474, 4 UN GAOR ESS Supp (No 1) 1 (1960).

tance in the resultant *Certain Expenses* case in which France and the Soviet Union contended that they could not be financially responsible for an action taken in violation of the Charter.[102] These two states formed the opinion that only the Security Council could undertake enforcement action. They believed that since the action in question (which they assumed was enforcement action) was undertaken by the General Assembly, it exceeded its authority under the Charter and as such they could not be held liable for expenses incurred.

Resolution 678 regarding the Iraqi-Kuwait conflict generated enormous reaction from the international legal community.[103] This resolution, adopted after the allied forces affirmed the right of self-defence in support of Kuwait, authorised military actions against Iraq, while preserving Kuwait's right to individual and collective self-defence. An interesting question is whether Resolution 678 made the resultant action an exercise of decentralised enforcement action in which the Security Council delegated its powers to states already acting under Article 51. Opinions differ widely amongst legal scholars on this issue and it is not intended to join issues in this regard.[104]

The Kosovo and Iraqi crises of 1999 and 2003 exemplify the height of operational failure of the UN collective security, particularly concerning the authorisation of enforcement action. Legal writers have commented extensively on these two crises.[105] A remarkable turning point in the Kosovo case was the adoption of Resolution 1244 by the Security Council.[106] This resolution established the KFOR composed of international and NATO forces subject to joint command by the UN and NATO.[107] Operation Allied Force, the codename for NATO's intervention in Kosovo, clearly fell outside Chapter VII in the sense that it was not taken pursuant to a delegated authority by the Council. The action was entirely conducted according to the prescription of NATO planners. Command and control was a matter purely for NATO military commanders. The UN had nothing whatsoever to do with the action until the adoption of Resolution 1244.

[102] ICJ Reports (1962), 151.

[103] See particularly John Quigley, above note 11; Krisch, above note 11; ND White, 'The Legality of the Threat of Force against Iraq', (1999) 30 *Security Dialogue* 75; C Tomuschat, 'Using Force against Iraq', (1998) 73 *Friedenswarte* 75; Lobel and Ratner, above note 92.

[104] See generally John Quigley above note 11; Yoram Dinstein above note 11; White and Ulgen, above note 18; Eugene Rostow, above note 21.

[105] For Kosovo, see Antonio Cassese, '*Ex Injuria ius Oritur*: Are We Moving Towards Legitimation of Forcible Humanitarian Countermeasures in the World Community?' (1999) 10 *European Journal of International Law* 23; Dino Kritsiotis, 'The Kosovo Crisis and NATO's Application of Armed Force Against the Federal Republic of Yugoslavia', (2000) 49 *International and Comparative Law Quarterly* 330.

[106] UN Doc S/RES/1244 (10 July 1999).

[107] See Annex 3 of Resolution 1244.

Moreover, Resolution 1244 was adopted on the understanding that it would not be interpreted or viewed as an endorsement of NATO's military action in Kosovo.[108] Neither Resolutions 1483,[109] which allocated a 'vital role' to the UN in Iraq, nor any other resolutions[110] adopted at the close of 2003 on the Iraqi conflict was of the same magnitude as 1244 in terms of bringing the conflict under UN control.

Whatever may be the legal pedigree and justifications of the above actions, one most common fundamental point agreeable by most writers is that in Korea, Iraq-Kuwait, Congo, and the Kosovo crises, the Security Council virtually abdicated its responsibility.[111] Although one may agree that the action against in Iraq 1990 represents the best instance of collective security since the formation of the UN, it is still deplorable that command and control was entirely left in the hands of the US, the same fate that the action in Korea suffered.[112] Kosovo was different in that the UN was not really involved in the enforcement action taken against the Federal Republic of Yugoslavia (FRY) by NATO member states.

The problem of command and control is a real and daunting one that has pushed UN collective security to a crossroads.[113] Often states, especially the United States,[114] insist on command of their own troops as a condition for participating in a collective security mission.[115] Where this is the case, the UN practically has little choice other than to accept or reject this condition and face whatever the consequences might be. Accepting means the possibility of the action being perceived as an illegitimate one, and an essentially unilateral action with multilateral *imprimatur*.

Article 47 of the Charter provides for the establishment of a Military Staff Committee to assist the Security Council on:

108 See Russia's argument in the Security Council debate leading to the adoption of 1244; SC 4011th mtg, 10 June 1999.

109 UN Doc S/RES/1483(2003).

110 UN Doc S/RES/1500(2003).

111 See Christine Chinkin, 'The State that Acts Alone: Bully, Good Samaritan or Iconoclast?' (2000) (11) *European Journal of International Law* 33; Pierre-Marie Dupuy, 'The Place and Role of Unilateralism in Contemporary International Law' (2000) 11 *European Journal of International Law* 19; Michael Reisman, 'Unilateral Action and the Transformations of the World Constitutive Process: The Special Problem of Humanitarian Intervention' (2000)(11) *European Journal of International Law*, 3; Quigley, above note 11; Krisch, above note 92 .

112 See Lie, above note 57 at 334.

113 For a definition of this term see Patricia Chilton, Otfried Nassauer, Dan Plesch and Jamie Patten (Whitaker), *NATO, Peacekeeping, and the United Nations* (London, British American Security Information Council, 1994) 33; Boutros Boutros-Ghali, *Report of the Secretary-General on the Work of the Organisation*, 2 September 1994 at 56.

114 See Goldman, above note 22. William Durch, 'Faultlines: UN Operations in the Former Yugoslavia' in Olatara Otunu and Michael Doyle (eds), *Peacemaking and Peacekeeping for the New Century* (Oxford, Rowman and Littlefield Publishers Inc, 1996) 193 at 213–15; and William Durch, 'Introduction to Anarchy: Humanitarian Intervention and "State-Building" in Somalia' in Otunu and Doyle (eds), 311 at 335–39.

115 ECOWAS insisted on commanding actions of its UN contingent in Sierra Leone as a precondition for rejoining the mission after its initial withdrawal. See Chapter 5 for analysis.

> all questions relating to the Security Council's military requirements for the maintenance of international peace and security, the employment and command of forces placed at its disposal, the regulation of armaments, and possible disarmament.

Regarding control, the Charter vests its collective security decisions, be it under Chapter VII or Chapter VIII, in the Security Council through the MSC.[116] The Charter obligates regional organisations to report whatever actions they may take to the Security Council.[117] Where states apply force in self-defence, they are obligated to immediately inform the Security Council of the measures so adopted.[118] However, where states are not acting in either manner, but are merely responding to requests in the Security Council's resolutions authorising enforcement action, then they must comply with the directives contained in enabling resolutions, as in 678.[119]

3.4.2. Absence of Obligation to Report

The problem of command and control and the reluctance/inability of the Security Council to superintend its delegated functions will be well appreciated if one remembers that this is not simply 'a nice and rather metaphysical legal issue, but an extremely practical one'.[120] The choice of actions by states acting on their own or under the auspices of the UN is determinative of the practical questions of the 'control and direction of hostilities in the Gulf, their termination, and the substance of settlement they produce'.[121]

James Baker, the US Secretary of State during the Gulf Crisis (1990–91), explained why the MSC was not involved in the Security Council's handling of that conflict. Once troops were put under the MSC, 'you begin getting into questions of whether or not there should be a UN command of forces, whether or not the Military Staff Committee should give *directions* to the multinational force, and questions of that kind, which we don't think, under these circumstances, are things that we ought to invite.'[122] Since the UN did not provide for its own command of the troops taking part in the action in the Persian Gulf, it was no surprise that the requirement of report contained in Resolution 678 was to no practical avail.

[116] For a full analysis of the Military Staff Committee, see Goldman, above note 22, 8.
[117] Art 54 UN Charter.
[118] Art 51 UN Charter.
[119] Operative para 4.
[120] Rostow, above note 21 at 506, cited in Franck, above note 38 at 296.
[121] *Ibid.*
[122] *US Policy in the Persian Gulf: Hearing before the Senate Committee on Foreign Relations*, 101st Cong, 2d Sess 107, (pt 1) (1990).

The mission of the UN in Sierra Leone (2001), as will be seen in Chapter 5, has pushed the loss of command and control of delegated action by the UN to an alarming level. Nigeria, leading other ECOWAS states, is executing its own mandate, which it declared in advance to be one of enforcement.[123]

What these instances indicate is that it does not matter much whether the Security Council delegates its power to states acting as such or to regional organisations. There will always be a problem with command and control where the Security Council resorts to decentralised enforcement action. However, whereas the Security Council may hold regional organisations accountable to their obligation under Article 54, it has no power as to where it delegates its powers to states acting as such. This is particularly so where the enabling resolution does not impose any such duties on states.

If the Security Council fails to supervise powers delegated by it, the action might be highjacked by the beneficiaries and used to further unilateral rather than collective purposes. This may affect the legitimacy of the action. No doubt such actions may be effective; for instance, the expelling of Iraqi forces from Kuwait. However, this does not mean that the action is a proper exercise of collective security power, especially when, despite Resolution 687 formally terminating the action, the allied forces continue to bomb the state on the grounds of self-defence and breach of Resolution 687 which according to United States and United Kingdom entitles them to act under Resolution 678.[124]

3.5. THE FACTORS MILITATING AGAINST THE CENTRALISED COLLECTIVE SECURITY SYSTEM

3.5.1. The Veto Power: A Critique of Existing Proposals for Reform

The veto constitutes the single most debilitating hindrance to the realisation of Chapter VII collective security.[125] States, regional organisations

[123] For an analysis, see Ademola Abass, 'The Implementation of ECOWAS New Protocol and Security Council Resolution 1270 in Sierra Leone: New Development in Regional Intervention' (2002) 10 *University of Miami Journal of International and Comparative Law* (Special Issue) 177; Madu Onuora, Segun Ayeoyenikan and Tunji Oketunbi, 'ECOWAS to Deploy 3,000 Troops to Sierra Leone', http://www.ngrguardiannews.com.

[124] 'UK Materials on International Law' (1992) 63 *British Yearbook of International Law* 824.

[125] See discussion in Chapter 1. See also Dwight Lee, 'The Genesis of the Veto' (1947) *International Organisation* 33; JL Brierly, 'The Covenant and the Charter' (1946) *British Yearbook of International Law* 83 at 89–90. For a comprehensive account of these proposals, see Bardo Fassbender, *UN Security Council Reform and the Right of Veto: A Constitutional Perspective* (The Hague, Kluwer Law International, 1998); For a comprehensive account of how the veto was used at this period, see Anjali Patil, *The UN Veto in World Affairs, 1946–1990: A Complete Record and Case Histories of the Security Council's Veto* (London, Mansell, 1992).

and writers have advanced several proposals regarding the use of the veto by its custodians.[126] The iniquitous manner in which the veto has been invoked has not only caused paralysis to UN collective security, it has also created a deepening distrust and contempt between the Security Council members and the other members of the UN[127].

Since 1979, UN member states have embarked on proposing reforms of the Security Council 'geared towards increasing diversity and numeric representation for non-permanent members'.[128] This changed with the end of the Cold War with many Third World states clamouring for a more radical overhaul of the Security Council.[129] The US is disinclined towards any reform that does not guarantee Japan and Germany[130] permanent seats in the Security Council, a position supported by Britain and France, amongst others,[131] although it was not as categorical with the issue of veto to the two. Germany[132] proposed an enlargement of the Security Council, but Mexico[133] and Italy rejected all suggestions for the expansion of the veto carriers, with the latter subscribing to the idea of semi-pernanent membership.[134]

For regional organisations, the reform of the veto is tied to the reform of the Security Council at large. Suggestions have ranged from allocating seats to regional organisations on rotational basis for five years with indefinite renewability to granting of Security Council membership to ethnically and culturally (rather than geographically) identified organisations.[135] African States, under the auspices of the now defunct OAU, advocated two permanent seats for the continent.[136]

[126] Maurice Bertrand (ed), *A New Charter for a World Organization*? (The Hague, Kluwer Law International, 1997); Bardo Fassbender, above note 125.

[127] On the question of veto and the historical circumstances surrounding its inclusion in the Charter, see Russell, above note 13; Mohammed Bedjaoui, *The New World Order and the Security Council: Testing the Legality of its Acts* (Dordrecht, Martinus Nijhoff Publishers, 1994).

[128] Michael J Kelly, 'UN Security Council Permanent Membership: A New Proposal for a Twenty-First Century Council' (2000) *Seton Hall Law Review* 319 at 329.

[129] *Ibid*. See General Assembly Resolution 47/62, Question of Equitable Representation and Increase in the Membership of the Security Council (UN Doc. A/RES/47/62), cited by Kelly, quoting Sam Daws, *The Reform of the UN Security Council: Introduction,* in Paul Taylor et al (eds), 1997 *Documents on Reform of the United Nations*, 415.

[130] See Christopher Wren, 'Revising the UN Security Council: All Agree They Don't Agree' (1995) *New York Times*, November 15, at A9, cited by Kelly, above note 128 at 331.

[131] Press Release, GA/9689) (December, 16 1999),

[132] See Kelly, above note 128.

[133] See the statement of Manuel Tello (Mexican representative) at the General Assembly's meeting (9689).

[134] Kelly, above note 128 at 333; See also Turkey's position on the issue, Reform of the Security Council: Position Paper of Turkey, September, 15, 1995, UN Doc A/AC.247/5(I).

[135] See the proposal by Syria, Press Release, United Nations General Assembly Continues Debate on Security Council Reform with Focus on Changing Veto, Permanent Membership, UN Doc GA/9692 (Dec, 20 1999).

[136] See the Harare Declaration of the Assembly of Heads of State and Government of the OAU on the Reform of the United Nations Security Council, June 4, 1997, UN Doc A/AC.247/1997/CPR11 (June 27, 1997). See also Fassbender, at 250; Martin Andjaba, Namibia representative to the General Assembly Meeting (9689).

Professor Wortley blazed the academic trail in the search for Security Council reform, especially in respect of the veto. Writing as early as 1946, Wortley contended that 'there is no theoretical reason why Members of the United Nations—for example, the five permanent members of the Security Council—should not enter into treaties with each other, or with the Security Council itself, limiting in advance the right to use the individual veto in defined circumstances'.[137] However, the practical problem with such postulations, he noted, was that '*if made with the Security Council* the treaty would be subject not only to the veto of a permanent member, but also to that of the five of the non-permanent members'.[138]

Other commentators have made more radical suggestions.[139] For some, the enlargement of the veto-carrying membership of Security Council will go a long way in addressing the problem, and should extend to as many as 10 members.[140] It has even been argued that the inclusion of one or more countries from the Third World would stem the clamour for democratisation of the UN system by the Third World and boost the waning image of the Security Council as an undemocratic forum.[141] At the extreme are those who believe that nothing short of a total abolition of the current Charter of the UN, and its replacement by a more realistic one, can restore the lost ideal of collective security as it was envisaged at San Francisco.[142]

Many of these proposals are not likely to be actualised for hindrances of law and dictates of reality. As Bailey noted, there is 'no evidence that any of the five permanent members is at present willing to give up the right of veto'.[143] In fact the prospect of achieving such a feat on the part of all permanent members of the Security Council would seem to be remote in the light of Article 109(2) of the Charter requiring that all permanent members of the Security Council must consent to recommendations for alterations of the Charter. Article 108 is of the same nature.

Furthermore, an abrogation of the veto, assuming that proposition goes beyond a figment of the academic imagination, is not a panacea to the problem of collective security. A relocation of collective security powers entirely in the General Assembly or in all members of the Security Council,

[137] BA Wortley, 'The Veto and the Security Council Provisions of the Charter' (1946) 43 *British Yearbook of International Law* 95 at 109.

[138] *Ibid.*

[139] Maurice, above note 126; Alexander W Rudzinski, 'The So-Called Double Veto' (1951) 45 *American Journal of International Law* 443.

[140] See particularly, David Whittaker, *United Nations in the Contemporary World* (1997), at 50.

[141] See Obiora Chinedu Okafor, 'The Global Process of Legitimation and the Legitimacy of Good Governance' (1997) 14 *Arizona Journal of International and Comparative Law* 117.

[142] Bertrand, above note 126. For more comprehensive account of academic proposals, see Kelly, above note 128 at 336 *et seq.*

[143] Sydney Bailey, 'The Security Council' in Philip Alston (ed), *The United Nations and Human Rights: A Critical Appraisal* (Oxford, Clarendon Press, 1992).

as one may be tempted to suggest, will not be a credible option for situations requiring expeditious decisions.

Moreover, there seems to be a real dilemma for the UN regarding a possible expansion of the veto-carrying membership of the Security Council or the enlargement of its non-permanent membership. Potential problems with expansion of the veto were well articulated by the Mexican representative during the General Assembly meeting.[144] Admittedly, increasing the number of veto wielders appears quite justifiable. Yet, there is a need to balance this expansion with another real need to ensure that collective security will be administered with the effectiveness required by the Charter. This, it is submitted, will be sacrificed just as it was in the days of the League of Nations.[145] The problems created by the Cold War as regard implementation of Charter collective security cannot be remedied by endowing more states with the veto power.[146] If the permanent Security Council were to be enlarged in the future, laying down objective criteria for selecting candidates would be a daunting task.

3.5.2. The Selectivity of Collective Security

The greatest threat yet to the effective implementation of the UN collective security in the post-Cold War era is the notorious selectiveness of the Security Council's response to breaches of peace and other conflict situations.[147] This problem has led to the loss of confidence in the Security Council by states which, rightly or wrongly, believe that the Security Council is biased against their interests.

Writers have paid very little attention to the problem of selective collective security,[148] sometimes blaming the Security Council's lacklustre reaction to conflicts on logistic problems.[149] Often, the Security Council's reluctance to tackle some conflicts, especially in Africa, is believed to be due to the widespread nature of such conflicts.[150]

[144] See Manuel Tello (Mexico), 9689, above note 133.

[145] Edward Carr, *The Twenty Years Crisis 1919–1939: An Introduction to the Study of International Relations* (London, Macmillan, 1939).

[146] For similar argument see David Caron, 'The Legitimacy of the Collective Authority of the Security Council', (1993) 87 *American Journal of International Law* 552.

[147] Martii Koskenniemi, above note 33 at 460; See Olivier Russbach, *ONU Contre ONU: Le Droit International Confisqué* (1994).

[148] See Professor Elihu Lauterpacht's *Foreword* to Marc Weller (ed), *Regional Peacekeeping and International Enforcement: The Liberian Crisis,* Cambridge International Documents Series, vol 6, (Cambridge, Cambridge University Press, 1994), at ix. But see Professor Burns Weston analysis of factors influencing decision-making in the Security Council, quoted in Akehurst (Malanczuk), above note 21, 428–29. See also below note 168.

[149] See Hilaire McCoubrey and Justin Morris, *Regional Peacekeeping in the Post-Cold War Era* (The Hague, Kluwer Law International, 2000), particularly at 132–34.

[150] See Georg Nolte, 'Restoring Peace by Regional Action: International Legal Aspects of the Liberian Conflict' 23 *ZaöRV* 53/3, 603.

Article 39 of the UN Charter permits the Security Council to make a determination that a situation exists which constitutes a 'threat to the peace, breach of the peace, or act of aggression'. It further authorises the Security Council to 'make recommendation or decide what measures shall be taken in accordance with Articles 41 and 42, to maintain or restore international peace and security'. International lawyers' perception of the exact scope of this provision is as diverse as the situations in which the Security Council has deployed it. While some lawyers believe that the Security Council must exercise this power with fairness,[151] others believe that a threat or breach to the peace is what the Security Council says it is in its unboundable wisdom.[152] The Security Council, acting under Article 39, is entirely at liberty to characterise any situation least deserving as one that falls under the provision, and the most desperate case as undeserving of its attention. With this in its armoury, it is all too easy for the Security Council to make Article 39 determination as it pleases.

Apart from Article 39, Article 2(7) of the Charter, which, *inter alia*, forbids the UN to intervene in matters that are essentially within the domestic jurisdiction of any State, provides another opportunity for the Security Council to be selective. As Thomas Franck observed, this article is the '"Greenwich foot" by which the actions taken by the Security Council in the name of "collective security" are judged'.[153] Unless the Security Council characterises a situation as one falling under Article 39, it may not unleash the measures contained in Articles 40–42.

The problem with Articles 2(7) and 39 is that, unless one is able to demonstrate that they have been applied *mala fides* in particular instances, it is difficult to impugn their deployment since they do not contain self-regulatory standards against which their application can be measured. In contrast, Article 24(1), which bestows collective legitimacy on the Security Council, remains the only means by which a principled application of Articles 39 and 2(7) by the Security Council can be determined. This is because Article 24(1) provides some measure of internal regulation. It confers upon the Security Council the responsibility to act on behalf of the international community *in order to ensure prompt and effective action*. In addition, some of the main purposes for the establishment of the UN are to prevent wars, violations of human rights, to maintain international peace and security, and so on, as stated in Articles 1 and 24(2) of the Charter. These articles constitute some check on the extent to which the Security Council can be capricious in functioning under Articles 39 and 2(7) in particular.

[151] See Thomas Franck above note 38; Gerry Simpson, 'Is International Law Fair?' (1996) 17 *Michigan Journal of International Law* 615.

[152] Hans Kelsen, *The Law of the United Nations: A Critical Analysis of its Fundamental Problems* (London, Stevens, 1964), 727; Akehurst's (Malanczuk ed,) above note 21 at 426; Yoram Dinstein, *War, Aggression and Self-Defence* (Cambridge, Cambridge University Press, 3rd edn, 2001) at 251.

[153] Thomas Franck, above note 38 at 219.

However, a reckoning of Security Council action or inaction in most African conflicts reveals that Articles 24(1) and Article 1 have played little role in guiding the Security Council when it receives emergency calls from member states. The Security Council did receive emergency calls from Liberia (1989–97), Sierra Leone (1997–2001) and Rwanda (1994). In virtually all of these cases its response had been similar: the UN could not get involved in such conflicts.[154] In contrast to African situations, an overthrow of a democratic government in Haiti (as the one in Sierra Leone) attracted the Security Council's 'ground-breaking' decision to intervene in the internal affairs of a member state.[155] Such double standards in the practice of the Security Council continue to raise concerns. As Professor Elihu Lauterpacht has noted:

> it is painful to ask, and even more painful to be unable satisfactorily to answer, the question why it is that the conscience of the international community is so rightly (albeit insufficiently) exercised over the first of these episodes (Yugoslavia conflict) and is so relatively unconcerned with, to the extent that it is aware of, the horrors of the second (Liberian conflict).[156]

The answer to this question surely oscillates in the dissonance between the letter of the law and the politics of its implementation.

3.5.3. The Security Council and the Legitimacy Crisis

States do not always accept that the collective security decisions of the Security Council are free from hidden motives.[157] One can point to the outbreak of the crisis in Sierra Leone (1997). The Security Council was initially not keen to intervene, arguably because some of its permanent members, especially the United States, were not interested.[158] The Secretary-General

[154] For official positions, See Javier Pérez de Cuéllar's statement as regard the Liberian conflict, *West Africa* 3851 (1–7 July 1991), 1076; Larry King Live: Interview with Boutros-Boutros Ghali (Cable Network News Broadcast, December 22, 1994) Transcript no 1312, available in Lexis, New Library, CNN File. See also Peter Daniel DiPaola, 'A Noble Sacrifice? *Jus Ad Bellum* and the International Community's Gamble in Chechnya' (1997) 4 *Indiana Journal of Global Legal Studies* 435.

[155] For analysis, see David Malone, 'Haiti and the International Community: A Case Study' (1997) 39 (2) *Survival* 126; David Malone, *Decision-Making in the UN Security Council: The Case of Haiti, 1991–1997* (Oxford, Clarendon, 1998).

[156] Elihu Lauterpacht in Weller, above note 148, ix.

[157] For instance in the Gulf crisis, the Colombian representative predicted, just before the adoption of Resolution 665, which authorised the use of maritime forces to implement the economic sanctions imposed by the Security Council on Iraq, that 'We are under no illusion that when the Council comes to vote on this draft resolution it will be establishing a naval blockade'. See UN Doc S/PV2938, 21, quoted by David Caron, above note 146 at 554.

[158] It is generally believed that the killing of 18 American troops in Somalia discouraged US involvement in African conflicts. Some have even suggested that the end of the Cold War and the consequent cessation of the East/West contest for satellite states means that Africa, with low economic importance to the West, is not a real priority for Western countries.

Kofi Anan has expressed the view that after the Somalia crisis, Western members of the UN should not be expected to be interested in intervening in African conflicts.[159]

In collective security discourse, *legitimacy* of the Security Council's collective action has become a vexatious issue amongst states and writers. The belief is now strong, especially amongst writers, that the standards, conducts and processes of Security Council's actions and decisions must be measured in accordance with the purposes and objectives of the Charter.[160] This is a remarkable departure from the classical position that the Security Council does not have to justify its action by reference to *justice* and *fairness*, and may indeed act contrary to the ethos of both.[161]

In broad terms, the functioning of the Security Council has been discussed in legal literature on two fronts: the *principled justification* (legality) for the Security Council's collective actions and the *acceptability* (legitimacy) of the process of decisions by the Security Council.[162] However, since we have commented, in first part, on the decentralised enforcement action, we do not intend to inquire into the theme of legality all over again. Nor is it the intention here to undertake an elaborate analysis of how and what principled justifications the Security Council offers when it authorises collective actions. On both issues, as well as doctrinal consideration of

[159] See statement made by the Secretary-General in Paris, France, Wednesday 3 May 2000, http://www.nytimes.com/library/world/africa.

[160] Although many scholars have commented on the theme of legitimacy in the work of the Security Council, particular mention must be made of Thomas Franck, *The Power of Legitimacy Among Nations* (1990); Sean Murphy, 'The Security Council, Legitimacy, and the Concept of Collective Security After the Cold War' (1994) 32 *Columbia Journal of Transnational Law* 201; David Caron, above note 146 at 552; J Frowein, 'Legal Consequences for International Law Enforcement' in Jost Delbrück (ed), *The Future of International Law: New Scenarios, New Law?: Proceedings of an International Symposium of the Kiel Institute of International Law*, March 25 to 27, 1992 (Berlin, Duncker & Humblot, 1993) 111; Andrew Boyd, *Fifteen Men on A Powder Keg: A History of the UN Security Council* (London, Methuen, 1971).

[161] Kelsen, Dinstein, above note 11; Koskenniemi, above note 33.

[162] See David Caron and Thomas Franck, above notes and respectively. Both Franck and Caron developed the principled justification thesis by ascertaining the modalities by which the Security Council justifies its decisions to take collective actions. The analysis offered by Thomas Franck however is the more relevant to this chapter. Franck's conception of legitimacy is based on a concrete analytical imperative, which presents legitimacy as one of the two composite independent variables on which the idea of fairness rests; the other composite is justice. Thus, in Franck, we confront the legitimacy of a rule as a function of 'certain intrinsic properties both of the rule and of the process by which it was made; and the process of its interpretation by judges and officials' (Franck, above note 38 at 26). The holistic analytical approach adopted by Franck has a notable advantage over all others: it links legitimacy with other processes such as the making and interpretation of rules. This approach is to be distinguished, for instance, from John Stuart Mill's approach which seeks to separate legitimacy from other concepts such as justice. See JS Mill, *Utilitarianism: On Liberty; Considerations on Representative Government* (edited by Geraint Williams) (London, Dent, 1993) especially Chapter 5. Since our discussion of legitimacy in the functioning of the Security Council invariably touches on the fairness or justice of circumstances in which the Council exercises its legitimate functions under the Charter, we adopt the framework offered by Franck as being more apt and representative of our undertaking.

legitimacy, there is excellent coverage in the legal literature.[163] One last caveat is that the analysis below does not engage in discussing the various headings of legitimacy, such as the normative and the sociological concepts of legitimacy, being of no relevance to our pursuit. Rather, this section raises three fundamental issues for consideration. First, it tries to understand legitimacy in the functioning of the Security Council. Second, it determines how to recognise loss of legitimacy by the Security Council. Third, it considers what the effects of the loss of legitimacy are on the ability of the Security Council to act on behalf of the international community.

3.5.4. Legitimacy in the Context of the Security Council's Functioning

In the parlance of international governance, legitimacy connotes the authority, both legal and moral, of the organs of international organisations tasked with certain functions, to take collective actions and decisions on behalf of the entirety of its members.[164] In the context of UN collective security, legitimacy refers to the collective justification of how the Security Council deploys its legal (and/or moral?) authority to decide on and implement the collective measures contained in Chapter VII of the UN Charter.[165] Thus two activities are engaged in atypical legitimacy contests or challenges: decision-making and execution. As Franck has noted, to assert its legitimacy, 'the Council must be seen to be acting in accordance with established procedures and limitations'.[166] According to Justice Mohammed Bedjaoui, 'the Council must also persuade states that it is exercising its powers justly'.[167] To challenge the legitimacy of the Security Council is to assail or impugn its decision-making process and deny that its execution meets the requirements of collectivity.

Legitimacy derives, and is largely dependent on, legality. Legality, in its simplest formulation, implies the legal *ability* to perform a task. To claim that an act is legal is to affirm that its performance is underwritten by a legal rule. A challenge to the legitimacy of an act assumes the existence of legality in the first place. An illegal act may be legitimatised through a subsequent process of collective adoption. An illegitimate act is one done without conformity to legal principles.[168] The relationship between legitimacy

163 *Ibid.*
164 See Thomas Franck, above note 38, 218.
165 *Ibid.*
166 *Ibid.*
167 Bedjaoui, 'Du Contrôle de Légalité des Actes du Conseil de Sécurité' in *Nouveaux itinéraires en Droit, Hommage à François Rigaux* (1993) cited by Franck, *Fairness*, above note 38 at 218.
168 In a similar vein, David Caron argues that 'even if an organization acts in accordance with its rules, it nonetheless may be viewed as illegitimate against some broader frame', above note 146 at 559.

and legality is that one (legitimacy) depends on another (legality) for survival. We cannot query the legitimacy of an act unless it is legal *ab initio*. An illegal act is the best candidate for illegitimacy.

In the functioning of the Security Council, allegations of illegitimacy resonate, as David Caron observes, in that 'space between the promises of preamble to the Charter of the organization and the realities of the compromises in the text that follows, a space in which there is discretion regarding the use of authority'.[169] Many agree that the Security Council is free to apply its discretion, as it deems fit. Thomas Franck noted however, this discretion 'is to be exercised *bona fides* and *intra vires*, in accordance with these specific procedures and substantive standards spelt out in the Charter'.[170]

Challenges to the Security Council's legitimacy can be expressed through various mediums and in respect of different aspects of the Security Council's engagements. States often perceive the potential to betray the promise made to them by the UN to have been already built directly into the Charter in the form of veto in 1945.[171] Former colonial African states often impugn the legitimacy of the Security Council (and the UN itself) on the grounds that when the UN Charter was concluded, most African members were colonies and did not contribute to the legal principles embodied by the Charter.

Allegations of illegitimacy may arise from critics' assessment of particular actions by the Security Council. For instance, as regards the Libyan sanctions, Mr Badi Ali, Chairman of the Islamic Committee for Palestine North Carolina once argued that 'the United Nations has been brought in to do the dirty work of the British-American alliance against the Muslim world and the third world countries'.[172] Professors Martti Koskenniemi and Burns Weston have also raised concerns. Weston asserts that 'the process by which Security Council Resolution 678 was won, while perhaps legally correct *strictu sensu*, confirms how complete the power of the United States over the UN policing mechanism had become in the absence of Cold War opposition'.[173] According to Koskenniemi, 'the Council has not reflected the collective interests of United Nations members as a whole, but only the special interests and factual predominance of the United States and its Western allies within the Council'.[174] Thomas Franck vividly portrayed the functioning of the Security Council as the Americans going to the British, the two of them getting the French aboard,

[169] Above note 146 at 560.

[170] Franck, above note 38 at 220.

[171] See Caron, above note 146 at 60.

[172] *Ibid*, at 563.

[173] Burns Weston, 'Security Council Resolution 678 and Persian Gulf Decision Making: Precarious Legitimacy', (1991) 85 *American Journal of International Law* 516.

[174] Martii Koskenniemi, above note 33 at 460–61.

and then trying to co-opt the Russians and hoping that the Chinese will go along because the resolution says it is not creating a precedent.[175]

True, states and writers frequently cast doubts on the integrity of the Security Council's decision-making processes and its collective actions. The question is whether such doubts invariably evidence a loss of legitimacy by the Security Council? Put differently, does the simple fact that states and writers challenge its legitimacy mean that the Security Council has, in actual fact, lost its legitimacy to act on behalf of the international community?

3.5.5. Proving the Loss of Legitimacy by the Security Council

How can we determine whether the Security Council has lost the legitimacy to take collective actions, especially on behalf of those states that feel sidelined by its selectivity? No easy answer to this can be proposed. However, general guidelines can be laid down for that purpose. The main justification for this inquiry is that without establishing that the Security Council has lost some of its legitimacy, it will be impossible to justify the resort by states to alternative collective security measures outside the framework of the Charter, as we shall discuss in Chapter 5.

The clearest indication of loss of legitimacy, by any UN organ for that matter, is mostly given by states themselves, although frequently by writers too. Often, states react to Security Council's actions on their behalf with cynicism, indignation, and indifference. An example of this was the reaction by many states to the Security Council's decision in 1992 to impose sanctions[176] on Libya.[177] Also, the costly prevarication of the Security Council in the face unravelling genocide in Rwanda led to outcry amongst many states, especially those in Africa, that the UN had abandoned the continent altogether.[178] Occasionally, top UN officials make statements that generally tend to reveal crisis in the legitimacy of the organ.[179] The argument may be made that the inscrutability that often characterises the working of the Security Council leads states and writers as well, to contest the collective basis of such decisions.[180] It has been asserted that 'informal

[175] Referred to by Paul Szasz in Jost Delbrück's *Allocation*, above note 31 at 68.

[176] UN Doc S/RES/748 (31 March 1992) paras 4–6.

[177] *Question of Interpretation and Application of the 1971 Montreal Convention Arising from the Aerial Incident at Lockerbie* (*Libya v US*), ICJ Reports (1992), 3, (henceforth *Lockerbie Case*).

[178] For a good account of this episode see Hilaire McCoubrey and Justin Morris, *Regional Peacekeeping in the Post-Cold War Era* (The Hague, Kluwer Law International, 2000), 132–34.

[179] See for instance the statement of Secretary-General Kofi Anan to the effect that after the conflicts in Somalia and Rwanda, the international community would have little courage to be involved in African conflicts, http://www.nytimes.com/library/world/africa/050500 sierra-leone-assess.html.

[180] See Martii Koskenniemi, above note 33; Thomas Franck, above note 38 at 230.

consultation of the Council now outnumbers the formal meetings, which have become mere ceremonial events, typically of very short duration'.[181]

The categories of challenges to the loss of Security Council's legitimacy are not closed. However, it is one thing for the Security Council to take crucial decisions outside the 'horseshoe' table in New York; it is another to conclude that such a process is *automatically* blighted by illegitimacy. The question then is, when can states' *responses* to Security Council's actions be said to amount to a successful challenge to the latter's legitimacy?

For an action by the Security Council to be illegitimate, it must be demonstrated that a majority of states disagree with the decision-making process and the execution of that action, and not just one or a handful of states. Where the number of states that disagree with the Security Council's functioning in a given case outweighs those who agree with it, this may be a good indication that those states believe that the Security Council's action is illegitimate, that is, does not represent their collective interest. Conversely where the majority of states approve of a Security Council action, it does not tarnish its legitimacy if only a few members disagree.[182] It is contended that good reasons for an action may not make it legitimate if it does not meet with the approval of the majority. The bombing of the FRY in 1999 by NATO forces might be explicable on humanitarian grounds, but this does not mean that the act itself was legitimate.

These propositions can be validated by a consideration of three examples of conflict situations: the *Lockerbie* affair, the Gulf Crisis (1991) and the Rwandan genocide. In the *Lockerbie* affair, several states criticised the decision of the Security Council to impose sanctions on Libya while the issue was before the ICJ, despite that it purportedly took the decision on behalf of all states.[183] With respect to the Iraqi–Kuwait conflict, virtually all states agreed with the adoption of Resolution 678, despite the fact that a few states, such as Yemen, Cuba and Colombia, disagreed with the timing of that resolution.[184] This does not make the Security Council's action less legitimate.

[181] JOC Jonah, 'Differing State Perspectives on the United Nations in the Post-Cold War Perspective', *Academic Council on the United Nations System* (ACUNS) Reports and Papers (1993) No 4, at 11.

[182] For a similar view, see David Caron contending that 'isolated allegations of illegitimacy by actors at the margins of an organization would likely have little significance for the organization as a whole', above note 146 at 558.

[183] For analysis, see Thomas Franck, above note 38 at 241–42; Nigel White, 'To Review or not To Review' (1999) 12 *Leiden Journal of International Law* 401. See also discussion above.

[184] Yemen and Cuba argued that the adoption of the resolution mandating enforcement action against Iraq was in violation of Chapter VII Art 42 which provides that once the Security Council imposes non-military measures under Art 41, it must wait for such to take full effect before proceeding to impose Art 42 measures. This process, those states claimed, was not followed. Colombia specifically argued that the delegation of the enforcement powers by the Security Council by Resolution 678 without spelling out the beneficiaries and detailing the modalities of control raised concerns. See UN Doc S/PV2938 (1990) at 21.

The approach adopted by the Security Council in the Rwandan genocide was heavily criticised by many states and writers as being less than desirable in such a situation.[185] The Security Council was thought to have delayed considerably in authorising action, aside from the fact that when the situation became desperate, the Security Council had not even placed Rwanda on its agenda.[186] Inaction or ineffective action by the Security Council, in this kind of situation, could amount to acting or omitting to act illegitimately, leading to outcry amongst states.[187] For in this set of circumstances, it is all too normal for alleging states to sense betrayal of 'what is believed to be the promise and spirit of the organization'.[188]

Furthermore, the extremely delicate venture of the Security Council in the *Lockerbie* affair could be rightly regarded as an illegitimate deployment of its discretionary power under Article 39. Resorting to Article 39 at a time when Libya had brought a case before the ICJ does not seem to accord to a principled deployment of Security Council's powers under the Charter. A subsequent imposition of sanctions on Libya, in our opinion, would appear to be an illegitimate exercise of collective security even if the action itself is *legal* under Article 103 of the UN Charter, the defining matrix of the relationship between the UN and states, regarding the latter's obligations under the Charter and under other international agreements.[189]

Another serious determinant of the loss of legitimacy by the Security Council—and one that is rarely noted—is the degree to which UN member states have started relocating confidence in regional organisations. We will say more on this issue later when we come to the effects of the loss of legitimacy.

The assertion that 'if the UN loses its credibility, the Security Council would still be able to order governments about', even if such ordering about should be regarded as 'having lost its international sheen' and 'looks more like big-power bullying'[190] is unduly optimistic. The Security Council may not be able to order states around for two reasons. First, in the absence of troops obtained under an Article 43 agreement, the Security Council cannot *decide* on collective security, at least on military matters, but can only authorise states to act. States may choose to or not act since there is no obligation on them under Article 25 to execute non binding decisions of the Security Council. This ends the Security Council's ability to enforce its orders by military means, though it can still order non military measures.

[185] See Justin and McCoubrey above note 178 for analysis.

[186] *Ibid.*

[187] David Caron recognised that illegitimacy may arise out of inaction. See Caron, above note 146.

[188] *Ibid*, at 559.

[189] But see Nigel White, above note 66.

[190] 'Open the Club', *The Economist* August 29, 1992 at 14.

Where the Security Council recommends that states take certain actions against a transgressor, it will have neither the practical means to deal with the transgressor by itself nor the legal capacity to compel states to implement its decisions. In addition, states may resort to the General Assembly and prevent any action by the Council by refusing to approve the necessary fiscal arrangements necessary for the Security Council action assuming that permanent members of the Security Council decide to act alone despite states' non co-operation. Indeed, a resort to bullying states, assuming that is factually and legally possible, is the clearest indication that the Security Council has lost its legitimacy altogether.

As we shall see later, what might happen is that most states will commence diverting attention from the UN. This they will do by becoming more active in regional organisations. They may also become less committed to fulfilling their financial obligations to the UN. The fact that several states regularly fall in arrears of their contributions to the UN, while at the same time they generously fund their regional organisations may be expressive of the fact that they no longer trust the credibility of the Security Council's actions on their behalf.[191]

3.6.6. Implications of Loss of Legitimacy for Centralised Collective Security

The following discussion is divided into two sub-sections. The first considers the short-term effect of loss of legitimacy and the second, those that are long-term. The short-term effects are (1) the inability of the Security Council to adopt some resolutions, (2) lack of optimal participation by states in its actions. Long-term effects include (1) gradual and systemic growth in the members' apathy, leading to defection to regional organisations such as NATO, ECOWAS and the EU. Finally, (2) there is a real possibility of the collapse of the UN collective security system.

3.5.6.1 Short-Term Effects of Loss of Legitimacy

Inability to Adopt Resolutions It has been claimed that the inability of the Security Council to adopt certain resolutions is the most significant effect of the loss of legitimacy by the UN.[192] The problem with the Security

[191] An instructive example of this might be Nigeria, a country that reportedly spent 3 billion US dollars in order to implement ECOWAS' mandate in Liberia. The country also was largely responsible for the largest human and material arrangements for the ECOWAS missions in Sierra Leone. See Ademola Abass, above note 123.

[192] For instance, out of the five examples of how the perception of illegitimacy may work against the Security Council stated by David Caron, four deal with the Council's inability to adopt resolutions. See David Caron above note 146 at 558. See Thomas Franck, above note 38 at 230.

Council resolutions, as Thomas Franck stated, is that 'they speak in the covered language of diplomacy, sometimes out of political necessity, sometimes out of the drafters' professional habit.'[193] Whatever may be the pedigree of these resolutions, 'they often fail to address issues of fairness, which leaves Council actions vulnerable to attack as exercises in unprincipled power'.[194] Once the deployment of the Security Council's function is blemished by unprincipled power and lack consideration of justness and fairness, it becomes difficult to garner support for such resolutions.

Whether illegitimacy leads to the failure of the Security Council to adopt resolutions, or whether it presents difficulties in building domestic support towards implementing resolutions or leads to slow consensus-building, it certainly undermines the Security Council's ability to undertake collective actions.[195] It does not matter whether such a consequence results from intentional or accidental actions and strategies adopted by the Security Council.[196] Once the Security Council resorts to an unprincipled deployment of its powers, such will adversely affect its functioning even if the powers are themselves legally exercised.

Lack of Optimal Participation by States It is not in every situation that loss of legitimacy may prevent the Security Council from adopting a resolution. On the contrary, it is possible that 'a determined political majority can hypothetically dispense with such fairness discourse, and in practice sometimes does so in the name of decisiveness and the need for an expeditious response to a crisis'.[197] Let us assume that, despite perceived illegitimacy, all the permanent members of the Security Council agree to a resolution authorising economic sanctions against a state. By virtue of Article 25 of the Charter, states must implement such a resolution.[198]

With resolutions authorising states to undertake enforcement action against a state, things are different. In this case, while it may be possible for the Security Council to adopt enforcement resolutions in the name of expediency and decisiveness, 'the action taken will be judged by standards of legitimacy and fairness, and that judgment will affect the capacity of the decisions made to pull the community towards compliance'.[199] Again, let us suppose that the Security Council is able to adopt an enforcement resolution, the major difficulty will then be for the Security Council to garner enough support amongst states to implement its recommendations. Resolutions recommending military actions against member states

[193] Thomas Franck, above note 38 at 230.
[194] *Ibid.*
[195] David Caron, above note 146 at 558.
[196] *Ibid*, at 558.
[197] Franck, at 219.
[198] See above.
[199] *Ibid.*

are not of the same legal character as those authorising economic measures. In this case, the ability of the Security Council to motivate the community of states to support its resolution depends largely on how such states perceive its decision making process, even if the decision is in itself lawful.

3.5.6.2. Long-Term Effects of Loss of Legitimacy

The Growth of Apathy and Tactical Withdrawal from the UN In the long run, it is possible that the UN collective security system could suffer more harm if the Security Council continued to deploy its powers in an unprincipled manner. As Secretary-General Boutros-Boutros Ghali observed in the *Agenda for Peace*, 'the principles of the Charter must be applied consistently, not selectively, for if the perception should be of the latter, trust will wane and with it the moral authority which is the greatest and most unique quality of that instrument'.[200]

It can be argued that the legitimacy crisis of the Security Council is partly responsible for the growth in the involvement of regional organisations in collective security tasks. Movement towards enhancing regional collective security capacity is already noticeable in Africa and Europe. Due to the perception that the Security Council is less vigorously committed to African conflicts,[201] many African states have started looking more inwardly for solutions to their collective security problems. The adoption by ECOWAS of a new Protocol in December 1999 attested to this development.[202] This Protocol empowers ECOWAS to undertake any form of intervention—including those covered by Article 53 UN Charter—without the prior authorisation of the UN. Although more will be said about this Protocol in Chapter 5, it suffices here to make certain observations. When asked by this writer why the Protocol was adopted by ECOWAS states despite the glaring fact that its operation would undermine the UN's primacy in collective security matters, the ECOWAS Legal Affairs Director responded that the countries in the sub-region did not have a modicum of faith in the UN to respond to any crisis in Africa.[203]

The fact that the UN did not respond to the Liberia crisis (1989–97) until about three years after the outbreak of the conflict, and only *after* ECOWAS had deployed its Monitoring Group, ECOMOG, did not bode

[200] Secretary-General Boutros-Boutros Ghali, *Agenda for Peace*, UN Doc A/47/277-S/24111 of 17 June 1992.

[201] See Koskeniemmi; Elihu Lauterpacht, above notes 33 and 148 respectively.

[202] For the text and commentary on the Protocol relating to Mechanism for Conflict Prevention, Management, Resolution, Peace-Keeping and Security, see Ademola Abass, 'The New Collective Security Mechanism of ECOWAS: Innovations and Problems' (2000) 5(2) *Journal of Conflict and Security Law* 211–59 (treaty annexed).

[203] This interview took place during an internship carried out at the ECOWAS Headquarters in Abuja, Nigeria, between March 22 and April 5 2000.

well for UN collective security in Africa. On 2 March 2001, the Assembly of Heads of State and Government (AHSG) of the Organisation of African Unity (OAU) established the African Union (AU), a new continental organisation that replaced the OAU, and imbued it with powers to undertake all action without deference to the Security Council.[204] As we shall see in Chapter 5, the AU Constitutive Act[205] empowers the Organisation to undertake enforcement action on its own authority.[206] This new authority seems to counter-balance the UN collective security activities in Africa.

Similarly, Europe appears to have borrowed a leaf from Africa in this regard. In December 2000, member states of the Europe Union (EU) meeting in Brussels proposed the establishment of the Rapid Reaction Force (RRF) as a collective security mechanism.[207] This force will undertake collective security actions 'where NATO as a whole is not engaged to launch and then to conduct EU-led military operations in response to international crises.'[208] The RRF would have the capacity to deploy between 50,000–60,000 troops by 2003. It is important to note a few points on the proposed force. First, it was made clear that 'NATO remains the foundation of the collective defence of its members, and will continue to have an important role in crisis management.' Second, it stated that '[t]hese forces should be self-sustaining with necessary command, control and intelligence capabilities.'[209]

Predictably NATO will be wary in future about responding in circumstances where none of its members has been attacked. Therefore, the new mechanism can be seen as an alternative. The UN's relevance in this hemisphere might decline further since between NATO and the RRF it should be expected that an effective mechanism for tackling all acts of aggressions or other peace threatening situations in Europe will be found.

The Total Collapse of the UN Collective Security System It may seem too drastic to suggest that the ultimate consequence of illegitimate functioning of the Security Council is the probable collapse of the whole UN collective security system. Nevertheless, there has been some indication that such a consequence is not unthinkable. Writing on the possibility of massive withdrawal of member states from the UN, Thomas Franck argued that if the abuse of powers by the Security Council continues, then there is a real

[204] For analysis see Ademola Abass above note 123.

[205] For analysis, see Ademola Abass and Mashood Baderin, 'Towards Effective Collective Security and Human Rights in Africa: An Assessment of the Constitutive Act of the African Union', (2002/1) XLIX *Netherlands International Law Review* 1.

[206] Art 4.

[207] See The Presidency Report to the Helsinki European Council on 'Strengthening the Common European Policy on Security and Defence and on "Non-Military Crisis Management"', Annex IV. See http://europa.eu.int/council/off/conclu/dec/99/dec99_en.htm#security.

[208] *Ibid*, 28 of 51.

[209] *Ibid*, 30 of 51.

possibility of over the next few years 30 or 40 states might walk out of the United Nations.[210]

Franck's suggestion may be a little too pessimistic. However, even if states do not commit an *en masse* withdrawal from the UN, his warning is by no means a 'strained reading of the situation' as Paul Szasz suggested.[211]

Whether states withdraw *en masse* from the UN or decide to embark upon a gradual relegation of their responsibility, commitment and allegiance to the organisation, the same effect may eventually result. UN collective security will suffer constant erosion. States' trust in the UN will definitely wane. Morale will become low. A relocation of states' trust and confidence in regional organisations will surely hasten the process of collapse of the UN collective security system. African states, which have notably received the least attention from the Security Council, may become uninterested in contributing to troops in respect of non-African conflicts. The Security Council may adopt resolutions, but most states will be reluctant to provide it with troops necessary to implement its decisions. The Security Council will obligate states under Article 25, but they may capitalise on the non-fulfilment of Article 43 agreement as reasons for non-compliance. Going it alone by the permanent members of the Security Council is not a guarantee of success. Further discontent among the five permanent members must be expected in the future. As some of the permanent members' appetite for illegitimacy grows so also will the insecurity of the others increase. Affected by the unresponsiveness, disdain and indifference of most countries, UN collective security faces an uncertain future.

3.6. CONCLUSION

Centralised collective security embodied by Chapter VII of the UN Charter has failed to materialise for several reasons that have been explored. This failure, as seen in our analysis, is due to serious problems with the working of the Security Council itself, the custodian of the Charter's collective security system.

By delegating its enforcement powers to states acting individually or under the auspices of regional arrangements, the Security Council attempted to circumvent the impact of the veto on collective security. However, the absence of in-built control mechanisms in enabling resolutions means that the Security Council cannot supervise states when they implement the mandate it entrusts to them.

[210] See Paul Szasz in Delbrück's *Allocation* above note 31 at 68–69.
[211] *Ibid.*

Furthermore, where the main actors to whom the Security Council delegates collective powers are permanent members of the Security Council, there is always a problem with guiding the guardian. This problem was noticeable in the Korean and Iraq-Kuwait crises. Decentralised enforcement action has thus not been a very effective replacement for centralised collective security.

As this chapter has demonstrated, we cannot determine the loss of legitimacy by the Security Council from evidence gained mainly from populist calls for reform of the Security Council or mere disenchantment with its handling of isolated cases. Certainly, there is always room for states to disagree with particular acts of the Security Council. As Andrew Boyd noted, 'the first time the tool is used there are almost bound to be complaints, from one quarter or another, that it is bent sinisterly'.[212] However, if the tool is used repeatedly in the same manner, this may suggest that there is a genuine case for the complaints made by certain sections of the community which think the tool is almost invariably bent sinisterly towards them.

As already hinted, regional organisations have started responding to the failure or ineffectiveness of collective security administered by the Security Council. Before dealing with the new developments in regional collective security system (Chapter 5), it is necessary to discuss the basis for regional organisations' possessing collective security powers conferred on the Security Council under Article 24(1) of the UN Charter. The discussion in the next chapter thus follows naturally from the analysis of the breakdown of the system in Chapters VII and VIII as already discussed.

[212] Andrew Boyd, above note 160 at 222.

4

Regional Organisations and Residual Responsibility for Collective Security

INTRODUCTION

WHAT HAPPENS WHEN the collective security system entrusted to the Security Council under Chapter VII fails?

The ultimate beneficiaries of Charter collective security are states, which in 1945 conferred on the Security Council the competence to take collective actions on their behalf. However, when the Charter was being negotiated, it was envisaged that situations might arise whereby the Security Council might not be able to maintain international peace and security. Therefore, the Charter contains certain mechanisms or remedies designed to protect states in default of Security Council action.

As the analyses in chapters 2 and 3 revealed, various developments since 1945 have pushed the relevant provisions of the Charter beyond their previous limits. The hope and attempts of making collective action more efficient under the Security Council's administration after the Cold War continue to prove elusive. The terrorist attacks on the US in 2001 and the conflict in Iraq (2003) are latest reminders that the Charter provisions on collective security, as well as its protective mechanisms, particularly Article 51, fall short of what can guarantee an effective collective security system in the contemporary world order.

This chapter examines whether regional organisations could play a residual role for the maintenance of peace and security in situations where the Security Council fails to act or is prevented from doing so, and the Charter protections themselves fail to protect states. The *raison d'être* of this inquiry is the recurring claim of regional organisations that they are naturally responsible for the maintenance of peace and security within their domains,[1] and that in doing so, they do not have to await Security Council approval.[2]

[1] ECOWAS and AU for instance. See A/Dec 9/5/90, 30 May 1990; *First Session of the Community Standing Mediation Committee* Decision A/Dec 3/8/90.

[2] See ECOWAS' justification for the adoption of its new Protocol for Collective Security in Ademola Abass, 'The New Collective Security Mechanism of ECOWAS: Innovations and Problems', (2000) 5(2) *Journal of Conflict and Security Law* 211–59 (treaty annexed).

This claim entails two issues. First, regional organisations now regard themselves as heirs apparent to the Security Council's responsibility for the maintenance of peace and security in their regions, once circumstances adjudged by them warrant their intervention.[3] Second, regional organisations' practice since the end of the Cold War shows that they no longer condition their intervention in members' conflicts on the failure or decline by the Security Council to mediate in such conflicts. Thus, as will be seen in the next chapter, regional organisations have intervened in conflicts even before the Security Council has had any chance to consider the matter.[4]

Yet, the Charter does not explicitly nominate any organ(s) of the UN or other international organisations for that matter to subrogate the Security Council whenever it fails to act, although it describes the Security Council's competence over peace and security as only *primary*. Therefore, the legality of such practice as developed by regional organisations after the Cold War, whereby they authorise collective security measures, like enforcement action, on the authority of their own treaties, can only be constructed on valid normative principles. To establish such principles, this chapter inquires into how states exercised collective security powers (if there were any) before the advent of the UN. By doing this, it seeks to determine the exact nature of the power which states (a) possessed before the advent of the UN, (b) conferred on the Security Council in 1945, and consider (c) whether such powers revert to regional organisations through states.[5]

Given that the Charter contains provisions designed to protect states in situations where collective security is not activated, a consideration of the adequacy or suitability of such in-built mechanisms is necessary. This assessment is to serve as a foundation for a subsequent construct of regional organisations' residual role proposed in this chapter.

This chapter does not go into an examination of whether the General Assembly or any other organ of the UN possesses residual responsibility for the maintenance of international peace and security.[6] Whether the

[3] For a discussion of such circumstances, see chapter 5.

[4] An example of this is the intervention of ECOWAS in the conflict in Cote d'Ivoire in September 2002.

[5] See generally J Delbrück (ed), *Allocation of law Enforcement Authority in the International System: Proceedings of an International Symposium of the Kiel Institute of International Law, March 23 to 25, 1994* (Berlin, Duncker & Humblot, 1995) 39 at 46 (hereafter Delbrück's *Allocation*); Bruno Simma (ed), *The Charter of the United Nations: A Commentary* (Oxford, Oxford University Press, 1st edn, 1994) 404 (hereafter Simma's *Commentary*); Bruno Simma (ed), *The Charter of the United Nations: A Commentary*, (Oxford, Oxford University Press, 2002), vol 2, 807 *et seq*.

[6] Nor do we tackle the question whether in its action on behalf of the international community the Security Council is accountable to states individually or through the General Assembly. For a discussion of this see Dan Sarooshi, *The United Nations and the Development of Collective Security: The Delegation by the UN Security Council of its Chapter VII Powers* (Oxford, Clarendon Press, 1999) 20 *et seq*; N D White, 'The Legality of Bombing in the Name of Humanity' (2000) 5(1) *Journal of Conflict and Security Law* 27 at 37 *et seq*; For analysis of this debate, see ND White, *Keeping the Peace* 2nd edn, (Manchester, Manchester University Press, 2nd edn, 1997) 150 *et seq*; Yoram Dinstein, below note 9, chapter 10.

General Assembly has or does not have a residual responsibility for peace and security, especially in terms of authorising the use of force, can now be regarded as moot following the non-utilisation of the *Uniting for Peace Resolution* for a similar purpose as during the 1950s and 60s or even in the present dispensation. In addition, the post-Cold War era has witnessed the Security Council rather than the General Assembly assuming responsibility for peacekeeping operations.[7] This means that the situation will hardly arise in the future whereby disagreement in the Security Council concerning whether or not to authorise enforcement action will prevent it from recommending or authorising peacekeeping operations.[8]

4.1. COLLECTIVE SECURITY: A GENERAL OVERVIEW

It is common for writers to refer to 'collective security' as connoting the exclusive power of the Security Council to use force in order to maintain peace and security.[9] Yet, this phrase is mentioned nowhere in the UN Charter. It is often suggested that there is only one type of collective security—the so-called *ideal* collective security—and that for a collective security system to be ideal, it must encompass all states in the world.[10] The term collective security is often used to distinguish between different types of

[7] See discussion in the last chapter.

[8] It was this sort of disagreement that prevented the Security Council from authorising enforcement action against North Korea when it attacked South Korea in 1950 and also disabled the Security Council during the Suez Canal conflict because the permanent Security Council members involved in the crisis, France and the United Kingdom, could not agree with other members of the Security Council as to how the conflict should be resolved.

[9] Although there is a voluminous literature on the theme of peace and security at large, on collective security, see specifically KP Saksena, *The United Nations and Collective Security: A Historical Analysis* (Delhi, DK Publishing House, 1974); John FL Ross *Neutrality and International Sanctions: Sweden, Switzerland and Collective Security* (New York, Praeger, 1989); George Downs (ed), *Collective Security Beyond the Cold War* (Michigan, The University of Michigan Press, 1994); Hans Kelsen, 'Collective Security and Collective Self Defence under the Charter of the United Nations' (1948) *American Journal of International Law* 783; Yoram Dinstein, *War, Aggression and Self Defence* (Cambridge, Cambridge University Press, 3rd edn, 2001); Van Alstyne and Richard Warner, *American Crisis Diplomacy: The Quest for Collective Security, 1918–1952*, (Stanford, Stanford University Press, 1952); Thomas G Weiss, *Collective Security in a Changing World* (Colorado, Lynne Rienner Publishers, 1993); Thomas G Weiss (ed), *Beyond UN Subcontracting: Task-Sharing with Regional Security Arrangements and Service-Providing NGOs* (London, Macmillan Press Ltd, 1998); JS Matthews, 'Redefining Security' (1989) 68 (2) *Foreign Affairs* 162; Edward C Luck, 'Whose Collective Security?' (1992) 15(2) *Washington Quarterly* 43; Stanley Hoffmann, 'Delusions of World Order' (1992) 39(7) *New York Review*, 38; Thomas G Weiss and James G Blight (eds), *The Suffering Grass: Superpowers and Regional Conflict in Southern Africa and the Caribbean Basin* (Boulder, Lynne Rienner, 1992); Ernst B Haas, 'The Collective Management of International Conflict, 1954–84', United Nations Institute for training research, *The United Nations and the Maintenance of International Peace and Security* (Dordrecht, Nijhoff, 1987).

[10] See MS Nious and PC Ordeshook, 'The Prospect for a New International Order Based On Collective Security' in George Downs (ed), *Collective Security Beyond the Cold War* (Michigan, The University of Michigan Press, 1994) 69.

security arrangements. Thus, a distinction is made between collective security arrangements and other types of arrangements such as the balance of power.[11] Questions frequently raised in the literature, concerning collective security include: what is collective security? When can an 'act' be deemed to be in the exercise of collective security powers? By whom or which body may such acts be undertaken? What is or must be the nature of an act that constitutes collective security? Can there be said to be an ideal collective security? What is the exact nature of the collective security ingrained in the UN Charter? What is *collective* about which *security*?

4.2. THE MEANING OF 'COLLECTIVE SECURITY'

Several writers have attempted to define 'collective security'. Approaches differ. 'Collective security' is sometimes defined from the perspective of the *historical agents* responsible for its regulation, such as the League of Nations or the UN. Elsewhere, definitions are based on ill-conceived, subjective notions—international community, collective interest, and security.[12] Certain difficulties attend these approaches. One is that they depend on external factors such as regulating *agents* like the UN or the League of Nations for validity. Another is that such approaches are based on understanding notions such as 'international community' and so on.

4.2.1. The 'Collectivity' of a Collective Security Action: The Period before the UN Charter

To say that an act is 'collective' one would naturally seem to mean that it has been performed by the totality, or the majority, of those who have the competence, legal or otherwise, to do so. A minor portion of all those involved in regulating collective security mechanism may take a 'collective' action on behalf of the rest. However, such actors must have been empowered to so act either by the constituent instrument of the society in question or by the totality of its membership. It is submitted that an unauthorised actor may undertake an action on behalf of others, without the initial concurrence or authority of those with the requisite competence to do so, provided that this act is subsequently adopted expressly or by

[11] Hans Kelsen, above note 9. But see Hans Kelsen, *The Law of the United Nations* (London, Stevens and Sons Limited, 1964), 923. See also ND White and Özlem Ülgen 'The Security Council and the Decentralised Military Option: Constitutionality and Function', (1997) XLIV (3) *Netherlands International Law Review* 378, at 383, (observing that 'one facet of a collective security organisation which distinguishes it from a defensive pact is that it is normally designed not merely to take defensive action, it can also enforce peace by removing not only the aggressor, but also situations that threaten the peace').

[12] See generally George Downs, above note 9.

necessary implication by the competent authority. By this method the erstwhile illegal and unilateral act becomes legal and collective through a process that can be described as legitimation.

Collective security pre-dated the UN Charter and the content of the pre-Charter collective security was much wider than that embodied by the Charter. Unfortunately, legal writers commonly assume that 'collective security' is synonymous with 'enforcement action', the specific term adopted by the Charter, and that collective security consists only in those actions ordained by the Security Council.[13] This assumption is misleading and underlines the legal construct of 'collective security' and the collective perception of how it works in practice.

The thrust of contemporary legal opinions is that 'collective security' depends upon a subjective, political decision by the Security Council and not just on *any* international body.[14] The correctness of this view is doubtful for several reasons, and challengeable on many fronts. As already noted, the Charter is silent on the term collective security. It does not explicitly decree that the maintenance of peace and security is an exclusive preserve of the Security Council. There is no doubt that Article 24(1) confers on the Security Council primary responsibility for the maintenance of international peace and security, and that under Chapter VII, only it may undertake enforcement action. Thus, even in the partially decentralised scheme of Chapter VIII, regional arrangements cannot undertake enforcement action except with the authorisation of the Security Council.[15]

Yet, the view that 'collective security' depends only on the Security Council obviously assumes that 'collective security' is the same thing as 'enforcement action'. Enforcement action can be defined as the deployment of the combined force of the international community for the purpose of enforcing international legal norms as accepted by the comity of nations.[16] As a Charter rule, *only* the Security Council may initiate enforcement action. An exception to this is where it delegates such powers to regional organisations under Chapter VIII or through other discretionary methods it may decide to adopt in the exercise of its power under Article 39 of the Charter.

[13] Sarooshi, above note 6, 14.

[14] See generally George Downs, above note 9.

[15] Klaus Dicke in Delbrück's *Allocation*, above note 5, 104.

[16] Morrison defines 'enforcement actions' as 'action which would itself be a violation of international law, if taken without either some special 'justification' or without the contemporaneous consent or acquiescence of the target state'. See Morrison in Delbrück's *Allocation*, above note 5, 43. This definition seems problematic in the opinion of this writer. An action cannot be 'enforcement' with the contemporaneous consent or acquiescence of a target state. To speak of a consensual enforcement action is contradictory in terms.

4.2.2. Collective Security and Enforcement Action: A Distinction

There are many differences between collective security and enforcement action despite attempts by writers to treat the terms as the same. Whereas enforcement action refers to the use of force in order to *restore* or *maintain* peace and security, collective security connotes both the *proactive* and *reactive* application of collective measures (which need not be of military nature) for the creation or preservation of peace and security. The difference between these two conceptions is of practical significance and carries serious legal implications.

Conceptually, collective security incorporates enforcement action. Insofar as the latter implies a *reactive* use of force, it constitutes only an element of collective security. For instance, pacific settlement, which does not involve the use of force to enforce peace, is another component of collective security, as are peace-building and peacekeeping. Unlike enforcement action, peacekeepers cannot use force to determine the outcome of a dispute.[17] They may only use force in self-defence. Yet, peacekeeping operations often include the imposition of collective measures intended to maintain the *status quo* between fighters or to secure a cease-fire agreement.[18] Whatever purpose such measures serve, they are never imposed against any of the parties. The same can be said of peace-building operations, which normally take place after the end of hostilities, in order to encourage warring factions to reconcile their differences.[19] While the Charter does not create these types of action by itself, they are widely regarded in general international law as legitimate components of collective security insofar as they are concerned with the preservation of peace and security by means concordant with Charter objectives.

Thus to speak of collective security as a 'system where a collective measure is taken *against* a member of a community that has violated a community-defined value' is truthful only to the extent that the definition adopts the wider term 'collective measure' as against the narrow term

[17] See Rosalyn Higgins, 'Peace and Security, Achievements and Failure' (1995) 6 *European Journal of International Law* 445; Elgin Clemons, 'No Peace to Keep: Six and Three-Quarters Peacekeepers' (1993) 26 *International Law and Politics* 107; Theodore C Sorensen, 'United States Policy on United Nations Peace-Keeping Operations' (1993) 18 *Yale Journal of International Law* 425; Stephen Chan, 'And What Do Peacekeeping Troops Do Apart from Burying the Dead, Then?' (1997) XIII(5) *International Relations* 27; White, *Keeping the Peace*, above note 6.

[18] An example of this is the imposition of an arms embargo on rebel factions in Liberia by ECOWAS and the UN. See Decision A/DEC.1/8/90 On the Ceasefire and Establishment of an ECOWAS Ceasefire Monitoring Group for Liberia, *First Session of the Community Standing Mediation Committee*, Banjul, 6–7 August 1990.

[19] The UN missions in Cambodia and Namibia are good examples of peace-building operations. See W Michael Reisman, 'Peacemaking' (1993) 18 *Yale Journal of International Law* 415.

enforcement action.[20] However, the definition is too restrictive to adequately represent the concept because by using 'against' it perceives collective security as being coterminous with enforcement action. Collective measures need not be *against* any of the parties to a conflict.

The definition of collective security offered by Ernst Haas seems to be the most useful in conceptualising collective security, especially within the context of the UN Charter. Haas regards collective security as the,

> Technique used by intergovernmental organizations to restrain the use of force among the members. It provides the norms and procedures for dealing with acts of aggression; it also includes the norms and procedures for inducing members to delay hostilities, norms and procedures summed up under the labels "pacific settlement of disputes". Finally [it] also comprises the organization's own ability to use force against a member if pacific settlement fails.[21]

The utility of this definition consists mainly in its incorporation of the diverse ingredients that make up a proper collective security system, a methodological approach not common in most legal writings on the subject.

First, the definition recognises that collective security is primarily concerned with the ability of an intergovernmental organisation to restrain the use of force by its own members.[22] The adoption of *intergovernmental* contrasts sharply with the more endemic conception of collective security as a province of *only* the Security Council (on behalf of the UN) and not just *any* intergovernmental organisation. The reference to *own* underscores the major distinction between collective security and defensive alliances whose primary task remains the repulsion of armed attacks against one or more of its member states.[23]

Second, Haas regards collective security as a much more commodious paradigm than enforcement action. By bringing pacific settlement of disputes (enshrined in Chapter VI of the Charter) within collective security, Haas's definition supports our earlier submission that collective security combines both reactive and preventive uses of force. Finally, the definition places pacific settlement at the *core* of collective security, with enforcement action coming to play only in the event of the failure of pacific settlement.

[20] Sarooshi, above note 6 at 5; See also Hendl K, 'Reflections on the Role, Functions and Procedures of the Security Council' (1987) 6 *Recueil des Cours*, 206 at 297 arguing, in part, that the use of force against an 'aggressor' is the core of a system of collective security (cited by Sarooshi, at fn 15).

[21] Ernst Haas, 'Collective Security and the Future International System' in Falk and Black (eds), *The Future of international Legal Order* (Princeton, Princeton University Press, 1969), 225.

[22] Cf Yoram Dinstein, 'Collective Security postulates the Institutionalization of the lawful use of force in the international community', above note 9 at 246, citing G Schwarzenberger and ED Brown, *A Manual of International Law* (Abingdon, Professional Books, 6th edn, 1976) at 153.

[23] See discussion in chapter 1.

It is contended that collective security is neither the prerogative nor the *domaine résérvé* of the Security Council.[24] To argue otherwise is not only to confuse the term with enforcement action, but also to extend the meaning of enforcement action beyond all acceptable legal limits. Enforcement action is typical of, but not coterminous with, collective security. Lest, it is to assert that the General Assembly cannot engage in collective security simply because it can only recommend enforcement action, or that when states undertake peacekeeping operations they are not performing collective security tasks since conceptually such operations do not include enforcement action.

4.2.3. The Benefit of a Broader Definition of Collective Security to Regional Organisations

Treaties adopted by regional organisations since the end of the Cold War have contained the phrase 'collective security' despite the absence of the term in the UN Charter. In some cases, such treaties detail the content of what these organisations believe to amount to collective security measures. These include the imposition of economic sanctions on recalcitrant states, the authorisation of inquiry and collection of information from member states, which may potentially lead to conflict. The explicit incorporation of such preventive measures into the ECOWAS 1999 Protocol[25] demonstrates that in the post-Cold War period, regional organisations regard their collective security functions as broader than the use of combined military force to preserve peace and security.

The advantage of liberally defining collective security is that it enables regional organisations to resort to such muscular activities as the imposition of economic sanctions in order to enforce peace without the authorisation of the Security Council.[26] Consequently, regional organisations potentially create a division between the use of military force (which is caught outright by Article 53(1) if undertaken without the authorisation of the Security Council), and economic sanctions (which they could use to achieve the same enforcement objectives, but without violating the Charter).

[24] See Niels Blokker, 'Is the Authorization Authorized? Powers and Practice of the UN Security Council to Authorize the Use of Force by 'Coalitions of the Able and Willing' (2000) 11(3) *European Journal of International Law* 541.

[25] See Ademola Abass, above note 2.

[26] See the imposition of sanctions on Iraq, ECOWAS member states on Liberian and Sierra Leone rebels and the OAS on Haiti, as examples. In all these cases, these sanctions were designed to force the targets to comply with either resolutions of the UN (in the case of Iraq) or concerned regional organisations (in cases of ECOWAS and the OAS). See David Cortright and George A Lopez, *The Sanctions Decade: Assessing UN Strategies in the 1990s* (Colorado, Lynne Rienner Publishers, 2000) for a complete record of the use of sanctions in the 1990s. See discussion in chapter 3.

4.3. STATES AND COLLECTIVE SECURITY BEFORE THE UN CHARTER

4.3.1. Collective Security and Bilateral and Multilateral Treaties

An earlier development in the law of treaties indicates the codification of rules empowering states to combine forces in order to prevent or repulse delinquent behaviours in the international community.[27]

The earliest recorded instance of such was the *Placaat*, a declaration issued by the Dutch government, in 1584, declaring all the ports of Flanders then remaining in the power of Spain to be blockaded.[28] The Dutch government conceived the blockade provided for by the *Placaat* as 'the right of siege on an unprecedented scale'.[29] The principles of the *Placaat* were later to be extended by treaties such as the 1655 *Anglo-French Treaty* which *prohibited commerce* of all kinds with towns and places 'besieged, blockaded or invested'.[30] This treaty, it is contended, qualifies as the first known international treaty on the use of economic measures as a means of collective security. The *Anglo-Swedish Treaty* of 1661, the *Dutch-Algerine Treaty* of 1662, the *Dutch-Swedish Treaty* of 1667, all concerned this issue in one form or the other and to different degrees.[31]

Although most of these treaties evolved in the context of war and the status of neutral states, they soon began to be put to a different use. Hugo Grotius, in his highly influential work in 1625, distinguished between blockade objects used only in war, and those that could indeed be applied in a period of peace. This distinction was not made by the *Placaat*.[32] A revised *Placaat* in 1630 enabled the Dutch authorities to arrest neutral ships sailing within any distance of an enemy's port, but which might have also *breached* the blockade.[33] More than half a century after the *Placaat*, the *Peace of Westphalia*,[34] was signed in 1648. This peace treaty has been credited with setting up a 'scheme for collective security',[35] forming the basis of

[27] Antonio Cassese, *International Law* (Oxford, Oxford University Press, 2001).

[28] 2 Twiss 247. By this instrument, the Dutch states-general 'made [the resolutions of the Placaat] known to all kings and nations whereby, they forbade all merchants to carry to the Spaniards provisions or any other goods whatsoever, under the penalty of being treated as enemies' quoting Grotius, *Hist De Rebus Belgicis*, 1.8, also cited by John Westlake *International Law, Part II, War* (Cambridge, Cambridge University Press, 1913), 199.

[29] Westlake, above note 28 at 256.

[30] Dumont, t 6, pt 2, 121, cited in Westlake, above note 28 at 260.

[31] For a full discussion of these treaties, see Westlake, above note 28 at 253–76.

[32] See Hugo Grotius, *De jure belli ac pacis*, 1. 3, c. 1, and 5, cited by Westlake above note 28, 257–58.

[33] See Robinson's *Collection Maritima*, 158, cited by Westlake, above note 28 at 259.

[34] See Saksena, above n 9 at 5 citing FL Schuman, *The Commonwealth of Man* (1952) 353. The *Treaty of Westphalia* had enjoined all the 'High Contracting parties to defend and protect all and every article of the peace against anyone . . . and to join the injured party, and assist him with counsel and force to repel the injury'.

[35] Cassese, above note 27 at 21.

states' relations in modern society.[36] The *Peace of Westphalia* consisted of two treaties: the Treaty of Münster and the Treaty of Osnabrück, signed in two different towns of Westphalia, but both forming 'an integrated whole'[37]. The Treaty of Münster provided that a state which had become a subject of threat to peace or any serious violation was not to resort to war until a three-year cooling-off period within which the transgressed state was to explore peaceful means of settling the dispute.[38] In the event of a failure to secure a pacific settlement, the injured state was entitled to commence a war and all the signatories to the treaty were to assist it by using force. The assisting states were also duty-bound to refrain from giving assistance to the offender or allow its troops to pass through their territories.[39]

The effect of the *Peace of Westphalia,* apart from concluding 'a most appalling war'[40] in Europe, was that it established a 'collective security system [which] hinged on the following notions: (i) a sweeping ban on the use of force; (ii) a prohibition on individual self-defence, except after the expiry of a long period; (iii) the duty of all States other than the victim of a wrong to act in collective self-defence'.[41]

The scheme of collective security established by the *Peace of Westphalia* was, however, never put into effect for reasons that included its ambitious nature and the fact that its tenets clashed with the predisposition of many of its signatories.[42] Nevertheless, the *Peace of Westphalia* introduced a collective security system to the international relations of states with rudiments that were to form the basis of the League of Nations in 1919, particularly with regard to the moratorium between the time a state is attacked and when it resorts to war.

The collective security thrust of the *Peace of Westphalia* was consolidated by the Treaty of Paris (the Holy Alliance) of 20 November 1815, establishing what became popularly known as the Concert of Europe. This treaty envisaged 'a system of collective security based on the agreement of the big Powers, designed to forestall or stifle any recurrence of Bonapartism, either in France or elsewhere.'[43] The Paris Treaty was originally intended to outlaw revolutionary movements, such that could overthrow monarchies in

[36] The Treaty of Peace, which concluded the ferocious war that started as a religious war, but snowballed into a contest for military hegemony amongst several European countries, was concluded in the Westphalian towns of Münster and Osnabrück. See text in C Parry (ed), *The Consolidated Treaty Series*, vol i at 198–269 and 319–56 (Dobbs Ferry, New York, Oceana Publications, 1969–86). See also Antonio Cassese, above note 27, 21.

[37] Cassese, above note 27, 21.

[38] Article 124.

[39] Article 3.

[40] Cassese, above note 27 at 21.

[41] *Ibid*, at 420, fn 4.

[42] *Ibid*.

[43] *Ibid*, 25.

Europe. The Concert of Europe strengthened this objective in 1820 by a protocol ratified by Austria, Russia, and Prussia.[44]

Unlike the *Peace of Westphalia*, the collective security provisions contained in the Treaty of Paris were applied twice in its history. These were in 1821 and 1823 when Austrian troops (dispatched to Naples and Turin) and the French troops (dispatched to Spain), on behalf of the Holy Alliance, suppressed liberal insurgents' attempts at independence.[45]

The incident of states coming together and using both military and non-military force to *preserve* peace or correct international anomalies permeate state practice from antiquity. According to Oppenheim this power was either 'universally recognised by custom . . . or laid down by law-making treaties'.[46] The first recorded incident of naval blockade occurred in 1827 when Great Britain, France and Russia declared a blockade against a coast which was to later belong to the Kingdom of Greece.[47] Afterwards, in 1831 Great Britain and France imposed a pacific blockade against the Netherlands, Great Britain against Grenada in 1837, and France against Portugal in 1831, to mention but a few instances.[48]

There is a conclusion to draw from the above account. Even if the collective security system established by such treaties as the *Peace of Westphalia* had failed to materialise, and, as Antonio Cassese put it, became a 'dead letter',[49] they clearly confirm that states possessed collective security powers before the advent of the UN. The fact that the Concert of Europe applied the Treaty of Paris supports the position taken by this writer that collective security, in terms of enforcement action and pacific settlement of international disputes, predated both the League of Nations and the UN.

4.3.2. Regionalisation of Collective Security before the UN Charter

Several precursors of the UN, especially the Inter-American System, provided in their constitutive instruments for fairly comprehensive systems of collective security. The earliest indication of the wider development of collective security on a regional basis could be said to have started with the so-called Monroe Doctrine of the United States of America.[50] In his mes-

44 *Ibid.*

45 *Ibid.*

46 L Oppenheim, *International Law: A Treatise*, 7th edition, H Lauterpacht (ed) (1948).

47 See Westlake, above note 28, 11.

48 For comprehensive reviews of these cases, see Hogan, *Pacific Blockade*, 88, cited in Westlake, above note 28, 12.

49 Cassese, above note 27 at 21.

50 Post 1945, the response of the Eastern Bloc, led by the Soviet Union, to the Monroe Doctrine was the Brezhnev Doctrine. On this doctrine, see John Norton Moore and Robert F Turner *International Law and the Brezhnev Doctrine* (Lanham, University Press of America, 1987).

sage to Congress on 2 December 1823, President Monroe declared that American States would intervene in any action from Europe that was likely to undermine the American continent or the independence of South American republics. The *Montevideo Conference* of 1933 sought to *preserve* peace by providing for the doctrine of non-intervention amongst American States. In 1936, the *Convention for the Maintenance, Preservation and Reestablishment of Peace,*[51] became perhaps the first modern treaty on collective security insofar as it dealt with the question of *preservation* of peace.[52]

The inroads made by these conventions were further consolidated by subsequent agreements, such as the 1938 *Declaration of Lima* and the *Resolutions of Habana* 1940 by which American States affirmed the principles of Monroe Doctrine 'against all foreign intervention or activity that may threaten them'.[53] The convergence of these early conventions was reflected in *the Bogota Pact*, which became the first Charter of the Organisation of American States (OAS) in 1948.[54] The OAS Charter had used the phrase 'collective security'[55] thus becoming the first international organisation to do so. The same term is contained in all its amending protocols.[56]

The observation to make here is that the adoption of the term 'collective security' by the OAS Charter, and its subsequent protocols, was not an accident of drafting. It was a culmination of gradually evolved practice dating back to at least more than half a century in the Americas before the UN was conceived. Indeed, it was this constant practice by American States that motivated them to begin to devise similar systems, although one under a much broader organisation, during the Second World War. To then argue that states did not possess collective security power (or as writers normally put it, enforcement power) before the emergence of the UN is to ignore the significance of treaty law, *opinio juris* and state practice before the advent of the UN.

[51] *See International Conference of American States*, vol II, p 188; (1934) 28 *American Journal of International Law* (Supp) 75.

[52] For a general comprehensive review of the evolution of the Inter-American System, see Charles G Fenwick, 'The Inter-American Regional System: Fifty Years of Progress' (1956) 50 *American Journal of International Law* 19.

[53] *Ibid*, at 21–22.

[54] As amended by the Protocol of Amendment to the Organisation of American States 'Protocol of Buenos Aires', signed on February 27, 1967 at the Third Inter-American Conference; Protocol of Amendment 'Cartagena Protocol' signed at Indias de Cartagena, approved on 5 December 1985 by the Fourteenth Special Session of the General Assembly; Protocol of Amendment to the OAS Charter Protocol of Washington, approved by the Sixteenth Special Session of the General Assembly 14 December 1992; and the Protocol of Amendment of the OAS Charter 'Protocol of Managua' adopted at the Nineteenth Special Session of the General Assembly 10 June 1993. OES/Ser X/11 (English) Treaty Series No 61. See also (1986) 25 *International Legal Materials* 529; General Assembly Document OEA/Ser P AG/doc 16 (XIV-E/85) rev 2, Feb 26, 1986.

[55] See Chapter VI of the OAS Charter, especially Arts 28 and 29.

[56] Above note 54.

4.4. COLLECTIVE SECURITY AND CONTEMPORARY INTERNATIONAL LAW

4.4.1. The League of Nations and the Kellogg-Briand Pact

The idea of a universal collective security system first emerged in the middle of the First World War. US President Woodrow Wilson pioneered the concept of universal collective security in the modern day context. In expressing support for the *League Enforcement Peace Plan* in 1916, the President enthused that 'the world is now upon the eve of a great consummation when some common force will be brought into existence . . . when coercion will be summoned not to the service of political ambition or selfish hostility, but to the service of a *common* order, a *common* justice, and a *common* peace'.[57]

The Wilsonian notion of collective security was a radical departure from the pre-World War I idea of security or the limited Kellogg-Briand Pact of 1928[58] which, although it attempted to extend the restriction placed on the use of force by the League, did not quite succeed. As rightly noted elsewhere,[59] before the First World War the idea of global security was based on the highly precarious notion of balance of power, having minimal deterrent effect. The notion of global security predominant during that period was that one set of the world's greatest military powers would maintain peace by balancing its powers against another set. In Wilsonian terms, this system is a 'disentangling alliance—the alliance disentangle the peoples of the world from those combinations in which they seek their own separate and private interests.'[60]

In reality, there is nothing *collective* about balance of power systems since they are not concerned with repelling aggression through collective action but by a handful of powerful states. Its objective is merely to serve as a visual deterrent in a more or less anarchical world. What President Wilson proposed instead was 'a single, overwhelming, powerful group of nations who shall be the trustee of peace of the world.'[61]

Unfortunately, President Wilson's idea for a common peace fell through at the Paris deliberations that led to the emergence of the League Covenant. 'Everyone wanted a strong League of Nations to guarantee a

[57] See Ray S Baker and WE Dodd (eds), *The Public Papers of Woodrow Wilson, New Democracy, II*, 186–87.

[58] General Treaty for Renunciation of War as an Instrument of National Policy (Kellogg Briand Pact of Paris), 1928, 94 *League of Nations Treaty Series* 57; Dinstein, above note 9, chapter 4.

[59] See Inis Claude, Jr, *Power and International Relations* (New York, 1962), 11.

[60] Woodrow Wilson, cited in James Brown Scott (ed), *President Wilson's Foreign Policy* (New York, Oxford University Press, 1981), 191. Also cited in KP Saksena, above note 9 at 9.

[61] See Baker and Dodd (eds), above note 57 at 343, cited in Saksena, above note 9 at 9.

treaty in which each first got what he wanted.'[62] The notion of the League interfering with national policies of member states was rejected outright by all. France's proposal for an international police force was rejected[63] and Britain preferred the sustenance of the old balance of power to fresh military commitments.[64] Paradoxically, the death knell of the Wilsonian concept of collective security was tolled by the American Congress.[65] Thus, while it could be said that in theory the League of Nations established the first regime of global collective security, several well-known factors militated against its practical utility.[66]

The contribution of the Kellogg-Briand Pact of 1928[67] to the emergence of collective security in the modern context, or more specifically, on the international law prohibiting the use of force by states, cannot be overlooked. Article II of the Kellogg-Briand Pact provided that 'the settlement or solution of all disputes or conflict or conflicts of whatever nature or of whatever origin they may be, which may arise among them, shall never be sought except by pacific means'.

The Kellogg-Briand Pact was significant as it, *prima facie*, became the first major attempt to prohibit the use of force by all states in resolving their disputes. As is widely known, the League Covenant did not totally prohibit the use of force by states. It only created a reprieve, a sort of cooling off period in which states were not supposed to use force to repel an attack for a given period of time.[68] This was to enable the League Council or the Permanent Court of International Justice (PCIJ) to undertake the necessary actions to address a dispute submitted to it by contentious parties. Thus, provided states complied with the three-month moratorium required by the Covenant, any subsequent recourse to war or other forms of armed reprisal by the restrained state was legal. Thus, the Kellogg-Briand Pact was a remarkable improvement on the League Covenant in the sense that it did not afford states any opportunity to resort to war as the League did.

[62] See Ray Stannard Baker, *What Wilson did in Paris* (New York, Harper & Brothers, 1992), 69.

[63] Miller, *The Drafting of the Covenant*, (New York, GP Putnam, 1928).

[64] *Ibid*.

[65] See Saksena, above note 9 at 12.

[66] Akehurst's *Modern Introduction to International Law* (P Malanczuk, ed,) (New York, Routledge, 1997) 25 *et seq*.

[67] The General Treaty for the Renunciation of War as an Instrument of National Policy, 27 August 1928, 94 *League of Nations Treaty Series*, 57. See Julius Stone, *Legal Controls of International Conflicts: A Treatise on the Dynamics of Disputes—and War—Law* (London, Stevens & Sons, 1954) 324.

[68] In this connection, the Covenant of the League of Nations in Arts 12, 13, and 15 only provided states with a 'cooling-off period of three months'. This idea of 'cooling off' was probably borrowed by the drafters of the Covenant from the Bryan Treaties, containing a provision on 'procrastination'. See Julius Stone, above note 67 at 167.

However, although it denounced force, the Kellogg-Briand Pact did not establish a collective security regime, unlike the League of Nations. There were no institutional organs or structures, such as the League Council or the Security Council, to implement its objectives. There were no provisions for sanctions against its breachers.[69] No formal mechanisms existed for settling disputes amongst its signatories.

The Kellogg-Briand Pact was weakened by several factors. Its major sponsors, especially the United States and Britain, expressly excluded its application to their areas of influence in the world.[70] In addition, writers have questioned the legal character of the Pact on the basis that it only exerts moral pressure on its signatories not to resort to war.[71] There are also no provisions in the Pact regulating the use of self-defence by states in case of attacks.[72] Nor did the Kellogg-Briand Pact recognise the role to be played by regional organisations such as was recognised, although to a limited extent, by Article 21 of the League Covenant, and Chapter VIII of the UN Charter. Without these salient features, a security arrangement cannot be regarded as a collective security system.

The Pact prohibited war, but not the use of force. Many writers hold the view that the use of force by states survived, at least in part, the Kellogg-Briand Pact.[73] Such writers argued that states retained the right to resort to reprisals despite the Pact. Other writers are more sceptical about this position. Professor Brownlie noted that the Pact certainly prohibited war as a mode of settlement.[74] Although Professor Brownlie did not go as far as confirm that reprisal survived Kellogg-Briand Pact, he did agree that the 'controversy as to whether the Covenant and the Pact prohibited reprisals indicated that their status as measures of self-help was far from secure . . . [and that] unambiguous prohibition of forcible reprisals was finally accomplished by the Charter of the United Nations'.[75] He indeed conceded that 'between the appearance of the Kellogg-Briand Pact and the outbreak of war in 1939 a vast body of state practice had . . . created customary rules restricting resort to force which negatived the assumptions of those who drafted the League Covenant'.[76]

69 It has however been argued that this does not make the Pact ineffective as 'it is not unusual for international treaties to provide for no sanctions in case of violations of their terms'. See Constantine Antonopolous, *The Unilateral use of force by States in International Law* (Athens, Ant N Sakkloulas Publishers, 1997) 21.

70 Denys Myers, *Origin and Conclusions of the Paris Pact and the Renunciation of War* (New York, Garland Publishers, 1972).

71 But see Ian Brownlie, *International Law and the Use of Force by States* (Oxford, Clarendon Press, 1963) 83.

72 Hindmarsh, *Force in Peace*, (1933), 124, 167–68. See also *Dissenting Opinion of Judge Pal in the Trial of War Criminals in the Far East*, (1956), 37, *et seq*.

73 Cassese, above note 27 at 33. See also Keller, *Die nichtkriegeriesche militärische Gewaltmanahme* (Berlin, 1934); Bustamante y Sirven, *Droit international public*, iv. 97 *et seq*.

74 Brownlie, above note 71 at 218.

75 *Ibid*, at 222 *et seq*.

76 *Ibid*, at 218.

It is submitted that the customary right of states to use force survived the Kellogg-Briand Pact, if not in its entirety, in the form of use of force that falls short of war. It is true, as Professor Brownlie has argued, that 'if forcible reprisals were taken against a state which was prepared to regard the action as creating a formal state of war they failed in their object and might lead to a serious conflict'.[77] However, the mere possibility of such characterisation by a belligerent would not obliterate the fine distinction between the term war, used by the Pact, and lesser military actions, such as reprisals. Hence Julius Stone noted that;

> [u]nless the terms of the Pact be a dead letter . . . this Pact narrowed the field for the exercise of forcible or coercive procedures to circumstances not amounting to a dispute or conflict, or to cases in which the application of these measures was not designed to settle or resolve a dispute or conflict, but had some milder objective.[78]

Even in its prohibition of war, Antonio Cassese argued that the Pact 'was unable to supplant the customary rule authorizing war, in that it did not turn into a customary rule abrogating the previous one'.[79] The fact that the UN Charter adopted the phrase 'use of force', instead of the term 'war' found in the Pact would seem to vindicate the view that customary right to resort to milder forms of military actions survived the Kellogg-Briand Pact or, *de minimis*, secured the controversy surrounding the subject.

4.4.2. The UN Charter and Collective Security

In the context of the UN Charter, the Wilsonian concept of collective security was embodied by the two different views held by Second World War US President, Frank Roosevelt, and his Secretary of State, Cordell Hull.

In Hull's view, only through the establishment of a global organisation, comprising all states, might peace and security be maintained throughout the world.[80] This coincided with the approach of President Roosevelt. Roosevelt, however, saw little political wisdom in establishing the kind of partnership suggested by Hull, between the strong and weak states, which were in no position to defend themselves against powerful aggressions. Instead of entrusting the collective security system to the hands of both the strong and weak states, Roosevelt proposed a system of trusteeship in which all powers would be given to the former who would then guarantee security of the latter who would be disarmed.[81]

[77] Brownlie, above note 71 at 220.
[78] Julius Stone, above note 67, at 286.
[79] Above note 27 at 34
[80] Ruth B Russell, *A History of the United Nations Charter: The Role of the United States 1940–1945* (Washington, DC, The Brookings Institution, 1958) 2.
[81] *Ibid.*

Roosevelt's and Hull's ideas juxtaposed with those of the British wartime Prime Minister, Winston Churchill. Churchill believed strongly in the organisation of collective security around regional security systems. According to him, 'it was only the countries whose interests were directly affected by a dispute who could be expected to apply themselves with sufficient vigour to secure a settlement' which, however, would still be subject to the World Council of the League.[82]

The original conception of an ideal collective security system suggested by Hull differs significantly from how the authors of the UN Charter eventually expressed themselves in Chapter VII. Whereas Hull had envisioned a system whereby all states, powerful or weak, would jointly operate the machinery for international peace and security, the resultant collective security of the Charter vested security powers almost exclusively in the powerful states, while at the same time providing a margin of decentralisation in Chapter VIII.

The emergence of the UN Charter in 1945 settled, once and for all, doubts about the possibility of establishing a universal collective security for the world community. In addition, many adjunct issues, such as the collectivity of an action, the competent authority to undertake collective security measures, and the nature of a collective measure, to mention but a few of the queries associated with collective security, seemed to have finally been laid to rest.

Furthermore, the old debate about whether states possessed police powers before the advent of the Charter could also be said to temporarily have remained only of academic interest upon the advent of the Charter. The Charter codified both the undoubted customary right of self-defence of states and attempted to resolve the controversy about international police power by speaking to the collective powers of states in several of its provisions. Hence, the rules governing collective security run through Article 24, Chapters VI, VII and VIII of the UN Charter.

However, despite the bold intervention by the UN Charter, especially in the areas of the use of collective police force by states, and the creative contribution of Article 2(4) to the law of use of force, old problems about collective security have resurfaced and new ones have emerged. The debate as to whether states possessed police powers in international law has revived. The exact impact of Article 24(1) provision on states' police power continues to elicit controversial responses from legal writers.[83]

[82] *Ibid*, at 105.

[83] See generally Delbrück's *Allocation*, above note 5, 15; Simma's *Commentary* above note 5 at 404.

4.5. COLLECTIVE SECURITY AND ARTICLE 24 OF THE CHARTER

Article 24(1) provides that:

> In order to ensure prompt and effective action by the United Nations, its Members confer on the Security Council primary responsibility for the maintenance of international peace and security, and agree that in carrying out its duties under this responsibility the Security Council acts on their behalf.

This provision embodies the vision of UN collective security. It not only designates the Security Council as possessing a primary responsibility for the maintenance of international peace and security, but also spells out the *nature* of the relationship this article creates between the Security Council and states. The article also declares that states 'confer' the responsibility on the Security Council.

Interpreting Article 24(1) literally, the relationship between the Security Council and the founding states is much akin to the one between principal and agent in ordinary legal parlance. This is because by endowing the Security Council with certain responsibilities, states designated it to act on *their* behalf although based on certain enumerated conditions. The only difference between the transaction under Article 24(1) and a typical agency relationship would appear to be that, whereas in an ordinary transaction an agent *cannot always* presume the principal's express or implied authority, the second part of Article 24(1) entails a presumption that the Security Council *represents* states at all times, provided it acts in furtherance of the responsibility so conferred on it.[84] In this way, the Security Council does not need to always seek recourse to states each time it wishes to act on their behalf. Both future express and implied authorisation of states required by the Security Council to function on their behalf could be said to have been secured once and for all in 1945.

Despite the relative precision of Article 24(1), a literal construction of the transaction between States and Security Council under that article could render the Security Council ineffective in practice. It would mean that states could collectively withdraw their authority from the Security Council at a future date, as may a principal from an agent who has breached a term of the agency agreement.[85] In addition, it may mean that

[84] The fact that Art 25 provides that 'The Members of the United Nations agree to accept and carry out the decisions of the Security Council in accordance with the present Charter' supports the contention by this writer that Art 24(1) avoids the need for the Security Council to secure states' authorisation whenever it wants to act on their behalf. Hence, they agree in advance to implement the Security Council's decisions for as long as they conform to the Charter, a caveat that must be understood to incorporate the terms on the basis of which states conferred the primary responsibility on the Security Council. But see Hans Kelsen above note 11 at 280 describing the formula of Art 25 as motivated by the sovereignty-dogma.

[85] On accountability see Sarooshi, above note 6.

the Security Council shall be accountable to states when it acts on their behalf, as agents do to their principals, and could be subject to penalty by states, just as a principal could discipline an erring agent either by curtailing his authority or totally divesting him of such altogether.

In the *Reparation for Injuries* case, the ICJ gave a clear indication as to the conception of the nature of the responsibility entrusted to the Organisation (and by extension, its organs) by the founders of the UN. Although the Court's advisory opinion was in respect to the legal personality of the UN, the Court held, in a clear but indirect reference to Article 24(1), that

> It [the UN] is at present the supreme type of international organization . . . It must be acknowledged that its members, by entrusting certain functions to it, with the attendant duties and responsibilities, have clothed it with the competence required to enable those functions to be effectively discharged.[86]

It must be pointed out that while the Court referred to the 'entrusting' of certain functions to the UN by its members, it also mentioned that the UN has 'attendant duties and responsibilities'. However, the Court did not say what should happen to the functions entrusted to the Security Council by states, should it fail to discharge the attendant duties and responsibilities.

From this construction of Article 24(1), three issues can be identified as constituting major concerns to international lawyers. First, on what authority does the Security Council possess its powers under Article 24(1)? Second, to which body may the Security Council be accountable for the use of that power? Third, if the Security Council is only conferred primary responsibility over those powers, which body retains residual responsibility? While the analysis below deals with the first and third issues, matters of accountability of the Security Council goes beyond the scope of this book.

4.5.1. Authority of the Security Council's Collective Security Powers

In order to determine whether states possess residual responsibility for the maintenance of international peace and security under Article 24(1), the first question to be asked is: by what authority is the Security Council conferred with such powers under Article 24(1)?

There are two contending views on this issue. According to one perspective, states did not possess police powers (a traditional equivalence of the power to maintain international peace and security under Article 24(1)) before the creation of the UN. As such, they could not claim the residuary of what they did not initially retain.[87]

[86] ICJ Reports (1949), 174, 182.

[87] Proponents of this view include Delbrück (Simma's *Commentary*, above note 5, 397–406, at 404); Hans Kelsen (above note 11 at 280); In the context of this debate, 'police power' is analogous to 'enforcement action' which states delegated to the UN Security Council in 1945.

As Delbrück argues, 'an interpretation of 24(1) which is based on the premise of a delegation by the members states of the powers granted to the SC under this provision cannot be upheld. The SC is an organ of the UN and therefore derives its powers from the UN Charter itself'.[88] Thus, as an organ of the UN, the 'SC acts on behalf of the Organization and not on behalf of individual member states. Accordingly, its actions and decisions are attributed to the UN Organization as a whole and not to individual members'.[89] This view, which we shall refer to as the 'absolute' theory, had earlier been proposed by Kelsen. Kelsen argued that the provision of Article 24(1) according to which member states 'agree that in carrying out its duties under this responsibility, the Security Council acts on their behalf'[90] is legally erroneous and superfluous. Dahm concurred to this view although, unlike Kelsen, he accepted the hierarchisation of the organs of the UN.[91]

Despite the position taken by Kelsen, Delbrück, Dahm, and other writers[92] other commentators argue the opposite. Degni-Segui,[93] for instance, contends that it was states that delegated the powers to maintain international peace and security to the Security Council. Proposing the basis of his thesis, in which he agrees with Professor Virally,[94] Degni-Segui argues that:

> Après avoir conféré au Conseil de sécurité la responsibilité principale du maintien de la paix, les Etats membres de l'Organisation prennent soin de spécifier qu'ils conviennent qu'en s'acquittant de sa tâche celui-ci "agit en leur nom". Cette disposition contient l'affirmation d'une véritable délégation de "pouvoirs" consentie par les Etats. Elle appelle des observations portant aussi bien sur l'objet que sur le bénéficiaé de la délégation.
>
> L'objet de la délégation ne semble pas a priori poser probléme. A s'entenir à la lettre du texte, c'est la fonction primordiale du maintien de la paix qui est transféréé de la sphère de competénce de chacun des Etats membres à celle du Conseil de sécurité. Cette fonction est transmise avec les pouvoirs y afférents. Cela revient à dire qu'il s'agit en fait d'une délégation de pouvoirs. Mais en poussant l'analyse plus loin l'on n'aura aucune peine à découvrir que la délégation porte en définitive sur la souveraineté. La fonction du maintien de la paix constitue, en effet, une prérogative de puissance publique, qui participe de la

It is the power by means of which a group of states could use collective force (thought to be military force) to correct an international wrong committed by another state.

[88] Simma's *Commentary*, above note 5 at 404.

[89] *Ibid.*

[90] Hans Kelsen, above note 11 at 281, also quoted by Delbrück in Simma's *Commentary*, above note 5 at 404.

[91] Dahm, G, *Völkerrecht*, ii (1961), cited by Delbrück in Simma's *Commentary* above note 5 at 404 fn 35.

[92] See also White, 'Legality of bombing' above note 6, 27 at 36–39.

[93] Jean-Pierre Cot and Alain Pellet, *La Charte des Nations Unies: Commentaire article par article sous la direction de* (Paris, Economica, 2nd ed, 1991) (hereafter Cot and Pellet).

[94] M Virally, *L'Organisation mondiale* (Paris, Collection U, 1972).

souveraineté de l'Etat. La délégation intervenant dans un tel domaine, on peut s'accorder avec le professeur VIRALLY pour sountenir qu'elle "ne eut s'analyser qu' en une délégation de souveraineté"[95]

The view taken by Dengi-Segui, Virally, and Sarooshi, reflects and extends a much earlier contention by Fawcett[96] and Oppenheim.[97] These commentators posit that states indeed possessed the power to use force either to *deter* unruly behaviour in the international community or to *preserve* international peace and security as a whole. As already remarked, states' international police power before the Charter was either universally recognised by custom or laid down by law-making treaties.[98] In this connection, Oppenheim further noted that,

> As a matter of both history and of principle the prohibition of intervention must be regarded primarily as a restriction which international law imposes upon states for the protection of the independence of other members of the international community [that] the notion and the prohibition of intervention *cannot* accurately extend to collective action undertaken in the general interest of states or for the collective enforcement of international law.[99]

This passage could be interpreted to mean that states enjoyed a customary right to use collective military force and that the Charter has not totally abrogated such rights although it might have shrunken it. The only restriction placed by Article 24(1) would seem to be that, where states claim the residuary of such rights as now codified by the Charter, it must be for the purpose of their general interests or for the collective enforcement of international law or where the Security Council fails to comply with the terms of the powers conferred under Article 24(1).[100]

According to Hersch Lauterpacht, 'if a State in time of peace or war violates such rules of the Law of nations as are universally recognised by customs or are laid down in law-making treaties, other States have a right to intervene and to make the delinquent submit to the rules concerned'.[101] Fawcett was in agreement with this notion when he observed that the international police power of states 'has often been exercized in the past century and a half by the great powers, acting either alone or in concert, to correct misrule, local civil strife or neutralise alien intervention, where

[95] Cot and Pellet, above note 93 at 450, *et seq*. Also quoted by Sarooshi, above note 6 at 26–27.

[96] JES Fawcett, *The Law of Nations*, (London, Allen Lane, The Penguin Press, 1968) at chapter 8.

[97] Sir Robert Jennings and Sir Arthur Watts (eds), *Oppenheim's International Law, vol 1, Peace* (London, Longman, 9th edn, 1992).

[98] L Oppenheim, *International Law: A Treatise*, H Lauterpacht (ed), (London, Longman, 8th edn, 1955), 305–20.

[99] *Ibid*, 319.

[100] We shall consider this proposition in great detail in chapter 6 when we consider the power of regional arrangements to retain enforcement action under Art 24(1).

[101] Above note 98 at 308. See also Sarooshi, above note 6 at 29.

those conditions have appeared seriously to threaten their interests and security'.[102]

The views expressed by Degni-Segui, Virally, Sarooshi, Fawcett and Oppenheim represent the correct interpretation of Article 24(1) of the UN Charter. As seen in the analysis of treaties and state practice before the emergence of the UN Charter, states not only possessed enforcement powers, they also had collective security powers that were provided for by treaties like the *Peace of Westphalia* and the *Treaty of Paris*. That states used some of these powers is not in doubt with regard particularly to the Treaty of Paris, which established the Concert of Europe.

The contention that a delegation of 'sovereign rights by member states . . . only refer to the founding of the Organization'[103] not only does not reflect the position of states vis-à-vis international police powers before the Charter, but also places too much emphasis on the formal procedure by which states may confer or transfer their power to whichever entities they desire. States may delegate part of their power to an organisation they form, through the constitutive instrument of such organisation. However, to argue, as Delbrück has, that the Security Council derives its power from the Charter, and that it was the Charter, and not the states, that conferred the enforcement power on the Security Council not only strains commonsense, but also is to conclude that the Charter created and animated itself.

Before considering the issue of residual responsibility, it is necessary to briefly examine the Charter provisions concerning the protection of states against armed attacks and aggressions in situations the Security Council is incapacitated. The analysis here answers a question that might be asked, namely what is the need for residual responsibility when the Charter itself contains remedies for states in the face of inaction by the Security Council?

4.5.2 The UN Collective Security and the Protective Mechanism

Under the UN Charter, there are three protections or remedies for states in situations where collective security is not or has not been activated. These are self-defence (Article 51), actions against former enemy states (Article 107), and surrogate collective action (Article 106). These provisions constitute exceptions to the prohibition of threat or use of force under Article 2(4) of the Charter. Furthermore, their activation is mostly not subject to prior authorisation by the Security Council since their action depends on the inaction of that organ.

[102] Fawcett J, 'Intervention in International Law', (1961-II) *Recueil des Cours*, 103, also cited by Sarooshi, above note 6 at 28.

[103] Delbrück in Simma's *Commentary*, above note 5 at 404.

In reality, the right of self-defence remains the only Charter protection left for states in the absence of collective security. Article 106, which contains the transitional security arrangement designed to protect states until the special agreement in Article 43 is concerned, although outside the normative framework of Chapter VII, is still subject to unanimity of the Security Council. Thus, as seen in the discussion of surrogate collective security in chapter 3, any transitional security arrangement under the Security Council can be defeated by the veto power, amongst other inhibitions. Article 107, the other protection, is now regarded as moribund as all former enemy states, against whose actions the provisions protect states, are currently members of the UN.

Article 51 states that,

> Nothing in the present Charter shall impair the inherent right of individual or collective self-defence if an armed attack occurs against a Member of the United Nations, until the Security Council has taken measures necessary to maintain international peace and security. Measures taken by members in the exercise of this right of self-defence shall be immediately reported to the Security Council and shall not in any way affect the authority and responsibility of the Security Council under the present Charter to take at any time such action as it deems necessary in order to maintain or restore international peace and security.

Article 51 has been a subject of extensive commentary. The main focus here, however, is to examine the nature of the protection it affords states in the context of contemporary challenges to peace and security.

Article 51 avail states if, and only if, such states have been subjected to armed attacks, a notion that is nowhere defined in the Charter. Although nothing in this provision states that such armed attack must equally originate from another state, the consensus among international lawyers is that authors of an armed attack, as contemplated under Article 51, can only be states. In support of this view is the fact that the prohibition in Article 2(4), to which Article 51 constitutes an exception, relates only to states.

The main problem with Article 51, in the context of this analysis, is that it does not protect states that have not been subject of armed attacks. This problem is different from the well-known issue as to whether Article 51 accommodates anticipatory self-defence, a term connoting the right of states to defend themselves *before* an actual attack has occurred, and which is of no relevance to this analysis.

As an exception to Article 2(4), it is not difficult to understand the historical rationale for designing Article 51 with the notion of armed attack in mind. Accordingly, the exercise of the right of self-defence can only be triggered by a breach of the activities prohibited under Article 2(4). Thus, since it is only the use or threat of force by one state against another that may activate Article 51, it logically follows that it is only such breaches that self-defence can respond to. However, this leaves unaddressed the fate of states which have been subject of unarmed attacks (in the meaning of Article 51) by either states or amorphous entities like terrorist organisations. Thus, when terrorists attacked the US in September 2001, Article 51 temporary went to sleep, and probably innocently too, until the US could fathom a tangible and credible nexus between the Al Qaeda Group, thought to be responsible for the attacks, and the state of Afghanistan, believed to have shielded it.

Without establishing a connection between Afghanistan and Al Qaeda it would have been difficult, to say the least, for the US to satisfy the requirements of Article 51 and afford itself the protection therefrom. First, the US would have had to prove that the use of commercial airliners to ram its buildings amounted to 'armed attacks' for the purpose of exercising the right of self-defence. Second, there would have also been a legal conundrum as to the basis for either attacking Al Qaeda Group or Afghanistan under Article 51.

The problem identified above with regard to the requirements of Article 51 in the modern day context is illustrated to a greater extent by the attack on Iraq by the coalition led by the US in March 2003. Clearly, unlike the Afghanistan case, the US found no credible nexus between Al Qaeda and Sadam Hussein's Iraq, even if it passionately believed that the Bathist regime in Baghdad supported terrorism against its interests. To attack Iraq under Article 51, in the absence of any connection between the two entities or imputation of the crime of Al Qaeda to Iraq for the purpose of responsibility, would have raised myriad legal problems such as discussed above. Not acting, assuming that there was a genuine threat posed by Sadam against American interests, would have meant that the US would have either had to suicidally await an attack by Iraq first, in order to fulfil Article 51, or put unbearable pressure on its provisions in order to pre-empt Iraq under anticipatory self-defence, as it eventually did.

Whether suggestions in some quarters that the prohibition of force in Article 2(4) be redrafted to include force used by non-state entities,[104] as the logical means of addressing the problem, is debatable. However, until a disentangling of Articles 2(4) and 51 is achieved one way or the other, the right of self-defence remains an inadequate protection for states which have been subjected to attacks by states using unconventional means or by groups not recognised by the UN Charter as capable of triggering the right of self-defence.

[104] Ann-Marie Slaughter and William Burke White, 'An International Constitutional Moment' (2002) 43 *Harvard International Law Journal* 1.

4.5.3. Who Possesses Residual Responsibility for International Peace and Security Under Article 24(1)?

Whatever may be the correct answer to the question as to who endowed the Security Council with its powers over international peace and security is of little relevance when determining which entity retains residual responsibility under Article 24(1). Article 24, it is contended, is a self-contained legal regime. This article created certain conditions under which the primary responsibility of the Security Council over peace and security is established. It confers on the Security Council primary responsibility for the maintenance of peace and security 'in order to ensure prompt and effective action'. What this means is that the power conferred, transferred or delegated to the Security Council by states or the Charter, is not a *carte blanche,* but one subject to the compliance by the Security Council with certain conditions.[105]

4.5.3.1. A Critique of the 'Absolute' Theory

The power contained in Article 24(1) is based on a corresponding duty that the Security Council shall perform its own obligation by taking *effective* and *prompt* action in deserving situations and acting in accordance with the purposes of the Charter. The non-fulfilment of these conditions, it is submitted, should be deemed to postpone the primacy so created in favour of the Security Council. In other words, should the Security Council not act *promptly* and *effectively*—both factors being cumulative—it forfeits its primacy in terms of responsibility for the maintenance of peace and security.[106]

The above contention can be justified in social contract theory, which establishes rights-based obligations, given the great impact constitutional practices and arrangements of UN Founding States had on the San Francisco Conference and the conception of the UN Charter, as explained below.[107] The basis of social contract theory between ruler and subjects is to be found in the simple proposition of the contractarian philosophers[108]

[105] For similar a view, see Thomas Franck, *Fairness in International Law and Institution* (Oxford, Clarendon Press, 1995) arguing that 'it is apparent that the Council has broad discretion, but that is to be exercised *bona fide* and *intra vires,*' 220; the separate opinion of Judge Weeramantry in the *Lockerbie* case, note at para 61. But see Yoram Dinstein, above n 9 at 250 contending that the 'Charter seems to give it [Security Council] a *carte blanche* in evaluating any given situation'.

[106] It is instructive to point out that Article 1 of the Charter also states that the Purpose of the United Nations are 'to maintain international peace and security, and to that end: to take effective collective measures for the prevention and removal of the threat to the peace, and for the suppression of acts of aggression or other breaches of peace'.

[107] For a similar view, see Paul Taylor, *International Organization in the Modern World: The Regional and the Global Process* (London, St Martin's Press, 1993) 5 *et seq*.

[108] Thomas Hobbes, *Leviathan* (London, Collins, 1651 (1962)); John Locke, *Two Treatises of Civil Government* (London, Everyman, 1690 (1924)).

that monarchs rule by virtue of the consent of the subjects, who have voluntarily subordinated themselves to the ruler in return for the ruler observing certain constraints on the exercise of power.[109] By analogy, such a theory can be applied in an analytical framework of the relationship between states and the Security Council vis-à-vis the voluntary conferral of collective security powers by the former on the latter in return for certain obligations to be performed by the latter. The basis for states conferring such power on the Security Council is to ensure 'prompt and effective action' by the UN, and it is only in complying with these conditions that states agree that the Security Council acts on their behalf.

The similarity between the nature of the transaction that took place between states and the Security Council in 1945 and the social contract theory is illustrated by an examination of the basis of the 'absolute' theory. Scholars who maintain that only the Security Council can act on behalf of the international community of states and that its power to do so cannot residually revert to states argue, *inter alia*, that states did not possess such rights before the UN was formed. In a way this resembles the contention of the classical contractarian philosophers such as Thomas Hobbes and John Locke. Both thinkers based their contract theories upon their understanding of the state of nature, which is the state presumed to have existed prior to the creation of any law.[110] Hobbes portrayed this as a state of permanent war of all against all in which there are 'no arts, no letters, no society; and which is worst of all, continual fear and danger of violence'.[111] Although Locke's view was much more benign[112] than Hobbes', he nevertheless agreed that the state of nature was such that necessitated the existence of law.[113]

If the analogy of *state of nature* of man's affairs before his social contract with his ruler to protect him, is applied to the *state of nature* of states under general international law before they made a contract with the Security Council, certain striking consequences result. First, like humans, states felt there was a need to regulate the way they conducted their international relations, especially as regard wars and security, which compelled them to transfer their power over such to the Security Council. The Preamble to the UN Charter, 'We the peoples of the world' portrays this desire for difference thus making peoples the focus of states relations with the UN. In this way, states acted like humans in the context of social contract.

However, it cannot be said that the state of nature of states under general international law was entirely like that of humans before the social contract. States, as already argued, had effective and organised ways of

[109] Mark Tebbit, *Philosophy of Law: An Introduction* (London, Routledge, 2000), 81.
[110] *Ibid*, 82.
[111] Hobbes, 1962 above note 108, at 143.
[112] *Ibid*.
[113] *Ibid*.

conducting their international relations and did not conduct a free-for-all and all-against-all war as humans did. To that extent, the state of the nature of the 'absolute' theory is faulty and not applicable to the contract that took place between states and the Security Council under Article 24(1). What this means then is that there was a contract between states and the Security Council in 1945 but at the background of that contract, there was no void that characterised the state of nature which underlined the social contract theory. Therefore Locke's view that social contract 'was a strictly conditional trade by those who voluntarily became subjects, granting the sovereign or sovereign body the right to rule on condition that he or they administer justice efficiently, as well as simply enforcing the peace', is to be preferred.

This submission is reinforced by John Ralws' elucidation of the social contract theory.[114] Rawls proposed the 'veil of ignorance' as underlining social contract theory. By this he means the fact that parties to the social contract are called upon to reflect on principles of justice to be adopted by the society in which they subsequently have to live. The contract would then involve the endorsement, in advance, of these principles which would govern a just society, each subject would be 'veiled' from all knowledge of their natural endowment of intelligence or practical ability. States could be said to have been operating under the Rawlsian veil of ignorance when they conferred their collective security powers on the Security Council in 1945 insofar as they could not be taken to have known all the endowment and practical ability that would govern their affairs in the future. Even for thinkers like David Hume who did not agree with Locke's defence of tacit consent, contemporary obligation has to be justified on the basis of actual benefit to be derived from a state which is generally obeyed.[115]

The application of the contractarian theory to the relationship between the Security Council and states in the context of the conferral of power by the latter to the former under Article 24(1) of the UN Charter was informed by certain historical considerations. Some of the states that took part in the San Francisco conference brought their domestic constitutional practices to bear on their conception of the Charter provisions and how these should be interpreted. The United States, in particular, drew heavily on the relationship between the Federal Government and the component states, in prescribing the manners in which the relationship between the UN and its organs, on the one hand, and the UN organs and member states, on the other, should be construed. John Foster Dulles, representing the United States, stated that:

[114] John Rawls, *A Theory of Justice* (Oxford, Oxford University Press, 1972).
[115] David Hume, *A Treatise of Human Nature* (London, Fontana, 1972 (1789)). For an analysis, see Tebbit, above note 109 at 83 *et seq*.

> The United States had had a long experience in dealing with a parallel problem, i. e., the relationship between the forty-eight states and the Federal Government. Today, the Federal Government of the United States exercised an authority undreamed of when the Constitution was formed, and the people of the United States were grateful for the simple conceptions in their Constitution. In a like manner . . . if the Charter contained simple and broad principles future generations would be thankful.[116]

Such flexible and broad conception of the Charter provisions, as advocated by Dulles, was amplified by US Ambassador Benjamin Cohen on the occasion of the General Assembly adopting the *Uniting for Peace Resolution*[117] in 1950. The US, leading several other states, had proposed that the General Assembly should adopt the Uniting for Peace resolution despite the fact that such resolution would give the Assembly the powers in the face of an impassed Security Council. Some states, especially the Soviet Union, had challenged this proposal on the ground, *inter alia*, that it was capable of distorting the drafters' allocation of functions between the Security Council and the General Assembly.[118] Benjamin Cohen had argued that the US constitutional practice allowed for 'executive agreements' supplementing the formal treaty power, and the recognition of 'implied powers' of Congress by the Supreme Court's decision in *McCulloh v Maryland*.[119] He then touted these American precedents as creative examples for the United Nations to emulate in construing its own constitutive instruments'.[120] As Thomas Franck has succinctly noted,

> Historically, *contractarianism* emphasized legitimacy in defining a community of rights and of the means to assert and defend those rights. It is self-evident that contractarian theory readily explains the origin, if not the modern nature, of international law and organization. States, too, have been seen by international legal theory as free and autonomous international "persons" associating for limited utilitarian purposes in a community to which they delegate certain powers so as to secure, in return the benefit of peace, order, and mutual support . . . From this it follows that states, like persons in the state of nature, are equal in their "statehood", which is restrained only to the extent that they have agreed voluntarily to be associated in a common enterprise and have defined the limits on their rights and autonomy in a reciprocal fashion.[121]

[116] 6 UNCIO, Commission I, Committee I, Doc 1019, I/1/42 June 16, 1945, 507, at 508, quoted in Thomas Franck, *Recourse to Force*: *State Actions against Threats and Armed Attacks* (Cambridge, Cambridge University Press, 2002), 13.

[117] GAOR, 5th Sess, Annexes, vol 2, Item 68, UN Doc A/1377 (1950).

[118] See GA Res 377(V). GAOR, 5th Sess, 302nd Plen Meeting, 3 Nov, 1950, A/PV302, 341 at 347.

[119] 4 *Wheat* 316 (1819).

[120] Benjamin V Cohen, *The United Nations, Constitutional Developments, Growths, Possibilities* (1961), 18–19, cited in Franck, above note 116, at 33.

[121] Thomas Franck, above note 116 at 28. (Emphasis added.)

The presence of the term 'primary responsibility' in Article 24(1), it is submitted, negates any proposition that at San Francisco the Security Council was intended to possess exclusive authority over the maintenance of peace and security. Had this been the intention, the Charter author would have undoubtedly adopted the more specific term 'exclusive'. Nothing in the *travaux préparatoires* of the Charter disclosed any such intention. Given the vehemence of the super powers on the powers of the Security Council at the conference, it is unimaginable that they would have allowed such a phrase in the Charter had they intended a different one.

4.5.3.2. Regional Organisations and Residual Responsibility for the Maintenance of Peace and Security: A Proposal

A theory that regional organisations possess residual responsibility for the maintenance of international peace and security, in default of action by the Security Council, can be constructed on our previous conclusion that it was states, rather than the Charter, that imbued the Security Council with primary responsibility for collective security. The UN is a creation of a treaty. The activities of the organs that act on its behalf must as such conform to the powers assigned to it by parties to the treaty.[122]

In its practice, the Security Council has formed the view that 'if the Council did not act or did not take a particular action, it would be failing to discharge the responsibility conferred upon it under the Charter'.[123] This perception by the Security Council of the effect of Article 24 has been contradicted by those who claim that 'it is the Security Council rather than some other organ or agency, which should act'.[124] This issue arose in connection with 'actions by regional organizations, subsidiary bodies, the Secretary-General, and most especially the General Assembly'.[125]

It is proposed that states, especially when operating under the auspices of regional organisations, may act in the defence of collective interests where both the Security Council and the General Assembly have failed to discharge their obligations. As already shown, in the case of social contract, a sovereign loses its power to act on behalf of its subjects if it is unable to protect them. In such circumstances, power reverts to the people. In the same vein, states may repossess the power to undertake collective security if the Security Council fails to act for the purpose for which they conferred the power on it.

[122] See Thomas Franck, above note 105 at 219.

[123] Leeland Goodrich, Edvard Hambro and Anne Simons, *Charter of the United Nations: Commentary and Documents* (New York, Columbia University Press, 3rd Revised edn, 1969) at 203.

[124] *Ibid* at 203.

[125] *Ibid*, at 203.

Since states, like peoples under social contract, transferred their powers to the Security Council in 1945 collectively, they can only repossess the same on a collective basis. Regional organisations present the best collective basis upon which residual power over collective security can revert to states, given their competence under Chapter VIII. A stronger case of legitimacy of such residual power is established where such a regional organisation is permitted by its treaty law to so act. A case for states acting as regional organisations is also supported by the fact that the claim of residuality is more vigorously made and more pronounced by states acting as regional organisations than those acting per se. This theme will be developed more fully in the next chapter.

It might be argued that the phrase 'prompt and effective' was not intended to constrain the functioning of the Security Council or to determine the validity of its actions. It might even be said that by declining to act in a particular situation the Security Council may be in lawful exercise of its discretion under Chapter VII.

The basis for proposing residual competence for collective security can be further expounded as follows. Article 24(1) created a legal obligation as between the Security Council and states or as between the Security Council and the rest of the international community for whose benefit the States must be understood to have created the power under Article 24. The terms of Article 24(1)—'prompt' and 'effective'—constitute the raison d'être for the grant of power to the Security Council by states or the Charter itself. Hence, the fulfilment of those terms by the Security Council, it is submitted, constitutes a *conditio sine qua non* for the enjoyment of that power by the Security Council. As Franck correctly argued, the legality of 'actions by any UN organ must be judged by reference to the Charter as a "constitution" of delegated powers'.[126] Therefore, as with the social contract, failure to observe those conditions upon which the law contained in Article 24(1) was based leads to reversion of those powers to states. It is not enough that the Security Council has taken a measure in a given situation; that measure must be prompt and effective.

The transfer of power, or, as it is referred to in the Charter, the conferment of power on the Security Council by states is a legal act in itself, having either contractual or constitutional effects.[127] As Dan Ciobanu has argued, in international law,

> legal acts may be categorized as acts simple and conditional. The intrinsic validity of some acts belonging to the latter category depends on the fulfilment of the

[126] Thomas Franck, 'The Power of Appreciation: Who is the Ultimate Guardian of UN Legality?' (1992) 86 *American Journal of International Law* 519 at 592.

[127] But see Hans Kelsen, above note 11 at 280 on his perception of the conferral or transfer of power by Members of the United Nations to its organs as having 'contractual' character.

condition precedent, which may be expressly provided for in a legal text, or could, as a necessary corollary, be inferred from the context.[128]

Considering Article 24(1), not only is the act of transferring states' police power a legal act, the exercise of that power by the Security Council, in the exact manner prescribed by the Charter, has legal consequences.[129] When the Security Council exercises that power, it does so, not on its own behalf, but on behalf of states. The intrinsic validity of the exercise of that power by the Security Council, it is submitted, must inextricably depend on the Security Council's compliance with those conditions attached to the power. In order words, those terms constitute *conditio sine qua non* for the purpose of the validity of the Security Council's exercise of power under Article 24(1).

In the case concerning the *Interpretation of the Statute of the Memel Territory*,[130] the Lithuanian Government argued that a recourse to the Permanent Court of International Justice was admissible only *after* the failure of the procedure initiated before the Council of the League of Nations under paragraph I of Article 17 of the Convention of Paris of 1924.[131] Although in that case the Permanent Court did not find that the text of the statute would have actually implied the condition, it pronounced on the meaning of *condition precedent*.[132] The International Court of Justice has had to consider this issue in the context of the case concerning the *Competence of the General Assembly for the Admission of a State to the United Nations*.[133] The issue for determination in this case was the effect of certain terms contained in Article 4(2) of the UN Charter. This article provides that 'the admission of any such State to Membership in the United Nations will be effected by a decision of the General Assembly upon the recommendation of the Security Council'. As to the effect of the conditions 'effect' and 'recommendation' the Court held, *inter alia*, that it 'has no doubt as to the meaning of the text. It requires two things to *effect* admission: a recommendation of the Security Council and a decision of the General Assembly'.[134]

The conditions contained in Article 24(1) constitute *conditio sine qua non* for the validity of the exercise of responsibility conferred on the Security Council. A *conditio sine qua non* may be *precedent*, *subsequent* or even *concurrent*.[135] A condition is precedent when it delays the investing of a right

[128] Dan Ciobanu, *Preliminary Objections related to the Jurisdiction of the United Nations Political Organs* (The Hague, Martinus Nijhoff, 1975), 78.
[129] Article 24(1) uses the word 'primary' to describe the position of the Security Council vis-a-vis that power and the unspecified secondary beneficiaries.
[130] PCIJ, Ser C No 59, 78.
[131] PCIJ, Ser C No 59, 78, cited in Ciobanu, above note 128, at 78–79.
[132] PCIJ, Ser A/B No 47, 248.
[133] *Ibid*, at 248.
[134] *Ibid*.
[135] Ciobanu, above note 128 at 79 *et seq*.

until the occurrence of a particular event.[136] Conversely, a condition subsequent is one which provides for the defeat of an interest on the occurrence or non occurrence of a particular act.[137] However, where the performance of one party depends on the performance by the other at the same time, then the condition is said to be concurrent.

The conditions contained in Article 24(1) are of concurrent nature. The article vests certain rights in the Security Council only insofar as it can promptly and effectively act. The right itself is to act *before* any other organ or state can so do. Thus, the non-acting of any other organ or state in a particular case simultaneously as the Security Council depends on whether the Security Council can be said to be *acting* in accordance to those stipulations. Promptness and effectiveness in this situation cannot amount to conditions precedent because the determination of those intrinsic qualities can only be done *after* the act has been undertaken or while the act lasts.

A condition precedent on the other hand is aimed at *a priori* determination of the act. For instance, in determining the allocation of competence between the General Assembly and the Security Council, Kelsen noted that the:

> words "while the Security Council is exercising . . . the functions" may be interpreted to mean: while a dispute or situation is still on the agenda of the Council. But it may also be interpreted to mean: while the Security Council is actually exercising its functions; so that when the Council because of the exercise of the veto right is reduced to inaction, it should not be considered as "exercising" its functions.[138]

The net effect of this is that the restriction placed on the General Assembly to make recommendations on issues as may be the subject of the Security Council's action is only temporary in order to avoid conflicts between the two.

In the same vein, one may construe the conditions of Article 24(1) as constituting a temporary restraint on states and other organs of the UN not to act as long as the Security Council can be said to be taking prompt and effective action in respect of a situation. Where the Security Council declines to put a matter on its agenda or is prevented from doing so by the veto, it is submitted that the restriction is thereby lifted. A system of collective security, it has been argued, should provide more, and not less, security.[139] Therefore, regardless of what the origin of the Charter enforcement power is, Article 24(1) is not devoid of all legal effects.[140]

[136] Ciobanu, above note 128 at 79 *et seq*.
[137] See *Re Macleay* (1875) LR 20 Eq 186. See also *Re Da Costa* [1912] 1 Ch 377, at 3.
[138] Kelsen, above note 11 at 217.
[139] Torsten Stein in Delbrück's *Allocation*, above note 5 at 117.
[140] See Sarooshi, above note 6 at 29 *et seq*.

An argument that it was the Charter, and not states, that conferred the powers contained in Article 24(1) on the Security Council, does not prejudice the conclusion above. Nor does the position that states did not possess collective military power before the advent of the Charter affect the substance of our position. This is because, in itself, Article 24(1) does not confer upon the Security Council an *unconditional* power to be enjoyed perpetually and *in vacuo*. It is a power created or given to the Security Council, through the instrument of the Charter to discharge a particular responsibility, to the temporary *exclusion* of all others only, and if *only* in the exercise of that power the Security Council fulfils the conditions attached to the power itself. If we accept the contention by Schachter[141] and Noncic[142] to the contrary, there will be little sense in states surrendering part of their sovereignty and the powers to guarantee their continued existence to organs of international organisations they create.[143]

4.6. CONCLUSION

As seen in the above analysis, the term collective security was neither an invention of the UN nor was its development in international law begun with the enthronement of the UN Charter at the head of international legal order. Clearly, states had, from time immemorial, organised themselves into more or less collective security systems as and when occasions demanded.

From a survey of bilateral and multilateral treaties of old down to the emergence of the UN Charter, we saw that the standards of collective security that developed and permeated the gamut of international society varied according to the vagaries and sophistication of the relevant periods and the historical circumstances that prompted, instigated or catalysed its evolution.

Moreover, it was clear from the analysis that the Founding States impressed on the provisions of the UN Charter their domestic constitutional arrangements and practices as they pondered the future development of collective security under the auspices of the UN at San Francisco. It was in this connection that states fashioned a primary role for the Security Council, over peace and security, cryptically retaining for themselves, and in accordance with the principles of contractarianism, residual responsibility for peace and security in the default of the Security Council.

[141] Oscar Schachter, 'In Defense of International Rules on the Use of Force' (1986) 53 *University of Chicago Law Review* 113 at 125–26.

[142] D Ninčić, *The Problem of Sovereignty in the Charter and Practice of the United Nations* (1970), 72 at 76–77, cited by Ciobanu, above note 128.

[143] See also John Murphy, 'Force and Arms' in Christopher Joyner (ed), *The United Nations and International Law* (Cambridge, Cambridge University Press, 1997) at 102.

Our inquiry into history showed clearly that states collectively transferred their enforcement power to the Security Council in 1945; that that transfer was on the basis of certain identified conditions; and that failure by the Security Council to fulfil those conditions caused the powers transferred to it to revert to states. However, such repossession of powers can only be done on a collective basis since it was on the same basis that states transferred power in the first place. Thus, we proposed that regional organisations are the best candidates to assume such a residual role.

As will be seen in the next chapter, regional organisations have stepped fully into this role. The close working relationship between the UN and regional organisations and more importantly, the monumental constitutional changes that have taken place within many regional organisations, discussed in the next chapter, justify the proposition that regional organisations play a residual role in collective security.

5

Regional Intervention after the Cold War

INTRODUCTION

REGIONAL ORGANISATIONS ARE the only entities explicitly recognised by the UN Charter to which the Security Council may delegate its Chapter VII powers. As seen in Chapter 2, the provisions concerning regional arrangements under Chapter VIII have undergone tremendous changes since the UN's inception. Between 1945 and 1990, regional organisations exerted enormous pressure on such Charter terms as 'authorisation' and 'enforcement action'. Yet, throughout this period, regional organisations managed to adhere to the formalistic framework of regional arrangements under Chapter VIII, stepping outside of it only by default, but quickly stepping back whenever a permanent Security Council member (usually the Soviet Union) raised concerns.

Events since 1990 however show a different picture of regional organisations altogether. While cooperating with the UN to a greater extent than before,[1] regional organisations have become hyper active in regional conflicts. In Liberia (1989–97),[2] Sierra Leone (1997–),[3] Niger Republic

[1] See the *Repertory of Practice of United Nations Organs*, II, 443. Bruno Simma (ed), *The Charter of the United Nations: A Commentary* (Oxford, Oxford University Press, 1st edn, 1994), 689, (hereafter Bruno Simma's *Commentary*). This scenario changed with the end of the Cold War. Hence, in 1994, the Secretary-General invited a host of regional organisations—the OAS, OAU, ECOWAS, WEU, NATO and the Arab League to attend. See 28 *United Nations Yearbook*. See Christine Gray, *International Law and the Use of Force* (Oxford, Oxford University Press, 2000), 204–5. But see *United Nations—Organization of African Unity Co-operation Agreement* of 15 November 1965, *548 United Nations Treaty Series* 316.

[2] Georg Nolte, 'Restoring Peace by Regional Action: International Legal Aspects of the Liberian Conflict', 23 *ZaöR V* 53/3, 603; Kofi Oteng Kufor, 'The Legality of the Intervention in the Liberian Civil War By the Economic Community of West African States' (1993) (5) *African Journal of International and Comparative Law* 525; Funmi Olonisakin, *Reinventing Peacekeeping in Africa: Conceptual and Legal Issues in ECOMOG Operations* (The Hague, Kluwer Law International, 2000)

[3] Karsten Nowrot and Emily Schabacker, 'The Use of Force to Restore Democracy: International Legal Implications of the ECOWAS Intervention in Sierra Leone' (1998) 14(2) *American University Journal of International Law* 321; A Conteh, 'Sierra Leone and the Norms of Non-Intervention: Evolution and Practice' (1995) 7 *African Journal of International and Comparative Law* 166; Ademola Abass, 'The Implementation of ECOWAS New Protocol and Security Council Resolution 1270 in Sierra Leone: New Developments in Regional Intervention' (2002) 10(1) *University of Miami International and Comparative Law Review* 177.

(1999)[4], Guinea-Bissau (1998)[5], and Federal Republic of Yugoslavia (FRY) (1999)[6], regional organisations intervened in conflicts to varying degrees. In at least three of these cases—Liberia, Sierra Leone and FRY—such interventions generated huge controversy, particularly with regards to the legality of those actions under Chapter VIII. To be certain, all three cases involved the use of military force by respective organisations without authorisation by the Security Council.

Before 1990, regional actions consisted mainly of peacekeeping operations.[7] Examples include the OAU's[8] actions in Chad (1981),[9] Congo (1960–63)[10]; the Arab League's[11] intervention in the Iraq-Kuwait crisis (1961–63),[12] and the Lebanese conflict[13] (1976). Only very rarely did regional organisations impose such controversial measures[14] as the OAS's action during Cuban Missile and Dominican crises.

[4] *Final Communiqué*, Meeting of Foreign Affairs Ministers of ECOWAS, Lome, Togo 24–25 May 1999, http://www.Sierra-leone.org/ecowas052599.html.

[5] *Final Communiqué Extraordinary Summit of Heads of State and Government* of ECOWAS 11 April 2001, Abuja, Nigeria. http://www.Sierra-leone.org/ecowas041101.html. See also *Outline of the ECOWAS Peace Plan for Guinea-Bissau* (1998) on file with the author; Additional Protocol to the Abuja Accord of November 1st 1998 Concerning the Formation of the Government of unity of Guinea-Bissau, Lome, Togo, 15th December 1998, on file with the author.

[6] Bruno Simma, 'NATO, the UN and the Use of Force: Legal Aspects' (1999) 10(1) *European Journal of International Law* 1.

[7] For example the Arab League and the Lebanese conflict and the Organisation of American States (OAS) and the Dominican crisis.

[8] OAU Charter (1964) 3 *International Legal Materials* 1116.

[9] See Gino J Naldi, *The Organization of African Unity* (London, Mansel Publishing Ltd, 2nd edn, 1999); Amadu Sesay, 'The Limits of Peace-Keeping by Regional Organisations: The OAU Peace-Keeping Force in Chad', (1991) 11 *Conflict Quarterly* 7–26; G Naldi, 'Peacekeeping Attempts by the OAU', (1985) 34 *International and Comparative Law Quarterly* 593; J-P Cot, 'The Role of the Inter-African Peacekeeping Force in Chad', in Cassese (ed), *The Current Legal Regulation of the Use of Force* (Dordrecht, Martinus Nijhoff, 1986), 167.

[10] For a detailed analysis see G Abi-Saab, *The United Nations Operations in the Congo 1960–1964* (Oxford, Oxford University Press, 1978); R Higgins, *United Nations Peacekeeping* 1947–1967, *Documents and Commentary: 3, Africa* (Oxford, Oxford University Press, 1980). For an account of the political circumstances of the Congo crisis see William J Durch, *The Evolution of UN Peacekeeping: Case Study and Comparative Analysis*, (New York, St Martin's Press, 1993).

[11] Established in May 1945. See text of the League Pact, see (1945) 39 *American Journal of International Law* Supp, 266. See I Pogany, 'The Arab League and Regional Peacekeeping', (1987) XXXIV *Netherlands International Law Review* 54.

[12] See Hussein Hassounna, *The League of Arab States and Regional Disputes: A Study of Middle East Conflicts* (New York, Oceana, 1975); Robert W McDonald, *The League of Arab States: A Study in the Dynamics of Regional Organization* (Princeton, Princeton University Press, 1965).

[13] See Yair Evron *War and intervention in Lebanon*: *The Israeli-Syrian Deterrence Dialogue* (London, Croom Helm, 1987); Marianne Heiberg, *Lebanon, Political Playground of the Middle East: The Role of Peacekeeping* (Oslo, NUPI, 1989); Istvan Pogany, *The Arab League and Peacekeeping in the Lebanon* (Aldershot, Avebury, 1987).

[14] See discussion in Chapter 3 on the OAS quarantine against Cuba.

During the Cold War, regional organisations justified their interventions in members' conflicts on the bases of *invitation* by member states,[15] and/or in order to prevent or halt humanitarian disasters.[16] From 1990, regional organisations have asserted the legal competence to take enforcement actions on the authority of their own treaties, without deference to the Security Council. Often, such treaties dispense with host state consent, thereby purporting to empower regional organisations to act, not only beyond Chapter VIII of the UN Charter, but also outside principles of general international law.[17]

The focus of this chapter is to examine regional intervention since the end of the Cold War. It raises three fundamental issues for consideration. First, it analyses the principles enunciated in the post Cold War regional treaties and practice. Second, it considers the effect of the new *right* of intervention, asserted by regional organisations, on the customary principle which obligates states to obtain the consent of host states, even if these are their members, before intervening in their conflicts. Third, the chapter evaluates the justifications for regionally authorised enforcement action and considers how such fit into the overall schemes of collective security. The chapter concludes by urging a greater autonomy for regional organisations over collective security than the Charter currently accords them.

5.1. AN OVERVIEW OF REGIONAL COLLECTIVE SECURITY AFTER THE COLD WAR

The Liberian conflict (1987–99) was epoch-making, not only in the development of the law of regional collective security, but also in the fostering of a new relationship between the UN and regional organisations. During that conflict, the UN and ECOWAS inaugurated a 'joint-peacekeeping' operation for the first time in the history of collective security.[18] It is thus the most instructive place to start an overview of regional organisations' practice after the Cold War.

Upon the outbreak of violence in Liberia in 1990, following armed insurgence levelled against Samuel Doe's government by the National Patriotic Front of Liberia (NPFL), ECOWAS deployed its Monitoring

[15] See the Communiqué issued by the office of the Presidency of the Lebanon, 16 June 1976, text in J Nielsen (ed), *International Documents on Palestine 1976* (1978) cited by Pogany, above note 11, on the intervention of the Arab League in the Lebanese conflict.

[16] A/Dec 1/8/90 of *First Session of the Community [ECOWAS] Standing Mediation Committee*, Banjul, The Gambia 6–7 August 1990, ECOWAS claimed to be 'gravely concerned about the destructive armed conflict going on in Liberia and profound disruptive effect that civil war is having on normal life in Liberia'.

[17] Cf Gray, above note 1 at 209.

[18] UN Doc S/RES/866 adopted at its 3281st mtg, 22 September 1993.

Group (ECOMOG)[19] to, among other things, keep the peace in Liberia until an amicable solution could be reached among contending parties. This objective at once proved unattainable mainly due to the antagonism of the NPFL towards ECOMOG force[20], which it believed was dominated by the pro-Doe Nigeria. Furthermore, while ECOWAS arguably obtained the consent of Samuel Doe's government to deploy to Liberia, it did not consult with Charles Taylor's NPFL, the largest and the most significant rebel faction in the conflict. The NPFL saw this as an indication that the presence of ECOMOG in Liberia was intended to protect Doe's government against the uprising. What is noteworthy in this affair was that following the death of Samuel Doe, ECOWAS resorted to an all-out military action to prevent the NPFL from capturing the seat of power in Monrovia.[21] This action was widely regarded as enforcement action undertaken without the Security Council's authorisation,[22] although some commentators argued that the Security Council eventually accorded it a retroactive approval.[23] However, it was clear from its relevant *travaux préparatoires* that ECOWAS clearly intended enforcement action *ab initio*.[24] According to the Guinean President who was one of the proponents of the ECOWAS Peace Plan for Liberia, 'we do not need the permission of any party involved in the conflict to implement the decisions reached in Banjul. So, with or without the agreement of any of the parties, ECOWAS troops will be in Liberia'.[25]

ECOMOG troops were deployed to Liberia after the Security Council had declined a request by the Liberian government to intervene in the conflict.[26] Nonetheless, in 1993 the UN despatched a mission—the United Nations Observer Mission in Liberia (UNOMIL)[27]—to Liberia. This mission was mandated, amongst other things, to supervise the implementation of the Cotonou Peace Plan by ECOWAS.[28] UNOMIL ran into a series of difficulties partly due to the problems associated with the implementa-

[19] A/DEC.3/8/90, *First Session of the Community Standing Mediation Committee*, Banjul, The Gambia, 1990.

[20] Established on 7 August 1990 by the ECOWAS Standing Mediation Committee on the Liberia conflict by its Decision A/DEC 1/8 90 (hereafter *Decision 1990*) in Banjul, Republic of The Gambia. See UN Doc S/21485 of 10 August 1990 (annex), 2. See also M Weller (ed), *Regional Peace-Keeping and International Enforcement: The Liberian Crisis*, (hereafter M Weller) Cambridge International Law Series vol 6, (Cambridge, Cambridge University Press, 1994), 67.

[21] Ramsbotham and Woodhouse, *Encyclopaedia of International Peacekeeping Operations* (California, ABC-CLIO, 1999).

[22] Kufor, above note 2; Gray, above note 1.

[23] See Nolte, above note 2.

[24] Decision A/Dec 1/8/90.

[25] *Africa Research Bulletin*, 15 September 1990, 9802.

[26] See discussion in Chapter 3.

[27] UN Doc S/RES/866

[28] See *Report of the UN Secretary-General on Liberia*, UN Doc S/26422, 9 September 1993, 4.

tion of the Cotonou Peace Plan[29] and partly due to its own mandate.[30] This led to the reduction in its size in 1994.[31] The 1996 Abuja II Peace Agreement[32] provided a better framework for both UNOMIL and ECOMOG to function. UNOMIL largely complemented ECOWAS and, in turn, the latter afforded it protection when it ran into trouble with the NPFL.[33]

Similarly, following the overthrow of President Tejan Kabbah's democratic government in 25 May 1997 by elements of the Sierra Leone National Army (SLNA), ECOWAS altered ECOMOG's mandate in Sierra Leone.[34] While the Liberian conflict lasted, ECOMOG troops were stationed in Sierra Leone under a Status of Force Agreement (SOFA),[35] concluded with the Sierra Leonean government, in order to prevent a spread of the Liberian crisis to Sierra Leone. This became necessary given the reported trans-border infiltration of rebels between the two countries and the rumoured assistance rendered to the NPFL faction by elements of the Revolutionary United Front (RUF) of Sierra Leone led by Fodah Sankoh.[36]

However, unlike the Liberian crisis where ECOMOG had arguably set out initially as a 'peacekeeping force', ECOMOG commenced undisguised *enforcement* action in Sierra Leone from the start in order to reverse the May coup.[37] It indeed stated this clearly as its main objective.[38] As with Liberia, ECOWAS enforcement in Sierra Leone was taken without the Security Council's authorisation,[39] although, as in Liberia, it subsequently

[29] For details see Funmi Olonisakin, above note 2; Clement Adibe, 'The Liberian Conflict and the ECOWAS-UN Partnership' in Thomas Weiss (ed), *Beyond Subcontracting: Task-Sharing with Regional Security Arrangements and Service-Providing NGOs* (Basingstoke, Macmillan, 1998), 67–90.

[30] The UN Secretary-General explained the nature of UNOMIL mandate thus: 'The role foreseen for the United Nations in the implementation of the Cotonou Peace Agreement is predicated on the assumption that the ECOMOG force will be in a position to perform the wide-ranging tasks entrusted to it by the Liberian parties'. Report of the Secretary-General on Liberia UN Doc S/26422.

[31] UN Doc S/1995/158; 1994 *United Nations Yearbook* 371.

[32] See Olonisakin, above note 2 for analysis.

[33] UN Doc S/RES 1014, 1020, 1041, 1059, 1071, and 1083 repeatedly called for ECOMOG to afford protection for UNOMIL.

[34] Decision A/DEC 7/8/97 Extending the Mandate of ECOMOG to cover Sierra Leone, Abuja, 28–9 August 1997, (Twentieth Session of the Authority of Heads of State and Government), Art 1.

[35] For a renewal or negotiation of a new SOFA with Sierra Leone, see *Final Communiqué Meeting of Chiefs of Defence Staff of Contributing States to ECOMOG* in Sierra Leone Abuja, 15 April 1999.

[36] *Ibid*, at para g.

[37] *Third Report of the ECOWAS Committee of Five on Sierra Leone to the United Nations Pursuant to Resolution S/RES* 1132 (1997) of 8 October 1997. Here, ECOWAS reported on its destruction of one of the airfields developed by the Junta.

[38] *Final Communiqué* 1996/1997 (on file with the author).

[39] Art 6 of the *Twentieth Session of the Authority of Heads of State and Government*, above, states that the 'subregional forces shall employ all necessary means to implement this decision'.

operated in conjunction with United Nations Mission in Sierra Leone (UNAMSIL).[40]

The NATO/UN operation during the disintegration of the former Yugoslavia had all the elements of experimentalism. NATO's cooperation with the UN informally began on 16 July 1992 when, through its operation 'Maritime Monitor', NATO ships entered the Adriatic Sea in order to monitor compliance with Security Council Resolutions 713[41] and 757[42]. The former resolution imposed a 'general and complete embargo on all deliveries of weapons and military equipment to Yugoslavia', while the latter imposed economic sanctions against the Federal Republic of Yugoslavia (Serbia and Montenegro).[43] In 1992, the Security Council adopted Resolution 787 under Chapter VIII.[44] This resolution stated, *inter alia*, that:

> [a]cting under Chapter VII and Chapter VIII, the Security Council calls upon States acting nationally or through regional agencies or organisations as may be necessary under the authority of the Security Council to halt all inward and outward maritime shipping in order to inspect and verify their cargoes and destinations and to ensure strict implementation of the provisions of resolutions 713 (1991) and 757 (1992).[45]

Relying on this resolution, NATO, which is not regarded as a regional arrangement under Chapter VIII,[46] implemented an interdiction of all ships in the Danube and the Adriatic. Resolution 787 was consolidated by Resolution 816.[47] Though this latter resolution was not adopted under Chapter VIII, it recalled the provisions of that chapter, therefore having similar effects as though it had been specifically adopted under Chapter VIII.

[40] Full discussion below. For the purpose of our analysis, the intervention in Sierra Leone shall be divided into two phases. The first phase covers the period following the overthrow of Kabbah's government in May 1997 and the intervention of the Nigerian ECOMOG Contingents in the same year through to the withdrawal of that contingent and the Ghanaian and Guinean as well between December 1999 and January 2000. The second phase starts with the re-entry of these contingents into the crisis in May 2000. The main parameters for this demarcation include the following. In the first phase, the operation of ECOWAS had been pursued under its previous legal regimes as represented by the PMAD and the Non-Aggression Protocol. In addition, in the first phase, ECOWAS and UNAMSIL had operated more or less separately, with separate command regimes and divergent mandates. On the other hand, in the second phase of the intervention, ECOWAS operated under its new legal regime. Also, its forces (ECOMOG) formed part of UNAMSIL, although it implemented a separate mandate from the UN and remained effectively under its own command regime. For a discussion of the joint action of the UN and ECOWAS in Sierra Leone, see Ademola Abass, above note 3.

[41] UN Doc S/RES/713, 25 September 1991.

[42] UN Doc S/RES/757, 30 May 1992.

[43] For an excellent review of NATO-UN cooperation in Yugoslavia, see Dick A Leurdijk, 'The UN and NATO in the Former Yugoslavia' in Weiss (ed), above note 29, 49–66.

[44] UN Doc S/RES/787, 16 Nov 1992.

[45] *Ibid*, para 12.

[46] See Rosalyn Higgins, 'Peace and Security: Achievement and Failures' (1995) 6 *European Journal of International Law* 445.

[47] UN Doc S/RES/816, 31 March 1993.

The NATO/UN relationship in Yugoslavia oscillated between different operational phases. Unlike operation 'Maritime Monitor' which NATO conducted alone, NATO operated under Resolution 816 in *cooperation* with the United Nations Protection Force (UNPROFOR)[48] in order to enforce a total flight ban on the airspace of Bosnia and Herzegovina. NATO provided air support for purposes authorised by the Security Council, leading to a situation which, according to Secretary-General Boutros-Boutros Ghali, raised 'unprecedented issues of command and control'.[49] However, there were also instances in which the Security Council supported NATO using force without specific authorisation by it. Following the massacre at the marketplace in Sarajevo in February 1994,[50] the Secretary-General asked NATO to authorise air strikes.[51] In implementing this, NATO relied entirely on its own resources. It stipulated an ultimatum for the withdrawal of heavy weapons of Bosnians and Serbs from designated areas. Moreover, in the aftermath of the massacre of civilians in Srebrenica in July 1995,[52] NATO took decisions, without involving the Security Council, that any further attacks on safe areas would be met by a firm action by NATO forces.[53]

On 14 December 1995, the 'General Framework Agreement for Peace in Bosnia and Herzegovina' was concluded in Dayton, Ohio, United States. Following this Agreement the Security Council adopted Resolution 1031[54] authorising the establishment of the International Forces under NATO's command.[55] The North Atlantic Council (NAC) endorsed this on 16 December. On 20 December 1995, the UN Secretary-General in a letter to the NAC confirmed the end of UNPROFOR and the ascension of IFOR to its responsibilities.[56]

The interaction of the Organisation for Security and Cooperation in Europe (OSCE),[57] the Commonwealth of Independent States (CIS)[58] and the UN's various missions in the Transcaucasian region of the former Soviet Union is also significant when chronicling the development of the UN/regional organisation relationship after the Cold War. This was the

[48] UN Doc S/RES/743, 21 February 1992.

[49] Leurdijk, above note 43, 54–55.

[50] *Ibid*.

[51] See NATO resolution on 'Recasting Euro-Atlantic Security', NATO Doc AR 295 SA (1998).

[52] See Lars-Eric Wahlgren, 'Start and End of Srebrenica' in William Durch (ed), UN *Peacekeeping, American Policy and Uncivil Wars of the 1990s* (New York, St Martins Press, 1996), 168.

[53] *Ibid*, 57–58.

[54] UN Doc. S/RES/1031 15 December 1995.

[55] Operative para. 14.

[56] *Ibid*.

[57] The CSCE was established in 1975. See (1975) 14 *International Legal Materials* 1292. But see generally (1993) *United Nations Yearbook* 219 on CSCE.

[58] *Ibid*.

first time the UN and regional organisations had *formally* agreed on a delineation of responsibilities over conflicts. In the Georgian conflict,[59] the UN took the lead in Abkhazia while the OSCE took the lead in South Ossetia. In addition, this case demonstrates the impact the presence of a regional hegemon (Russia) could have on joint-action between the UN and regional organisations.

The conflict in Georgia grew out of the events around the Georgia's transition to independence in 1989–90.[60] Two of Georgia's numerous ethnic minorities, the Ossets and the Abkhaz, had been fighting before the disintegration of the Soviet Union. This led to a declaration of secession by the South Ossetian Autonomous Oblast of the Republic of Georgia, a declaration effectively quashed by the Georgian Supreme Soviet.[61] An early intervention by the Soviet Interior Ministry forces was withdrawn following the collapse of the Soviet Union.[62] A meeting of the warring parties, at the instigation of President Boris Yeltsin, secured a cease-fire in the conflict. In 1992, the President of Georgia, Eduard Shevardnadze, invited the OSCE to intervene in order to 'promote negotiations on a peaceful political settlement of the conflict'.[63] The OSCE established its Mission to Georgia in Tbilisi.

The conflict in Abkhazia exploded almost at the time when hostilities were subsiding in South Ossetia.[64] An overthrow of the government of Zviad Gamsakhudia in November 1991 had triggered a chain reaction across the land, pitching two rival factions, the Georgian National Guard and the Georgian forces, against each other.[65] The conflict spiralled, leading to a declaration of independence by Abkhaz. Georgia (now under President Shevardnadze) appealed to the UN to save Georgia from total collapse. This was while a Russia-brokered cease-fire of July 27 1993 tattered.[66] The UN responded with a small observer group, the United Nations Observer Mission to Georgia (UNOMIG) in late 1993.[67] In October 1994, based on an agreement between Moscow and President Shevardnadze in June 1994, Russian forces were deployed to Mingrelia

[59] See Leurdijk, above note 43.

[60] For an excellent documentation and review of this case, see Neil MacFarlane, 'The CIS and the OSCE in Georgia's Wars' in Thomas Weiss, above note 29, 115–36 especially at 120.

[61] *Ibid*, 119.

[62] *Ibid*.

[63] *OSCE Handbook* 1996 (Vienna, OSCE, 1996), 21, also cited by Neil MacFarlane, above note 60 at 119.

[64] S M Chervonnaya, *Abkhazia-1992: Post-Kommunisticheskaya Vandeya* (Moscow, Mosgorpechat, 1993).

[65] Leurdijk, above note 43.

[66] UN Doc S/RES/854, 6 August 1993.

[67] UN Doc S/RES/858, 24 August 1993. See Neil MacFarlane, L Minear and S Shenfield, *Armed Conflict in Georgia: A Case Study in Humanitarian Action and Peacekeeping* (Providence, RI, Watson Institute, 1995), Occasional paper No 27; S Hunter, *The Transcaucasus in Transition: Nation-Building and Conflict* (Washington DC, CSIS, 1994).

and suppressed the conflict.[68] Subsequently, the CIS deployed a peacekeeping operation to Georgia, based on the agreement by all parties to the conflict, in order to legitimise the Russian intervention and to bring the action under the auspices of the CIS.[69] The Security Council endorsed this move and also expanded UNOMIG by Resolution 937,[70] following the introduction of the Commonwealth of Independent States Peacekeeping Force (CISPKF) into the conflict.[71]

The mandate of the OSCE Mission to Georgia ranged from negotiating with the parties to the conflict, facilitating a political settlement of the conflict,[72] maintaining early warning capacity, to building confidence among the locals.[73] It accomplished most of its mandate through cooperation with the UN. It designated a special representative, Ambassador Gyarmati, for Georgia, while the UN designated Ambassador Edward Brunner.[74] Both the OSCE and UN worked effectively together and eventually arranged that the UN should lead on the matter on political settlement with the OSCE working in the area of human rights. Both indeed agreed on a joint Human Rights office in Abkhazia.

It must be noted that the OSCE had declared itself a regional organisation under Chapter VIII of the UN Charter shortly before this operation.[75] Its Helsinki Declaration spelt out its peacekeeping activities to include operations as varied as deployment of civilian personnel and large deployment of forces.[76] However, it is clear from its Helsinki Declaration that the OSCE would not take enforcement action. Hence, in the case of Georgia, the OSCE Mission in South Ossetia did not transcend its peacekeeping mandate. Its mandate was in fact the most conservative of the various actors involved in the management of the Georgian conflict, containing no explicit humanitarian or other functions. This contrasts sharply with the operation of CISPKF in Abkhaz. The CISPKF mandate was to 'promote the safe return of refugees and displaced persons, especially to the Gali District'.[77] There were no set

[68] P Baev, *Russia's Peacekeeping in the Caucasus*, Norwegian Institute of International Affairs/Western European Union Conference on 'Peacekeeping in Europe: Assessing UN and Regional Perspectives', Oslo, 17–18 November 1994, mimeograph, also cited by MacFarlane, above note 60 at note 15.

[69] MacFarlane, above note 60, 122.

[70] UN Doc S/RES/937, 21 July 1994.

[71] Discussion below.

[72] UN Doc S/RES/876 19 October 1993.

[73] MacFarlane, above note 60 at 123 *et seq*.

[74] On this issue, see CSCE, *Third Meeting of the Council: Summary of Conclusions* (Stockholm, CSCE, 1992), 12.

[75] *CSCE Helsinki Documents* 1992, 32.

[76] For excellent discussion of the CSCE activities see Adrian Hyde-Price, 'Future Security Systems for Europe' in C McInnes (ed), *Security & Strategy in the New Europe* (London, Routledge, 1992) 37–58; Harard Mueller 'A United Nations of Europe and North America', (1991) 21(1) *Arms Control Today* 3.

[77] Protocol to the Agreement on a Cease-Fire and Separation of Forces, mimeograph, cited by MacFarlane, above note 60, 125.

rules of engagement in the enabling instrument, and the mandate was ambiguous enough to accommodate enforcement action. The only restraint on the CISPKF mandate was that its implementation was to be supervised by UNOMIG.

As with its South Ossetia Mission, the OSCE mission in the crisis between Armenia and Azerbaijan in respect of the Armenians of the Nagorny-Karabakh[78] in Azerbaijan had remained largely a peacekeeping one.[79] This was despite the escalation of the conflict brought about by the seizure of the Agdam in the Azerbaijani Republic. Although the OSCE's plans to send troops to the conflict failed to materialise, the UN had largely ceded the leading role in that conflict to the organisation. The OSCE had effectively co-operated with the UN which particularly endorsed the efforts of the 'Minsk Group of the CSCE to achieve a peaceful solution to the conflict, including efforts to implement resolution 822 (1993)'.[80]

Nowhere is the fostering of UN/regional organisation relationship after the Cold War better portrayed than the operation of the OAS in Haiti.[81] The crisis arose from the following facts. The democratic government of Jean-Bertrand Aristide, sworn into office on 7 February 1991, was overthrown in September of that year by a military junta led by General Raul Cedras. The response by the OAS to the coup was swift and revealing. Under the provisions of the Santiago Commitment to Democracy and Development and Renewal of Inter-America System,[82] the OAS Ministers of Foreign Affairs immediately convened a meeting between 2–3 October. The Meeting adopted a resolution that rejected the coup, called for diplomatic isolation of the junta, and recognised the legitimacy of the toppled Aristide regime.[83]

On 8 October, following its botched attempt to mediate with the junta at Port-au-Prince, the OAS Mission of Foreign Ministers adopted a resolution urging member states to 'freeze the assets of the Haitian State and to impose a trade embargo on Haiti, except for humanitarian aid'.[84] On October 7, the General Committee of the UN General Assembly decided, quite unusually, to send the Haiti matter to the General Assembly directly instead of through one of the Assembly's surbodinate bodies.[85] Four days later, the General Assembly adopted a resolution stipulating, *inter alia* 'the immediate restoration of the legitimate government'.[86] The UN Secretary-General also became deeply involved in the Haiti affair. He encouraged

[78] UN Doc S/RES/822, 30 April 1993.
[79] UN Doc S/RES/853, 29 July 1993.
[80] *Ibid*, operative para 6.
[81] For a full account of this conflict, see David Malone, *Decision-Making in the UN Security Council: The Case of Haiti, 1990–1997* (Oxford, Oxford University Press, 1998).
[82] OAS-AG/RES 1080 (XXI-)/91/5 June 1991.
[83] OAS-MRE/RES/1/91.
[84] OAS-MRE/RES/2/91, 8.
[85] GA/8219, 7 October 1991. See also Malone, above note 81 at 65.
[86] UNGA R/46/7 11 October 1991.

initiatives among several world leaders on the role of the UN in Haiti.[87] The Security Council President endorsed the OAS resolution and indeed called for the restoration of the legitimate government of Haiti.[88]

The first attempt to involve the UN was through a resolution adopted by the OAS Foreign Affairs Ministers on 13 December 1992 which sought to 'explore the possibility and advisability of bringing the Haitian situation to the attention of the United Nations Security Council as a means of bringing about global enforcement of the trade embargo recommended by the OAS'.[89] On 9 February 1993, the UN and OAS established the Mission *Civile Internationale sur les Droits de L'Homme en Haiti* (MICIVIH), a civilian mission to spearhead the joint effort.[90] The decisive involvement of the Security Council came in the form of the unanimously adopted Resolution 841[91] imposing an arms and fuel embargo on Haiti. It must be pointed out that this resolution came following a decision by the OAS in June 1993 that the 18-month old OAS voluntary sanctions were ineffective.[92] This forced the junta to participate in the famous 'proximity talks' at Governor Island, New York, resulting in an agreement signed on 3 July 1993. In response, the UN suspended sanctions on Haiti[93] only to reintroduce[94] them when the junta reneged on its obligations under the Governor Island Agreement and prevented UNMIH[95] troops from entering Haiti.

A series of events[96] led the United States (and the OAS) to back a military solution, under UN auspices, to the Haitian crisis. On 31 July 1994, the Security Council adopted Resolution 940 mandating, *inter alia*, the use of 'all necessary means to facilitate the departure from Haiti of the military leadership'.[97] The US-led Multinational Force (MFN) landed in Haiti in September.[98] After successfully putting down the minimal challenge from the Haitian security in Cap-Haïtien, it took over the control of Haiti. Cedras and colleagues fled on 12 October and Aristide returned to Haiti on 15 October. The military action dubbed *Operation Uphold Democracy* was a success, handing over its responsibilities to the UNMIH on 31 March 1995.

[87] See Malone, above note 81 at 78 *et seq*.
[88] UN Doc S/PV3011, 3 October 1991.
[89] OAS-MRE/RES4/92.
[90] A/RES/47/20B 23 April 1993.
[91] UN Doc S/RES/841, 16 June 1993.
[92] OAS-MRE/RES 5/93 6 June 1993.
[93] UN Doc S/RES/861, 27 August 1993.
[94] UN Doc S/RES/873, 13 October 1993.
[95] This was approved by Security Council, UN Doc S/RES/867 23 February 1993.
[96] These events include: the martyrdom of activist Randall Robinson, who commenced a protracted hunger-strike to force Washington to drop the forcible repatriation of Haitian refugees; serious political heat turned on the Democratic party in the US by the Congressional Black Caucus; failure of sanctions and embargo to achieve the collective objective of the international community, unilateral withdrawal of the US troops from the sea port in Port-au-Prince.
[97] UN Doc S/RES/940, 31 July 1994.
[98] Malone, above note 81.

The above cases demonstrate the varied phases of regional interventions and the nature of the relationship that has developed between the UN and regional organisations since the end of Cold War. In the Georgian conflicts, the UN left it to the OSCE to seek an end to the Abkhazia crisis by its own means, while it took the lead in South Ossetia. In Liberia, the UN stepped into the matter only after ECOWAS had taken the lead. In Yugoslavia, the UN formally delegated powers to another organisation without being able to effectively supervise its use. In Haiti, the OAS created an enabling environment for the UN to intervene in the conflict. The success of these missions was to a large extent due to the cooperation between concerned regional organisations and the UN.

The examples of ECOWAS[99] and NATO[100] (unauthorised) enforcement actions constitute a clear but unusual departure from the framework of Chapter VIII and the trend in state practice during the Cold War.[101] This practice has grown even wider since ECOWAS missions in Liberia and Sierra Leone, and NATO's action against FRY. The Constituent Treaty of the African Union,[102] a new organisation that replaced the Organisation of African Unity (OAU) in 2001, empowers the organisation to take enforcement action. In January 2004, the AU affirmed its right to undertake military intervention in respect of members' conflicts.[103] Similarly, the practice of ECOWAS in Liberia and Sierra Leone has been codified by its new Protocol, which gives the sub-regional organisation significant powers to undertake enforcement action without Security Council authorisation.[104]

The most articulate explication of the UN/regional organisation relationship is to be found in the *Agenda for Peace*.[105] The *Agenda* identifies *preventive diplomacy, peacekeeping, peacebuilding* and *peacemaking* as the boundaries beyond which regional organisations may not aspire.[106] For the

[99] George Nolte, above note 2, 23 *ZaöR V* 53/3, 603; Kufor, above note 2.

[100] Bruno Simma, 'The NATO, the UN and the Use of force; Legal Aspects', (1999) 10(1) *European Journal of International Law* 1.

[101] See S Neil MacFarlane and Thomas G. Weiss, 'Regional Organizations and Regional Security' (1992) 2(1) *Security Studies* 6 at 7.

[102] For a commentary on this treaty see Ademola Abass and Mashood Baderin, 'Towards Effective Collective Security and Human Rights Protection in Africa: An Assessment of the Constitutive Act of the New African Union' (2002) XLIX *Netherlands International Law Review* 1.

[103] 'AU Okays Military Intervention in Member-Nations' *The Guardian* (Nigeria) 1 January 2004, 64.

[104] See Abass, above note 3.

[105] *An Agenda for Peace: Preventive diplomacy, peacemaking and peace-keeping. Report of the Secretary-General pursuant to the statement adopted by the Summit Meeting of the Security Council on 31 January 1992*, UN GAOR, 47th Sess, Agenda item 10, at 1, UN Doc A/A47, UN Doc S/2411 (1992).

[106] The concept of peacemaking, in the contemplation of the *Agenda*, had included the use of force by peacekeeping troops in order to implement their mandate. Such a use of force could indeed go beyond the boundary of traditional peacekeeping permitting force only in self-defence. Muscular peacekeeping, or multi-dimensional peacekeeping, the types of which the UN Under Secretary-General Kofi Annan (as he then was) said demanded 'teeth' and 'muscle' blurs the distinction between peacekeeping and enforcement action. For a full

Agenda, like the UN Charter, competence over enforcement actions resides with the UN. Hence, the *Agenda* does not include enforcement action in the regional organisations' syllabus, although it permits them to undertake 'muscular' peacekeeping operations.[107] According to Secretary-General Boutros Boutros-Ghali, if regional organisations were allowed to take enforcement action on their own, serious problems of control would arise.[108]

5.2. AN ASSESSMENT OF THE DEBATE ABOUT THE RELATIONSHIP BETWEEN THE UN AND REGIONAL ORGANISATIONS

The academic debate surrounding the post Cold War UN / regional organisation relationship underscores the deepening conceptual difficulty that characterises the subject matter.[109] Partly responsible for this is the assumption that the rise in regional interventions is due to the post-Cold War 'rediscovery [on the part of the Security Council] of and *enthusiasm for Chapter VIII* of the United Nations Charter'.[110] In this section we analyse this debate with a view to revealing its deficiencies before analysing cases in which regional organisations authorised enforcement actions entirely on their own.

5.2.1. Subsidiarity, Burden-sharing, Burden-shifting and Subcontracting: Different Concepts, Common Mistakes

Epithets commonly found in the legal literature on the subject matter include *subsidiarity*, *burden-sharing*, *burden-shifting* and *sub-contracting*.[111]

The principle of *subsidiarity* connotes the allocation of political authorities in 'a tiered' regime believed to be first used in the creation of the

enunciation of this type of peacekeeping, see Kofi Annan, UN Under-Secretary-General for Peacekeeping Operations, *NATO Review*, October 1993, at 4, cited by R Higgins, above note 46.

[107] For a critique of muscular peacekeeping, see R Higgins, above note 46, at 458–60.

[108] The *Report of the Secretary-General on the Work of the Organization. Supplement to an Agenda for Peace: Position paper of the Secretary-General on the Occasion of the Fiftieth Anniversary of the United Nations*, (hereafter Supplement to Agenda) UN Doc S/1995/1 (1995), UN Doc A/50/60, UN GAOR, 50th Sess, indeed clearly demarcated between peacekeeping operations and enforcement action.

[109] See Weiss above note 101; Eric Berman, 'The Security Council's Increasing Reliance on Burden-Sharing: Collaboration or Abrogation?', (1998) 4 (1) *International Peacekeeping* 1; David O'Brien, 'The Search for Subsidiarity: The UN, African Regional Organisations and Humanitarian Action' (2000) 7(3) *International Peacekeeping* 57.

[110] Berman, above note 109 (Emphasis added).

[111] Berman adopts 'burden-sharing' in his analysis, O'Brien adopts 'subsidiarity', 'burden-sharing' and 'burden-shifting'; MacFarlane and Weiss prefer not to adopt a conceptual paradigm.

Central Commission for Navigation of the Rhine in 1815.[112] According to one of its advocates, it is a principle of power allocation which favours delegating power to a lower authority.[113] Other writers conceive this concept as being capable of 'both expansion and restriction of authority by linking governance to the issue of competencies'.[114]

Burden-sharing and burden-shifting although appearing somewhat analogous are, in fact, operationally dissimilar. In addition, they have little in common with subsidiarity with which they are often confused. Whereas burden-sharing connotes 'an exchange of resources among authorities to realize common objectives',[115] burden-shifting implies the 'devolution of responsibility for humanitarian response without due concern for whether the capacity exists to respond effectively'.[116] Sub-contracting, on the other hand, is commonly regarded as the delegating of an authority to act by a superior organ to an inferior one.[117] Thus, subsidiarity subsumes burden-sharing and subcontracting insofar as it implies the pattern of distribution of powers and responsibilities between the UN and regional organisations. To that extent they are treated here as ejusdem generis.

The concept of burden-shifting denotes the passing of the responsibility from one organisation to the other, in this context, from the UN to concerned regional organisations. This concept assumes that a humanitarian effort by UN and regional organisations invariably implies distribution of burdens between the UN and regional organisations. Hence, it is often argued that:

> [w]estern governments that are either reluctant to commit military or civilian personnel to politically volatile and physically dangerous situations, or are unwilling to underwrite the costs of assistance in regions where their narrowly defined national interest do not lie[118]

find this concept appealing. It suffices to mention here that it is both limiting and inaccurate to construe the relationship between the UN and regional arrangement *mainly* in terms of its financial implications or burden allocation.

Whereas some of the regional actions already discussed provide numerous instances of subcontracting, several do not. The NATO/UN joint action in Yugoslavia (1991–95) can be classified as 'burden-sharing' both

[112] See Genvieve Peterson, 'Political Inequality at the Congress of Vienna' (1945) 60(4) *Political Science Quarterly* 544, cited in David O' Brien, above note 109 at 59.

[113] O' Brien above note 109 at 58.

[114] See Andy W Knight 'Towards a Subsidiarity Model of Peacemaking and Preventive Diplomacy: Making Chapter VIII of the UN Charter Operational' (1996) 17 *Third World Quarterly* 49.

[115] O'Brien, above note 109 at 58.

[116] *Ibid.*

[117] O'Brien traced the development of this 'tied' system to the creation of the Central Commission for the Navigation of the Rhine in 1815, above note 109 at 60.

[118] *Ibid.*

before and after the Dayton Agreement.[119] On 28 February 1994, NATO aircraft shot down four Serbian aircraft that had violated the no-flight zone. Following that, NATO provided air cover for UNPROFOR to implement its mandate. Finally, NATO enforced the 'exclusion zones' around the safe areas without the authorisation of the Security Council.[120] However, in all these circumstances, there was either a formal delegation of power to NATO, which it arguably exceeded, or an initiation of actions by NATO, based on permissible grounds. Such grounds include the fact that the designation of 'safe areas' was done by the UN while NATO decided on their enforcement. To a large extent, this analysis can be applied to the relationship between the UN/OAS *mutantis mutandi*.

However, the UN/ECOWAS operation in Liberia and Sierra Leone cannot really be described as falling under any of the above conceptual frameworks. For example, concerning the two conflicts some writers argued that the UN *delegated*[121] powers to ECOWAS to intervene; that ECOWAS acted as a subcontractor of the UN.[122] This view is erroneous. In Liberia, the UN had declined to intervene in the crisis when the Liberian government invited it to do so in 1991,[123] and did not get involved until about three years after ECOWAS had deployed its monitoring group to that country.[124]

The fallacy of the assumption that the UN/ECOWAS relationship was one of subcontract is even more striking in the first phase of the Sierra

[119] For a similar view see Leurdijk, above note 43, 54–57.

[120] *Ibid.*

[121] Sarooshi, for instance, wrote that 'In its response to the *coup* . . . the Security Council delegate (sic) to ECOWAS by resolution 1132 the power to carry out a naval interdiction against the country (Sierra Leone)' See D Sarooshi, '*The Development of Collective Security: The Delegation by the UN Security Council of its Chapter VII Power*' (Oxford, Clarendon Press, 1999) at 249, fn. 4. While it is true that Resolution 1132 directly referred to ECOWAS, it was a misnomer to say that it *delegated* the power of interdiction to ECOWAS. ECOWAS had already commenced interdiction fully under its own directive (A/Dec 7/8/97) exactly two months before the UN adopted its first resolution on Sierra Leone (1132). All this resolution did, according to ECOWAS, was merely '*reiterating* support for the ECOWAS effort in the Sierra Leone and the imposition of sanctions on the illegal regime in Sierra Leone'. Communiqué of the *Fifth Meeting of the Ministers of foreign Affairs of the Committee of five on Sierra Leone* (on file with the author).

[122] But see Marten Zwanenburg, 'Double Standards in Peacekeeping? Subcontracting Peacekeeping and International Humanitarian Law' (1999) 12 *Leiden Journal of International Law* 753.

[123] The inability of the UN and OAU to intervene in the Liberian crisis has been attributed to the doctrine of 'non-intervention'. The representative of the Liberian Interim Government noted in January 1991, upon his invitation to address the Security Council, that the principle of 'non-interference has hampered the effectiveness of the Council', UN Doc. S/PV.2974 of 22 January 1991, 3. See also Funmi Olonisakin, *Reinventing Peacekeeping in Africa: Conceptual and Legal Issues in ECOMOG Operations* (The Hague, Kluwer Law International, 2000) 114. Georg Nolte noted that the Liberian issue 'was not even put on its (Security Council's) agenda,' above note 2 at 632.

[124] It has been argued however by Ramsbotham and Woodhouse, above note 21, that when the UN Secretary-General tried to raise the issue of Liberia in the Security Council on 28 May 1990, this attempt 'was blocked by African governments led by Nigeria, which was keen to keep external interference out of the region', at 139.

Leone crisis (1997–99) where the two organisations implemented different mandates[125] and ECOWAS had been acting long before the UN intervened. There is no basis to ground the relationship as being one of sub–contracting. The term 'sub-contracting', in this context, denotes situations whereby 'regional organisations are requested or invited *by* the Security Council to execute tasks within terms set by the Council'.[126] It requires a formal delegation of power by one organisation to the other as in the UN/NATO case in Yugoslavia. Subsidiarity, on the other hand, suggests the allocation of political authorities in a 'tiered' regime. Regional organisations are not in a tiered-relationship with the UN in the way that a federal government with the component states.

It would be inconceivable to see regional organisations as subsidiaries of the UN. They are not organically linked with the UN and as such cannot be its subsidiaries. In Liberia and Sierra Leone, ECOWAS acted on its own terms with little or no real connection to the mission established by the Security Council.[127] The UN had not requested ECOWAS to intervene in Liberia and Sierra Leone. Neither did ECOWAS operate within the terms set by the Security Council in either situation.[128] It decided and operated enforcement action in both cases, especially in Sierra Leone, whereas UNAMSIL implemented a peacekeeping mandate. It paid its own bills in both cases and commanded its own troops. How then, the question must be asked, could the UN be regarded as having *delegated* the power to intervene in Liberia and Sierra Leone to ECOWAS?

5.3. REGIONALLY AUTHORISED ENFORCEMENT ACTIONS OR DECENTRALISED COLLECTIVE SECURITY

What does the phrase 'decentralised collective security' mean? Does it suggest that regional organisations may supplant the UN in the maintenance of peace and security even in their regions, or that they act in violation of the principles and objectives of the UN Charter?

[125] See Ademola Abass, above note 3.

[126] Leurdijk, above note 43 at 62.

[127] Ramsbotham's and Woodhouse's (above note 21) assessment of the Liberia case seems to be more representative of the reality of the situation. These writers argue that '[a]lthough in the Cotonou Agreement the UN's coordinating role was seen to be complementary to ECOMOG's security role, the relationship was not made clear', at 141.

[128] Although it might be argued that while ECOWAS acted under its own legal regime it was still mandated by the UN, this is not actually so as we shall see later in the discussion. The *authorisation* the UN granted ECOWAS was the one enjoining ECOWAS to implement the mandate contained in resolution 1132 concerning interdiction of ships heading towards Sierra Leone. As we argue later, this *authorisation* is redundant since ECOWAS had already commenced full interdiction before this resolution was adopted. While nothing prevents the UN according retroactive authorisation on an organisation, in the circumstances of the present case the authorisation did not amount to that.

As used here, decentralised collective security refers to a *system whereby regional organisations are able to perform such functions including, but not limited to, peacekeeping, peacebuilding, peacemaking, pacific settlement of disputes and enforcement action, empowered by legal regimes other than the Charter, and in circumstances as may dispense with Security Council authorisation.* It is the implementation of collective security by regional organisations *within* and *beyond* the legal regulation of Chapter VIII. Decentralised collective security is distinguishable from decentralised enforcement action which is contained in Chapter VIII. The latter refers to the *utilisation* of regional organisations for enforcement action by the Security Council under Article 53(1).

The authorisation of states 'acting nationally or through *regional agencies or organisations*' by Resolution 787[129] in Yugoslavia was an example of decentralised enforcement action under Chapter VIII.[130] Accordingly, the power to act under Chapter VIII was officially delegated to regional organisations by the Security Council, as prescribed by Article 53(1) of the Charter, and the beneficial regional organisations or agencies were to act 'under the authority of the Security Council'.[131] Here was the first case of the Security Council *utilising* regional organisations or agencies in the language of Chapter VIII. Another example of decentralised enforcement action is typified by that part of Resolution 787 which calls on states acting 'nationally'. Although such states do not act under regional arrangements, and hence not subject to the reporting obligation in Article 54, they are theoretically under the Security Council control as may be specified in the enabling resolutions and the Security Council's practice.[132]

The main legal problems of decentralised collective security are Articles 53(1) and 2(4).[133] In other words, the question may be asked: How may we justify regionally authorised enforcement action when Article 53(1) requires Security Council authorisation as a condition for valid regional enforcement action?

5.3.1. ECOWAS' Justifications for Beyond Chapter VIII Action and Third States' Responses

During a Security Council debate in 1997,[134] ECOWAS proffered many justifications for its unauthorised enforcement action in Sierra Leone. First, it argued that it was left 'with no option but to adopt a set of measures in

[129] UN Doc S/RES/787 16 Nov 1992.
[130] Emphasis added.
[131] See discussion above.
[132] See discussion in Chapter 3.
[133] Discussion about Article 2(4) in the next chapter.
[134] S/PV 3822 8 Oct, 1997, at 4.

the form of sanction and embargo as a means of pressuring the regime in Freetown to appreciate the futility of its situation'. It also claimed that there was a real need to avoid a repeat of the Liberia tragedy. With regards to its use of force without Security Council's authorisation, ECOWAS claimed that 'it was recognized that the other two options, including negotiation and sanctions cum blockade, could not be achieved without the use of some military force'.[135]

Moreover, ECOWAS claimed that it was 'sufficiently seized of the matter.'[136] It extended this basis in 1999 by claiming that it was the natural organisation that could effectively find solutions to conflicts in West Africa, and that in the circumstances ensuing in Sierra Leone the UNAMSIL peacekeeping mandate was not a realistic option.[137]

After advancing its justification, ECOWAS then formally requested the Security Council's authority to 'carry out its tasks as mandated by the ECOWAS summit'.[138] One quick observation to make here is that the authorisation requested by ECOWAS is in respect of tasks which included the use of force as decided by ECOWAS summit.

ECOWAS persisted in its line of justification when it eventually restored President Kabbah's government in Sierra Leone in 1998 through the use of force.[139] Interestingly, not only did the Security Council fail to admonish ECOWAS during its meeting immediately following this action, but also 'commends the important role that the Economic Community of West African States (ECOWAS) has continued to play towards peaceful resolution of the crisis'.[140] Furthermore, the Security Council failed to condemn ECOWAS unauthorised action against the junta in its subsequent meetings.[141]

On 13 July 1998, the Security Council returned fully to discuss ECOWAS role in Sierra Leone. Individual members expressed what they thought of ECOWAS's forcible action. Austria, speaking on behalf of European Union, 'commend[s] the important role that ECOWAS has continued to

[135] S/PV 3797, 11 July 1997.

[136] *Ibid*, at 4.

[137] In the Preamble to the Twentieth Session of the Authority of Heads of State and Government, (Abuja, Nigeria, 28–29 August 1999), ECOWAS noted that 'the ECOWAS Monitoring Group (ECOMOG) in Liberia is the only Force in the Sub-region capable of prompt response to any requests in this regard and has the relevant expertise to achieve this purpose'. See Decision A Dec 7/8/97 *Extending the Scope of Activity and Mandate of ECOMOG to cover Sierra Leone* (on file with the author).

[138] *Ibid*, 4.

[139] UN Doc S/RES 1156, 16 March 1998 '[w]elcomes the return to Sierra Leone of its democratically elected government on 10 March 1998'; UN Doc S/RES/1162, 17 April 1998, '[c]ommends the Economic Community of West African States (ECOWAS) and its Military Observer Group (sic) (ECOMOG), deployed in Sierra Leone, on the important role they are playing in support of the objectives related to the restoration of peace and security'.

[140] S/PV 3857, 26 Feb 1998, at 2.

[141] S/PV 3861 16 March 1998.

play towards the peaceful resolution of the crisis'.[142] The United Kingdom followed suit, noting particularly that 'ECOMOG deserves our gratitude'.[143] Apart from commending ECOWAS for doing a 'commendable job' Kenya observed that 'Sierra Leone would not be where it is today without the heroic and superb efforts of ECOMOG'.[144]

More endorsement came from other Security Council members such as The Gambia[145] and US.[146] Japan, which had been somewhat ambivalent about ECOWAS involvement, also commended the organisation.[147] The best defence of ECOWAS' action, and indeed, of regionally authorised enforcement actions, came from Costa Rica. Mr Niehaus, speaking on behalf of that country, stated that Costa Rica,

> firmly believes in the importance of regional and subregional organizations. In this case, the Economic Community of West African States (ECOWAS), has played a crucial role, and the ECOWAS Monitoring Group (ECOMOG) continues to be the body entrusted with monitoring security and maintaining stability in Sierra Leone.[148]

China called ECOWAS action 'a positive role'[149] while Sweden called for an encouragement of 'ECOMOG to co-ordinate its efforts with UNOMSIL'. Sweden also pointed out that the 'joint efforts of the United Nations and ECOMOG, as a subregional organization, are well in line with the overall ambition of the international community to support and strengthen African peacekeeping capacity'.[150]

Of all the Security Council members only France exercised some restraint, although it did not condemn the action. It stressed that the cooperation between ECOWAS and UN must be along 'the desired lines between the United Nations and the regional organization in which we place our trust'. Brazil noted that the restoration of the legitimate President 'was not followed by peace',[151] but blamed this on the fighters of the rebel group, RUF. The resolution 1181 was unanimously adopted without any condemnation of ECOWAS by any Security Council member.

From the above, it is clear that the Security Council's endorsement of ECOWAS action was much bolder than advocates of implicit authorisation recognised. Apparently, the Security Council knew that ECOWAS had not conformed to the relevant provisions of the Charter on this

142 S/PV 3902, 13 July 1998.
143 *Ibid*, at 4.
144 *Ibid*, 6.
145 *Ibid*, 13.
146 *Ibid*, 14.
147 *Ibid*, 8.
148 *Ibid*, 9.
149 *Ibid*, 11.
150 *Ibid*, at 11.
151 *Ibid*, 12.

occasion, specifically Article 53(1) and 2(4) of the Charter. Yet, it commended ECOWAS, not on one but several occasions. The Security Council, as the UK put it, 'applaud the vital role played by the Economic Community of West African States'.[152] Without ECOMOG's effort to bring about peace and preserve security, UK argued, 'there would not be a peace process for us to support'.[153] Instances of states' disapproval of ECOWAS actions in Sierra Leone are difficult to find; the handful antagonisms there are exist only within the academic community.

In summary, Chapter VIII forms part of a holistic structure of the UN collective security system. Thus, its operation entails a *modus operandi* based on certain expectations that the Security Council will authorise a regional action default its own action, subject to a reasonable exercise of its discretion. A non-realisation of these expectations must of necessity elicit a *modus vivendi* by means of which regional organisations may cope with the gaps created by the Security Council's inaction and/or inability to authorise regional actions.

Thus, where the Security Council declines to intervene in a conflict despite a formal request by the affected state, a regional organisation already operating in that region may take whatever action it deems appropriate in the circumstances.[154] For if the Security Council is unwilling to intervene in a particular conflict, it may not be inclined to authorise regional organisations to do so as this may mean its own indirect involvement. Furthermore, where a regional organisation intervenes in a conflict in default of the UN's involvement, the concerned regional organisation may continue to implement its own mandate even if the UN decides eventually on a different one. The justification for this is that the UN often issues peacekeeping mandates to its missions in situations where there is no peace to keep. The irony of such inadequate mandates is that it often falls to the regional organisation, as it did to ECOWAS, to protect UN mission against enemy fire.[155] The question is if the UN genuinely believed that the mandate it issued to UNAMSIL was appropriate to the situation in Sierra Leone, why did it require ECOMOG to protect its personnel? And if ECOWAS had accepted to implement a peacekeeping mandate in the face of the war, as the UN had wanted it to, from where would it have gotten the capacity to protect not only its own troops, but also the additional burden of UNAMSIL?

The Security Council, through Resolution 1270,[156] issued a peacekeeping mandate for the forces of the United Nations Mission in Sierra

[152] S/PV 4035, 20 August 1999, 4.
[153] *Ibid.*
[154] See discussion in Chapter 3.
[155] S/PV 4035 20 August 1999, 7.
[156] UN Doc S/RES/1270, 22 October 1999.

Leone (UNAMSIL), which, upon deployment, had to operate alongside ECOMOG troops which had assumed an enforcement mandate.[157] The constant frictions resulting from the divergent mandates of the two organisations, apart from the perennial conflict about command and control, led to the withdrawal of the Nigerian, Ghanaian, and the Guinean contingents from the ECOWAS mission.[158] When the Nigerian contingent agreed to return to Sierra Leone, although this time as part and parcel of UNAMSIL, ECOWAS had *insisted* on implementing an enforcement mandate against the rebel faction. It also retained the command and control of its forces. The insistence by ECOWAS on its own mandate therefore precludes any presumption that by operating as part of UNAMSIL, ECOWAS functioned under the UN and not ECOWAS mandate.

5.4. THE RATIONALE FOR REGIONALLY AUTHORISED ENFORCEMENT ACTION

5.4.1. The Emerging Principles in the Law and Practice of Regional Collective Security

Several emerging principles concerning intervention by regional organisations in the conflicts or other peace-threatening situations occurring within their regions can be identified from the laws and practice of regional organisations since the end of the Cold War. There is the principle that now purports to *replace* the member states' consent authorising regional organisations to intervene in *intra* or *inter*-state conflicts by a new *right* of intervention.[159] In addition, there is the principle that empowers regional organisations to decide on what measures may be necessary to mitigate conflicts or other peace-threatening situations.[160] Lastly, there is the principle that imposes an *obligation* on member states of some regional organisations to comply with decisions of these organisations even if they are in the process of withdrawing their membership.[161] We consider these principles in detail below.

[157] 'Nigeria Sets Interventions Terms', BBC News: World Africa, 10 May 2000 http://www.bbc.co.uk/hienglish/world/africa/newid_743000/743219.stm. Madu Onuorah, Segun Ayeoyenikan and Tunji Oketunbi, 'ECOWAS to Deploy 3,000 troops to Sierra Leone' http:www.ngrguardiannews.com.

[158] Documents on file with the author.

[159] Article 10 ECOWAS Mechanism; Article 4(h) AU Act.

[160] Article 10 ECOWAS Mechanism.

[161] *Ibid*, Article 27.

5.4.1.1. *The Replacement of Host State Consent with the New Right of Intervention*

No direct provision of the UN Charter governs peacekeeping operations.[162] Nevertheless, some principles have evolved through the practice of the UN and states alike, which have found general acceptance amongst states and writers as forming the legal basis of peacekeeping.[163] The first of these is that peacekeepers must seek and obtain the consent of, or be invited by, the *host* state, before they can intervene in a conflict.[164] Also, peacekeepers must be completely *impartial* and must not use force to determine the outcome of the conflict. Finally, peacekeepers must not use force except in *self-defence*.[165] These principles could be said to form the *corpus* of customary international law on peacekeeping operations. Thus, international lawyers do not generally regard the absence of specific Charter rules for regulating peacekeeping operations as incapacitating these principles.

[162] See Ramsbotham and Woodhouse, above note 21, noting that 'Peacekeeping is not mentioned in the UN Charter', at xi. See also Dan Ciobanu, 'The Power of the Security Council to Organize Peace-Keeping Operations' in A Cassese, above note 9 at 15, arguing that '[I]t is general knowledge that the Charter of the United Nations does not provide *in terminis* the power of the Security Council to organize peace-keeping operations, and the *travaux preparatoires* of the San Francisco Conference do not suggest that the founding fathers of the Organization would have really contemplated them.' Attempts by writers to ascribe definitions to the term peacekeeping have only resulted in some confusion. See Paul Diehl, *International Peacekeeping* (Maryland, John Hopkins University Press, 1994), 4. He however observed that 'one distinguishing attribute of peacekeeping is the performance of a noncoercive mission', at 5. See also James Boyd, *United Nations Peace-keeping operations: A Military and Political Appraisal* (New York, Praeger Publishers, 1972), at 10 noting that 'despite the emergence of a new pattern of 'peace-keeping', there is still no fully-agreed upon definition of the term. Ramsbotham and Tom Woodhouse adopted the definition of peacekeeping given by the UN in its official peacekeeping account, the *Blue Helmet*, stating that 'A Peacekeeping operation has come to be defined as an operation involving military personnel, but without enforcement powers, undertaken by the United Nations to help maintain or restore peace and security in areas of conflict', *id*, xi.

[163] See IJ Rikhye, *Preparation and Training of United Nations Peace-Keeping Forces* (Adelphi Papers No 9) (London, Institute for Strategic Studies, 1964); Ernest Lefever, *Crisis in Congo* (Washington DC, The Brookings Institution, 1965).

[164] *United Nations Blue Book Series*, Vol VIII, *The United Nations in Somalia* 1992–1996 (New York, Department of Public Information, 1996). The UN varied the requirement of Host State consent in Somalia, noting that, 'unlike conventional peace-keeping operations, the force could not be deployed at the request or with the consent of a host government (since there was no Government), or on the basis of an agreement among the parties to the conflict.' *Id*, 3. See also the First Report of the Secretary-General Dag Hammarskjold, stating, *inter alia*, that '. . . while the General Assembly is entitled to establish the Force (UNEF I) with the consent of those parties which contribute units to the Force, it could not request Force to be stationed or operate on the territory of a given country without the consent of the Government of that country'. (A/3302 6 November 1956, para 9). See R Higgins, 'A General Assessment of United Nations Peace-Keeping' in A Cassese (ed), *United Nations Peace-Keeping* (Alphen aan den Rijn, Sijthoff & Noordhoff, 1978), 1.

[165] But see the *Agenda for Peace*.

As stated earlier on, in its intervention in Liberia in 1990, ECOWAS had acted contrary to all the norms of peacekeeping. Its purported invitation by the Samuel Doe regime was controversial for lack of compliance with the procedures laid down in the relevant treaty.[166] Apart from that, the intervention of ECOWAS did not receive the consent of one of the main rival factions in the conflict.[167] In addition, ECOMOG used force against one of the rebel factions in Liberia to the extent that surpassed what is customarily permissible under the law of peacekeeping. Finally, ECOWAS did not seek the authorisation of the Security Council as it was required to do by Article 53(1) of the UN Charter when it commenced enforcement action against one of the warring factions in 1991.

As noted above, certain members of ECOWAS which withdrew from Sierra Leone[168] returned as part of UNAMSIL.[169] Upon its return, ECOWAS applied the provisions of its new Protocol adopted in November 1999, especially those entitling it to undertake enforcement action without the Security Council authorisation and to decide on whatever mandate it pleased.[170] It also laid down specific conditions and its rules of engagement in the conflict although, this time, it was to function as part of UNAMSIL.[171]

What is paramount to us here, however, is the nature and specific impact of the provision of Article 10 of ECOWAS' new Protocol on the requirement of Host State consent. This Article states that the Mediation and Security Committee (MSC) of ECOWAS '*shall* authorise all forms of interventions'.[172]

Article 10 allocates to ECOWAS a special type of power. This power has transformed ECOWAS into a supra-national organisation enjoying

[166] Gray argued that 'it is clear that the normal decision-making processes of ECOWAS were not followed', above note 1 at 213. Similarly, Kofi Oteng Kufor argued that the 'decision making process was subverted', above note 2 at 538. But see Georg Nolte, above note 2, arguing that '[ex]isting precedents show that the institutional aspects of collective security organisations are not normally meant to be exclusive', 615.

[167] Ramsbotham and Woodhouse argue observed that 'ECOMOG's ambivalent role was a fundamental problem . . . as recently as April 1993 it had mounted a full-scale assault on the NPFL, with rockets launchers, naval gunfire, and ground attack aircraft,' above note 21 at 143.

[168] Security Council Resolution 1289 'takes note of the decision of the Governments of Nigeria, Guinea and Ghana to withdraw their remaining ECOMOG contingents from Sierra Leone,' as reported in the letter to the Secretary General of 23 December 1999.' UN Doc S/RES/1289 (2000) para 7.

[169] 'Nigeria Sets Intervention Terms', BBC News: World Africa, 10 May 2000 http://www.bbc.co.uk/hienglish/world/africa/newsid_743000/743219.stm. The Security Council recognised these modalities during its 4139 meeting, S/PV. 4139 p 11.

[170] Article 10(c) empowers the Mediation and Security Council (MSC) to, *inter alia*, 'authorise all forms of intervention and decide particularly on the deployment of political and military mission'.

[171] *Ibid*.

[172] Text in Abass, 'The New Collective Security Mechanism of ECOWAS: Innovations and Problems' (2000) 5(2) *Journal of conflict and Security* 211.

greater powers than the component members that established it.[173] Article 10 does not *only* empower ECOWAS to *forcibly* intervene in a conflict involving one or more member states, it imposes some responsibility on member states to comply with the exercise of power by ECOWAS.[174] ECOWAS members have thus agreed in advance to comply when ECOWAS exercises its powers to intervene in their conflicts. An invitation by a host state for an intervention by ECOWAS appears now to be legally superfluous in the light of Article 10. This Article has apparently abolished or desegregated the consent of ECOWAS member states, which ECOWAS would normally be required to obtain *before* it may intervene in their conflicts.

5.4.1.2. *Effects of the New Provisions*

Insofar as ECOWAS member states ratified the new protocol, notwithstanding that it purportedly terminates their *right* to formally invite ECOWAS to intervene in their conflicts, this new power accorded ECOWAS takes precedence over the customary law with respect to Host State consent. Article 26 of ECOWAS new Protocol lists five parties who may *now* initiate an intervention upon the outbreak of a conflict. These are: the Authority of Heads of State and Government of ECOWAS, the MSC, a member state, the Executive Secretary of ECOWAS, and the Organisation of African Unity or the United Nations. It must be pointed out that this provision does not specifically speak to a member state who may be experiencing a conflict.

The creation of the powers to intervene seems to be the unique achievement of ECOWAS Protocol, and definitely the most revolutionary legal provision that has evolved from ECOWAS' practice since its involvement in collective security functions commenced in 1990. In fact, the tenets of Article 10 constitute a major advancement over the collective security system of the UN Charter itself. For Article 2(7) of the UN Charter prohibits the organisation from intervening in 'matters which are essentially within the domestic jurisdiction of any State', subject only to Chapter VII provisions.

The validity of transforming host state consent into a treaty obligation derives, not only from the existence of affirmative state practice to that effect, but largely from the fact that states made a conscious choice to change the status of the principle from a soft law obligation into treaty law.[175]

[173] HG Schermers and NM Blokkers, *International Institutional Law*, (The Hague, Martinus Nijhoff Publishers, 3rd edn, 1995), 59–62.

[174] See a discussion of this below.

[175] For a similar argument, see CM Chinkin, 'The Challenge of Soft Law: Development and Change in International Law' (1989) 38 *International and Comparative Law Quarterly* 30 at 37.

Similar provisions establishing the same principle as Article 10 of ECOWAS 1999 Protocol, and many other principles, are to be found in the Article 4(h) of the Constitutive Act of the African Union (hereafter the AU Act).[176] This article provides that the Union has the '*right* to intervene in a Member State pursuant to a decision in respect of grave circumstances, namely: war crimes, genocide and crimes against humanity'.[177] As with the Article 10 of ECOWAS Protocol, this article has also adopted the term 'right' to describe the nature of the power accorded the new organisation by member states.

When compared to Article 19 of the OAU Charter,[178] it is clear that the AU Act's intended effect is much more than merely encouraging member states to pursue pacific settlement of their disputes. Although it might be said that Article 4 contains only a principle, the AU affirmed in January 2004 that it has right to militarily intervene in member states' conflicts.[179]

Moreover, it is entirely up to a member state, according to Article 4(j), 'to request intervention from the Union in order to restore peace and security'. However, based on Article 4(h), the absence of such requests will not prevent the Union from acting *suo motu*. Thus, there is no requirement of consent in the AU Act. Member States have a *privilege* to request an intervention, but no more. Conversely, the Union has a *right* to intervene entirely on its own initiative.[180] The *right* of the Union is independent of the preference of concerned member states. Theoretically speaking, a rejection of an intervention by a member state may easily be overturned by an affirmation of two-third majority of the Assembly of Heads of State and government.[181] Another important principle found in the AU Act is that the Union will only intervene in a member State where there is occurrence of war crimes, genocide and crimes against humanity.[182] The Act does not define what these terms mean. Nor does it specify who determines their occurrences. It is plausible to assume that events in Somalia, and particularly Rwanda, motivated this provision.[183]

[176] *Council of Ministers Seventy-fourth Ordinary Session/Ninth Ordinary Session of the AEC*, 2–7 July 2001. CM/2210 (LXXIV).

[177] For a definition of these terms, see the Statute of the International Criminal Court (Rome Statute) (1998) 37 *International Legal Materials* 999–1019. Articles 6, 7 and 8 define 'genocide', 'crime against humanity' and 'war crimes' respectively.

[178] Article 19 of the OAU Charter states that 'Member States pledge to settle all disputes among themselves by peaceful means and, to this end decide to establish a Commission of Mediation, Conciliation, and Arbitration' 3 *International Legal Materials*, 116.

[179] See above.

[180] See Abass and Baderin, above note 102.

[181] Article 7(1) Constitutive Act of the African Union.

[182] Article 4(h) Constitutive Act of the African Union.

[183] See the *Report of the Secretary-General on the Implementation of the Sitre Decision on The African Union* (EAHG/DEC 1 (V)), especially the section on the 'Political underpinnings of the Transformation of the OAU to the African Union', at 2.

There is no provision in the Act obligating the Union to report actions which it authorises to the Security Council under Article 54 of the UN Charter as was the case with the previous legal regimes.[184] This raises the question whether the AU will formally request Security Council's authorisation before taking an enforcement action as Article 53(1) requires. The intentions of the AU in this regard have been made much clearer with the adoption of its *Protocol Relating to the Establishment of the Peace and Security Council*[185] of the Union which entered into force on 26th of December 2003 upon the deposition by Nigeria of the 27th instrument of ratification of the protocol.[186] Article 13 of the Protocol provides for an 'African Standby Force'. This force is to be deployed, according to paragraphs 3, to a wide range of activities including intervention, humanitarian assistance, and any other functions as may be mandated by the Peace and Security Council of the Assembly.

Paragraph 4 of Article 13 states that in undertaking these functions, the African Standby Force shall, 'where appropriate, cooperate with the United Nations and its Agencies'. Does this mean that the AU will seek an authorisation from the Security Council prior to an enforcement action?

This writer put this question to the director of the Peace and Security department of AU on 2 February 2004, given the fact that Article 16 of the protocol allocated 'primary responsibility for promoting peace, stability and security in Africa' to the Union. In his response, Ambassador Sam Ibok gave a categorical 'no' as answer. In his explanation, the AU director stated that 'We [AU] are not an arm of the United Nations. We accept the UN's global authority but we will not wait for the UN to authorise an action that we intend to take. You [this writer] yourself know the politics associated with the Security Council's authorisation'.[187] Pressed further on the issue, the director added that 'we [AU] are in a tacit agreement with the United Nations on this and there is an understanding to that effect'.

Whilst it might be said that this interpretation does not constitute AU practice, precedents suggest that opinions usually given by officials of African regional organisations, especially those that deal directly with the concerned instruments, often portray the collective stance of the respective organisations on the issues. For instance, when asked a similar question by this writer in 2000, the director of ECOWAS Legal Department, Mr Roger Laloupo, gave a similar answer. Needless to add

[184] *Final Communiqué, Eighth Meeting of Foreign Ministers of the Committee of Five On Sierra Leone*, New York, 5–6 Feb 1998.

[185] Adopted during the First Ordinary Session of the Assembly of the Union, Durban, South Africa 9 July 2002, on http://www.africa-union.org/home/welcome.htm.

[186] Press Release No 117/2003.

[187] This interview was conducted via a telephone directly between me and this director. Time of interview was between 9:30 and 10:15 am 2 February 2004. Transcript available with the author.

that his interpretation was followed to the letter when ECOWAS went to Sierra Leone.

The final treaty to be considered as regards the evolution of the principle which now seems to have abrogated the customary rule of host state consent, as we shall later prove, is the SADC Protocol on Politics and Security (hereafter SADC Protocol).[188]

Although SADC was established between 1994/95,[189] its Defence Protocol was adopted only in 1997.[190] Article 2 of the protocol states that SADC functions are to (a) protect the people and safeguard the development of the region against instability arising from the breakdown of law and order and inter-state conflict; (e) mediate in inter-state and intra-state disputes and conflicts. Article 2(g), being the most detailed of these provisions empowers SADC 'where a conflict does occur, to seek to end this as quickly as possible through diplomatic means. Only where such means fail would the Organ consider *necessary measures* to restore peace and stability. Such measures shall be immediately reported to the OAU and/or the UN for their consideration under the provisions of their respective Charters'.

Obviously, this provision is far reaching in several respects. Apart from adhering to the traditional framework of Chapter VIII which encourages regional organisations to seek pacific settlement of their disputes it obligates SADC to comply with the obligation stated in Article 54 of the UN Charter. Not only that, it obligates an *immediate* reporting of measures taken to the UN or OAU or both. Thus, *prima facie*, one is tempted to conclude that SADC is an exception to other regional organisations. However, the treaty also provides that SADC will take *necessary measures* to restore peace and order where diplomatic means fail. Since these necessary measures are to be taken once diplomatic measures fail, they can only be enforcement actions.

The outbreak of conflict in the Democratic Republic of Congo (DRC)[191] demonstrated that SADC would undertake primary responsibility in its region if the UN did not intervene in its members conflicts. SADC successfully brought all the nine parties to the conflict in the DRC to conclude the Lusaka Peace Agreement, in Lusaka, Zambia in 1999.[192] It held two further summits on August 7 and 14 in order to seek means of ensuring

[188] (1993) 32 *International Legal Materials* 116. See also Hilaire McCoubrey and Justin Morris, *Regional Peacekeeping in the Cold War Era* (The Hague, Kluwer Law International, 2000) (hereafter Morris and McCoubrey), 140–50.

[189] For a comprehensive review of the Southern Africa Security structure see J Cilliers, 'The Evolving Security Architecture in Southern Africa' (1995) 4 *African Security Review* 40.

[190] McCoubrey and Morris, above note 188, 140–50.

[191] See the statement of Nancy Soderberg, the US representative to the Security Council Meeting held in the first week of August 2000, Integrated Regional Information Networks (IRIN), 7 August 2000, http://www.relief.int/IRIN/cea/countrystories/drc.

[192] UN Doc S/1999/815.

compliance with the ceasefire by the conflicting parties.[193] These Peace Agreements like those of ECOWAS in Liberia and Sierra Leone formed the basis of UN's intervention in the conflict.

SADC did not apply the provision of Article 2 empowering it to use *necessary measures* when President Laurent Kabila unilaterally suspended the Lusaka Accord in August 2000.[194] This does not however mean that SADC has no *legal* capacity to so act or that it will not act in the future. It may be that the sudden assassination of President Laurent Kabila forestalled such an action, especially since the new government headed by his son is widely perceived to be more amenable to diplomatic resolution of the conflict.

NATO's intervention[195] in the Kosovo crisis, to some extent, indicates a moving in the direction of autonomous regime of collective security by this organisation. NATO's action in Kosovo, according to the analyses of most international lawyers,[196] failed the test of the UN Charter as well as its own treaty, which restricts its activities to the Atlantic area, except when its members are attacked from outside.[197] However, if NATO's action in Kosovo is analysed against the background of the new strategy adopted during its 1992 Rome Summit[198] one may discern a deliberate move by NATO towards a decentralised collective security system.[199] During the Alliance's fiftieth birthday anniversary in Washington in 1999 Strobe Talbott, the American Deputy Secretary of State, informed the world that NATO was hammering out a new 'strategic concept' to define its role in the 21st century. He stated that:

> In that project [transformation of NATO] . . . we must be ambitious. NATO was founded and designed to deal with the Soviet Union Warsaw Pact. That state and that alliance are gone, and so is the threat they posed . . . This isn't to say that NATO's original task of collective defense is no longer at the core of the Alliance's mission. NATO must maintain its capacity enshrined in Art V of the Treaty of Washington, to deter and if necessary defeat what might be called classic aggression. Such threat could arise in the future. But it is less likely to do so if NATO remains robust and ready.

[193] UN Doc S/RES/1316, 23 August 2000.

[194] IRIN, DRC, 24 August 2000.

[195] See previous chapters.

[196] See particularly Bruno Simma, above note 1; Dino Kristiotis, 'The Kosovo Crisis and NATO's Application of Armed force against the Federal Republic of Yugoslavia' (2000) 49 *International and Comparative Law Quarterly* 330; ND White, 'The Legality of Bombing in the Name of Humanity' (2000) 5(1) *Journal of Conflict and Security Law* 27; Nico Krisch, 'Unilateral Enforcement of the Collective Will: Kosovo, Iraq, and the Security Council' (1999) 3 *Max Planck Yearbook of United Nations* 59.

[197] See Articles 6 and 5 respectively.

[198] Professor Higgins hinted at this when she noted that 'NATO has in fact systematically adopted a new role—that of "peace support operations" . . . by adopting its "New Strategic Concept" at its Rome Summit in late 1992'. See R Higgins, above note 46, 453.

[199] For various views about NATO's new concept, see Michael Brenner (ed), *NATO and Collective Security* (London, Macmillan Press Ltd, 1998).

> However, that is not enough if NATO is to remain relevant at all times. With the end of the Cold War, new less spectacular, but more diversified threats have arisen. Disputes over ethnicity, religion or territory, can, as we've already seen, trigger armed conflict, which in turn can generate cross-border political instability, refugee flows and humanitarian crises that endanger European security.[200]

These statements touch on the core of decentralised collective security. NATO understood clearly the changed nature of the post-Cold War conflict and also recognised the imperativeness of fashioning a commensurate response to it. It recognised that in order to do this, it could not limit itself to the original functions ingrained in Article V of its Treaty. While that must remain the core of its existence, new actions must now be brought in.

An expansion of NATO's tasks beyond the realm of collective self-defence to the arena of collective security necessarily means that there must be a reconfiguration of the alliance's relationship with the UN. Strobe Talbot, declared that NATO member states are not,

> suggesting that NATO act in splendid isolation from or high-handed defiance of-United Nations or the OSCE . . . At the same time, we must be careful not to subordinate NATO to any other international body or compromise the integrity of its command structure. We will try to act in concert with other organizations . . . but the alliance must reserve the right and the freedom to act when its members, by consensus, deem it necessary.[201]

This statement is significant to the nature of the relationship between NATO and the UN. It indeed indicates a move in the direction of greater autonomy. NATO, the above statement indicates, may act in isolation, insofar as it is not a splendid isolation, and may defy the UN or OSCE inasmuch as the defiance is not high-handed. Who determines when isolation is splendid and defiance high-handed? The answer must be NATO. The alliance would act in concert with others, but must be careful not to subordinate NATO to *any* other international body. The only international organisation that may expect subordination from NATO, and all other organisations, is the UN. Thus, the insertion of the word 'any' is for emphasis, to drive the point home that the new NATO would not be constrained in the task of collective security. After the cessation of hostilities in Kosovo, and the adoption of Resolution 1244[202] by the Security Council, the integrity of NATO command, which Talbott warned against being compromised, was maintained. Although the resultant mission, the KFOR was composed by the member states of the UN and NATO, the command regime was a joint one.[203]

200 See Bruno Simma, above note 1 at 14–15.
201 *Ibid*.
202 UN Doc S/RES/1244, 10 June 1999.
203 *Ibid* (Annex 2).

It is too early to conclude how NATO will act in the future vis-à-vis the UN, and a single episode in Kosovo does not justify an assertion that NATO will again act without Security Council authorisation. However, it is most likely that the alliance will review its treaty in the near future with a view to incorporating the radical contents of its new strategic concept. In this regard, it must be expected that any future efforts by NATO at reviewing or amending its treaty are likely to deal decisively with the twin questions of whether it can undertake *enforcement* action without authorisation from the Security Council, and whether it can be classified as a regional arrangement within Chapter VIII.

The adoption of a Treaty of Nice[204] by the European Union Summit in December 2000 culminated in the establishment of a Rapid Reaction Force (RRF) for Europe. Although the instruments for taking this decision are to be found in several summits and conferences held by different organs of the EU, two documents are particularly significant in discussing the nature of the new force. These are the Presidency Report to the Helsinki European Council on *Strengthening the Common European Security and Defence* and on *Non-Military Crisis Management of the Union*[205] and the Report on Strengthening the Common European Security and Defence Policy.[206] Whist it is still uncertain whether the EU will adopt a separate treaty in order to implement the objectives of its new security system, the Helsinki report contains certain proposals for this purpose. According to the report, the central goal of the RRF is to be deployed with military and collective capabilities in the field of command and control, intelligence and strategic transport.[207]

Article 19 of the Nice Treaty[208] raises some questions as per what the relationship between an EU-led operation and the UN might be. This article states that,

> Member States which are also members of the United Nations Security Council will concert and keep other Member States fully informed. Member States which are permanent members of the Security Council will, in the execution of their functions, ensure the defence of the position and interests of the Union, without prejudice to their responsibilities under the provisions of the United Nations Charter.

[204] Treaty of the European Union (as amended by the Nice Treaty), Provisional Text Approved by the Intergovernmental Conference of Institutional reform SN 533/00 Brussels, 12 December 2000 (14.12) (OR Fr), (hereafter Nice Treaty).

[205] (Hereafter Helsinki Report). See Press Release Library/Miscellaneous, Brussels (11-12-1999)-Nr 00300/1/99. See also http://www.weu.int/eng/about.htm.

[206] Feira European Council: The Report on Strengthening the Common European Security and Defence Policy (hereafter Feira Report), http://eu.int/pecs/military/en/Feira.htm.

[207] Helsinki Report, above note 205 at 20.

[208] SN 533/00 *Conference of the Representatives of the Government of the Member States*, Brussels, 12 December 2000 (14.12) (Or Fr).

What is the exact import of this provision? It can be argued that Article 19 may become, in practice, the instrument by which the EU might circumvent the Security Council in a conflict situation. This provision imposes two different obligations; one on the EU states that are ordinary members of the Council and the other, on EU states which are permanent members of the Council. What is the nature of EU interest and how may the EU members of the Security Council *ensure* the defence of such in the execution of their functions?

It is contended that Article 19 imposes a crucial obligation on France and the United Kingdom, being the EU states which are also permanent members of the Security Council. A strict adherence of these states to the provisions of that article will most likely impact on Articles 39, 103, and 53 of the UN Charter. Since the EU is a regional arrangement, there is no doubt that the missions it will lead under the auspices of the RRF will be perceived as regional actions. A defence of EU interest in a manner inconsistent with the UN decisions obviously may be in derogation of the prevalence of the UN Charter over other international treaties as guaranteed in Article 103.

However, in practice, it may be quite difficult to determine when the EU member states, which are permanent Security Council members, are actually acting under the guidance of the Article 19 of the Nice Treaty. The permanent members of the Security Council are not required to state reasons for exercising their veto in a particular context. Therefore, where, for instance, a non-EU permanent Security Council member proposes a solution to a conflict which might not be the one favoured by the EU permanent Council members, the latter may in fact invoke their veto to avoid the proposal. The real motivation for such a use of veto power may actually be a consideration that the proposed measure will conflict with certain EU interests in the matter. Hence, the veto is used to ensure the defence of the EU position.

Similarly, it remains to be seen whether the EU, upon occurrence of conflicts in its region, will defer action until the Security Council has made a determination under Article 39 of the Charter. In the light of Article 19 of the Nice Treaty, this seems unlikely to be so.

5.4.1.3 *The Reconceptualisation of the Notion of Peace and Security and the 'Non-Intervention' Principle in the Law and Practice of Collective Security after the Cold War*

A major factor in the development of regionally authorised enforcement action is the new interpretation accorded the phrase 'peace and security' and the relaxing of the 'non-intervention' principle in the practice of the UN and regional organisations after the Cold War. Paradoxically, it is the Security Council's liberal interpretation of acts which constitute threats to international peace and security that was catalytic to regional organisations developing new rules of intervention. The Cold War period witnessed many re-iterations of the principle of non-intervention by regional organisations.[209] Article 3 of the OAU Charter forbade interference in the internal affairs of member states.[210] Article 3 of the OAS Charter contains similar provisions.[211] Attempts by regional organisations to relax the non-intervention principle during the Cold War met with resistance from member states. The OAU intervention in the conflict in the former Spanish colony of the Western Sahara between Morocco and Polisario Front led to the withdrawal of Morocco from the OAU in 1984.[212] Likewise, although the OAU intervention in the Chadian (1981) conflict was expressly requested by President Goukouni, he had covertly withdrawn his consent and became very hostile to the organisation when he thought that the OAU was not acting to suppress the insurrection against him.[213]

The UN itself had generally abided by the provisions of Article 2(7) of its Charter forbidding it to intervene in matters which are essentially within the domestic jurisdiction of member states. Most of UN interventions during the Cold War were predicated on matters which were clearly in violation of Article 2(4) of the Charter, such as the invasion of South Korea by North Korea. Others, such as the Congo's crisis, were matters that would normally constitute threats to international peace and security,[214] thereby removing the protection afforded states by Article 2(7) and

[209] See GA Res 2131, UN GAOR, 20th Sess, Supp No 14, UN Doc A/6014 (1965) adopted by 109 member states with one abstention (by the United Kingdom); Declaration on Principles of International Law Concerning Friendly Relations and Cooperation Among States in Accordance with the Charter of the United Nations, GA Res. 2625, UNGAOR, 25th Sess, Supp No 28, at 21, UN Doc A/8028 (1970) (unanimously adopted); Definition of Aggression, GA Res 3314, UN GAOR, 29th Sess, Supp No 31, at 142, UN Doc A/9631 (1974); Declaration of the Inadmissibility of Intervention and Interference in the internal Affairs of States, GA Res 36/301, UN GAOR, 36th Sess, Supp No 31, UN Doc A/36/761; and finally, Declaration on the Enhancement of the Effectiveness of the Principle of refraining from the Threat or Use of Force, GA Res 42/44, UN GAOR, 42nd Sess, Supp No 41, at UN Doc A/42/41(1987). For a history and principle of the doctrine of 'non-intervention' see Dino Kritsiotis, 'Reappraising Policy Objections to Humanitarian Intervention' (1998) 19 *Michigan Journal of International Law* 1005 at 1008.

[210] 3 *International Legal Materials* (1964) 1116. See Naldi, above note ; A Sesay, 'The Limits of Peace-keeping by Regional Organizations: The OAU Peacekeeping Force in Chad' (1991) 11 *Conflict Quarterly* 7; J-P Cot, 'The Role of the Inter-African Peacekeeping Force in Chad, 1981–1982 in A Cassese (ed), *The Current Legal Regulation of the Use of Force* (The Hague, Martinus Nijhoff Publishers, 1986), 167.

[211] 30 April 1948, 2 UST 2394; 119 *United Nations Treaty Series* 3, reprinted in 33 *International Legal Materials* (1994) 981.

[212] See Naldi, above note 9 at 595.

[213] *Keesing's Contemporary Archives* (1982) 31677–80.

[214] M Akehurst, *A Modern Introduction to International Law* (London, Allen & Unwin, 6th edn, 1987) (noting that 'a threat to the peace is whatever the Security Council says is a threat to the peace'), 219; See also, Y Dinstein, *War, Aggression and Self-Defence* (Cambridge, Grotius Publications, 3rd edn, 2001) 251; G Cohen Jonathan, 'Article 39' in J-P Cot and A Pellet (eds), *La Charte des Nations Unies* (Paris, Economica, 1985), 645. But see discussion in Chapter 3 on the legal competence of regional organisations to perform this task.

placing the matters within the Security Council's competence under Chapter VII.[215] Mere violations of human rights, even when substantial as in Uganda during Idi Amin's regime, did not inspire intervention by the UN as such matters were then largely perceived as caught by Article 2(7). Although individual UN member states were able to act in such circumstances, as the Tanzanian invasion of Uganda demonstrates, they did not claim the right to do so in terms of the hostile acts constituting a threat to international peace and security. They justified their actions on the basis of self-defence. As John Murphy noted, the 'UN Charter does not speak to intervention by states'.[216] Louis Sohn also affirmed that, 'the Charter does not expressly provide any guidance to States facing a more limited situation which might lead to international friction or give rise to a dispute'.[217]

In its practice after the Cold War era, the Security Council has widened the frontiers of activities that it perceives as breaching or threatening international 'peace and security' and have devised a means of circumventing the Article 2(7) restraint.[218] Thus, '[m]atters once solely of local concern now have impact across national borders'.[219] Such are matters over which the UN can now simultaneously exercise competence together with its member states. As Dan Ciobanu has argued, 'the field of human rights [is] an example of concurrent jurisdiction *ratione materiae* between the United Nations and its Members'.[220] For instance, Resolution 688 concerning the Iraq-Kuwait crisis recalled Article 2(7) of the Charter and then held that the 'massive flow of refugees towards and across international frontiers and cross-border incursions . . . threaten international peace and security in the region'.[221] The Security Council through its Resolutions 841[222] and 940[223] regarding the Haiti crisis in 1993 made a similar determination.[224] However, the concept of *erga omnes*—that is, obligations in which the entire community of states has a legal interest, and under which any states may apply counter-measures against an offending state—does not justify a unilateral intervention by one state in the internal affairs of others.[225]

215 See discussion in Chapter 3.

216 John F Murphy, 'Force and Arms' in Christopher Joyner (ed), *The United Nations and International Law* (Cambridge, Cambridge University Press, 1999) 97 at 98.

217 *Ibid*, at 30.

218 See ND White and R Cryer, 'Unilateral Enforcement of Resolution 687: A Threat Too Far?' (1999) 29 *California Western International Law Journal* 243.

219 Oscar Schachter in Joyner (ed), above note 216 at 10

220 D Ciobanu, *Preliminary Objections Related to the Jurisdiction of the United Nations Political Organs* (The Hague, Martinus Nijhoff, 1975), 50.

221 UN Doc S/RES/688, 5 April 1991.

222 UN Doc S/RES 841, 13 October 1993.

223 UN Doc S/RES/940, 31 July 1993.

224 For a discussion, see David Malone, 'Haiti and the International Community: A Case Study' (1997) 39 (2) *Survival* 126.

225 One example of an 'erga omnes' case is when the International Court of justice (ICJ) directed that all states must deny recognition to acts of South Africa relating to Namibia in its 1971 advisory opinion concerning that country. See (1971) ICJ Reports at 55–56.

Similarly, regional organisations have relaxed their principle of non-intervention by reconceptualising acts that may now threaten peace and security in their hemispheres.[226] Furthermore, unlike the UN, they have gone a step further to specifically identify such acts in their treaties and reserve the right to designate other acts as such as circumstances may dictate in the future.[227] Article 58 of the Revised Treaty of the Economic Community of West African States provides that 'Member States undertake to safeguard and consolidate relations conducive to the maintenance of peace, stability and security within the region'.[228] It is noteworthy in that provision that the phrase 'peace, stability and security' has been adopted, not just 'peace and security' as in the UN Charter.

Notably, the original treaty of ECOWAS had contained no similar provisions. Neither did the *Protocol on Non-Aggression*[229] nor the *Protocol relating to Mutual Assistance and Defence* (PMAD)[230] which merely recited the prohibition contained in Article 2(4) of the Charter. These were the two instruments that formed the basis of ECOWAS collective security activities from 1978 to 1999. Yet, ECOWAS had formed the view, in the preamble to the PMAD that 'economic progress cannot be achieved unless the conditions for the necessary security are ensured in all Member States of the Community'.[231] Thus as early as 1981, ECOWAS had identified a nexus between the quest for regional stability and economic viability of member states. It was only a matter of time before ECOWAS would come up with a more pragmatic instrument to pursue this agenda.

[226] According to Mr Diarra, ECOWAS Deputy Secretary-General, '[t]here is definitely a growing importance of the necessity of subregional organizations such as ECOWAS involving themselves in the affairs of a country which previously have been considered purely internal matters and which governments would have guarded jealously . . . if the old trend of sweeping everything under the carpet is allowed to continue, crises will continue to break out', Nicole Itano, 'Ivory Coast tests African Union', *Christian Science Monitor*, 7 October 2002, http://www.csmonitor.com/2002/1007/p0601 – woaf.html.

[227] Article 4(h) Constitutive Act of the African Union.

[228] See Revised Treaty of ECOWAS, (as amended by the Revised treaty) 24th July 1993 (1996) *International Legal Materials* 660. From the wording of this provision, it seems that the obligation imposed on member states by this article is a specific one and not a 'soft' obligation open to variation by member states. For instance, the *Final Communiqué of Ministerial Meeting on A Mechanism for Prevention, Management and Resolution of Conflicts and Peacekeeping*, Yamoussoukro, 11–12 March 1998, (on file with the author), directed that 'the provisions of Chapter X, notably Article 58 of the revised ECOWAS Treaty, should be complied with'. Accordingly, the *Protocol Relating to the Mechanism for Conflict Prevention, Management, Resolution, Peacekeeping and Security* in 1999 in pursuance of this article was unanimously adopted by member states, notwithstanding that its provisions contain principles and precepts that derogate from the sovereign rights of these states in respect of certain issues such as already discussed. For the text of and commentary on this Protocol, see Abass, above note 172.

[229] Adopted on April 22 1978. See text in Weller (ed), above note 20, 18.

[230] Adopted 29 May 1981. See ECOWAS Doc A/SP3/5/81. Printed also in the *Official Journal of ECOWAS*, vol 3, June 1981 pp 9–13. See M Weller, above note 20, 19.

[231] *Ibid.*

In the preamble to its most recent treaty on collective security[232], ECOWAS recognised formally that 'good governance, the rule of law and sustainable development are essential for peace and conflict prevention'. The inclusion of 'good governance and the rule of law' in this treaty, is indicative of a substantial paradigmatic shift in ECOWAS' conception of what is, and what guarantees, 'peace and security' in its region. It is however a regionalisation of the UN's wider practice. For example, during the Haiti crisis, the General Assembly adopted a resolution demanding 'the immediate restoration of the legitimate government . . . and observance of human rights in Haiti.'[233] The effect of this is that ECOWAS reconstrued the notion of 'peace and security' differently from what it had held under its constituent treaty (as revised) and the two protocols of 1978 and 1981.[234]

In a very interesting development, the phrase 'peace, security and stability' has dramatically appeared in the Constitutive Act of the African Union.[235] In the preamble to the Act, the African Union recognises that the 'scourge of conflict in Africa constitutes a major impediment to the socio-economic development of the continent and the need to promote peace, security and *stability* as a prerequisite for the implementation of our development and integration agenda'.[236] In addition, as with ECOWAS' new treaty, Article 4(m) of the AU Act obligates the Union to respect 'democratic principles, human rights, the rule of law and good governance'.[237] In the *CSSDCA*[238] *Declaration* the Assembly of Heads of State and Government, determined *inter alia*, that 'HIV/AIDS and other pandemics on the continent constitute a threat to human security'.[239] In addition, the movement of refugees and displaced persons were also declared as constituting 'threat to peace and security of the continent'.[240]

Although Article 4(g) of the AU Act reaffirms the principle of 'non-interference' in the internal affairs of Member States, it also empowers the Union 'to intervene in a Member State pursuant to a decision of the Assembly in respect of grave circumstances, namely: war crimes, genocide and crimes against humanity'.[241] The implication of this provision is quite telling. Under the old arrangement, there was no similar provision so that

232 See Abass, above note 172.

233 UNGA Resolution 46/7, 11 October 1991.

234 Following the overthrow of the government of Guinea-Bissau, ECOWAS decided that the coup d' tat 'was a violation of the Abuja and Lome Agreements'. See *Meeting of Ministers of foreign Affairs*, Lome, Togo, 24–25 May 1999 (on file with the author), at para 16.

235 See above note 102.

236 *Ibid*.

237 Article 4(m).

238 AHG/Decl 4 (XXXVI). *Conference on Security, Stability, Development and Cooperation in Africa* 8–9 May 2000, Abuja, Nigeria.

239 *Ibid*, Principle k.

240 Principle g.

241 Article 4(h).

where such acts existed in member states as might constitute threats to peace, security and stability of the region, there was nothing the OAU could do, except, if invited, peacekeeping. Thus, the principle of non-interference is now accompanied under Article 4(h) of the Constitutive Act with the conferment on the Union of the right to intervene.[242]

Likewise, the preamble to the *Protocol on Defence and Security of the Southern African Development Community* (SADC) affirms 'the primary role of the United Nations Security Council in the maintenance of international peace and security'.[243] Nevertheless, it states, that the organisation shall 'mediate in *inter*-state and *intra*-state disputes and conflicts' of member states.[244] It is interesting to note that the phrase 'peace and stability' is also found in the protocol.[245]

The gradual but steady movement of regional organisations towards a more autonomous regime of collective security can no longer be denied in legal analysis. Different reasons account for different regional practices in this area. African regional organisations in particular have decisively departed from the traditional notions of 'peace and security', and the customary international law principle of 'non intervention'. This might be in realisation of the fact that Africa cannot achieve real peace, stability and security without devising ways of tackling the perennial conflicts occurring within the territories of Member States. It seems therefore appropriate to observe that it is mostly countries which have least benefited from the UN collective security system that are more prone to devising alternative approaches towards maintaining peace and security in their region. That the UN and the Western members of its Security Council have little commitment to African conflicts is clear.[246]

The UN cannot be expected to find solutions to all the world conflicts. Thus, in its practice, the UN has become somehow selective in terms of what conflicts to respond to, when, and by what means.[247] The UN's uneven response to conflicts was first recognised as a serious problem by Secretary-General Javier Pérez de Cuellar. In his last annual report in 1991, he complained about 'the lack of means at the disposal of the United Nations to maintain an *impartial* and *effective* global watch over situations of potential or incipient conflict'.[248] Secretary-General Kofi Annan was

242 Abass and Baderin, above note 102 at 31.

243 Principle 4.

244 Article 2(e), AU Act.

245 Article 2(g).

246 See Lauterpacht in his *Foreword* to Weller, (ed) above note 20, ix.

247 See O Schachter in Joyner (ed), above note 216 at 16; see also M. Koskenniemi, 'The Place of Law in Collective Security' (1996) 17 *Michigan Journal of International Law* 455 at 460 (arguing that the first problem of collective security 'relates to the Council's notorious selectiveness').

248 *Report of the Secretary-General on the Work of the Organisation*, UN GAOR, 46th Session, Supp No 1, at 3, UN Doc A/461/1 (1991).

even more blunt about the implications of the UN's selectivity. In a statement, he noted that:

> Already we know what happened after the tragedy in Somalia. We know that the international community and the Western countries were not ready to go to Rwanda. And after Sierra Leone, I think there's going to be little encouragement for any of them to get involved in operations in Africa.[249]

An effective intervention by the UN in all or most conflicts will require a pre-emptive move by that organisation. As expressed by the Prime Minister of Cape Verde during the debates of the first Security Council Summit at the level of heads of state in 1992:

> the best most efficient and longest-lasting security measure to avoid conflict is to invest in the solution of social problems and the eradication of poverty and underdevelopment and to promote a cult of respect for, and strict observance of, Charter principles, strict observance of the principle of the peaceful settlement of disputes.[250]

The potential problems of asking the UN to undertake such enormous tasks as preventive diplomacy, such that can prevent the outbreak of conflicts, were brought to light during the meeting.[251] The UN Secretary-General of the day, Boutros Boutros-Ghali warned that it would be difficult to achieve preventive diplomacy, as this would require 'means for observation, a sophisticated communications network and new financial resources.'[252] In addition, there is the need to obtain the consent of parties to the conflict, since factors that may result in a full-blown armed conflict are often essentially within the domestic jurisdiction of concerned states.[253] Thus, preventive diplomacy presents the UN with both legal (Article 2(7)) and practical (resource-orientated) obstacles.

The erratic nature of the Security Council's use of its discretionary powers makes it quite difficult to predict whether or not it will find a threat or a breach of peace and security in any given situation. And, if it does find one, whether it would take measures necessary to maintain international peace and security in particular situations as Article 39

249 Statement of the Secretary-General, Kofi Anan, made in Paris, France, on Wednesday 3 May 2000. Http://www.nytimes.com/library/world/africa/050500sierra-leone-assess.html.

250 *Provisional Verbatim Record of the Three Thousand and Forty Sixth Meeting, UN Doc S/PV 3046 (1992); United Nations Security Council Summit Meeting*, New York, 31 January 1992, 2, also published in UN SCOR, Supp. 47, Jan–March, UN Doc S/23500 (1992) 51–52.

251 The Security Council has indeed adopted a resolution of a purely pre-emptive nature, which linked the epidemic of AIDS with peace and security and urged actions in that regard, S/RES/1308, 17 July 2000.

252 See S/PV 3046, above note 150. Also cited by L Sohn, *Broadening the Role of United Nations, in Preventing, Mitigating or Ending International or Internal Conflicts that Threaten International Peace and Security*, International Rule of Law Center Occasional paper Series, Second Series, Number 1 (Washington, George Washington University Law School, 1997) 14.

253 *Ibid*, at 14.

states. While genocide unfolded in Rwanda, the Security Council had determined in Resolutions 918[254] and 929[255] that such an act constituted a threat under Article 39 of the Charter. Yet, it did not take what would seem to be a measure capable of maintaining international peace and security at the most crucial time of the crisis when Resolution 918 was adopted. By the time the Security Council adopted Resolution 929, the genocide was virtually over.[256] In Liberia, the Security Council declined intervention outright. In Sierra Leone it played a minimal role. In Kosovo, it found threats to peace and security but could go no further. Regional organisations therefore present an opportunity to mitigate the inequitable use of the veto power as well as address the problem of selective collective security as practised by the Security Council. It might be in recognition of this, and the many other problems, that the Security Council has reoriented itself to encouraging regional organisations to take more active roles in regional conflicts, welcoming their actions towards amicable solutions even when such solutions have been pursued through enforcement actions. Regional organisations are certainly more suited to mediating in members' conflicts than 'foreigners', and possess the requisite knowledge of dealing with the terrain. When their acts are well implemented and co-ordinated with those of the UN, they can be a useful complement to the activities of the UN itself. This was shown by the conflicts in Liberia, Sierra Leone, Georgia, and most importantly, Haiti.

5.5. THE PREFERENCE FOR DECENTRALISED RATHER THAN CENTRALISED COLLECTIVE SECURITY

By proposing a greater autonomy for regional organisations in collective security matters than Chapter VIII presently allows, it is not being suggested that such a development will invariably bring with it an advantage over the UN system. On the contrary, in many cases where they have intervened, regional organisations have experienced serious difficulties, such as shortages of manpower and expertise. Sometimes regional interventions tend to aggravate matters even if they eventually succeed in bringing the situations under control.[257] Often certain members of regional organisations are accused of harbouring hegemonial motives. For

[254] UN Doc S/RES/918, 17 May 1994.

[255] UN Doc S/RES/929, 22 June 1994.

[256] For a critique of the handling of the Rwandan case by the UN, see McCoubrey and Morris, above note 188, 132–34.

[257] An example of this could be seen in the initial opposition of the NPFL to the deployment of ECOMOG to Liberia. For a detailed account of ECOMOG clash with NPFL, see Nkem Agetua, *Operation Liberty: The Story of Major General Joshua Dogonyaro* (Lagos, Hona Communications, 1992); Segun Aderiye, 'ECOMOG Landing' in Vogt (ed*), The Liberian Crisis and ECOMG,* quoted by Clement Adibe, above note 29, at 73.

instance, the involvement of Nigeria in Liberia and Sierra Leone raised serious concerns among some writers who felt that Nigeria was pursuing an expansionist objective and an ambition to install puppet governments in those states.[258] The United States was also accused by some members of the OAS, especially during the Cold War, of dominating the regional organisation.[259]

Nevertheless, such accusations have not generally been levelled by ECOWAS member states in particular.[260] OAS member states have not repeated their allegations of US's hegemony since the end of the Cold War. On the contrary, when Nigeria decided not to send troops to Côte d'Ivoire in November 2002,[261] despite an ECOWAS decision to intervene in that country's conflict,[262] several ECOWAS states regretted Nigeria's decision and hoped it would be changed. According to the deputy Secretary-General of ECOWAS, Cheick Oumar Diarra, '[w]hat we are working on is to get Nigeria participating in this force because we cannot imagine an African contingent without Nigeria'.[263] Such responses by ECOWAS to a decision by one of its own suggests that ECOWAS member states do not perceive the role played by their most powerful member as inimical to the overall objective of ECOWAS. On the contrary, it clearly indicates recognition that the contribution of powerful member states such as Nigeria is virtually indispensable.[264]

Moreover, the fact that ECOWAS cannot undertake an enforcement action without the concurrence of a majority (not all) of its Member States

[258] MacFarlane and Weiss (above note 101, at 20) cited the case of Ivory Coast and other francophone countries which 'resisted (ECOMOG intervention) because of their discomfort with the assertiveness of the regional hegemon, a position reflecting not just their own concern about Nigeria preponderance, but that of their traditional patron, France'. There is no known record of any official resistance by either Ivory Coast or any other Francophone country to ECOWAS' intervention in Liberia on the basis of discomfort with a regional hegemon; these writers cite none. Certainly Ivory Coast did not vote against ECOMOG deployment.

[259] MacFarlane and Weiss regard the OAS intervention in the Dominican Republic in 1968 as a 'surrogate for the U. S. "peace-keeping" operation, hardly a model for the future from the point of view of Latin Americans', *ibid*, at 25.

[260] Occasional disagreement about modalities of intervention, composition of troops and the question of command do pitch ECOWAS members against one another sometimes. See for instance, Silvia Aloisi, 'West African Rivalries threaten Ivory Coast Force', 1 November 2002, http://www.alertnet.org/thenews/newsdesk/545003?view.

[261] 'Nigerian Troops not for Peacekeeping in Côte d'Ivoire_Lamido', 4 November, Vanguard (Lagos), http://allafrica.com.stories/200211040626.html; BBC News, 7 November 2002, http://news.bbc.co.uk/2/hi/africa/2414529, 'No Nigerian Troops for Ivory Coast' *The News* (Monrovia) 8 November, 2002.

[262] 'African Ministers agree to send 2,000 Troops to Ivory Coast', http://www.ananova.com/news/story/sm_697652.html', 'West African Army Chiefs Agree Buffer Force for Ivory Coast', 7 November 2002, http://allafrica.com/stories/200211070647.html

[263] *Ibid*, 2 of 3.

[264] Mr Diarra repeated his optimism about Nigeria joining the force to be deployed to Côte d'Ivoire when he said that '[w]e hope that Nigeria will agree to be part of the mission, we don't see the mission without Nigeria'. See http://allafrica.com/stories/200211070647.html 2 of 2.

means that a powerful state may not simply have its way. In addition, the absence of the veto in the functioning of ECOWAS and AU political organs means no single country can thwart or highjack the decision of the majority as is possible under the UN system. In a very interesting development, the AU has agreed to set up a UN-style Security Council, to be called Peace and Security Council.[265] This body will however not have the veto power and its decisions are to be taken unanimously or, if subject to vote, two-third majority.[266] Therefore, an intervention by a regional organisation in a member's conflict hardly suffers the legitimacy problem that some of Security Council's actions suffer.[267] Security Council's decisions to take some measures are often taken (or not taken)[268] against the wishes of the majority of UN member states. An example of such a decision taken by the Security Council was to impose economic sanctions on Libya in 1998, a decision that provoked discontent among several states.[269] In addition, states more readily identify with their regional organisations, socially, politically, and culturally. Such affinities make a decision for intervention by a regional organisation more readily acceptable than that of the Security Council. As John Burton wrote, 'the necessary first step of breaking up and uncovering issues is far more likely to take place in regional discussion than a centralized forum comprising one hundred nations'.[270]

The role played by the AU and ECOWAS in respect of the conflict in Côte d'Ivoire[271] illustrates some of the points being made here.[272] At the outbreak of the crisis on 19 September 2002, ECOWAS took the lead in finding an amicable resolution of the conflict. Within one month of its mediation, ECOWAS had brought the conflict under control, leading to a ceasefire agreement signed by all parties to the dispute on 17 October 2002.[273] ECOWAS Mediation Committee stepped up its search for a last-

[265] 'African Union to set up Security Council' *UN Integrated Regional Information Network*, February 4, 2003, http://allafrica.com/stories/200302040442.html Algeria has ratified the PSC.

[266] 'African Union's Peace and Security Council to have wide Powers', http://www.namibian.com.na/2002/july/africa/026E8729AF.html.

[267] See discussion in Chapters 3 and 4.

[268] An example of a decision not taken by the Security Council, despite the general clamour for it to do so, was to intervene to stop the genocide that unfolded in Rwanda in 1994.

[269] See discussion in Chapter 3.

[270] John Burton, *Peace Theory*, cited in Joseph Nye, *Peace in Parts: Integration and Conflict in Regional Organization* (Boston, Little, Brown, 1971), 129.

[271] Ofeibea Quist-Arcton, 'West African and AU Leaders for Ivory Coast Talks', 23 October 2002, http://allafrica.com/stories/200210230183.html, 'Mbeki Says Ivory Coast must Deal with Underlying Tension', 24 October, 2002, http://allafrica.com/stories/200210240070.html.

[272] Nicole Itano, 'Ivory Coast tests African Union', Christian Science Monitor, 7 October, 2002, http://www.csmonitor.com/2002/1007/p06s01-woaf.html.

[273] Silvia Aloisi, 'Peace Plan Raises Hope for end to Ivory Coast War', 18 October 2002, http://www.alertnet.org/thenews/newsdesk/536135; Rory Carroll, 'Ceasefire in Ivory Coast' *The Guardian* 18 October 2002, http://www.guardian.co.uk/international/story/0,3604,814346,00.html.

ing solution, putting pressure on President Laurent Gbagbo of Côte d' Ivoire to make concessions and negotiate with the rebels.[274]

It seems plausible to suggest that some of the factors that gave ECOWAS an edge in quickly bringing the conflict under its control are its familiarity with the terrain of conflict, the ECOWAS membership of Côte d'Ivoire and the fact that that country's president sits on ECOWAS' highest political organ. The precious time that would have been lost to the Security Council's lengthy and cumbersome procedures for seising it of such conflicts was capitalised on by ECOWAS' expeditious mechanism to stem the tide of violence. It might even be that the differences in the time zones of the Security Council members would have delayed matters for much longer.

5.6. CONCLUSION

Regional organisations have undoubtedly undergone significant transformation since the end of the Cold War. Not only have they increased their co-operation with the UN, they have also significantly enhanced their legal and practical capacities to undertake collective security functions. As is to be expected in such a situation, certain tensions have arisen between these organisations and the UN. This has led to a search by writers for conceptual frameworks to accommodate this development clearly not anticipated by the Charter. While these concepts are effective in describing certain aspects of the relationship, they are not particularly representational of the growing trend in the UN/regional organisation relationship. Nor is it any longer useful to keep regarding a radically growing and widely embraced practice as an aberration to the law. A better approach might be to begin to view decentralised collective security as a necessary development in the post Cold War international order. Of course, as the OSCE has demonstrated, some regional organisations will still prefer to limit their activities to classical peacekeeping; this does not mean all others invariably remain the same.

However, no one can credibly suggest that regional organisations should discard the UN Charter, no matter how impractical its provisions may have become. Hence, their activities, even if legal under their internal laws, must be reconcilable with the Charter provisions. The proposition that where the Security Council is unable or unwilling to act regional organisations are free to undertake enforcement action is not without fundamental problems. What if a member state of a regional organisation does not agree to intervention by the regional organisation, does this

[274] *Ibid*.

not violate Article 2(4)? What if such regional action conflicts with the obligations under the Charter such that Article 103 accords primacy? It is to an examination of the compatibility of regionally authorised enforcement action with the prohibition of the use of force in the UN Charter that the book now turns.

6

Regional Enforcement Action and the Prohibition of the Use of Force

INTRODUCTION

ARTICLE 2(4), THE MOST radical and fundamental provision of UN Charter, embodies the legal regulation of the use of force in international law. It prohibits UN members, in their international relations, from the 'threat or use of force against the territorial integrity or political independence of any State, or in any other manner inconsistent with the Purposes of the United Nations'.[1]

The customary status of the prohibition in Article 2(4) is confirmed by the unanimous opinion of jurists[2] states[3] and the ICJ.[4] The obligations contained in Article 2(4) are widely believed to have evolved into a *jus cogens* rule, that is a peremptory norm of general international law from which

[1] Bruno Simma (ed), *The Charter of the United Nations: A Commentary* (Oxford, Oxford University Press, 2nd edn, 2002); Jean-Pierre Cot et Alain Pellet (eds), *La Charte Des Nations Unies: Commentaire article par article* (Paris, Economica, 2e édition, 1991); Leland Goodrich, Edvard Hambro, and Particia Simons, *Charter of the United Nations: Commentary and Documents* (New York, Columbia University Press, 3rd and Revised edn, 1969).

[2] For instance Oscar Schachter notes that '[u]ntil 1945, there was no customary international prohibition on the resort to force', O Schachter, 'Coercion and Self-Determination: Constructing Charter 2(4)' (1984) 78 *American Journal of International Law* 642. Verdross, 'Jus Dispositivum and Jus Cogens in International Law' (1966) *60 American Journal of International Law* 5; Jiménez De Arechaga, 'International Law in the Past Third of a Century' (1978) 159 *Hague Recueil* 64; James Crawford, *The Creation of States in International Law* (Oxford, Clarendon Press, 1976); GA Christenson, 'The World Court and Jus Cogens' (1987) 81 *American Journal of international Law* 93; Weisburd, 'The Emptiness of the Concept of Ius Cogens, as Illustrated by the War in Bosnia-Herzegovina' (1995–96) 17 *Michigan Journal of International Law* 591, Ronzitti, below note 3, 153

[3] See for instance the views expressed by states participating at the Vienna Conference on Law of Treaties *UN Conference on the Law of Treaties; First and Second Session*, Vienna, 26 March–24 May 1968. *Official Records; Documents of the Conference*, New York, 1971 (Doc A/CONF 39/11/Add 2), 67–68, cited by Natalino Ronzitti, 'Use of Force, Jus Cogens and State Consent' in A Cassese (ed), *The Current Legal Regulation of the Use of Force* (Dordrecht, Martinus Nijhoff Publishers, 1986) 147 at 149.

[4] *Nicaragua* case below note 21, 99, at para 187 *et seq*.

no derogation is permitted and which can only be modified by a subsequent norm of general international law having the same character.[5]

Nonetheless, the exact scope of the rule in Article 2(4) has divided writers across generations. This schism was prompted by the last phrase of Article 2(4) forbidding the threat or use of force 'in any other manner inconsistent with the Purpose of the United Nations'. The issue is whether this imprecise phrase permits the threat or use of force in any manner *not* inconsistent with the Purposes of the UN. Differently formulated, are there other exceptions to Article 2(4) apart from those expressly recognised by the UN Charter? Certainly only actions taken in self-defence under Article 51, Chapter VII collective measures, and the now obsolete Article 107 may derogate from Article 2(4), as far as the Charter rules are concerned.

Despite these explicit exceptions, some writers have argued that the last part of Article 2(4) permits the threat or use of force in circumstances not inconsistent with the Purposes and Principles of the United Nations.[6] For others, the phrase should not be construed as expanding the scope of Article 2(4).[7] Specific streaks of this debate manifest in the doctrinal disagreement on whether extra-Charter uses of force for: humanitarian purposes,[8] protection of democracy,[9] prevention or halting the repression of

[5] Article 53 Vienna Convention on the Law of Treaties, 1969; Article 26 The Law Commission's Articles on State Responsibility, (2001), text and treaty in James Crawford, *The International Law Commission's Articles on State Responsibility: Introduction, Text and Commentaries* (Cambridge, Cambridge University Press, 2002) (hereafter ILC's *Commentary*).

[6] See below.

[7] See generally on this debate, Ian Brownlie, *International Law and the Use of Force by States*, (Oxford, Clarendon Press, 1963); Derek Bowett, *Self-Defence in International Law* (Manchester, Manchester University Press, 1958); Humphrey Waldock, 'The Regulation of the Use of force by Individual States in International Law' (1952) 81 *RCADI* 415; Thomas Franck, 'Who Killed Article 2(4)?' (1970) 64 *American Journal of International Law* 809; Louis Henkin, 'The Reports of the Death of Article 2(4) are Greatly Exaggerated' (1971) 65 *American Journal of International Law* 544; Antony D' Amato, 'The Invasion of Panama was a Lawful Response to Tyranny', (1990) *84 American Journal of International Law* 516; Oscar Schachter, 'The Right of States to Use Armed Force' (1984) 82 *Michigan Law Review*, 1620; Oscar Schachter, 'The Lawful Response to Unilateral Use of force' (1985) 10 *Yale Journal of International Law* 291; Rosalyn Higgins, *The Development of International Law through the Political Organs of the United Nations* (Oxford, Oxford University Press, 1963); Roberto Ago, 'Additive to the 8th Report on State responsibility', A/C-N.4/318/Add.5/7, *Yearbook of International Law Commission* (1980), II, I; ND White and A Abass, 'Countermeasures and Sanctions' in MD Evans (ed), *International Law* (Oxford, Oxford University Press, 2003), 505.

[8] Richard Lillich, 'Humanitarian Intervention: A Reply to Ian Brownlie and a Plea for Constructive Alternatives' in John Norton Moore (ed), *Law and Civil War in the Modern World* (Baltimore, Johns Hopkins University Press, 1974) 229–51; Ian Brownlie, 'Humanitarian Intervention' *id*, 217–28; Dino Kristiotis, 'Reappraising Policy Objections to Humanitarian Intervention' (1998) 19 *Michigan Journal of International Law* 1005; Fernando Teson, *Humanitarian Intervention: An Inquiry into Law and Morality* (New York, Transnational, 2nd edn, 1997); D Verfey, 'Humanitarian Intervention' in A Cassese (ed), *The Current Legal Regulation of the Use of Force Antonio*, (Dordrecht, Martinus Nijhoff , 1986), 57.

[9] Thomas Franck, 'The Emerging Rights to Democratic Governance', (1992) 86 *American Journal of International Law*, 46; James Crawford, 'Democracy and International Law' (1993) 44 *British Yearbook of International Law* 113; Sean Murphy, 'Democratic Legitimacy and the

ethnic minority and violation of human rights,[10] constitute permissible exceptions to Article 2(4).

Following terrorist attacks on targets in the United States on 11 September 2001,[11] some writers have even suggested that Article 2(4) should be expanded to incorporate a provision[12] which would specifically address the inviolability of civilians during armed conflicts. They argue that the current Article 2(4) cannot tackle the new warfare engendered by terrorist organisations operating on individual, non-state basis.

The doctrinal debate surrounding Article 2(4) assumed great practical significance during the NATO invasion of the Federal Republic of Yugoslavia (FRY).[13] In the case instituted by the FRY against ten NATO members before the International Court of Justice (ICJ), some of the respondents claimed that they acted out of humanitarian consideration for the plight of the ethnic Albanians in Kosovo.[14] NATO collectively claimed it acted in order to 'halt the violence and bring an end to the humanitarian catastrophe now unfolding in Kosovo'.[15]

Recognition of States and Governments' (1995) 48 *International and Comparative Law Quarterly* 545.

[10] Michael Reisman, *Hollow Victory: Humanitarian Intervention and Protection of Minorities* (1997) 91 *Proceedings of the American Society of International Law*, 431; Michael Reisman, 'Coercion and Self-Determination: Construing Charter Article 2(4)', (1984) 78 *American Journal of International Law* 642.

[11] UN Doc S/RES 1373(2001), 28 September, S/RES/1438 (2002), 14 October, S/RES/1440 (2002), 24 October, S/RES/1441 (2002) 14 November.

[12] Anne-Marie Slaughter and William Burke-White, 'An International Constitutional Moment' (2002) 43 *Harvard International Law Journal* 1. On the Iraqi crisis (2003) see Rüdiger Wolfrum, 'Iraq—A crisis for our System of Collective Security', 24-02-2003, www.mpil.de/en/wolfrum/einfo.html; Alain Dejammet, 'Ambiguities of UNSC 1441: Constructive and Not', 16-10-2003, http://edoc.mpil.de/fs/2003/eitel.cfm; Davis Brown, 'Enforcing Arms Control Agreements by Military Force: Iraq and the 800-Pound Gorilla', (2003) 26 *Hastings International and Comparative Law Review* 159; Vaughan Lowe, 'The Iraq Crisis: What Now?' (2003) 52(4) *International and Comparative Law Quarterly* 959.

[13] Bruno Simma, 'NATO, the UN and the Use of Force: Legal Aspects' (1999) 10(1) *European Journal of International Law* 1; Thomas Franck, 'Sidelined in Kosovo? The United Nations Demise Has Been Exaggerated' (1999) 78 *Foreign Affairs* 116–18; Edward Lutwakk, 'Give War a Chance', *id*, 36–44; Peter Rodman, 'The Fallout from Kosovo', *id* 45–51; William Hagen, 'The Lethal Nationalism', *id* 52–54; Edward Luck, 'A Road to Nowhere', *id* 118–19; Walter Rocker, 'America First?' *id*, 119–20; Michael Glennon, 'The New Interventionism, the Search for a just International Law' *id*, 2–7; Michael Glennon, 'Glennon Replies' *id*, 120–22; Chris Hedges, 'Kosovo's Next Masters?' *id*, 24–42; Vojtech Mastny, 'Did Nato Win the Cold War?' *id*, 176–89; Robert Hunter, 'Maximising Nato' *id* 190–203; Antonio Cassese, 'Ex Injuria ius Oritur. Are We Moving Towards Legitimation of Forcible Humanitarian Countermeasures in the World Community?' (1999) 10(1) *European Journal of International Law*; Dino Kristiotis, 'The Kosovo Crisis and NATO's Application of Armed Force against the Federal Republic of Yugoslavia' (2000) 49 *International and Comparative Law Quarterly*, 330; Nigel White, 'The Legality of Bombing in the Name of Humanity' (2000) 5(1) *Journal of Conflict and Security Law* 27.

[14] Below.

[15] NATO Press Release 1990 (040) cited by Christine Gray, *International Law and the Use of Force* (Oxford, Oxford University Press, 2000), 32.

Generally, states did not explicitly raise humanitarian intervention as a possible exception to Article 2(4) until the ECOWAS intervention in Liberia in 1990, followed by the United Kingdom's justification of *Operation Safe Haven* to protect the Iraqi Shiite and Kurdish populations from Iraq's repression in 1991.[16] Prior to 1990, humanitarian intervention was raised mainly by writers as a probable justification for actions such as the Indian intervention in Bangladesh,[17] Tanzania against Uganda[18] and Vietnam against Cambodia.[19]

Academic exposition of the omnibus clause in Article 2(4) 'in any other manner inconsistent' has been beclouded by discourse of *humanitarian intervention*, being perhaps the most morally persuasive of all the possible exceptions to Article 2(4). The chapter is not concerned with enquiring into the lawfulness or otherwise of this doctrine under Article 2(4). Nor is it tasked to investigate whether there could be derogation from Article 2(4) for *other* purposes. Apparently, there is a lack of agreement amongst writers as regard these subjects, especially humanitarian intervention.[20] Even when states have intervened in conflicts presumably out of humanitarian consideration, as many believed of Tanzania's invasion of Idi-Amin's Uganda, they hardly rely on humanitarian reasons in their official justifications.[21] As a matter of policy, kind-hearted states[22] have always subsumed humanitarian grounds under, or coupled it with, more legally tenable justifications like self-defence.[23] In addition to the divergence over humanitarian intervention, writers disagree totally on the exact impact of the phrase 'in any other manner inconsistent with the Purpose of the

[16] The speculation by Christine Gray (page 30) that 'this UK espousal of the doctrine of humanitarian intervention seems to have been the first open support by a state since the establishment of the UN' is incorrect. The UK's justification of *Operation Safe Haven* came after ECOWAS had decided to intervene in Liberia to stop the senseless killing out of grave 'concern for wanton destruction of human life and property and the displacement of persons occasioned by the conflict'. See Decision A/Dec 1/8/90 First Session of the Community Standing Mediation Committee on the *Ceasefire and Establishment of an ECOWAS Ceasefire Group for Liberia*, Banjul, The Gambia, 6–7 1990. But see Christine Gray, *International Law and the Use of Force* (Oxford, Oxford University Press, 2000), 30 *et seq*.

[17] 1971 *United Nations Yearbook* 144. See Thomas Franck and Nigel Rodley, 'After Bangladesh: The Law of Humanitarian Intervention by Military Force', (1973) 67 *American Journal of International Law* 275.

[18] 1979 *United Nations Yearbook* 262.

[19] 1979 *United Nations Yearbook* 271.

[20] For a similar view, see Schachter, 'The Right of States to Use Armed force', above note 2 at 1629.

[21] The ICJ seemed to recognise this when in Nicaragua case it observed that no 'general right of intervention in support of an opposition within another state exists in contemporary international law', *Nicaragua Case,* (Case Concerning Military and Paramilitary Activities in and Against Nicaragua) ICJ Reports (1986) at 209 at para 109.

[22] For a discussion, see Dino Kritsiotis, 'Reappraising Policy Objections to Humanitarian Intervention', (1998) 19 *Michigan Journal of International Law* 1005.

[23] *Ibid.*

United Nations' on the prohibition in Article 2(4).[24] This means that there is a lack of consensus on what type of force is not inconsistent with the Purpose of the UN.[25]

This chapter examines whether or not consensual interventions by regional organisations violate the peremptory norm in Article 2(4). The general trend in legal writing is to treat regional enforcement actions *merely* as an exception to the prohibition of the use of force.[26] This approach is justified when analysing regional enforcement actions within the orthodox framework of Chapter VIII since such actions are only possible with the permission of the Security Council.

However, as Professor Müllerson has argued, even if states are conservative in the sense of the absence of political will to draft new rules on the use of force and intervention, this does not necessarily mean that law too is as inertial as are these states.[27] The adoption of new treaties by regional organisations, the provisions of some of which empower them to take enforcement action without the authorisation of the Security Council, means that analysis of regional enforcement actions can no longer be safely regarded as merely an institutional exception to Article 2(4). If regional organisations dispense with the authorisation of the Security Council under Article 53(1), as they currently purport to do, that challenges the rule in Article 2(4). The prime task for this chapter therefore is to determine how treaties such as ECOWAS' 1999 Protocol and the Constitutive Act of the AU, which directly challenge the rule prohibiting the use of force in Article 2(4), fit into the wider context of the *jus ad bellum*.

In order to answer this question, the analysis below adopts two approaches. First, it determines whether the *consent* of members of regional organisations that their organisations may use force on their territories for various reasons, is a manifestation of a *principle shared* by those states. If this can be established, the next issue for determination is whether such states have accepted this principle as binding on them, that

[24] See for instance, Anthony D' Amato, above note 7.

[25] See Ian Brownlie, above note 7; Derek Bowett, *Self-Defence in International Law* (Manchester, Manchester University Press, 1958); Julius Stone, *Aggression, and World Order: A Critique of United Nations Theories of Aggression* (London, Stevens & Sons , 1958); Ruth Russell, *A History of the United Nations Charter: The Role of the United States 1940–1945* (Washington, DC, The Brookings Institution, 1958).

[26] One of the very few works which have taken a more critical approach towards the development of Article 2(4) by states and regional organisations after the Cold War is, Rein Müllerson, 'Jus Ad Bellum: Plus Ça Change (Le Monde) Plus C'est La Même Chose (Le Droit)?' (2002) 7 (2) *Journal of Conflict and Security Law* 149. On the inadequacy of Article 2(4) to meet the challenges of transnational acts such as terrorism which may not be directly linked to a state, see Richard Falk, 'Defining a Just War' *The Nation* 29 Oct 2001, also cited by Müllerson, above; EPJ Myjer and ND White, 'The Twin Towers Attack: An Unlimited Right to Self-Defence' (2002) 7(1) *Journal of Conflict and Security Law* 17.

[27] *Ibid*, particularly at 151 *et seq*.

is, whether there is *opinio juris necessitatis*. From this preliminary exercise, the chapter goes on to determine the impact of such principle and practice on Article 2(4).

6.1. CONSENSUAL INTERVENTION BY REGIONAL ORGANISATIONS: A CONSTITUTIONAL PRINCIPLE?[28]

As noted in Chapter 5, the Constitutive Act of the African Union explicitly enumerates the conditions that may trigger the AU intervention.[29] This is not so with the ECOWAS Protocol on Collective Security, which, though it has codified its well-entrenched intervention principles over a period of ten years (1989–99), did not specify its *casus foederis*.

It will be recalled that ECOWAS's principal justification for intervening in Liberia was 'to stop the senseless killing' and prevent humanitarian disasters,[30] a rationale that featured strongly in its subsequent interventions in Sierra Leone, Guinea-Bissau,[31] and the Niger Republic.[32] Therefore, notwithstanding absence of explicit grounds of intervention in its Protocol, ECOWAS member states have accepted, in principle and practice, certain conditions as warranting ECOWAS' *mandatory* intervention. To this extent, Article 22 (c) of ECOWAS 1999 Protocol charges ECOMOG with, *inter alia*, 'humanitarian intervention in support (sic) of humanitarian disaster'. Article 10 gives the Mediation and Security Council (MSC) the power to intervene through a wide variety of measures including 'peace-keeping',[33] 'humanitarian intervention'[34] and 'enforcement of sanctions'.[35]

The fact that it is not just peacekeeping, but also humanitarian intervention and enforcement of sanctions that appear in Articles 10 and 22 means that ECOWAS states accept that the organisation may use force beyond

[28] The consensual intervention advocated in this chapter, although based on consent like peacekeeping, is not of the same nature as peacekeeping. Whereas the consent of *all* parties to a conflict is required to a peacekeeping operation, only states need to give their consent to regional organisations for the purpose of using force to protect community values. Moreover, while in peacekeeping consent is required mostly, though not always, *after* the outbreak of conflicts, consent for forcible intervention may be given in *advance*. Furthermore, whereas force is limited to self-defence in peacekeeping operations, consensual intervention entails peace enforcement. Finally, unlike peacekeeping, consensual intervention is based on the principle of the concerned regional organisation determining the outcome of events.

[29] Article 4(h) African Union Act.

[30] See above.

[31] See *Additional Protocol to the Abuja Accord of November 1st 1998, Concerning the formation of the Government of Unity of Guinea Bissau* Lome, Togo, 15th 1998, on file with the author; *Agreement between the Government of Guinea Bissau and the Self-proclaimed Military Junta* 1st November 1998, Abuja, Nigeria, on file with the author.

[32] *Meetings of Ministers of Foreign Affairs*, Lome Togo, 24–5 1999, http://www.Sierra-leone.org/ecowas052599.html on file with the author.

[33] Article 22(b).

[34] Article 22(c).

[35] Article 22(d).

traditional peacekeeping frontiers. Thus, despite the fact that Charles Taylor had consolidated the hold of his NPFL on Liberia by capturing about 90% of the country, ECOWAS had insisted on a democratic transfer of power even if it meant at the end of the day that the same party would still win the elections.

Similarly, had ECOMOG been a peacekeeping operation *simpliciter* in Sierra Leone, it would not have mounted an attack on the military junta, which had already settled itself in power. ECOWAS said clearly *before* intervening in Liberia that its mission did not require the consent of any of the parties to the conflict.[36] It repeated this in the second phase of its intervention in Sierra Leone.[37] Thus, the so-called *invitation* by President Samuel Doe was superfluous since ECOWAS had already assumed the competence to intervene without such invitation. When it became apparent during the conflict that Doe was unsatisfied with the actions of ECOMOG troops to repel the insurrectionists,[38] he had been unable to withdraw his consent. However, had Doe decided to withdraw his consent, this would have been legally possible since ECOWAS had not adopted the treaty that 'froze' members' consent to its intervention in their conflicts. The fact that Doe chose not to withdraw strongly evidences an acceptance of the practice that was to later transform into law through the Collective Security Protocol.

Moreover, in the Sierra Leone case, when ECOWAS returned to that country following the withdrawal of its largest contingent, Nigeria, it did not require the specific consent of President Tejan Kabah to re-enter Sierra Leone.[39] It would appear that ECOWAS had dithered as to its legal grounding in the first phase of its intervention in Sierra Leone—when it had operated on the authority of Protocol for Mutual Assistance and Defence (PMAD)—and had acted upon a formal invitation by exiled President Kabah. However, this was not the case in the second phase in which it had operated fully on the authority of its new protocol, which have endowed it with powers including dispensing with Host State consent.

Furthermore, while NATO's intervention in Kosovo was not underwritten by any of the provisions of its treaty, it was *legitimatised* by a unanimous decision of all its members.[40] Whether such a decision could be validly reached by means other than an amendment of NATO's original treaty is a separate question which is not a remit of this chapter, as is

[36] See discussion in Chapter 5.
[37] *Ibid.*
[38] *Ibid.*
[39] See Ademola Abass, 'The Implementation of ECOWAS New Protocol and Security Council Resolution 1270 in Sierra Leone: New Developments in Regional Intervention'. (2002) 10(1) *University of Miami International and Comparative Law Review* 177.
[40] NATO Doc AR 295 SA (1998). But see Nigel White, above note 13, especially 36 *et seq.*

whether the unanimous agreement by 19 democracies could legally *extend* the task of NATO from collective self-defence to collective security. The point of interest to this chapter is that all NATO states agreed to the use of force by the alliance against FRY and none of them challenged the action.

It is instructive that not a single ECOWAS state has yet criticised or condemned its enforcement action in any of the cases in which it has intervened. Although, occasionally there is a tendency by one or two members, such as Burkina Faso and Côte d' Ivoire in the Liberian case,[41] to breach or not to implement the collective decisions of the Community, such internal wrangling has not generally developed into a challenge to ECOWAS actions by such derogating members. Indeed, such problems are promptly sorted out at the level of the Assembly of Heads of State and Government. Although the NPFL initially protested against ECOMOG deployment to Liberia, the basis of this objection was the perceived lopsided composition of the force rather than the legality of ECOWAS' intervention.[42]

There seems also to be emerging a gradual recognition or toleration by the international community that new regional exceptions to Article 2(4) may develop through state practice.[43] At the provisional stage of the FRY's suit against ten NATO states, Belgium sought support for NATO's action by indicating, *inter alia*, the non condemnation of a similar action by ECOWAS in Liberia and Sierra Leone by any of the UN organs.[44] In effect, Belgium seemed to argue that since no organ of the UN condemned ECOWAS actions in Liberia and Sierra Leone, then the action must be perceived as having been *tacitly* endorsed by the UN, or, *de minimis*, that the actions did not contravene the Charter provisions.

In contrast, there were serious condemnations of NATO's action against FRY in the Security Council.[45] It would appear that the difference between the international perception of NATO's action in Kosovo and ECOWAS' actions in Liberia and Sierra Leone lies in the difference in their legal implications. Whereas the Sierra Leone action was by a collection of states acting under a regional organisation, empowered by an enabling treaty, and acting in respect of a conflict affecting a member state, NATO's action in Kosovo was the exact opposite. This distinction, as we will later argue, makes all the difference between the legal basis for proposing a consensual intervention that may constitute permissible derogation from Article 2(4) and multilateral violation of that article by states acting in somewhat analogous circumstances.

[41] See Chapter 5.

[42] *Ibid.*

[43] Professor Müllerson argues that the customary process may not only be more natural and flexible but in today's circumstances even quicker in consolidating emerging tendencies into law. See above note 26 at 152 *et seq*.

[44] *Legality of Use of Force* (*Yugoslavia v Belgium*) CR99/15, 10 May 1999; (1999) ICJ Pleadings http://www.icj cij.org/icjwww/idocket/iybe/iybeframe.htm.

[45] UN Doc 4011th mtg, 10 June 1999. See analysis in Chapter 5.

Yet, to conclude, as Belgium did before the ICJ, that the acquiescence of the Security Council, the General Assembly and the rest of the international community to ECOWAS' enforcement actions amounts to an *acceptance* of such action is to assume that the intervention itself lawfully derogated from Article 2(4).[46] It is possible that, being a political rather than a judicial body, the Security Council may often have to overlook an illegality and predicate its actions on previous illegality of member states for pure political reasons.[47] It did with Resolution 1244 where, despite the contention by Russia that that resolution did not amount to an endorsement of NATO's action in Kosovo, the Security Council was content to work with NATO forces in the mission entrusted to KFOR. Therefore, since acquiescence itself, without more, cannot make legal an otherwise illegal act, it is proposed to consider the compatibility of ECOWAS consensual intervention with Article 2(4).

6.2. DETERMINING THE PEREMPTORY CHARACTER OF ARTICLE 2(4)

Article 53 of the Vienna Convention on the Law of Treaties[48] states that a 'treaty is void if, at the time of its conclusion, it conflicts with a peremptory norm of general international law'. The Convention further states that 'if a new peremptory norm of general international law emerges, any existing treaty which is in conflict with that norm becomes void and terminates'.[49]

In its Articles on Responsibilities of States for Internationally Wrongful Acts (ARSIWA) adopted in 2001, the International Law Commission (ILC) confirmed the peremptory character of the ban of the use of force. While Articles 20, 21, 22, 23, 24, and 25 of the ARSIWA recognise circumstances that may preclude wrongfulness of conducts otherwise inconsistent with international obligations, Article 26 expressly protects a peremptory norm from such exemptions.[50] According to this article, '[n]othing in this Chapter (Chapter V) precludes the wrongfulness of any act of a State which is not in conformity with an *obligation* arising under a peremptory

[46] For analysis of this case see Dino Kristiotis, 'The Kosovo Crisis and NATO's Application of armed force against the Federal Republic of Yugoslavia' (2000) 49 *International and Comparative Law Quarterly* 330.

[47] For instance, as seen in the last chapter, the Security Council did not condemn Operation Desert Fox against Iraq, following from a series of threats by the Allied states. The fact that the Security Council did not condemn these threats should not be seen as evidencing its acceptance of the action.

[48] Opened for signature on 23 May 1969, *United Nations Treaty Series Register*, No 18, 232, UN Doc A/CONF 39/27 (1969), reprinted in (1969) 63 *American Journal of International Law* 875, hereafter the Convention or VCLT.

[49] Article 64. For analysis see Yoram Dinstein, *War, Aggression and Self-Defence* (Cambridge, Cambridge University Press, 3rd edn, 2001), 94 *et seq*.

[50] See ILC's *Commentary*, above note 5. See Ronzitti, above note 3 at 148.

norm of general international law'.[51] Article 50 of the ARSIWA contains similar provisions concerning the prohibition of reprisals as a form of countermeasure. As the Special Rapporteur on the Law of Treaties, Fitzmaurice, once observed, '[a] treaty obligation the observance of which is incompatible with a new rule or prohibition of international law in the nature of *jus cogens* will justify (and require) non-observance of any treaty obligation involving such incompatibility'.[52]

Certainly, Article 2(4) contains norms that have a peremptory character out of which no state can contract.[53] However, does the prohibition of use of force in Article 2(4) mean that *any* use of force by states invariably breaches a *jus cogens* rule? What norms under Article 2(4) have become *peremptory* or does Article 2(4) consist only of a single, indivisible norm of international law? Is it not possible, and is it not necessary, to subject the different uses of force possible under Article 2(4) to the test of peremptory character in order to, as the ICJ did in the *Nicaragua* case, separate a gravest form of force from lesser ones?

Understandably, there is professional reluctance to inquire into the content of Article 2(4), and as Professor Ian Brownlie rightly noted, 'more authority exists for the category of *jus cogens* than exists for its particular content'.[54] In order to determine what *obligation* under Article 2(4) states may not contract out of, it is necessary to first ascertain what obligations under that article constitute a peremptory norm. As Ronzitti observed, 'in order to ascertain its precise scope . . . it is necessary to submit the particular conduct which is alleged to be in breach of the *jus cogens* prohibition to the . . . test'.[55]

6.2.1. The Tests of Peremptory Norms under Article 2(4)

Article 53 of the Vienna Convention on the Law of Treaties lays down two tests that must be passed before a norm of general international law can be regarded as having become *jus cogens*. These are that the norm in question must be (1) binding on all members of international community of states as a whole[56]; and (2) it must be accepted by the international community

[51] Article 26 of the ILC Articles on State Responsibility, text in ILC's *Commentary*, above note 5.

[52] Fitzmaurice, 'Fourth Report on the Law of Treaties', (1959) cited in ILC's *Commentary*, above note 5 at 187.

[53] Ronzitti, above note 3 at 149. Ronzitti, for instance, contends that 'the principle of *volenti non fit injuria* does not apply when a peremptory norm is violated', at 148. We shall return to this issue later.

[54] Ian Brownlie, *Principles of Public International Law* (Oxford, Clarendon Press, 1990) 514–15.

[55] Ronzitti, above note 3, at 153.

[56] ILC *Commentary*, above note 5 at 247.

that there can be no derogation from such a norm.[57] A further test might be the test of 'seriousness'[58] of breach as formulated in the Commentary to the ARSIWA. However, it seems that this requirement is merely complimentary to those laid down in the Article 53 of the VCLT and not intended to establish a new category, otherwise it would have been explicitly mentioned in the articles dealing with peremptory norms in the ARSIWA. Nevertheless, the fact that the 'seriousness' test is added in the commentary evidences the cogency attached by the ILC to the task of determining when a norm becomes peremptory in general international law. A 'serious' breach, to which peremptory norm applies is defined in the second paragraph of Article 40 as 'a gross or systematic failure by the responsible State to fulfil the obligation in question'.[59]

According to Ronzitti, 'the core of the peremptory rule is the sum of the State conducts which the essential components of the international community consider effectively forbidden by a ban from which absolutely no derogation is permitted'.[60] In the words of Dinstein:

> what marks out peremptory norms (constituting *jus cogens*), as compared to ordinary norms of general international law (amounting to mere *jus dispositivum*) [is that] the special standing of *jus cogens* is manifested less in enjoining States from contrary behaviour (violations), and more in aborting attempted derogations from the general norms.[61]

Professor Louis Henkin refers to peremptory norms as the 'principal norms of contemporary international law'.[62] Howsoever writers may explain the *raison d'être* tests, it seems well settled that writers agree on those two elements as guiding the passage of an ordinary norm into a peremptory one.[63] In the *Nicaragua* case,[64] the Court affirmed that although both the United States and Nicaragua agreed on the customary character of Article 2(4), it must satisfy itself that 'there exists in customary international law an *opinio juris* as to the binding character of such abstention'.[65]

[57] ILC's *Commentary*, above note 5 at 245 *et seq*.
[58] *Ibid*, at 247.
[59] *Ibid*.
[60] Above note 3 at 150.
[61] Above note 49 at 94, quoting Jerzy Sztucki, *Jus Cogens and the Vienna Convention on the Law of Treaties: A Critical Appraisal* (Wien, Springer, 1974), at 67–68.
[62] Loius Henkin, *How Nations Behave* (New York, Columbia University Press 1968), 129.
[63] See also G A Christenson, 'The World Court and Jus Cogens', (1987) 81 *American Journal of International Law* 93; G Gaja, 'Jus Cogens beyond the Vienna Convention' (1981) 172 *Recueil des Cours*, 271.
[64] Above note 21.
[65] *Ibid*, para 188.

6.2.2. What Norms are Exactly Peremptory Under Article 2(4)?

There is an extensive literature on the subject of *jus cogens* rules in international law.[66] There is also a substantial body of legal instruments which recognise certain norms of international law as constituting peremptory norms under general international law.[67] However, it is in the work of the International Law Commission that the concept of *jus cogens* has been more fully developed.[68]

The initial attempt by the ILC to designate certain norms as peremptory norms was criticised by jurists such as McNair,[69] Schwarzenberger,[70] Sztucki[71] and Theodor Meron.[72] Charles de Visscher[73] once pointed out that the proponent of a rule of *jus cogens* in relation to Article 53 VCLT will have a considerable burden of proof. However, the ILC further developed the idea of peremptory norm in the final version of its Articles on State Responsibility adopted in 2001. An examination of Articles 20 and 26 of these articles is crucial to a consideration of the content of Article 2(4) as *jus cogens*.

Article 20 of the ARSIWA provides that:

> valid consent by a State to the commission of a given act by another State precludes the wrongfulness of that act in relation to the former State to the extent within the limit of that consent.

The preclusion of wrongfulness by Article 20 on the basis of *consent* by the injured state does not apply, according to Article 26, to,

[66] Christenson GA, 'The World Court and Jus Cogens' (1987) 81 *American Journal of International Law* 93 at 101; J Sztucki, *Jus Cogens and the Vienna Convention on the Law of Treaties: A Critical Appraisal* (Wien, Springer, 1974); Lauri Hannikainen, *Peremptory Norms*: (jus cogens), in *International Law*: *Historical Development, Criteria, Present Status*, (Helsinki, Lakimiesliiton Kustannus (Finnish Lawyers' Publishing Company), 1988); Christos Rozakis, *The Concept of Jus Cogens in the Law of Treaties* (Amsterdam, Oxford, North-Holland Publishing Co, 1976); G Gaja, 'Jus Cogens beyond the Vienna Convention' (1981) 172 *Recueil des Cours* 271 at 301; E Suy, 'The Concept of Jus Cogens in Public International Law' 2 *Carnegie Endowment for International Peace*, Papers and Proceedings, The Concept of Jus Cogens in International Law 17 (1967); G Tunkin, 'Jus Cogens in Contemporary International Law' (1975) IV, *University of Toledo Law Review* 107; G Schwarzenberger, '*International Jus Cogens?*' (1965) 43 *Texas Law Review* (1965) 455.

[67] See the *Vienna Convention on the Law of Treaties*, Articles 53 and 64; *Restatement of the Law*: *The Foreign Relations Law of the United States, I*, American Law Institute, 28 (3rd edn, 1986).

[68] For a similar view, see Christenson, above note 66 at 96; see also ICJ in *Nicaragua* case, 99.

[69] Arnold McNair, *The Law of Treaties* (Oxford, Clarendon, 1961), especially at 213–15.

[70] Above note 66.

[71] Above note 66.

[72] Theodor Meron, 'On a Hierarchy of International Human Rights', (1986) 80 *American Journal of International Law* 1.

[73] Charles de Visscher, *Théories et réalités en droit international* (4th edn, 1970), 295–96, cited by Brownlie, at 514.

any act of a State which is not in conformity with an obligation arising from a peremptory norm of general international law.[74]

The ILC noted that the 'criteria for identifying peremptory norms of general international law are stringent' and that 'so far, relatively few peremptory norms have been recognised as such'.[75] The ILC has identified examples of such norms already affirmed by 'various tribunals, national and international' as those that 'are clearly accepted and recognised'.[76] These include 'the prohibition of aggression, genocide, slavery, racial discrimination, crimes against humanity and torture, and the right to self-determination'.[77] It must be stressed that, in the context of use of force, the ILC identified *only* the prohibition of aggression as a peremptory norm under Article 2(4). It did not identify other *types* of forces as constituting a peremptory norm in Article 2(4).

Similarly, the ICJ referred to the General Assembly's *Declaration on Friendly Relations* as a further affirmation of the customary recognition that the ban on force has a peremptory character.[78] It also quoted the ILC's characterisation of Article 2(4) that: 'the law concerning the prohibition of force in itself constitutes a conspicuous example of a rule in international law having the character of *jus cogens*'.[79] Nevertheless, the ICJ did not pronounce on the specific content of Article 2(4) that may have become peremptory norms. On the contrary, in a very interesting passage, the Court stated that '[a]s regards certain particular aspects of the principle (prohibition of force) in question, it will be necessary to distinguish the most grave forms of the use of force (those constituting an armed attack) from other less grave forms'.[80] It is submitted that the latter types of force must be regarded as those that have not been *clearly accepted or recognised* as peremptory norms in general international law. They are such that will fail the test of 'seriousness of breach' laid down in Article 40 of the ILC Articles on State Responsibility.

The most authoritative statement on the question of what norms under Article 2(4) are peremptory is stated by the ILC in its 2001 Commentary on its ARSIWA.[81] This is because the ILC's explication of the subject in the

[74] For analysis, see Ademola Abass, 'Consent Precluding Wrongfulness: A Critical Analysis', (2004) 53 *International and Comparative Law Quarterly* 211.

[75] ILC's *Commentary*, above note 5 at 188.

[76] *Ibid*.

[77] See the *Case Concerning East Timor* (Portugal and Australia) ICJ Reports 1995, 90 at 102, para 29.

[78] *Nicaragua* case, at 100.

[79] *Ibid*, 100, quoting from paragraph (1) of the Commentary of the Commission to Article 50 of its draft Articles on the Law of Treaties, (1966) II *International Law Commission Yearbook* at 247.

[80] *Nicaragua* case para. 101.

[81] It must be noted that the ICJ itself placed great reliance on the opinions and views of the ILC on peremptory norms in coming to its own conclusions in the *Nicaragua* case. See ICJ's reference to ILC's characterisation of peremptory norms on page 99 of *Nicaragua* case, quoting (1966) vol II *International Law Commission Yearbook* at 247. See also page 100.

ARSIWA clarifies its previous position as contained in its commentary on the Vienna Convention on the Law of Treaties.[82] Although Articles 40 and 41 dealing with 'serious obligations under peremptory norms of general international law' do not specifically list what these obligations are,[83] the *Commentary* in fact supplies a list. Having referred to the various statements of the ICJ in cases like *East Timor*, the *Application of the Convention on the Prevention and Punishment of the Crime of Genocide,* the ILC stated that 'among these prohibitions, it is generally agreed that the prohibition of aggression is to be regarded as peremptory'.[84] It supported this claim with its *Commentary* on Article 53 of the VCLT,[85] and the uncontradicted statements of the governments taking part in that conference.[86] The ILC, relying on international and national tribunal decisions,[87] also found as peremptory norms the prohibition against torture as defined in Article 1 of the Convention against Torture and Other Cruel, Inhuman or degrading Treatment or Punishment of 10 December 1984.[88]

The ILC stated that by mentioning some examples of peremptory norms it 'should be stressed that the examples . . . may not be exhaustive'. Nonetheless, it emphasised that Article 40 applies a further limitation for the purposes of the Chapter (Chapter 5 of Articles on State Responsibility), viz: that the breach should itself have been 'serious'.[89] Although, this limitation is to be applied *generally* when determining what norms qualify as peremptory, it is of a particular significance to the prohibition of the use of force and the issue of *jus cogens* under Article 2(4). It represents a clear desire by the ILC 'not to trivialize the breach'.[90]

Roberto Ago, the former Rapporteur of the ILC on State Responsibility, had made a similar distinction between aggression and *other* types of forces in his report on the state of necessity.[91] While he categorically mentioned *aggression* as being prohibited as a peremptory norm of inter-

[82] (1966) II *International Law Commission Yearbook* 247.

[83] The ILC states that 'it is not appropriate to set out examples of the peremptory norms referred to in the text of Article 40 itself, any more than it was in the text of Article 53 of the Vienna Convention', ILC's *Commentary,* above note 5 at 245.

[84] ILC's *Commentary,* above note 5, 246.

[85] *Ibid.*

[86] *Ibid, UN Conference on the Law of Treaties,* A/CONF 39/11, 294, 296–97, 300, 301, 303, 304, 306, 307, 311, 312, 318, 320, 322, 323–24, 326, cited by ILC's *Commentary,* above note 5 at 246 fn 679.

[87] The US Court of Appeals, 2nd Circuit, in *Siderman de Blake v Argentina,* 965 F 2d 699; (1992) *International Law Reports,* vol 103, 455; the UK Court of Appeal in *Al Adsani v Government of Kuwait,* (1996) International Law Reports, vol 107, 536 at 540–41; UK House of Lords in *R v Bow Street Metropolitan Magistrate, ex parte Pinochet Ugarte* (no 3), [1993] 2 *WLR,* 827.

[88] *United Nations Treaty Series,* vol 1460, 112.

[89] ILC's *Commentary,* above note 5, 247.

[90] *Ibid.*

[91] Roberto Ago, 'Addendum to the Eighth Report on State Responsibility' (1980) *Yearbook of International Law Commission* II, 1, 44.

national law, he hesitated to include the other category, including forcible self-determination, in the fold.[92] Professor Brownlie has also noted that 'certain portions of *jus cogens* are the subject of general agreement, including the rules on the use of force by states, self-determination, and genocide'.[93] He however observed that 'yet even here many problems of application remain, particularly in regard to the effect of self-determination on the transfer of territory'.[94] Another scholar, Professor Ronzitti, shares the concern raised by Professor Brownlie. Ronzitti argued in favour of the classification of the rule in Article 2(4) into two. The first is a 'behaviour which is held to be covered by the peremptory rule banning the use of force . . . [the second] a given action [which is] forbidden by a customary rule but not by a peremptory rule, if States, although convinced of the binding nature of the prohibition are not absolutely convinced of its inderogability'.[95]

The approach taken by the ILC in the final version of its ARSIWA is remarkably different from its early position on peremptory norms. For instance, in its comments on the draft Article 53 of the Vienna Convention on the Law of Treaties, the ILC had cited, as an example of a breach of peremptory norm, 'a treaty contemplating an unlawful use of force contrary to the principles of the Charter'. It would thus seem that specifically identifying *aggression* as an example of a peremptory norm and imposing the test of 'seriousness' of breach in its present commentary is more helpful than blandly regarding all unlawful uses of force as violative of peremptory norms.

The approach adopted by the ILC towards ascertaining the content of peremptory norms, in the final version of its Articles on State Responsibility, was entirely consistent with its practice. The ILC had observed that 'it would clearly be wrong to regard rules of *jus cogens* as immutable and incapable of modification in the light of future development'.[96] This was a departure from the ILC's initial tendency to treat peremptory norms as though 'their content were agreed'.[97] From this analysis, one may conclude that in the context of Article 2(4) only the prohibition of aggression has become a peremptory norm of international law.

However, since the content of Article 2(4) is wider than aggression,[98] it follows that there are other types of prohibitions under that article which

[92] *Ibid.*
[93] Brownlie, above note 54 at 515.
[94] *Ibid.*
[95] Above note 3 at 150.
[96] 'Report of the International Law Commission', 18th Session, [1966] II *International Law Commission Yearbook* 248.
[97] See Christenson, above note 66 at 98.
[98] See also Ronzitti, noting that 'in fact the peremptory rule banning the use of force does not exactly coincide with corresponding rule contained in Article 2(4) of the UN Charter', at 150.

have not become peremptory. For instance, intervention in the internal matters of another state for *humanitarian* reasons while unlawful under Article 2(4) does *not* seem to breach a peremptory norm of general international law. For instance, humanitarian intervention, though perhaps not permitted under Article 2(4),[99] cannot be described as aggression since it is not aimed against the territorial integrity or political independence of the target state. When Syria invaded Lebanon in 1976 purportedly on humanitarian grounds, it claimed to have done so in response to the request by the Lebanese people.[100] Syria also claimed that its presence in Lebanon was with the consent of the Lebanese government and that if the latter requested its withdrawal, it would do so.[101] More important is that when the Arab States met to discuss the issue in Cairo from 8–10 June 1976, they did not condemn Syrian action despite the fact that Syria had acted for hegemonic rather than humanitarian considerations.[102]

There is a lack of consensus on the definition of aggression. It is widely believed,[103] however, that aggression is the 'use of armed force by a State against the sovereignty, territorial integrity or political independence of another State or in any other manner inconsistent the Charter of the United Nations'.[104] In the light of this definition, neither peacekeeping operations that transcend permissible use of force nor humanitarian interventions can be regarded as aggression in the manner intended by Article 2(4). While both instances typify cases in which there is either lack of consent or the consented mandate has been exceeded, neither constitutes aggression, as that term is ordinarily understood. It is therefore submitted that non-aggressive uses of force do not violate a peremptory norm under Article 2(4) even if they violate the general ban on the use of force. We therefore advocate a distinction between the ban on force that gives rise to a peremptory obligation under Article 2(4) (aggression) and the threat or use of force that does not under Article 2(4).

During the Cold War, states regarded the use of force for *whatever* purposes as a violation of *jus cogens* rule. During the Vienna Conference on the law of treaties, several delegations confirmed this rule.[105] However, states now increasingly seem to accept that only aggression violates a peremp-

[99] See also Ronzitti, above note 3 at 155.

[100] See the transcript of the statement by President Hafez al-Assad of Syria to West German television, 9 September 1978, Damascus Domestic Service (unpublished), at 1, quoted in Ronzitti, above note 3 at 155.

[101] *Ibid*, at 2.

[102] See also Ronzitti, above note 3 at 155.

[103] For a similar view, see Dinstein, above note 49 at 115.

[104] Article 1, The General Assembly Consensus Definition of Aggression (hereafter Definition of Aggression), adopted in 1974.

[105] See for instance the views of Uruguay, Cyprus, Cuba, Ecuador, Italy, Phillipines, Switzerland, Norway, Nepal, Bielorussia, Malaysia, Poland and Lebanon, and Sierra Leone during the Vienna Conference on the Law of Treaties, UN Conference on the Law of Treaties, First Session, Vienna, 26 March–24 May 1968. *Official Records*, UN A/CONF 39/11, at 294.

tory norm under Article 2(4). Hence, the invasion of South Korea by North Korea, Kuwait by Iraq,[106] and the Falklands Islands by Argentina[107] have all been explicitly termed as aggressions by states, and in the Korean case, by the General Assembly. For instance in the Falklands/Malvinas conflict, Japan condemned Argentina's action as a breach of a peremptory norm of international law.[108]

If it is accepted that in the context of the use of force only aggression has been widely regarded as violating a *jus cogens* rule, then it is possible to argue that other uses of force prohibited by Article 2(4) do not violate a peremptory norm. This is because non-aggressive uses of force are not directed *against* the 'territorial integrity' and 'political independence' of other states. These dual idioms, according to Yoram Dinstein, 'may invite a rigid interpretation blunting the edge of Article 2(4)'.[109] Such *blunting* indeed manifests in the rather curious interpretation of Anthony D'Amato that unless a particular use of force permanently shrinks the size of a state or overthrows its leadership as such it does not violate Article 2(4).[110] While this emphasis on the *physical* damage done to a territorial state seems to be an extreme standard, the submission by Dinstein is more persuasive, although it must be qualified. According to him, 'the correct interpretation of Article 2(4) . . . is that *any* use of inter-State force by Member States for *whatever* reason is banned, unless explicitly allowed by the Charter'.[111] This view should not however be interpreted as meaning that no elements of Article 2(4) can be contracted out of by consent.

Dinstein in fact developed his thesis on the prohibition of the use of force as *jus cogens* by reference only to aggression and not *all* or *any* kinds of force.[112] He argued that,

> a pact of aggression ought not to be confused with a treaty, concluded between Arcadia and Numidia, colliding with ordinary rights of Utopia (i.e. rights derived from *jus dispositivinum*). The validity of an ordinary treaty between Arcadia and Numidia is not affected by the infringement of Utopia's rights. Arcadia and Numidia will bear international responsibility towards Utopia, but their treaty remains in force. By contrast, a pact of aggression, being in conflict with *jus cogens*, would be invalid.[113]

While there is no doubt that 'the principle of non-use of force belongs to the realm of *jus cogens*', it is incorrect to view this principle in terms of the totality of Article 2(4).[114] It is one thing to say that *any* use of force is

[106] See discussion in Chapter 3.
[107] SC 2350 mtg, 37 UN SCOR (1982).
[108] UN Doc S/PV2350, April 3, 1982, 27.
[109] Dinstein, above note 49 at 81.
[110] See above note 7.
[111] *Ibid*, at 82. (Emphasis added.)
[112] *Ibid*, at 93 *et seq*.
[113] *Ibid*, at 95.
[114] See the separate opinion of President Singh in the ICJ decision in *Nicaragua* case, at 153.

prohibited by Article 2(4) (as Dinstein correctly said) but it is another to assume that Article 2(4) in its entirety is *jus cogens* (as Dinstein assumes). What can be said is that Article 2(4) forbids *all* types of force, but not all types of force prohibited under Article 2(4) have become peremptory norms.

The separate contradictory opinions of Judges Singh[115] and Camara[116] in the *Nicaragua* case did not tally with the overall, cautious approach of the Court towards the determination of *jus cogens* rule in Article 2(4). The Court had clearly hierarchised uses of force when it came to an assessment of the forces allegedly used by the United States against Nicaragua.[117] The Court then noted that alongside certain descriptions which may refer to aggression, the test of the principles contained in the *Declaration on Friendly Relations*, as recalled by the Court, restrain states from threat or use of force in circumstances that constitute reprisals, depriving peoples of equal rights and self-determination, encouraging insurgent activities against other states and so on.[118] None of the instances listed by the Court preclude the use of non-aggressive force where the territorial state is in agreement to such.

It would thus seem that the ICJ had graduated the incidents of forces and compartmentalised them into different categories according to the gravity of the action. It had singled out direct and indirect aggression (the gravest form of the use of force) from other less grave forms. It is thus submitted that the approach adopted by the Court in *Nicaragua* supports our proposition that while indeed Article 2(4) prohibits all uses of force, it is only the prohibition of the gravest form of force (aggression) that has been accepted and recognised by states as constituting a peremptory norm of general international law.

There is no difficulty in ascertaining what the position is as regards aggression when we apply these tests. However, it is more difficult to establish *opinio juris* amongst states when we apply these tests to other elements of Article 2(4) and some categories of force. For instance, can it be said that a single instance of the threat of force passes the twin tests of peremptoriness in Article 53 VCLT?

Moreover, the position of the use of force in support of self-determination of peoples cannot be said to have been agreed by the totality of all members of the international community. There was controversy, especially during the Cold War, between the Western and Eastern blocs, and between the Colonial and the Colonised states, as to the exact impact of Article 2(4) on self-determination.[119] There is no need to restate this well-known debate

115 *Ibid.*

116 *Ibid*, at 199

117 At 101 at para 191. See above.

118 *Ibid.*

119 For an authoritative assessment of state practice regarding the perception of Article 2(4) by socialist states, see Kende, 'Twenty-five Years of Local Wars' (1971) 8 *Journal of Peace Research* 6.

here. It suffices to state that whether states regard Article 2(4) as banning the use of force by colonial people fighting for independence per se, or that such is permitted by Article 2(4)[120] (*but* not the use of force by insurgent groups within an independent state[121]) depends on which side of the ideological divide states found themselves.[122] Certainly, it is a controversy that was much guided by the ideological polarisation of the world during the Cold War in which the Western States rejected an interpretation of Article 2(4) that permits use of force for self-determination, whereas socialist countries favoured such an exegesis.[123] However, in the absence of a general agreement the use of force for the purpose of self-determination fails the test of peremptoriness. The first test of peremptoriness is that it must be agreed to by the international community as a 'whole'. Without this, we cannot proceed to determine the state of *opinio juris* in the non-derogability of that norm. Since there is no agreement by all the members of the international community as a whole on the first test, there is no need to go further.

6.3. CAN CONSENT PRECLUDE THE OPERATION OF ARTICLE 2(4) IN RESPECT OF REGIONAL ACTIONS NOT VIOLATING PEREMPTORY NORMS?

Article 20 of the ARSIWA expressly states that consent by a state to the commission of a given act by another state precludes wrongfulness of that act in relation to the former state to the extent that the act remains within the limits of that consent. However, as already noted above, consent, according to Article 26, does not operate to preclude an obligation arising out of a peremptory norm. Thus, in accordance with our analysis above, consent cannot excuse the violation of a *jus cogens* rule, such as the prohibition of aggression or genocide.

Consistently with our position that the content of Article 2(4) is divisible into rules violating peremptory norms (aggression) and rules violating a general prohibition but not peremptory norms (lesser forces), it can be

120 See for instance the position of Spain and Algeria in the Western Sahara case ICJ Pleadings, *Western Sahara*, vol IV, 499.

121 *Ibid*, see Morroco's position. See R Prevost, 'Observation sur l'avis consulatif de la Cour Internationale de Justice relatif au Sahara occidental ('terra nullius' et autodétermination)' (1976) 103 *Clunet* 854.

122 For an excellent review of this debate, see Paolo Rubino, 'Colonialism and the Use of Force by States' in A Cassese (ed), above note 3 at 133;

123 See for instance G Tunkin, *Theory of international Law* (Translated by William E Butler) (London, George Allen & Unwin, 1974); Dicanu, *Normele imperative in dreptul international—ius cogens* [*Peremptory Norms in International Law*] (Bucharest, Editura Academiei Republice Socialiste România, 1977), cited by Hanna Bokor-Szegö, 'The Attitude of Socialist States Towards the International Regulation of the Use of Force' in Antonio Cassese (ed), above note 3 at 453.

argued that consent given by states to regional organisations may preclude the application of Article 2(4) insofar as such relates to the second category of forces. Aggression, being the main indisputable example of a peremptory norm under both Article 2(4) and general international law, enjoys special protection. Thus, even if a state consents to the commission of aggression against it by another state, the aggressor is not thereby released from its obligation arising from a peremptory norm under Article 2(4). The aggressor cannot claim that he committed aggression with the consent of the attacked, hence *volenti non fit injuria* does not apply. In the context of the prohibition of the use of force, aggression must be regarded as a strict liability offence, the responsibility for which does not depend on the state of *mind* of the aggressor, and which cannot be precluded by consent of the attacked state. Thus, whereas states cannot contract out of obligations arising from a peremptory norm of general international law, they should be able to contract out of norms that do not possess a peremptory character. An agreement by states that their regional organisations can, in specified circumstances not involving aggression, use force on their territories, it is submitted, does not violate Article 2(4).

A deployment of force based on a *freely* given power for the same purpose it is applied, can neither be one used *against* the territorial integrity or political independence of the donors of that power, nor one used in any manner inconsistent with the purpose and principle of United Nations. As one commentator has argued,

> States have the power to consent to limitations on their independence. Indeed, states may surrender their independence altogether by merging with another state. Accordingly, states must be free to yield any lesser measure of their independence, in the form of a license to intervene.[124]

Other scholars support this view, stating that, considering that states may extinguish their legal personality altogether, 'it would seem strange if a state could not consent to a less drastic curtailment of its right of non intervention'.[125]

Examples of such a freely given consent to intervention could be seen in the Treaty of Protective Friendship between France and Monaco[126] (Article 4); Treaty of Friendship between Persia and Soviet Union (Article 6)[127] and the Treaty of Guarantee between Cyprus and Greece on the one

[124] David Whippman, 'Treaty-Based Intervention: Who Can Say No?' (1995) 62 *University of Chicago Law Review* 607 at 616.

[125] Ann Van Wynen Thomas and AJ Thomas, Jr, *Non-Intervention: The Law and Its Import in the Americas* (Southern Methodist, 1956), at 92, cited by Wippman, above note 124, at 617.

[126] 17th July 1918, Matens, *Nouveau Recueil Général des Traités*, 3e série, vol 11, at 314, cited in Ronzitti, above note 3 at 157.

[127] 26 February 1921, Societé des Nations, *Recueil des Traités et des engagemnets internationaux enregistrés par le Sécrétariat de la Société des Nations*, vol 9, No 268, at 383 *et seq* cited in Ronzitti, above note 3 at 157.

hand, and Turkey and the United Kingdom, on the other.[128] The crux of these treaties is that they empower states to deploy their troops to another state, such as French troops to Monaco, without the need to consult the territorial states for their consent in cases of emergency.[129] In fact Article 6 of the treaty between the Soviet Union and Persia permitted the former to deploy troops to Persia to defend its own interest. Article 4 of the Cyprus Treaty of Guarantee permits the three guarantor states (Greece, Turkey and the UK) to take certain measures individually or collectively to guarantee the fundamental provisions of the Cyprus constitution.

These treaties have been criticised as violating the peremptory norm of Article 2(4). According to Professor Reisman, '[h]owever a use of force under Article 6 might be rationalized, it necessarily infringes the territorial integrity of the target, and in so far as it is not invited by that state in that particular instance, it impairs its political independence'.[130] Ronzitti challenged Reisman's view, attributing it to 'a mistaken premiss (sic): the identification of the peremptory norm prohibiting the use of force in international relations with Art 2(4) of the UN Charter'.[131] Ronzitti argued that if 'our initial assumption is that only the more serious breaches of Art 2(4)—for example, aggression—are forbidden by a peremptory norm, the conclusion is different'.[132] Another commentator has stated that a determination of whether the entry of foreign troops into another's territory constitutes a breach of the peremptory rule prohibiting the use of force 'must inevitably depend on the circumstances, which would include the question of consent by the State concerned'.[133]

Whatever view is correct, it seems certain that an intervention by a country in another's affairs by consent does not violate a peremptory norm prohibiting the use of force. Although Professor Reisman maintained the view that no rationalisation of any use of force could make it an exception to the peremptory rule is Article 2(4), he nevertheless qualified his statement. He suggested that a use of force necessarily infringes the territorial integrity of the target insofar as it is not invited by that state. We can conclude from this is that a use of force that is based on the consent of the territorial state may violate the prohibition of force but not a peremptory norm of general international law.

The basis of this submission must be distinguished from two similar but unidentical premises. Firstly, this contention is not based on the *ends* of such

128 382 *United Nations Treaty Series*, No 5475.

129 Article 4 of the treaty between France and Monaco; Article 4, Treaty of Friendship between Persia and Soviet Union; Article 6 of Treaty of Guarantee.

130 W Michael Reisman, 'Termination of the USSR's Treaty Right of Intervention in Iran' (1980) 74 *American Journal of International Law* 144 at 153.

131 Ronzitti, above note 3 at 159.

132 *Ibid*.

133 Comment of Sir Francis Vallat on Art 29 of the Draft Articles on State Responsibility submitted by Roberto Ago to the ILC. See (1979) (I) *Yearbook of International Law Commission*, at 38 cited in Ronzitti, above note 3 at 160.

power, that is, not based on whether the use of force is for *humanitarian* purposes, good governance, or self-determination of minority groups. In fact, one of the main reasons for the inability of states and writers to agree on whether humanitarian intervention constitutes an exception to Article 2(4) is that it is a deployment of force without the consent of the territorial state. It is a sort of *deus ex machina*.

Secondly, the position is somewhat different in a situation of failed states as in Somalia where there was no functional government in existence. In such a situation, a regional organisation could undertake a consensual intervention if the failed state is a member of the regional organisation. In that case, the absence of a government would not prevent its intervention, because once state consent has been given in the form of ratification of the enabling treaty, there is no need for further consent before deployment. For instance, the fact that there was no effective government in Liberia when ECOWAS intervened vindicated this view. Although Samuel Doe was reported to have officially invited ECOMOG, it was clear, as we have already stated, that ECOWAS intended to undertake enforcement action in Liberia and the Committee responsible for the decision clearly indicated this by saying that no consent was required for what ECOWAS intended to do in Liberia. Analogously, if a member of the African Union were to experience crisis presently and such a state fails, this failure will not prevent an intervention by the Union because, by virtue of Article 4 of the Act, the Union can now intervene upon the decision of the Assembly of Heads of State and Government. Therefore, the advantage of desegregating consent by these treaties is that it dispenses with the need to obtain specific consent in a crisis situation.

The situation of unconsensual intervention, such as humanitarian intervention, contrasts sharply with the tenets of consensual intervention. Consensual intervention is constructed on the legal grounding that states (including the one against which the action is conducted) have granted their organisation the power to use force for the protection of collective interests as may be contained in the organisation's constitution. Authoritative writers have long recognised that 'the prohibition of intervention must be regarded primarily as a restriction which international law imposes upon states for the protection of the independence of other members of the international community'.[134] For this reason, the 'notion and prohibition of intervention cannot accurately extend to collective action undertaken in the general interest of states of for the collective enforcement of international law'.[135] As Natalino Ronzitti has observed, 'the consent of the territorial State operates as a circumstance precluding wrongfulness'.[136]

[134] Oppenheim's *International Law*, Sir Robert Jennings and Sir Arthur Watts (eds), (London, Longman, 9th edn, 1992)

[135] *Ibid*.

[136] Ronzitti, above note 3 at 148.

A consideration of the stance taken by the ILC in its Articles on State Responsibility and the ICJ in *East Timor* case, will shed light on the importance of consent in regard to wrongfulness of acts.

6.3.1. Consent in the ILC Articles on State Responsibility

The attitude of the International Law Commission towards defining *jus cogens* would seem to bear out the above proposition. The ILC observed that although circumstances precluding wrongfulness cannot justify or excuse a breach of a State's obligations under a peremptory rule, 'in applying some peremptory norms the *consent* of a particular State may be relevant. For example, a State may validly consent to a foreign military presence on its territory for a lawful purpose.'[137] But whether consent in particular cases is valid to excuse wrongfulness is a question of fact. The ILC, however, noted that 'whether consent has been validly given is a matter addressed by international law rules outside the framework of State'. Without doubt, such international rules must include issues such as who gives the consent, the legality of consent given, whether consent has been given freely or under duress, and others.[138]

The ILC further raised the possibility of the question being asked whether 'consent expressed by a regional authority could legitimize the sending of foreign troops into the territory of a State, or whether such consent could only be given by the central government'.[139] Although this question was raised in the context of whether it is the central or regional authority that could authorise an intervention in a federal state, it seems to have been assumed that it is in fact possible that authorised regional intervention is permissible by consent provided such consent emanate from the appropriate authority. In that case, the question of who should have granted the consent is a matter for the internal laws of the federation to resolve either alone or in conjunction with appropriate rules of international law.

The ILC went on to note further that while 'the rights conferred by international human rights treaties cannot be waived by their beneficiaries, but individual's free consent may be relevant to their application'.[140] The ILC also gave examples of humanitarian relief and rescue operations as instances where consent can preclude wrongfulness in international law. If this is so, there is no reason why states cannot consent to a regional treaty codifying such a use of force, and other types, provided none includes aggression.

[137] ILC's *Commentary*, above note 5 at 188.
[138] See Ademola Abass, above note 74.
[139] *Ibid*, at 164.
[140] *Ibid*, at 165.

It must be borne in mind that consent, or any other circumstances precluding wrongfulness in international law does not abrogate the particular obligation it precludes. It merely prevents its applicability for the period in which the precluding circumstance applies. In the context of consensual intervention, it is submitted that responsibility of a regional organisation is precluded the moment a state ratifies the organisation's treaty. In the *Gabčíkovo-Nagymaros Project* case, the ICJ had applied one of the circumstances precluding wrongfulness in international law and concluded that:

> The state of necessity claimed by Hungary—supposing it to have been established—thus could not permit the conclusion that . . . it had acted in accordance with its obligations under 1977 Treaty or that those obligations had ceased to be binding upon it. It would only permit the affirmation that, under the circumstances, Hungary would not incur international responsibility by acting as it did.[141]

The ILC maintained its very practical approach towards construing the impact of consent in determining the responsibility of states for acts to which they consent when it commented on Article 26. As stated above, this article states that 'nothing in the Chapter precludes the wrongfulness of any act of a State which is not in conformity with an obligation arising under a peremptory norm of general international law'.[142] Thus, to the question whether consensual regional enforcement action can preclude wrongfulness under Article 2(4), the answer is affirmative. Where there is an apparent conflict between primary obligations, one of which arises for a State directly under a peremptory norm of general international law, and other obligations, it is evident that such an obligation must prevail.[143]

However, whereas there can be said to be conflicting obligation between a prohibited use of force that has emerged into a peremptory norm (aggression), vis-à-vis consensual intervention, there is no such obligation in respect of ordinary prohibition which does not constitute a peremptory norm. It seems that great caution needs now to be exercised before invalidating a treaty simply because it contains an obligation that is prohibited by international law, even if such prohibited obligation is a peremptory norm. The ILC recognised that when it observed that:

> in theory one might envisage a conflict arising on a subsequent occasion between a treaty obligation, apparently lawful on its face and innocent in its purpose, and a peremptory norm. If such a case were to arise it would be too much to invalidate the treaty as a whole merely because its application in the given case was not foreseen.[144]

141 *Gabčíkovo-Nagymaros Project (Hungary/Slovakia)*, ICJ Reports (1997), 7, para 48, cited by ILC's *Commentary*, above note 5 at 160.

142 *Ibid*, 187.

143 *Ibid*, 187.

144 *Ibid*, 187.

This opinion by the ILC is extremely important to our analysis. It is clear that the position taken by the ILC, as expressed by this dictum, demonstrates a different approach to the provision of Articles 53 and 64 of the VCLT on the requirement of nullification of treaties which, at the time of conclusion, contradict a peremptory norm. This bold and imaginative approach by the ILC is to be commended especially when it is remembered that state consent is the very foundation of international law. Attempts to relocate some norms beyond the reach of states' consent may indeed be incongruent with such an orthodox basis for the development of international law. Although it must be pointed out that the ILC affirmed that the *desirability* of making it clear that the circumstances precluding wrongfulness do not excuse any derogation from a peremptory norm, it is submitted that uses of force which do not violate such norms preclude the general prohibition of Article 2(4).

6.3.2. State Consent and the ICJ

The approach taken to the question of consent by the ILC above seems to have found support in the approach taken by the ICJ in the *East Timor* case.[145] The case arose out of the conclusion of a treaty in 1989 by Australia and Indonesia concerning the delineation a continental shelf by the two states between 1971–72. Portugal brought an action before the ICJ claiming, *inter alia*, that the treaty violated the right of self-determination of the East Timorese people. Portugal therefore requested the Court to declare the conduct of Australia unlawful. Australia objected to the Court's exercising jurisdiction on this matter since, according to her, a determination of the issue sought by Portugal by the Court would affect the right of a third state (Indonesia) which was not a party to the case.[146] In response to Australia's objection, Portugal argued, quite correctly in our view, that the right to self-determination constitutes an obligation *erga omnes*, and is enforceable by all states irrespective of whether the culprit consents to the suit or not.

The Court agreed with the Portuguese position as to the justiciable basis of an obligation arising out of an *erga omnes* principle, holding in fact, that 'the right of peoples to self-determination, as it evolved from the Charter and from the United Nations practice . . . is irreproachable'.[147] It however held that,

> the *erga omnes* character of a norm and the rule of consent to jurisdiction are two different things. Whatever the nature of the obligations invoked, the Court

[145] *Case Concerning East Timor* (*Portugal v Australia*) ICJ Report (1995), 90.
[146] *Ibid*, at 100 *et seq*.
[147] *Ibid*, at 102 para 29.

> could not rule on the lawfulness of the conduct of a State when its judgement would imply an evaluation of the lawfulness of the conduct of another State which is not a party to the case. Where this is so, the Court cannot act, even if the right in question is a right erga omnes.[148]

The pronouncement of the Court clearly departs from the theoretical utopia of the academic writer who does not entertain any deviation from norms such *as erga omnes* or *jus cogens* even by consent. Although the Court had rendered its judgment in respect of an *erga omnes* principle it indeed said that 'whatever the nature of the obligations invoked'. This means that it would have made no difference to the Court had the East Timorese' right violated by Indonesia been *jus cogens*. It would have been expected by Portugal (and by most academic writers) that the obligation in question, being a serious norm under general international law, the Court would have disregarded the fact that Indonesia had not given her consent to the case. No doubt, the *ratio decidendi* of the Court seems to have been founded on the distinction to be made between the character of a norm in dispute and the need to secure consent from a party which might be affected by the outcome of the dispute. However, the principle of consent established by the Court in the *Monetary Gold* Case is distinguishable from the instant case in which the obligation sought to be preserved applied to all states.[149]

It would seem plausible to argue that in arriving at its conclusion in the *East Timor* case, the Court indirectly affirmed that we cannot throw away states consent when we seek to determine the lawfulness or rightfulness of an action regardless of what types of norms are involved.

6.4. CONCLUSION

From the above analysis, it can be seen that the ILC, the ICJ and even states do not share the seeming doctrinal rigidity of academic writers in determining what actions violate peremptory norms. The shift noticed both in the ILC's and Court's attitude may have been dictated by the need to approach the interpretation of the normative rules and principles of the UN Charter, and other instruments of international law, in a much more pragmatic way. Certainly, one cannot advocate that regional organisations should conclude treaties that authorise acts of aggression against erring member states. But that does not mean that within the general prohibition of force, states cannot avail themselves of some margin of appreciation as they may generally agree on, provided such powers do not encroach on peremptory norms.

[148] *Case Concerning East Timor* (*Portugal* v *Australia*) ICJ Report (1995), at 102 para 29.
[149] *Monetary Gold Removed from Rome in 1943* ICJ Report, (1954), 19.

Conclusion

THE LAW AND practice of collective security by regional organisations developed more rapidly in the first decade after the Cold War than in the first forty-five years of the UN's existence. As we have seen in the foregoing chapters, the development of the law and practice of collective security by regional organisations after the Cold War has been attended by many incidents. Such incidents include the adoption of treaties some provisions of which are either directly in conflict with some provisions of the UN Charter or challenge the very basis of some of those provisions. We discussed the reasons why such enforcement provisions such as are contained in the ECOWAS protocol and the AU Constitutive Act do not contravene Charter provisions. Our analysis in this regard focussed on issues such as consensual intervention and its relationship with the prohibition of the use of force under Article 2(4). We also examined the *jus cogens rule* in Article 2(4) in order to determine whether decentralised collective security impinges on the peremptory norms in that article.

There are several types of regional organisations currently in existence and it is indeed quite difficult to lay down trite criteria for determining which of them come under Chapter VIII regulation.

More interesting than the transformation of regional organisations either from purely economic grouping to multi-purpose organisations (for example, ECOWAS, SADC and CARICOM) or from collective defence to collective security organisation (for example NATO) is the attitude of the UN. One can safely observe that the days seem forever gone when the UN would be discouraged from enlisting the cooperation of an organisation simply because its constitutive treaty designates it as an organisation formed under Chapter VII (Article 51) as opposed to Chapter VIII. The involvement of NATO in the peacekeeping operations/enforcement action during the disintegration of the former Yugoslavia and the inclusion of NATO troops in the Kosovo Forces (KFOR) clearly demonstrate the new approach of the UN to regional organisations and defensive alliances. The Security Council continues to devise resolutions that invite states operating through regional organisations of their national governments to assist in finding solutions to conflicts. As we showed in our analysis (in chapters 2 and 5 especially) a greater emphasis is now placed on what regional organisations are doing rather than what their treaties say they can do. Nevertheless, we advised caution, on the part of the UN especially, not to completely allow flexibility to overtake legality. While there may be no real use in insisting at all times on regional organisations' complying with their treaties and the UN provisions, an unregulated regime can hardly ensure efficiency, coherence and the health of collective security. The operations of the UN and NATO in the former Yugoslavia, UN and ECOWAS in Sierra Leone, demonstrated that extreme flexibility is a recipe for chaos.

The Charter of the UN continues to remain the foundation for further development in the field of collective security. However, as our analysis in chapter 2 revealed, there is a dire need for reinforcement. If the UN Charter lays down specific legal prescriptions to regulate certain issues, it does not freeze such prescriptions or benchmark their limits. The Charter of the United Nations is a living instrument and must continue to generate further development, both in the law and practice of collective security. Through our analysis of the various ingredients of regional arrangement under Chapter VIII, we showed clearly that the UN Charter is not past the age of child bearing.

The Security Council, as the ultimate custodian of collective security, cannot afford to allow formality to overshadow intention. If a particular operation by a regional organisation does not conform exactly to the requirements of the UN Charter, the Security Council must temper law with pragmatism; it must be prepared to accommodate exigencies such that made it to devise a decentralised military option, in order to beat the stasis of the Cold War. This does not mean that the Security Council must allow undue and irrational exuberance by regional organisations to fetter its sense of purpose or constrain its administration of peace and security on behalf of the entire humanity. Rather what is being suggested here is that the Security Council must as and when necessary recognise the dictates of modern reality. It must continue to remember that the UN Charter is not a piece of domestic legislation an amendment of which may be secured by a few parliamentarians in the corridors of a legislative chamber. It is a most important document, devised by humanity for humanity and can only be altered by the entire humanity as represented by the memberships of the UN itself. Therefore, developments of its provisions by organs of the UN, states and regional organisations must be seen as a necessary tool for advancing the course of that humanity although within the confines of legality.

The view that only the Security Council may forever more use force on behalf of the international community is undoubtedly based on the provisions of the UN Charter. As we saw in our discussion in chapter 4, such provisions (as Article 24) are not devoid of legal effects. They are based on the anticipation that the Security Council shall fulfil its primary obligation for the maintenance of international peace and security. True, the Security Council has discretion as to when, where and by what means it must deploy the collective security machinery of the UN. It is extremely doubtful that the intention of states in 1945 was to concede their collective security power to an organ of the UN which might erratically decide how to use such powers without due regards to the donors. Arguments that the Security Council cannot be constrained as to how it deploys the powers conferred on it by states has been shown to be seriously flawed. Such arguments do not appear to be in touch with the reality of post Cold War collective security needs.

If the lessons learnt in Rwanda, Kosovo and other places, were to mean anything to the Security Council in particular, it is that there is a serious danger in allowing the dictates of national interests of Security Council members to becloud the collective responsibility entrusted to it under the Charter. Persistent selectivity in the application of collective security mechanisms will only breed more distrust in the system, weaken the system and consequently damage its credibility beyond repair. The League of Nations collapsed for many reasons. One significant factor was the disillusion suffered by several Member States in the Organisation's ability to guarantee peace and security on an equal basis to all nations. The attack on Ethiopia by Italy and the inability of the League to remedy the situation conspicuously demonstrated that the League was not the organisation to give the world the effective collective security it badly needed after the First World War.

Certainly states possessed collective security powers before the advent of the League of Nations and the UN. They undoubtedly gave those powers up to the Security Council so that the latter could administer it on their behalf. States could be taken to be operating under a 'veil of ignorance' as to what to expect in the future. After all, the view is commonly expressed nowadays that the Charter authors did not anticipate that civil wars would become such a perennial problem of collective security as they have today become. States could not have foreseen the entire dynamics of the world that would open before them after departing San Francisco. Therefore, it continues to be in their interest to keep addressing the problem of collective security through their regional organisations.

As we have already said, since states collectively yielded their power in 1945, they can only collectively repossess such powers in default of the Security Council. Since they also gave up the power through a constitutional instrument (the Charter) even if this be a unique piece of treaty, they can only repossess such powers through the same means. Hence, while we can rationalise ECOWAS 1999 protocol and the AU Act on this basis, the NATO's use of force on a mere consensus by its members, without a formal alteration of its constituent treaty, is difficult to defend. Repossessing powers already given to another organisation to use on one's behalf is difficult to justify in the absence of an enabling treaty. That does not mean that every modification must be accomplished by a treaty amendment.

The Security Council could not discharge its responsibility under Chapter VII during the Cold War. The abuse of the veto power, especially by the Soviet Union, rendered centralised collective security inoperable. However, the Security Council ingenuously resorted to performing its functions by means that circumvented the formality of the Charter, thereby avoiding the obstruction by the veto power. This was the mechanism of decentralised enforcement action by means of which the Security Council authorises or encourages states to implement its recommendations. As seen in our discussion in chapter 3, this mode proved extremely useful in resolving the Gulf crisis, arising from the Iraqi annexation of Kuwait and the Korean conflict in the 1950s. Nonetheless, this model, like the one under Chapter VII, depends mainly on whether the permanent members of the Security Council agree on an enforcement action.

For the General Assembly to subrogate the Security Council, as it did in the past, the Security Council must either procedurally transfer the particular matter on which its members do not agree to it, or the Assembly must fall back on the *Uniting for Peace* resolution devised by it for such situations. For some inscrutable reasons, the Western states, led by the United States, which had devised the *Uniting for Peace* in 1950, did not activate the resolution when Russia's threat prevented the Security Council from effectively dealing with the Kosovo crisis in 1999. The view has been expressed by some writers that it may be that NATO members were mindful that requesting the General Assembly to intervene in NATO's crisis could fetter them as to the type of weapons they could use and might have created a precedent for future purposes. With regards to the Iraqi crisis in 2003, it was obvious why the General Assembly could not have been activated, had states so intended.

Whatever may be responsible for the non-activation of the General Assembly, the resort to decentralised enforcement action by the Security Council is always attended by problems. Powerful participants such as the United States easily dominate these sorts of actions. Command and control of the operations are often shrouded in utmost secrecy so that the Security Council, which authorises them, is only informed of what actions these states take afterwards.

The fear expressed by functionalists like David Mitrany that regionalism would be inimical to universalism seems somewhat misplaced. Such a concern, as our analysis has shown, is behind the doctrinal conception of regionalism as being antagonistic to universalism. In the Cold War period when mistrust and mutual suspicion reigned, it was understandable to have believed that regionalism would lead (and in fact led) to the creation of regional blocs such as the Western and the Eastern Hemispheres policed by the Monroe and Brezhnev doctrines respectively. However, in the world order that emerged after the demise of the Cold War, complementarity, as opposed to exclusivity, has become the bastion of the relationship between the UN and regional organisations. Therefore, our analysis in chapter 5 revealed that while regional organisations continue to adopt treaties that strengthen their competence and authority in their domains of influence, they also continue to reserve roles for the UN. In many instances of joint-operations we reviewed, we noted that there was real cooperation between the UN and regional organisations. In some other situations, we identified areas in which the UN and regional organisations must continue to improve their relationships. It must be emphasised that such problems as emerged in the operations in the former Yugoslavia and Sierra Leone cannot be totally avoided in a typical joint-operation involving different organisations having different notions and ideas of peace and security and how to restore order. However, rather than seeing such disagreement and tension as the bane of joint-operations, they must be viewed as necessary attendants of the learning process such as the UN and regional organisations are currently going through.

The problem of regional hegemons is one of the dark sides to decentralised collective security. Some countries such as the United States and Nigeria have been accused of highjacking enforcement powers to further national interests. However, as we argued, especially in chapter 5, such views are not shared by member states of concerned regional organisations. True there is often disagreement about the modality of intervention or the question of which state must direct an operation. However, as already noted, evidence disclosed that such internal disgruntlement has not generally led to accusation of hegemonial motives.

Undoubtedly, the development of collective security by regional organisations can no longer be ignored. As we demonstrated in chapter 6, regional organisations no longer perceive Article 2(4) as refraining them from undertaking such actions as their members may empower them to. It may be too early to conclude that this has definitely become a new norm of international law, nevertheless, its potential in that regard cannot be discounted. As already mentioned, the establishment of the Peace and Security Council (PSC) by the AU in 2002 indicates that international law may yet witness more radical development by regional organisations.

The question to ask is what is the future of decentralised collective security? An attempt to answer this question must begin with an appreciation of the contribution that regional organisations have made so far. As is to be expected, the initial attempts by ECOWAS to mediate in Liberia backfired because the organisation pursued a peace enforcement action rather than the peacekeeping action its monitoring group was set up for. Such confusion could have been avoided by a clearer specification of mandates. Hence, when ECOWAS prepared to re-enter Sierra Leone, it clearly stated that it was going to enforce peace. Clarity of mandate thus became a helpful means of putting operations in a proper context. One can only hope that in the future regional organisations will work out details of operations carefully with the UN, as partners in progress, and avoid the rancor that marred the joint-operations of ECOWAS and UNAMSIL in Sierra Leone.

Also, funding of regional actions is a crucial determinant of the fate of regional collective security. So far, ECOWAS has been able to function largely because of the ability of the Nigerians to underwrite its expenses. Nonetheless, reliance on a single country for making the major contribution has its own disadvantages. If such a state, due to internal pressures or whatever, declines to participate in an action, this could potentially frustrate regional efforts. Perhaps, this is another area in which the UN can improve relations with regional organisations. Western states, which may not be interested in physically participating in certain conflicts, may be encouraged to assist regional organisations with financial and logistical supports. Situations where a single state supplies more than two-third of troops needed for an operation and underwrites the expenses incurred by the entire mission is not a very healthy one for the development of the capacity of regional organisations for collective security. In fact, such lop-sided responsibilities are good pretexts for hegemonial motives.

Development of institutional infrastructure has commenced in some regional organisations. This is within the framework of a reconceptualisation of collective security. A holistic notion of collective security, as we noted in our discussion in chapter 5, encompasses addressing issues that may ripen into full-blown conflicts. Creating a regional zonal system is one attractive technique which ECOWAS has adopted in this regard. Significantly the AU (still using the infrastructures of the OAU) also has credible institutional assets to undertake its responsibilities. Collating facts and figures about brewing problems is extremely helpful in understanding the nature of, and proposing solution to, conflicts. Apparently, the UN is incapable of putting in place such systems in the whole world. Therefore, an area of cooperation which will continue to guarantee the future of regional collective security is for the UN to continue to liaise with regional organisations for information collation. Such a *modus operandi* will ensure that there is a progression of understanding between the UN and regional organisations about developments within each region. Waiting until violence erupts and matters have been taken to the battlefield before cooperating with regional organisations is not a helpful approach. The realities of a conflict, the very excruciating circumstances of the war front, often affect the scope of communication and cooperation between the UN and regional organisations.

As witnessed in the former Yugoslavia, serious misunderstanding of issues by UN officers in charge of political decisions and NATO officials in charge of implementing the overall policies of the organisation brought disastrous consequences on the mission, leading to the seizure of several hundreds of UN personnel. When details of operations are well thought through and worked out between the UN and regional organisations, the reward can be very encouraging, as in the case of the OAS/UN mission in Haiti. Lack of understanding of regional dynamics may complicate the effectiveness of UN missions in many regions of the world. Thus, the UN needs to draw largely on the experience of regional organisations in this area. Happily, *the Supplement to the Agenda for Peace*[1] has identified areas of cooperation between the UN and regional organisations. These are (a) consultation; (b) diplomatic support; (c) operational support; (d) Co-deployment; and (e) joint operations. Some of these have already been achieved. These include diplomatic support (between the UN and OSCE), concerning constitutional issues relating to Abkhazia and the OSCE over Nagorny Karabakh, and co-deployment (ECOWAS/UN in Liberia).

When the UN and regional organisations cooperate effectively, this may narrow the chances of particular members of such organisations pursuing hegemonic motives. The activities of the UN and the OSCE arguably limited the extent to which Russia would have influenced events in Georgia between 1993–1994 had Russia been left all alone. This however does not mean that certain countries, by virtue of their position in the affected region or their influence within a regional organisation will not manifest a tendency towards proactiveness. Nigeria's occasional tendency in this direction is understandable. To simply assert that 'Nigeria's military rulers used Liberia as a rehearsal for their elaborate scheme to consolidate despotic rule in their own country'[2] begs the question. Such views do not explain why democratic leaders in such countries continue to support regional collective security.

No one can predict with certainty what the future holds for the extent to which the UN and regional organisations are able to cooperate and see each other as indispensable partners in the search for an enduring collective security. What is certain though is that regional organisations are not in conflict with the UN and they cannot supplant the function of the UN. They neither have the requisite capacity nor constitutional mandate to extend their operations throughout the world. Their primary spheres of operation remain their own regions and their objectives are as contained in their constitutions. Their ability to transcend their regional boundaries or take actions not specifically provided for by their treaties depends mainly on whether or not the Security Council deems it fit to utilise them to that extent and for such purposes.

An area in which regional organisations need to improve considerably upon in their collective security activities is accountability of their troops and personnel. The problem of human rights abuse by peacekeeping or

[1] A/50/60–S/1995/1, 3 January 1995.

[2] See Clement Adibe, 'The Liberian Conflict and ECOWAS—UN Partnership' in Thomas Weiss (ed), *Beyond UN Subcontracting: Task-Sharing with Regional Security Arrangements and Service-Providing NGO's* (New York, St Martin's Press, 1998) 67 at 84.

peace enforcement troops is becoming endemic. It is a problem the UN cannot be totally absolved from either. However, whereas there are adequate human rights mechanisms within the UN systems to address violations of rights by UN blue helmets, many regional organisations, especially the African ones, do not have such mechanisms. This means that unless there is enough political will on the part of the culprit state to investigate, and subsequently punish the offending troops, impunity of peacekeepers might gradually endanger the overall objectives of collective security missions. Again, the UN has a great and decisive role to play here. Since it has capacity for supervising and implementing human rights obligations amongst its Member States, it must ensure that its own troops, as well as those of regional organisations, respect the human rights of the people they have been deployed to protect. Killing defenceless civilians is as horrible as murdering peacekeeping troops.

The question whether the UN should issue its troops with a peacekeeping mandate in situations where there is no peace to keep is a rather complex one. It concerns the type of operation the UN is mindful to undertake in a given situation. However, where the UN deliberately issues a peacekeeping mandate in a situation where clearly only enforcement mandates will do, it opens itself to accusations of lack of commitment to the conflict. If, for instance, peacekeepers are deployed to situations where armed hostility is still probable, it is to be expected that they will be fired upon. Returning fire for fire is the only reasonable course of action but it guarantees that the UN will be drawn into the battle. In addition, if such UN troops have to operate alongside regional troops which may be implementing an enforcement mandate, tension will be inevitable and the overall cohesion of the mission may be unduly sacrificed.

The relationship that has developed between the UN and regional organisation in the aftermath of the Cold War is a reassuring one. In the future, the capacity of the UN and regional organisations to cooperate will undoubtedly expand as long as both sides continue to recognise areas of defects and improve on them. In the opinion of this writer, the future of collective security rests as much on the ability of regional organisations to effectively police their regions as on their ability to maintain good relations with the UN. The era that has been ushered in by the maiden joint action between the UN and regional organisation in Liberia is an era of complimentarity. The duty imposed on the Security Council under the Charter is to implement its responsibility for the maintenance of peace and security in a way that will make it attractive for regional organisations to continue to work with the UN.

Bibliography

A Abass, 'Consent Precluding State Responsibility: A Critical Analysis' (2004) 53 *International and Comparative Law Quarterly* 211.

—— 'The New Collective Security Mechanism of ECOWAS: Innovations and Problems' (2000) (5) 2 *Journal of Conflict and Security Law* 211.

—— 'The Implementation of ECOWAS New Protocol and Security Council Resolution 1270 in Sierra Leone: New Developments in Regional Intervention' (2002) 10 *University of Miami International and Comparative Law Review* 177.

—— 'The Security Council and the Challenges of Collective Security in the Twenty-First Century: What Role for African Regional Organisations?' in Douglas Lewis (ed), *Global Justice and the Quest for Justice* vl 1, *International and Regional Institutions* (Oxford, Hart Publishing, 2005).

A Abass and ND White, 'Countermeasures and Sanctions' in Malcolm D Evans (ed), *International Law*, (Oxford, Oxford University Press, 2003).

A Abass and Mashood Baderin, 'Towards Effective Collective Security and Human Rights Protection in Africa: An Assessment of the Constitutive Act of the African Union' (2002) XLXIV *Netherlands International Law Review* 1.

G Abi-Saab, *The United Nations Operation in the Congo, 1960–1964* (Oxford, Oxford University Press, 1978).

C Adibe, 'The Liberian Conflict and the ECOWAS-UN Partnership' in Thomas Weiss (ed), *Beyond Subcontracting: Task-Sharing with Regional Security Arrangements and Service-Providing NGOs* (London, Macmillan Press, 1998).

N Agetua, *Operation Liberty: The Story of Major General Joshua Dogonyaro* (Lagos, Hona Communications, 1992).

R Ago, 'Addendum to the Eighth Report on State Responsibility' (1980) *Yearbook of International Law Commission* II 1.

M Akehurst, 'Enforcement Actions by Regional Organisations with Special Reference to the Organization of American States' (1967) 42 *British Yearbook of International Law* 175.

—— *Modern Introduction to International Law*, P Malanczuk (ed), (London, Routledge, 1997).

M Alagappa, 'Regional Arrangements, the UN, and International Security: A Framework for Analysis' in Thomas Weiss (ed), *Beyond Subcontracting Task-Sharing with Regional Security Arrangements and Service-Providing NGOs* (London, Macmillan Press, 1998).

B Andemicael (ed), *Regionalism and the United Nations* (Dobbs Ferry, NY, published for UNITAR by Oceana Publications, 1979).

—— *The OAU and the UN: Relations between the Organization of African Unity and the United Nations* (New York, Published for the United Nations Institute for Training and Research by Africana Pub Co, 1976).

PV Anjali, *The UN Veto in World Affairs, 1946–1990: A Complete Record and Case Histories of the Security Council's Veto* (London, Mansell, 1992).

C Antonopoulos *The Unilateral Use of Force by States in International Law* (Athens, Ant N Sakkloulas Publishers, 1997).
C Archer, *International Organization* (London, Routledge, 2nd edn, 1992).
J de Arechaga, 'La Coordination des systèmes de l'ONU et de L'OEA pour de règlement pacifique des differends et la sécurité collective', (1964) 111 *Recueil des cours* 423.
—— 'International Law in the Past Third of a Century' (1978) 159 *Hague Recueil* 64.
P Baev, *Russia's Peacekeeping in the Caucasus*, Norwegian Institute of International Affairs / Western European Union Conference on 'Peacekeeping in Europe: Assessing UN and Regional Perspectives', Oslo, 17–18 November 1994.
S Bailey, 'The Security Council' in Philip Alston (ed), *The United Nations and Human Rights: A Critical Appraisal* (Oxford, Clarendon Press, 1992).
RS Baker and WE Dodd (ed), *The Public Papers of Woodrow Wilson, New Democracy, II*, 186–87.
—— *What Wilson did in Paris* (New York, Harper & Brothers, 1992).
J Beatson and MH Matthews, *Administrative Law: Cases and Materials* (Oxford, Clarendon Press, 1983).
J Beaufays, *Théorie du régionalisme* (Brussels, S Story-Scientia, 1985).
E Beckett, *The North Atlantic Treaty, the Brussels Treaty and the Charter of the United Nations* (London, Stevens & Sons, 1950).
M Bedjaoui, *The New World Order and the Security Council: Testing the Legality of its Acts* (Dordrecht, Martinus Nijhoff Publishers, 1994).
—— 'Du Contrôle de Légalité des Actes du Conseil de Sécurité' in *Nouveaux itinéraires en droit, Hommage à François Rigaux* (1993) cited by Franck, at 218.
EG Berman, 'The Security Council's Increasing Reliance on Burden-Sharing: Collaboration or Abrogation'? (1998) 4(1) *International Peacekeeping* 1.
Cyril E Black and Richard A Falk (eds), *The Future of International Legal Order: The Structure of the International Environment* (Princeton, Princeton University Press, 1972) Vol 4.
N Blokker, 'Is the Authorization Authorized? Powers and Practice of the UN Security Council to Authorize the Use of Force by "Coalitions of the Able and Willing"' (2000) 11(3) *European Journal of International Law* 541.
N Blokker and Muller, 'NATO as the UN Security Council's Instrument: Questions Marks from the Perspective of International Law' (1996) 9 *Leiden Journal of International Law* 419.
RT Bohan, 'The Dominican Case: Unilateral Intervention' (1966) 60 *American Journal of International Law* 809.
H Bokor-Szegö, 'The Attitude of Socialist States towards the International Regulation of the Use of Force' in A Cassese (ed), *The Current Regulation of the Use of Force* (Dordrecht, Martinus Nijhoff, 1986).
B Boutros-Ghali, *Agenda for Peace*, (1992) 31 *International Legal Materials* 953.
—— *An Agenda for Peace* (New York, United Nations, 1992).
—— 'The Arab League (1945–1970)' (1969) 25 *Revue Egyptienne de Droit International* 67.
DW Bowett, *Self-Defence in International Law* (Manchester, Manchester University Press, 1958).
—— 'Economic Coercion and Reprisal by States' (1972) 13 (1) *Virginia Journal of International Law* 1.

—— 'Economic Coercion: Past and Present' (1976) 16 *Virginia Journal of International Law* 245.

—— *The Law of International Institutions* (London, Sweet & Maxwell, 1982).

A Boyd, *Fifteen Men on A Powder Keg: A History of the UN Security Council* (London, Methuen, 1971).

J Boyd, *United Nations Peace-keeping Operations: A Military and Political Appraisal* (New York, Praeger Publishers, 1972).

M Brenner (ed), *NATO and Collective Security* (London, Macmillan Press Ltd, 1998).

JL Brierly, 'The Covenant and the Charter' (1946) *British Yearbook of International Law* 83.

I Brownlie, *International Law and the Use of Force by States* (Oxford, Clarendon University Press, 1963).

—— 'Humanitarian Intervention' in John Norton Moore (ed), *Law and Civil War in the Modern World* (Baltimore, Johns Hopkins University Press, 1974).

—— *Principles of Public International Law* (Oxford, Clarendon Press, 1990).

LC Buchheit, 'The Use of Nonviolent Coercion: A Study in Legality Under Article 2(4) of the Charter of the United Nations' in Richard Lillich (ed), *Economic Coercion and the New International Economic Order* (Virginia, The Michie Company Law Publishers, 1976).

J Burton, 'Functionalism and Resolution of Conflict' in AJR Groom and Paul Taylor (eds), *Functionalism: Theory and Practice in International Relations* (London, University of London Press, 1975).

AIL Campbell, 'The Limits of the Powers of International Organizations' (1983) 32 *International and Comparative Law Quarterly* 523.

D Caron, 'The Legitimacy of the Collective Authority of the Security Council' (1993) 87 *American Journal of International Law* 552.

E Carr, *The Twenty Years Crisis 1919–1939: An Introduction to the Study of International Relations* (London, Macmillan, 1939).

A Cassese, 'Ex Injuria ius Oritur. Are We Moving Towards Legitimation of Forcible Humanitarian Countermeasures in the World Community?' (1999) 10(1) *European Journal of International Law* 23.

—— (ed), *United Nations Peace-keeping: Legal Essays* (Alphen aan den Rijn, Sijthoff & Noordhoff, 1978).

—— (ed), *The Current Regulation of the Use of Force* (Dordrecht, Martinus Nijhoff , 1986).

—— *International Law* (Oxford, Oxford University Press, 2001).

Z Červenka, *The Organisation of African Unity and its Charter* (New York, Frederick A Praeger, 1968).

S Chan, 'And What Do Peacekeeping Troops Do Apart from Burying the Dead, Then?' (1997) XIII(5) *International Relations* 27.

A Chayes, 'Law and the Quarantine of Cuba' (1962/63) 41 *Foreign Affairs* 550.

SM Chervonnaya, *Abkhazia-1992: Post-Konnunisticheskaya Vandeya* (Moscow, Mosgorpechat, 1993).

E Childers, 'Gulf Crisis Lessons for the United Nations' (1992) 23(2) *Bulletin of Peace Proposals* 129.

P Chilton, O Nassauer, D Plesch and J Patten (Whitaker), *NATO, Peacekeeping, and the United Nations* (London, British American Security Information Council, 1994).

C Chinkin, 'The State that Acts Alone: Bully, Good Samaritan or Iconoclast?' 2000 (11) *European Journal of International Law* 33.
—— 'The Challenge of Soft Law: Development and Change in International Law', (1989) 38 *International and Comparative Law Quarterly* 30.
GA Christenson, 'The World Court and jus Cogens' (1987) 81 *American Journal of International Law* 93.
C Christol, 'Maritime Quarantine: The Naval Interdiction of Offensive Weapons and Associated Matériel to Cuba' (1962) 57 *American Journal of International Law* 525.
J Cilliers, 'The Evolving Security Architecture in Southern Africa' (1995) 4 *African Security Review* 40.
D Ciobanu, *Preliminary Objections related to the Jurisdiction of the United Nations Political Organs* (The Hague, Martinus Nijhoff, 1975).
—— 'The Power of the Security Council to Organize Peace-Keeping Operations' in A Cassese (ed), *The Current Regulation of the Use of Force* (Dordrecht, Martinus Nijhoff, 1986).
I Claude Jr, 'The OAS, the UN, and the United States' (1964) *International Conciliation* 547.
—— *Power and International Relations* (New York, Random House 1962).
—— 'Collective Legitimization as a Political Function of the United Nations', (1966) 20 *International Organization* 20.
IL Claude, *Swords into Plowshares: The Problems and Progress of International Organization* (New York, Random House, 4th edn, 1971).
R Clawson, (ed), *East-West Rivalry in the Third World: Security Issues and Regional Perspectives* (Wilmington, Del, Scholarly Resources, 1986).
E Clemons, 'No Peace to Keep: Six and Three-Quarters Peacekeepers' (1993) 26 *International Law and Politics* 107.
NJ Colletta and L Cullen, *Violent Conflict and the Transformation of Social Capital: Lessons from Cambodia, Rwanda, Guatemala, and Somalia* (Washington, DC, World Bank, 2000).
A Conteh, 'Sierra Leone and the Norms of Non-Intervention: Evolution and Practice' (1995) 7 *African Journal of International and Comparative Law* 166.
D Cortright and G Lopez, *The Sanctions Decade: Assessing UN Strategies in the 1990s* (London, Lynne Rienner Publishers, 2000).
—— *The Creation of States in International Law* (Oxford, Clarendon Press 1976).
J-P Cot, 'The Role of the Inter-African Peacekeeping Force in Chad' in A Cassese (ed), *The Current Regulation of the Use of Force* (Dordrecht, Martinus Nijhoff, 1986) 167.
J-P Cot et Alain Pellet (sous la direction de), *La Charte des Nations Unies: Commentaire: article par article* (Paris, Economica, 2e édition revue et augmentée, 1991).
J Crawford, *The International Law Commission's Articles on State Responsibility: Introduction, Text and Commentaries* (Cambridge, Cambridge University Press, 2002).
—— 'Democracy and International Law' (1993) 44 *British Yearbook of International Law* 113.
G Dahm, *Völkerrecht*, ii (1961).
A D'Amato, 'The Invasion of Panama was a Lawful Response to Tyranny' (1990) 84 *American Journal of International Law* 516.

L Damrosch, 'Retaliation or Arbitration—or Both? The 1978 United States–France Aviation Dispute' (1980) 74 *American Journal of International Law* 785.

I Dekker and E Myjer, 'Air Strikes on Bosnian Positions: Is NATO also Legally the Proper Instrument of the UN?' (1996) 9 *Leiden Journal of International Law* 413.

J Delbrück (ed), *Allocation of Law Enforcement Authority in the International System: Proceedings of an International Symposium of the Kiel Institute of International Law, March 23 to 25, 1994* (Berlin, Duncker & Humblot, 1995).

M Denys, *Origin and Conclusions of the Paris Pact and the Renunciation of War* (New York, Garland Publishers, 1972).

K Deutsch and W Isard, 'A Note on a Generalized Concept of Effective Distance' (1961) *Behavioural Science* 308–10.

—— et al, *Political Community and the North Atlantic Area* (Princeton, Princeton University Press, 1975).

C De Visscher, *Théories et réalités en droit international* (Paris, Pedone, 1970 4th edn).

E De Wet, 'The Relationship between the Security Council and Regional Organizations during Enforcement Action under Chapter VII of the United Nations Charter', (2002) 71 *Nordic Journal of International Law* 1.

P Diehl, *International Peacekeeping* (Maryland, John Hopkins University Press, 1994).

Y Dinstein, *War, Aggression and Self-Defence* (Cambridge, Cambridge University Press, 2nd edn, 2001).

PD DiPaola, 'A Noble Sacrifice? Jus Ad Bellum and the International Community's Gamble in Chechnya' (1997) 4 *Indiana Journal of Global Legal Studies* 435.

G Downs (ed), *Collective Security beyond the Cold War* (Ann Arbor, Mich, University of Michigan Press, 1994).

L Doyle, 'UN Has No Role in Running War' *Independent* (London), 11 February 1991, 2 (interview with Perez de Cuellar).

JC Dreier, *The OAS and the Hemisphere Crisis* (New York, Harper and Row 1962).

RM D'Sa, *The Relationship between the UN and OAU in the Fields of International Peace and Security and of Economic and Social Development* (unpublished PhD thesis), Faculty of Law, University of Birmingham (1982), vol 1.

PM Dupuy, 'Le droit des relations entre les organisations internationales' (1960) 100 *Recueil des cours* at 533.

—— 'The Place and Role of Unilateralism in Contemporary International Law'.

W Durch (ed), *The Evolution of UN Peacekeeping: Case Studies and Comparative Analysis* (New York, NY, St Martin's Press, 1993).

—— 'Faultlines: UN Operations in the Former Yugoslavia' in Olatara Otunu and Michael Doyle (eds), *Peacemaking and Peacekeeping for the New Century* (Oxford, Rowman and Littlefield Publishers Inc, 1996).

—— 'Introduction to Anarchy: Humanitarian Intervention and "State-Building" in Somalia', in Olatara Otunu and Michael Doyle (eds), *Peacemaking and Peacekeeping for the New Century* (Oxford, Rowman and Littlefield Publishers Inc, 1996).

A Eide, 'Peace-keeping and Enforcement by Regional Organizations' (1966) 3 *Journal of Peace Research* 125.

OY Elegab, *The Legality of Non-Forcible Counter-Measures in International Law* (Oxford, Clarendon Press, 1988).

A Etzioni, *Political Unification: A Comparative Study of Leaders and Forces* (New York, Rinehart & Winston, 1965).

R Falk, 'The Complexities of Humanitarian Intervention: A New World Order Challenge' (1996) 17 *Michigan Journal of International Law* 491.

T Farer, 'The Role of Regional Collective Security Arrangements' in Thomas Weiss (ed), *Collective Security in a Changing World* (London, Lynne Rienner Publishers, 1993).

—— 'Political and Economic Coercion in Contemporary International Law' (1985) 79 *American Journal of International Law* 407.

B Fassbender, *UN Security Council Reform and the Right of Veto: A Constitutional Perspective* (The Hague, Kluwer Law International, 1999).

J Fawcett, 'Intervention in International Law', (1961–II) *Hague Recueil des Cours* 103.

JES Fawcett, *The Law of Nations*, (London, Allen Lane, The Penguin Press, 1968).

L Fawcett, 'Regionalism in Historical Perspective' in Fawcett and Hurrell (eds), *Regionalism in World Politics: Regional Organization and International Order* (Oxford, Oxford University Press, 1995).

L Fawcett and Andrew Hurrell (eds), *Regionalism in World Politics: Regional Organization and International Order* (Oxford, Oxford University Press, 1995).

C Fenwick, 'The Inter-American Regional System: Fifty Years of Progress' (1956) 50 *American Journal of International Law* 18.

R Foot, 'Pacific Asia: The Development of Regional Dialogue' in Fawcett and Hurrell (eds), *Regionalism in World Politics: Regional Organization and International Order* (Oxford, Oxford University Press, 1995).

WTR Fox & Warner R Schilling, *European Security and the Atlantic System* (New York, Columbia University Press, 1973).

AG Frank, 'The Development of Underdevelopment' (1966) *Monthly Review* (September) 369.

T Franck, 'Sidelined in Kosovo? The United Nations Demise Has Been Exaggerated' (1999) 78 *Foreign Affairs* 116.

—— *Fairness in International Law and International Institution* (Oxford, Clarendon Press, 1995).

—— *The Power of Legitimacy Among Nations* (New York, OUP, 1990).

—— 'The Power of Appreciation: Who is the Ultimate Guardian of UN Legality?' (1992) 86 *American Journal of International Law* 519.

—— 'Who Killed Article 2(4)?' (1970) 64 *American Journal of International Law* 809.

—— 'The Emerging Rights to Democratic Governance' (1992) 86 *American Journal of International Law* 46.

T Frank and N Rodley, 'After Bangladesh: The Law of Humanitarian Intervention by Military Force' (1973) 67 *American Journal of International Law* 275.

W Friedmann, *The Changing Structure of International Law* (London, Stevens, 1964).

J Frowein, 'Legal Consequences for International Law Enforcement' in Jost Delbrück (ed), *The Future of International Law: New Scenarios, New Law?: Proceedings of an International Symposium of the Kiel Institute of International Law, March 25 to 27, 1992* (Berlin, Duncker & Humblot, 1993).

J Frowein and R Wolfrum, 'Security Council Control over regional Action' (1997) 1 *Max Planck Yearbook of United Nations Law* 129.

Y Funabaschi, 'The Asianization of Asia' (1993) 72 (5) *Foreign Affairs* 81.

G Gaja, 'Jus Cogens beyond the Vienna Convention' (1981) 172 *Recueil des Cours de l'Académie de Droit International* 271.

R Gerold, *Die Sicherung des Friedens durch die OAS*, (Berlin, Duncker and Humblot, 1971).
T Gill, 'Legal and Some Political Limitations on the Power of the UN Security Council to Exercise Its Enforcement Powers under Chapter VII of the Charter' (1995) 26 *Netherlands Yearbook of International Law* 33.
R Gilpin, *The Political Economy of International Relations* (Princeton, Princeton University Press, 1987).
P Gleijeses, *Shattered Hope: The Guatemalan Revolution and the United States, 1944–1954* (Princeton, Princeton University Press, 1991).
M Glennon, 'The New Interventionism, the Search for a just International Law' (1999) 78 *Foreign Affairs* 2.
—— 'Glennon Replies' (1999) 78 *Foreign Affairs* 120.
R Goldman, *Is it Time to Revive the UN Military Staff Committee*, Occasional Papers Series, (Los Angeles, California State University, 1990).
A Gomaa, *The Foundation of the League of Arab States* (London, Longman, 1977).
L Goodrich, E Hambro, A Patricia Simons, *Charter of the United Nations: Commentary and Documents* (New York, Columbia University Press, 3rd edn, 1969).
V Gowlland-Debbas (ed), *United Nations Sanctions and International Law* (The Hague, Kluwer Law International, 2001).
G Grandin, *The Blood of Guatemala: A History of Race and Nation* (Durham NC, Duke University Press, 2000).
C Gray, *International Law and the Use of Force* (Oxford, Oxford University Press, 2000).
—— 'After the Cease-Fire: Iraq, the Security Council and the Use of Force' (1994) 65 *British Yearbook of International Law* 135.
—— 'Bosnia and Herzergovina: Civil War or Inter-State Conflict? Characterization and Consequences', (1996) 67 *British Yearbook of International Law* 155.
LC Green, *The Contemporary Law of Armed Conflicts* (Manchester, Manchester University Press, 2nd edn, 2000).
C Greenwood, 'International Law and the NATO Intervention in Kosovo' (2000) 49 *International and Comparative Law Quarterly* 926.
AJR Groom, 'Functionalism in World Society' in AJR Groom and Paul Taylor (eds), *Functionalism: Theory and Practice in International Relations* (London, University of London Press, 1975).
H Grotius, *Hist. De Rebus Belgicis* (Eng transl Kelsey of 1646 edn).
E Haas, 'The Challenge of Regionalism' (1958) 12(4) *International Organization.*
—— *The Uniting of Europe: Political, Social, and Economic Forces, 1950–1957* (Stanford, Stanford University Press, 1968).
—— 'Collective Security and the Future International System' in Falk and Black (eds), *The Future of International Legal Order* (Princeton, Princeton University Press, 1969).
—— *Beyond the Nation-State: Functionalism and International Organization* (Stanford, Stanford University Press, 1964).
—— *The Obsolescence of Regional Integration Theory* (Berkeley, The University of California Press, 1976).
—— 'The Collective Management of International Conflict, 1954–84', United Nations Institute for Training Research, *The United Nations and the Maintenance of International Peace and Security* (Dordrecht, The Netherlands, Nijhoff, 1987).
W Hagen, 'The Lethal Nationalism' (1999) 78 *Foreign Affairs* 52–54.

G Haines, *European Integration* (Baltimore, The Johns Hopkins Press, 1957).
JW Halderman, 'Regional Enforcement Measures and the United Nations' (1963) 52 (1) *Georgetown Law Journal* 89.
L Hannikainen, *Peremptory Norms*: (jus cogens), in *International Law: Historical Development, Criteria, Present Status*, (Helsinki, Lakimiesliiton Kustannus (Finnish Lawyers' Publishing Company), 1988).
RJ Harrison, *Europe in Question: Theories of Regional Integration* (London, George Allen & Unwin Ltd, 1971).
H Hassounna, *The League of Arab States and Regional Disputes: A Study of Middle East Conflicts* (New York, Oceana Publications, 1975).
—— 'The Arab League of States and the United Nations: Relations in the Peaceful Settlement of Disputes' in Berhanykun Andemicael (ed), *Regionalism and the United Nations* (Dobbs Ferry, NY, published for UNITAR by Oceana Publications, 1979).
C Hedges, 'Kosovo's Next Masters?' (1999) 78 *Foreign Affairs* 24.
K Hendl, 'Reflections on the Role, Functions and Procedures of the Security Council' (1987) (6) *Hague Recueil des Cours* 206.
L Henkin, 'The Report of the Death of Article 2(4) are Greatly Exaggerated' (1971) 65 *American Journal of International Law* 544.
—— *How Nations Behave*: *Law and Policy*, (New York, Columbia University Press for the Council on Foreign Relations, 2nd edn, 1979).
A Henrikson, 'The Growth of Regional Organizations and the Role of the United Nations' in Louise Fawcett and Andrew Hurrell (eds), *Regionalism in World Politics*: *Regional Organization and International Order* (Oxford, Oxford University Press, 1995).
—— (ed), *Negotiating World* Order: *The Artisanship and Architecture of Global Diplomacy* (Wilmington, Del, Scholarly Resources Inc, 1986).
B Hettne, 'Neo-Mercantilism: The Pursuit of Regionness' (1993) 28 (3) *Cooperation and Conflict*.
R Higgins, 'Peace and Security: Achievements and Failures' (1995) *European Journal of International Law* 445.
—— *United Nations Peacekeeping, 1946–1967*: *Documents and Commentary vol 3, Africa* (Oxford, Oxford University Press, 1980).
—— 'A General Assessment of United Nations Peace-Keeping' in A Cassese (ed), *United Nations Peace-Keeping* (Alphen aan den Rijn, Sijthoff & Noordhoff, 1978), 1.
—— *The Development of International Law through the Political Organs of the United Nations* (Oxford, Oxford University Press, 1963).
A Hindmarsh, 'Self-Help in Time of Peace' (1932) 26 *American Journal of International Law* 515.
—— *Force in Peace*, (New York, Kennikat Press, 1973).
T Hobbes, *Leviathan* (London, Collins, 1962).
S Hoffmann, 'International Organization and the International System' in *Janus and Minerva*: *Essays in the Theory and Practice of International Politics* (Boulder, Westview Press, 1987).
—— 'Delusions of World Order' (1992) 39(7) *New York Review* 38.
OW Howard, *Southern Region of the United States* (Chapel Hill, NC, University of North Carolina Press, 1936).
D Hume, *A Treatise on Human Nature* (London, Fontana, 1972 [1789]).

W Hummer and M Schweitzer in Bruno Simma (ed), *The Charter of the United Nations: A Commentary* (Oxford, Oxford University Press, 2nd edn, 2002).

R Hunter, 'Maximising Nato' (1999) 78 *Foreign Affairs* 190.

S Hunter, *The Transcaucasus in Transition: Nation-Building and Conflict* (Washington DC, CSIS, 1994).

A Hurrell, 'Regionalism in Theoretical Perspectives' in Fawcett and Hurrell (eds), *Regionalism in World Politics: Regional Organization and International Order* (Oxford, Oxford University Press, 1995).

A Hyde-Price, 'Future Security Systems for Europe' in C McInnes (ed), *Security & Strategy in the New Europe* (London, Routledge, 1992).

R Immeman, *The CIA in Guatemala: The Foreign Policy of Intervention* (Austin, University of Texas Press, 1982).

H Jacobson, *Network of Interdependence: International Organization and the Global Political System* (New York, Alfred A Knopf, 2nd edn, 1984).

R Jennings and Sir A Watts (eds), Oppenheim's *International Law*, vol 1, *Peace* (London, 9th edn, Longman, 1992).

M Jensen (ed), *Regionalism in America,* (Madison, Wis, University of Wisconsin Press, 1951).

L Johnson, *Department of States Bulletin* (September 26, 1966) 4453.

JOC Jonah, 'Differing State Perspectives on the United Nations in the Post-Cold War Perspective', *Academic Council on the United Nations System* (ACUNS) Reports and Papers (1993) No 4, at 11.

GC Jonathan, 'Article 39', *La Charte des Nations Unies* (J-P Cot and A Pellet, eds) (Paris, Economica, 1985).

R Jordan, with Michael Bloome, *Political Leadership in NATO: A Study in Multinational Diplomacy* (Boulder, Colo, Westview Press, 1979).

M Keating, *The New Regionalism in Western Europe: Territorial Restructuring and Political Change* (Cheltenham, Edward Elgar Publishing Limited, 1998).

H Kelsen, 'Is the North Atlantic Treaty a Regional Arrangement?' (1950) *American Journal of International law* 162.

—— *Collective Security under International Law,* International Studies, Naval War College 1954 (1956).

—— *The Law of the United Nations* (London, Stevens & Sons, 1950).

—— 'Collective Security and Collective Self Defence under the Charter of the United Nations' (1948) *American Journal of International Law* 783.

—— 'Twenty-five Years of Local Wars' (1971) 8 *Journal of Peace Research* 6.

S Kinzer and S Schlensiger, *Bitter Fruit: The Untold Story of the American Coup in Guatemala* (New York, Doubleday, 1982).

F Kirgis, 'The Security Council's first Fifty Years' (1995) 89 *American Journal of International Law* 506.

AW Knight 'Towards a Subsidiarity Model of Peacemaking and Preventive Diplomacy: Making Chapter VIII of the UN Charter Operational' (1996) 17 *Third World Quarterly* 49.

T Koh, 'Summary and Conclusion' The Singapore Symposium: *The Changing Role of the United Nations in Conflict Resolution and Peace-keeping,* 13–15 March 1991 (New York, United Nations, 1991).

V Kononenko, Heads of Governments Grapple over CIS Charter in Attempt to Salvage Commonwealth Russ Press DIG, 13 Nov 1992.

M Koskenniemi, 'The Place of Law in Collective Security' (1996) 17 *Michigan Journal of International Law* 455.

R Kothari, *Footstep Into the Future: Diagnosis of the Present World and a Design for an Alternative* (New York, The Free Press, 1974).

E Kourula, 'Peace-keeping and Regional Arrangements' in Anthony Cassese (ed), *United Nations Peace-keeping: Legal Essays* (Alphens aan den Rijn, Sijthoff & Noordhoff, 1978).

F Kratochwil, 'Of System, Boundaries, and Territoriality' (1986) 43 (1) *World Politics*.

N Krisch, 'Unilateral Enforcement of the Collective Will: Kosovo, Iraq, and the Security Council', (1990) 3 *Max Plank Yearbook of United Nations* 59.

D Kristiotis, 'The Kosovo Crisis and NATO's Application of Armed Force against the Federal Republic of Yugoslavia' (2000) 49 *International and Comparative Law Quarterly* 330.

—— 'Reappraising Policy Objections to Humanitarian Intervention' (1998) 19 *Michigan Journal of International Law* 1005.

KO Kufor, 'The Legality of the Intervention in the Liberian Civil War By the Economic Community of West African States' (1993) (5) *African Journal of International and Comparative Law* 525.

—— 'Developments in the Resolution of the Liberian Conflict' (1994–95) 10(1*) The American University Journal of International Law and Policy* 373.

R Lavalle, 'The Law of United Nations and the Use of Force under the Relevant Security Council Resolutions of 1990 and 1991 to Resolve the Persian Gulf Crisis' (1992) 23 *Netherlands Yearbook of International Law* 3.

D Lee, 'The Genesis of the Veto' (1947) *International Organisation* 33.

E Lefever, *Crisis in Congo* (Washington DC, The Brookings Institution, 1965).

DA Leurdijk, 'Before and After Dayton: the UN and NATO in the Former Yugoslavia' in Thomas G Weiss (ed), *Beyond Subcontracting: Task-Sharing with Regional Security Arrangements and Service-Providing NGOs* (New York, St Martin's Press, 1998), 17.

—— *The United Nations and NATO in Former Yugoslavia, 1991–1996: Limits to Diplomacy and Force* (The Hague, Netherlands Atlantic Commission/ Netherlands Institute of International Relations, 'Clingendael', 1996).

T Lie, *In The Cause of Peace* (New York, Macmillan, 1954).

R Lillich (ed), *Economic Coercion and the New International Economic Order* (Virginia, The Michie Company Law Publishers, 1976).

—— 'Humanitarian Intervention: A Reply to Ian Brownlie and a Plea for Constructive Alternatives' in John Norton Moore (ed), *Law and Civil War in the Modern World* (Baltimore, Johns Hopkins University Press, 1974).

L Linderg, *The Political Dynamics of European Economic Integration* (Stanford, Stanford University Press, 1963).

FT Liu, 'Peacekeeping and Humanitarian Assistance' in Leon Gordenker and Thomas Weiss (eds), *Soldiers, Peacekeepers and Disasters*, (Basingstoke, Macmillan, 1991).

J Lobel and M Ratner, 'Bypassing the Security Council: Ambiguous Authorizations to Use Force, Cease-Fires and the Iraqi Inspection Regime' (1999) 93 *American Journal of International Law* 124.

J Locke, *Two Treatises of Civil Government* (London, Everyman, 1690 (1924)).

V Lowe, 'Precluding Wrongfulness or Responsibility: A Plea for Excuses' (1999) 10(2) *European Journal of International Law* 405.

E Luck, 'A Road to Nowhere' (1999) 78 *Foreign Affairs* 118.

—— 'Whose Collective Security?' (1992) 15(2) *Washington Quarterly* 43.

Y Lukacs (ed), *Documents on the Israeli-Palestinian Conflict* (Cambridge, Cambridge University Press 1984).

E Lutwakk, 'Give War a Chance' (1999) 78 *Foreign Affairs* 36.

SN MacFarlane, 'The CIS and the OSCE in Georgia's Wars' in TG Weiss (ed), *Beyond Subcontracting: Task-Sharing with Regional Security Arrangements and Service-Providing NGOs* (New York, St Martin's Press, 1998).

SN MacFarlane, L Minear and S Shenfield, *Armed Conflict in Georgia: A Case Study in Humanitarian Action and Peacekeeping* (Providence, RI, Watson Institute, 1995), Occasional paper No 27.

WT Mallison, 'Limited Naval Blockade or Quarantine Interdiction: National and Collective Defense Claims Valid Under International Law' (1962) 31 *George Washington University Law Review* 339.

D Malone, *Decision-Making in the Security Council: The Case of Haiti* (Oxford, Clarendon Press, 1998).

—— 'Haiti and the International Community: A Case Study' (1997) 39 (2) *Survival* 126.

H Marianne, *Lebanon, Political playground of the Middle East: The Role of Peacekeeping* (Oslo, NUPI, 1989).

V Mastny, 'Did Nato Win the Cold War?' (1999) 78 *Foreign Affairs* 176–89.

JS Matthews, 'Redefining Security' (1989) 68 (2) *Foreign Affairs* 162.

B Maurice, *The United Nations: Past, Present* and *Future*, (The Hague, Kluwer Law International, 1997).

B Maurice and D Warner (eds), *A New Charter for a Worldwide Organisation?* (The Hague, Kluwer Law International, 1997).

J Mayall, 'National Identity and the Revival of Regionalism' in Louise Fawcett and Andrew Hurrell (eds), *Regionalism in World Politics: Regional Organization and International Order* (Oxford, Oxford University Press, 1995).

—— *Nationalism and International Society* (Cambridge, Cambridge University Press, 1990).

H McCoubrey and J Morris, *Regional Peacekeeping in the Post-Cold War Era* (The Hague, Kluwer Law International, 2000).

RW McDonald, *The League of Arab States: A Study in the Dynamics of Regional Organization* (Princeton, Princeton University Press, 1965).

JPS McLaren, 'The Domonican Crisis: An Inter-American Dilemma' (1966) 4 *Canadian Yearbook of International Law* 178.

A McNair, *The Law of Treaties* (Oxford, Clarendon Press, 1961).

L Meeker, 'Defensive Quarantine and the Law' (1963) 57 *American Journal of International Law* 515.

T Meron, 'On a Hierarchy of International Human Rights' (1986) 80 *American Journal of International Law* 1.

EM Miller, 'Legal Aspects of the United Nations Action in the Congo' (1961) 55 *American Journal of International Law* 1.

—— *The Drafting of the Covenant* (New York, GP Putnam, 1928).

D Mitrany, *A Working Peace System* (Oxford, Oxford University Press, 1944).

HE Moore, *American Regionalism: A Cultural-Historical Approach to National Integration* (New York, Henry Holt, 1938).
J Moore, 'The Role of Regional Arrangements in the Maintenance of World Order', in Cyril Black and Richard Falk (eds), *The Future of International Legal Order* Vol III (Princeton, Princeton University Press, 1972).
J Moore and FR Turner, *International Law and Brezhnev Doctrine* (Lanham, University Press of America, 1987).
JN Moore, 'The Role of Regional Arrangements in the Maintenance of World Order' in Cyril E Black and Richard Falk (eds), *The Future of the International Legal Order vol 3*, (New Jersey, Princeton University Press, 1971).
FL Morrison in J Delbrück (ed), *Allocation of law Enforcement Authority in the International System: Proceedings of an International Symposium of the Kiel Institute of International Law, March 23 to 25, 1994* (Berlin, Duncker & Humblot, 1995).
H Mueller 'A United Nations of Europe and North America' (1991) 21(1) *Arms Control Today* 3.
R Müllerson, 'Jus Ad Bellum: Plus ÇA Change (Le Monde) Plus C'est La Même Chose (Le Droit)?' (2002) 7(2) *Journal of Conflict and Security Law* 149.
J Murphy, 'Force and Arms' in Christopher Joyner (ed), *The United Nations and International Law* (Cambridge, Cambridge University Press, 1997).
S Murphy, 'The Security Council, Legitimacy, and the Concept of Collective Security After the Cold War' (1994) 32 *Columbia Journal of Transnational Law* 201.
—— 'Democratic Legitimacy and the Recognition of States and Governments' (1995) 48 *International and Comparative Law Quarterly* 545.
GJ Naldi and Konstantinos D Magliveras, 'The African Union—A New Dawn for Africa?' (2002) 51(2) *International and Comparative Law Quarterly* 415.
—— *The Organization of African Unity: An Analysis of its Role* (London, Mansell, 2nd edn, 1999).
—— (ed), *Documents of the Organization of African Unity* (London, Mansell, 1992).
—— 'Peacekeeping Attempts by the OAU' (1985) 34 *International Comparative and Law Quarterly* 593.
I Neumann, (ed), *Regional Great Powers in International Politics* (London, Macmillan, 1992).
J Nielsen (ed), *International Documents on Palestine* 1976 (Washington, Institute for Palestine Studies 1978).
MS Nious and PC Ordeshook, 'The Prospect for a New International Order Based On Collective Security' in George Downs (ed), *Collective Security Beyond the Cold War* (Michigan, The University of Michigan Press, 1994).
G Nolte, 'Restoring Peace by Regional Action: International Legal Aspects of the Liberian Conflict', 23 *ZaöR V* 53/3 603.
D Noncic, *The Problem of Sovereignty in the Charter and Practice of the United Nations* (The Hague, Nijhoff, 1970).
K Nowrot and E Schabacker, 'The Use of Force to Restore Democracy: International Legal Implications of the ECOWAS Intervention in Sierra Leone' (1998) 14(2) *American University Journal of International Law Review* 321.
JS Nye, *International Regionalism* (Boston, Little Brown, 1962).
—— *Peace in Parts: Integration and Conflict in Regional Organization* (Boston, Little, Brown, 1971).

D O'Brien, 'The Search for Subsidiarity: The UN, African Regional Organizations and Humanitarian Action' (2000) 7(3) *International Peacekeeping* 57.
AC Ofodile, 'The Legality of ECOWAS Intervention in Liberia' (1994–95) 32 *Columbia Journal of Transnational Law* 381.
F Olonisakin, *Reinventing Peacekeeping in Africa: Conceptual and Legal Issues in ECOMOG Operations* (The Hague, Kluwer Law International, 2000).
L Oppenheim, *International Law: A Treatise* (Cambridge, Cambridge University Press, 7th edn, 1948, H Lauterpacht ed).
O Otunu and M Doyle (eds), *Peacemaking and Peacekeeping for the New Century* (Oxford, Rowman and Littlefield Publishers Inc, 1996).
CAA Packer and D Rukare, 'The New African Union and its Constitutive Act' (2002) 96(2) *American Journal of International Law* 365.
NJ Padelford, 'The OAU' (1964) 18 *International Organization* 521.
N Palmer, *The New Regionalism in Asia and the Pacific* (Lexington, Mass, Lexington Books, 1991).
C Parry (ed), *The Consolidated Treaty Series*, 155 vols (Dobbs Ferry, New York, Oceana Publications, 1969–86).
G Patterson, *Discrimination in International Trade: The Policy Issues 1945–1965* (Princeton, Princeton University Press, 1966).
JJ Paust and AP Blaustein, 'The Arab Oil Weapon—A Threat to International Peace' (1974) 68 *American Journal of International Law* 410.
C Pentland, *International Theory and European Integration* (London, Faber & Faber, 1973).
G Peterson, 'Political Inequality at the Congress of Vienna' (1945) 60 (4) *Political Science Quarterly* 544.
J Plano and R Riggs, *Forging World Order* (New York, Macmillan, 1967).
IO Pogany, 'The Arab League and Regional Peacekeeping' (1987) *Netherlands International Law Review* 54.
J Quigley 'The United States and the United Nations in the Persian Gulf War: New Order or Disorder?' (1992) 25 *Cornell International Law Journal* 1.
O Ramsbotham and T Woodhouse, *Encyclopaedia of International Peacekeeping Operations* (California, ABC-CLIO, 1999).
J Rawls, *A Theory of Justice* (Oxford, Oxford University Press, 1972).
WM Reisman, 'Peacemaking' (1993) 18 *Yale Journal of International Law* 415.
—— 'Hollow Victory: Humanitarian Intervention and Protection of Minorities', (1997) 91 *Proceedings of the American Society of International Law* 431.
—— 'Coercion and Self-Determination: Construing Charter Article 2(4)' (1984) 78 *American Journal of International Law* 642.
—— 'Termination of the USSR's Treaty Right of Intervention in Iran' (1980) 74 *American Journal of International Law* 144.
IJ Rikhye, *Preparation and Training of United Nations Peace-Keeping Forces* (Adelphi Papers No 9) (London, Institute for Strategic Studies, 1964).
C Robert, *Haiti* (Paris, Presses Universitaires de France, 2nd Revised edn, 1993).
AH Robertson, *The Law of International Institutions in Europe* (Manchester, Manchester University Press, 1961).
P Robson, 'The New Regionalism and the Developing Countries' (1993) 31(3) *Journal of Common Market Studies* 335.

W Rocker, 'America First?' (1999) 78 *Foreign Affairs* 119.
P Rodman, 'The Fallout from Kosovo' (1999) 78 *Foreign Affairs* 45.
N Ronzitti, 'Use of Force, Jus Cogens and State Consent' in Antonio Cassese (ed), *The Current Legal Regulation of the Use of Force* (Dordrecht, Martinus Nijhoff Publishers, 1986).
JFL Ross, *Neutrality and international Sanctions: Sweden, Switzerland and Collective Security* (New York, Praeger, 1989).
EV Rostow, 'Until What? Enforcement Action or Collective Self-Defense?' (1991) 85 *American Journal of International Law* 452.
W Rostow, 'The Coming Age of Regionalism' (1990) 74(5) *Encounter*.
C Rozakis, *The Concept of Jus Cogens in the Law of Treaties* (Amsterdam, North-Holland Publishing Co, 1976).
P Rubino, 'Colonialism and the Use of Force by States' in A Cassese (ed), *The Current Regulation of the Use of Force* (Dordrecht, Martinus Nijhoff , 1986).
AW Rudzinski, 'The So-Called Double Veto' (1951) 45 *American Journal of International Law* 443.
O Russbach, *ONU Contre ONU: Le Droit International Confisqué* (Paris, Ed la Découverte, 1994).
RB Russell, *A History of the United Nations Charter: The Role of the United States 1940–1945* (Washington DC, The Brookings Institution, 1958).
B Russett, *International Regions and the International Systems: A Study in Political Ecology* (Chicago, Rand McNally and Co, 1967).
—— *Power and Community in World Politics* (San Francisco, WH Freeman, 1974).
—— et al, 'World Handbook on Political and Social Indicators' (New Haven, Yale University Press, 1964).
KP Saksena, *The United Nations and Collective Security: A Historical Analysis* (Delhi, DK Publishing House, 1974).
D Sarooshi, *The United Nations and the Development of Collective Security: The Delegation by the UN Security Council of its Chapter VII Powers* (Oxford, Clarendon Press, 1999).
R Sato, J Wanadi, and S-J Han (eds), *Asian Security Issues: Regional and Global* (Berkeley, Institute of East Asian Studies, University of California, 1988).
O Schachter, 'In Defense of International Rules on the Use of Force,' (1986) 53 *University of Chicago Law Review* 113.
—— 'Coercion and Self-Determination: Constructing Charter 2(4)' (1984) 78 *American Journal of international Law* 642.
—— 'The Right of States to Use Armed Force' (1984) 82 *Michigan Law Review* 1620.
—— 'The Lawful Response to Unilateral Use of Force' (1985) 10 *Yale Journal of International Law* 291.
HG Schermers and NM Blokkers, *International Institutional Law*, (The Hague, Martinus Nijhoff Publishers, 3rd edn, 1995).
FL Schuman, *The Commonwealth of Man* (New York, Knopf, 1952).
G Schwarzenberger and ED Brown, *A Manual of International Law* (Abingdon, Professional Books, 6th edn, 1976).
—— *'International Jus Cogens?'* (1965) 43 *Texas Law Review* (1965) 455.
JB Scott (ed), *President Wilson's Foreign Policy* (New York, Oxford University Press, 1981).

A Sesay, 'The Limits of Peace-Keeping by Regional Organisations: The OAU Peace-Keeping Force in Chad' (1991) 11 *Conflict Quarterly* 7.

B Simma, *The Charter of the United Nations: A Commentary* (Oxford, Oxford University Press, 2nd edn, 2002).

—— *The Charter of the United Nations: A Commentary* (Oxford, Oxford University Press, 1994).

—— 'NATO, the UN and the Use of Force: Legal Aspects' (1999) 10(1) *European Journal of International Law* 1.

—— 'Regional Enforcement of Community Objectives' in Vera Gowlland-Debbas (ed), *United Nations Sanctions and International Law* (The Hague, Kluwer Law International, 2001).

—— 'Regional Enforcement of Community Objectives' in Vera Golland-Debbass (ed), *United Nations Sanctions and International Law* (The Hague, Kluwer Law International).

G Simpson, 'Is International Law Fair?' (1996) 17 *Michigan Journal of International Law* 615.

A-M Slaughter and W Burke-White, 'An International Constitutional Moment' (2002) 43 *Harvard International Law Journal* 1.

L Sohn, *Broadening the Role of the United Nations in Preventing, Mitigating or Ending International or Internal Conflicts that threaten International Peace and Security*, (Washington DC, International Rule of Law Center, The George Washington University Law School, 1997).

—— (ed), *Basic Documents of African Regional Organizations* (Dobbs Ferry, NY, Published for the Inter-American Institute of International Legal Studies by Oceana Publications, 1971–72).

—— 'The Authority of the United Nations to Establish and Maintain a Permanent United Nations Force' (1958) 52 *American Journal of International Law* 229.

TC Sorensen, 'United States Policy on United Nations Peace-Keeping Operations' (1993) 18 *Yale Journal of International Law* 425.

ER Stettinus, Jr, *Report to the President of the Results of the San Francisco Conference* (Department of State, June 26, 1945).

J Stone, *Aggression and World Order* (London, Stevens & Sons, 1958).

—— *Legal Controls of International Conflicts* (London, Stevens & Son, 1954).

HF Strauch, 'L'OAU et les conflits frontaliers' (1967) 22 *Revues française d'etudes politiques africaines* 59.

JS Sutterlin, *The United Nations and the Maintenance of International Peace and Security: A Challenge to be Met* (Connecticut, Praeger, 1995).

E Suy, 'The Concept of Jus Cogens in Public International Law' 2 *Carnegie Endowment for International Peace*, Papers and Proceedings, The Concept of Jus Cogens in International Law 17 (1967).

PC Szasz, 'Centralized and Decentralized Law Enforcement: The Security Council and the General Assembly Acting under Chapters VII and VIII' in Delbrück (ed), *Allocation of law Enforcement Authority in the International System: Proceedings of an International Symposium of the Kiel Institute of International Law, March 23 to 25, 1994* (Berlin, Duncker & Humblot, 1995).

J Sztucki, *Jus Cogens and the Vienna Convention on the Law of Treaties: A Critical Appraisal* (Wien, Springer, 1974).

T Szulc, *Dominican Diary* (New York, Delacorte Press, 1965).

T Szulc and KE Meyer, *The Cuban Invasion: The Chronicle of a Disaster*, (New York, Ballantine Books, 1962).

J Tascan, 'Searching for OAS/UN Task-Sharing Opportunities in Central America and Haiti' in Thomas Weiss (ed), *Beyond Subcontracting Task-Sharing with Regional Security Arrangements and Service-Providing NGOs* (London, MacMillan Press Ltd, 1998).

P Taylor, *International Organization in the Modern World: The Regional and Global Process* (London, Pinter, 1993).

M Tebbit, *Philosophy of Law: An Introduction* (London, Routledge, 2000).

F Teson, *Humanitarian Intervention: An Inquiry into Law and Morality*, (New York, Transnational, 2nd edn, 1997).

C Thomuschat, 'Using Force against Iraq' (1998) 73 *Friedenswarte* 75.

GI Tunkin, 'Jus Cogens in Contemporary International Law' (1975) IV, *University of Toledo Law Review* 107.

—— *Theory of International Law* (Translated by William E Butler) (London, George Allen & Unwin, 1974).

United Nations, *United Nations Blue Book Series*, Vol VIII, *The United Nations in Somalia 1992–1996* (New York, Dept of Public Information, 1996).

B Urquart, *Decolonization and World Peace* (Austin, Texas, University of Texas Press, 1989).

—— *Hammarskjöld* (New York, Harper Colophon Books, 1972).

—— 'The United Nations, Collective Security, and International Peacekeeping' in Henrikson (ed), *Negotiating World Order: The Artisanship and Architecture of Global Diplomacy* (Wilmington, Del, Scholarly Resources Inc, 1986), 62.

AH Vandenberg (ed), *The Private Papers of Senator Vandernberg* (London, Gollancs, 1952).

A Van Wyen Thomas and AJ Thomas jr, *The Organization of American States* (Dallas TX, Southern Methodist University Press, 1963).

MS Vazquez, 'La neuvième réunion de consultation des Ministres des Affaires Étrangères et l'affaire du Cuba' (1964) 10 *Annuaire français de droit international* 638.

A Verdross, 'Jus Dispositivum and Jus Cogens in International Law' (1966) 60 *American Journal of International Law* 5.

D Verfey, 'Humanitarian Intervention' in A Cassese (ed), *The Current Legal Regulation of the Use of Force Antonio* (Dordrecht, Martinus Nijhoff, 1986).

M Virally, *L'Organisation Mondiale* (Paris, Collection U, 1972).

M Vogt (ed), *The Liberian Crisis and ECOMOG: A Bold Attempt at Regional Peacekeeping* (Lagos, Gajumo Publishing, 1992).

Von Alfred Verdross and Bruno Simma, *Universelles Völkerrecht: Theorie und Praxis 3, völlig neu bearbeitete Aufl* (Berlin, Duncker & Humblot, 1984).

L-E Wahlgren, 'Start and End of Srebrenica' in William Durch (ed), *UN Peacekeeping, American Policy and Uncivil Wars of the 1990s* (New York, St Martins Press, 1996).

H Waldock, 'The Regulation of the Use of Force by Individual States in International Law' (1952) 81 *RCADI* 415.

M Wallace and D Singer, 'Intergovernmental Organisations in the Global System, 1815–1964: A Quantitative Description' (1970) XXIV *International Organisation* 272.

C Wallander, 'Institutional Assets and Adaptability: NATO After the Cold War' (2000) 54 *International Organization* 712.

C Walter, 'Security Council Control over Regional Action', (1997) *Max Planck Yearbook of United Nations Law* 1.

U Wannop, *The Regional Imperative: Regional Planning and Governance in Britain, Europe and the United States* (London, Jessica Kingsley, 1995).

VA and R Warner, *American Crisis Diplomacy: The Quest for Collective Security, 1918–1952*, (Stanford, Stanford University Press, 1952).

AM Weisburd, 'The Emptiness of the Concept of Ius Cogens, as Illustrated by the Law in Bosnia-Herzegovina' (1995–96) 17 *Michigan Journal of International Law* 591.

TG Weiss (ed), *Beyond Subcontracting: Task-Sharing with Regional Security Arrangements and Service-Providing NGOs* (New York, St Martin's Press, 1998).

—— (ed), *Collective Security in a Changing World* (London, Lynne Rienner Publishers, 1993).

TG Weiss and JG Blight (eds), *The Suffering Grass: Superpowers and Regional Conflict in Southern Africa and the Caribbean Basin* (Boulder, Lynne Rienner, 1992).

TG Weiss and McFarlane, 'Regional Organizations and Regional Security' (1992) 2(1) *Security Studies* 5.

M Weller (ed), *Regional Peacekeeping and International Enforcement: The Liberian Crisis*, Cambridge International Documents Series, Vol 6, (Cambridge, Cambridge University Press, 1994).

J Westlake, *International Law, Part II, War* (Cambridge, Cambridge University Press, 1913).

B Weston, 'Security Council Resolution 678 and Persian Gulf Decision Making: Precarious Legitimacy' (1991) 85 *American Journal of International Law* 516.

ND White, 'The Legality of Bombing in the Name of Humanity' (2000) 5(1) *Journal of Conflict and Security Law* 27.

—— *Keeping the Peace* (Manchester, Manchester University Press, 2nd edn, 1997).

—— 'To Review or Not to Review', (1999) 12 *Leiden Journal of International Law* 401.

ND White and R Cryer, 'Unilateral Enforcement of Resolution 687: A Threat Too Far?' (1999) 29 *California Western International Law Journal* 243.

ND White and Özlem Ülgen, 'The Security Council and the Decentralised Military Option: Constitutionality and Function' (1997) XLIV *Netherlands International Law Review* 378.

F Wilcox, 'Regionalism and the United Nations' (1965) *International Organization*, 19(3) 789.

M Williams, 'Re-articulating the Third World Coalition: The Role of the Environmental Agenda' (1993) 14(1) *Third World Quarterly* 7.

D Wippman, 'Enforcing the peace: ECOWAS and the Liberian Civil War' in Lori F Damrosch (ed), *Enforcing Restraint: Collective Intervention in Internal Conflicts* (New York, Council of Foreign Relations, 1993).

—— 'Treaty-Based Intervention: Who Can Say No?' (1995) 62 *University of Chicago Law Review* 607.

J Wolf, 'Regional Arrangements and the UN Charter' 6 *Encyclopaedia of International Law* 289.

J Wolf, 'Regional Arrangements and the UN Charter' (1983) 6 *Encyclopaedia of Public International Law* 289.

R Wolfrum, 'Der Beitrag Regionaler Abmachungen zur Friedenssicherung: Moglichkeiten und Grenzen', (1993) 1 *ZaöRV* 53 (1993) 576.

BA Wortley, 'The Veto and the Security Council Provisions of the Charter' (1946) 43 *British Yearbook of International Law* 95.

E Wouters, 'The Prospects for Regionalism in World Affairs' in Cyril E Black and Richard A Falk (eds), *The Future of International Legal Order*, Vol 1 (Princeton, Princeton University Press, 1969).

Q Wright, 'The Middle East Problem' (1970) 64 *American Journal of International Law* 270.

A Wyatt-Walter, 'Regionalism, Globalization, and World Economic Order' in Fawcett and Hurrel (eds), *Regionalism in World Politics: Regional Organization and International Order* (Oxford, Oxford University Press, 1995).

E Yair, *War and Intervention in Lebanon: The Israeli-Syrian Deterrence Dialogue* (London, Croom Helm, 1987).

R Yalem, 'Regionalism and World Order' (1962) 38 *International Affairs* 460.

O Young, 'Political Discontinuities in International System' (1968) 20(3) *World Politics* 369.

M Zwanenburg, 'Double Standards in Peacekeeping? Subcontracting Peace-keeping and International Humanitarian Law' (1999) 12 *Leiden Journal of International Law* 53.

Index